THE ODYSSEY
OF A WOMAN
FIELD SCIENTIST

A STORY OF PASSION, PERSISTENCE, AND PATIENCE

For Alice —
in appreciation for
our long friendship
Love,
Jean

JEAN H. LANGENHEIM

To order additional copies of this book, contact:
Xlibris Corporation
1-888-795-4274
www.Xlibris.com
Orders@Xlibris.com
56302

CONTENTS

PART IV   CHANGING COURSE

Dedicated to Mother and the many students and friends
who have shared this odyssey with me—and for women, especially,
who aspire to travel similar, but now more open, trails.

INTRODUCTION

I had not thought seriously about writing my life story until after a gala seventy-fifth birthday party given to me by my surrogate family of former graduate students. Colleagues and others had broached the idea, but I only became tantalized to do it after this event—realizing that I now had the time to reflect upon the extraordinary changes I've witnessed in my long professional odyssey. I'm writing these reflections as a memoir, a remarkably elastic genre that allows a narrative of my personal adventures and a thoughtful discussion of my professional career doing research and teaching in plant ecology, paleobotany, and ethnobotany, crossing the boundaries of botany, geology, and chemistry in so doing.

The varied parts of my life are like the threads of a tapestry. Some of the boldest and brightest threads were spun and then woven early in my life—not only my interests in geology and natural history but also my enduring love of train and air travel, of art and companion animals, as well my fascination with the variety of cultures and political issues that have shaped our world. These threads have been strengthened by the teachers, researchers, and special experiences that have influenced me at the many institutions with which I've been associated. Some of the warp and woof of my life comes from my years of marriage. Other threads appear and then disappear in their prominence. Together they have resulted in a complex, interwoven fabric that is my life's tapestry.

As a child of the Great Depression, and having lived through World War II in my high school and college years, I learned perseverance in overcoming obstructions and limitations. Many of the interests in natural history and world travel I developed as a youth have played a significant role in the direction of my professional life. Doing doctoral studies under the supervision of a leading figure in plant ecology/geobotany at the University of Minnesota in the late 1940s and early 1950s, I was a latter-day pioneer woman in these areas. I was allowed to do PhD research because I was married and my husband and I could do our dissertations in tandem. After obtaining my PhD, I faced many professional limitations during the 1950s and into the 1960s, such as restrictions imposed by institutional nepotism regulations initiated during the Depression as well as society's lack of expectations for women outside the traditional role of housewife. I had to be an opportunist in adapting to these difficulties, but I had the good fortune to be able to follow some of my multifarious interests. Through continued interaction with leaders in plant ecology and evolution at University of California at Berkeley and University of Illinois at Urbana, I participated in research during a time of conceptual advances in these disciplines. I was able to observe or study flora and vegetation from arctic-alpine environments to the tropics, and, through international travel, to intertwine my interests in different cultures and political systems.

In the early 1960s, at midlife, I surmounted the major personal challenge of divorce, and moved into a period of professional advancement through an appointment as a scholar of the newly established Radcliffe Institute for Independent Studies. With this support, that of several faculty members and associated appointments at Harvard, I was part of American society's transition from limited expectations to greater professional opportunities for women and dramatic changes in their status.

I again was fortunate to capitalize on the diversity of my previous experience to return to the University of California and join the faculty at the new campus at Santa Cruz (UCSC) in 1966. It was an intriguing move from the oldest US university, full of rich tradition, to a new campus bursting with innovation. It also would be a contrast to my days as a wife of a faculty member while at UC Berkeley. To the educational experiment of undergraduate residential colleges within a research university at UCSC, I brought experience in having taught part-time at several small liberal arts colleges as well as having done research at four major universities. Subsequently, I lived through the period of being the token woman in numerous situations; I was not an activist fighting on the front lines, so to speak, but tried to demonstrate the capability of women through my own hard work and accomplishments.

At UCSC I enjoyed living in a residential college as a part of its development, doing innovative teaching, and designing a research program of my own, which I executed with teams of graduate students. Change was occurring rapidly across ecological and evolutionary studies during the 1960s and into the 1970s. I investigated questions at the boundaries of botany and geology (in both geobotany and paleobotany) and chemistry (in paleobotany, ecology, and ethnobotany). I used my paleobotanical studies of amber as evolutionary background to move my research into the new subfield of chemical ecology; through this I contributed to the expansion of research in tropical ecology. The very nature of this research took me to many parts of the world where I could witness both New and Old World vegetation and see how science and scientists interact in different cultures. I also developed research on Pacific Coast plants and participated in the beginning of agroecology. All of these activities were enhanced by the continuous and rapid technological advances in chemical instrumentation and computers. The impact of the Internet and electronic communication on research cannot be overstated.

I not only participated actively in building the UCSC campus but also extended my activities to national and international arenas. My timing was such that I was present in the early days and participated in the development of organizations that would become premier in their areas, such as the Rocky Mountain Biological Laboratory, the Organization for Tropical Studies, and the International Society for Chemical Ecology. While serving as the first woman president of the Association for Tropical Biology and the International Society of Chemical Ecology and the second woman president both for the Ecological Society of America and the Society of Economic Botany, I had the opportunity to observe how the role of science in society and the role of women had changed during the twentieth and early twenty-first centuries.

Although I accepted the university's special retirement package in 1994, I have remained active in campus activities, especially those concerning graduate students, as an Emeritus and Research Professor.

I have chosen to tell my life's story chronologically—the way I have lived it. I have, however, grouped some major activities that spanned a number of years, providing a sense of continuity in these cases. Remembering is a tricky business and there are several levels of accuracy in my account. My memories of some threads are still vivid, whereas others are misty. Some I can verify empirically, but evidence for others is irrecoverable. Although some of the stories I have included are imperfect recollections, they have not been sacrificed because verifiable data are now lost.

I also have the advantage of being an inveterate letter writer. Until my mother's death in 1978, I wrote many letters to her recounting my adventures from places such as Colombia, Mexico, Brazilian Amazon, and Africa. She saved many of these letters, having enjoyed accompanying me vicariously. And, I was surprised recently to receive a packet of letters I had written to a young soldier from Yale whom I had met during World War II; one of his children sent them to me after his death. I derived some information from field notebooks and from the plethora of photographs I have taken over many years. And since this is the odyssey of an academic scientist, documentation of my life can be found in the records of numerous universities, national and international committees, and professional societies as well as from my publications, those of my students and collaborators, and those of other scientists whose research I have put into my own historical perspective.

The particular time span of my life greatly influences my story. To facilitate understanding of some of the significant changes that are relevant to my odyssey, following this Introduction I have included a timeline. On the same timescale as my life story, I have compared selected historic events, some indicators of the changing status of women, and milestones in ecology of particular importance to my areas of interest. My hope is that the timeline can be a useful reference as I place each chapter of my life in its larger context.

Memoir is a new genre for me. Throughout my life I have described my experiences and reactions to events in many letters, but the narrative style I have tried to develop here is alien to my experience in professional scientific writing. Furthermore, I could not think of writing without referring to the writings of others. Although not cited in the text, a chapter-wise reference list is appended at the end of the book.

So many wonderful people have influenced my odyssey over the years, and most of these names appear in the pages that follow. An exception is a discussion of all the graduate students I have either sponsored or cosponsored. Space does not allow me to include the following students who obtained masters degrees, but nonetheless were integral members of the lab family. I would feel remiss not to at least mention them here: David Wilson, Craig Foster, Robert McGinley, Rita Belserene, Jan Allison, Leslie Linn, Juan José Jimenez, Marc Buchanan, Catherine Courtney, and Yael Lachman.

I gratefully acknowledge those friends and colleagues who have given much time and thought to reading and commenting on parts or even entire drafts of this manuscript. Their willingness to be a sounding board to me has been invaluable in writing such a complicated autobiography. And for me, it was fascinating to analyze the differences in their perspectives on my life. Much of whatever success this writing venture has can be attributed to their inputs. I especially want to thank Anne Hayes for her persistence in assisting with copy editing, and for insightful comments throughout the volume by Sue Martin, Karen Holl, Lincoln Taiz, Ingrid Parker, John and Jill Thompson, John Jordan, Deborah Letourneau, and Susanne Altermann. Others who have read parts or given continual encouragement for which I am grateful are: Pete Holloran, Karen Tenney, Elizabeth Bell, Jonathan Krupp (also of great assistance with scanning many photographs), Teresa Rao, Teresa Payne, and Erica Lann-Clark (input from a nonscientist perspective), Gail and Leroy Fail, Aaron Hicks, Susanne Arrhenius, and Emma Jean Bowman. I am grateful for Adelia Barber making several maps and Amy Whitesides' addition to all of them. The timeline came into existence with the help of Sue Martin in particular, as well as contributions from Susanne Altermann, Aaron Hicks, and finally by Amy Whitesides. I appreciate Dotty Hollinger's typing of early drafts and Linda Frazho's assisting with the collation of photos and preparing the index list, among other essential tasks.

All royalties from this book will be donated to the Jean H. Langenheim Graduate Fellowship in Plant Ecology and Evolution at the University of California at Santa Cruz. I encourage readers to make donations as well to this fellowship through the UC Santa Cruz Foundation, 2155 Delaware Ave., Santa Cruz, CA 95060 (http://giving.ucsc.edu/).

TIMELINE

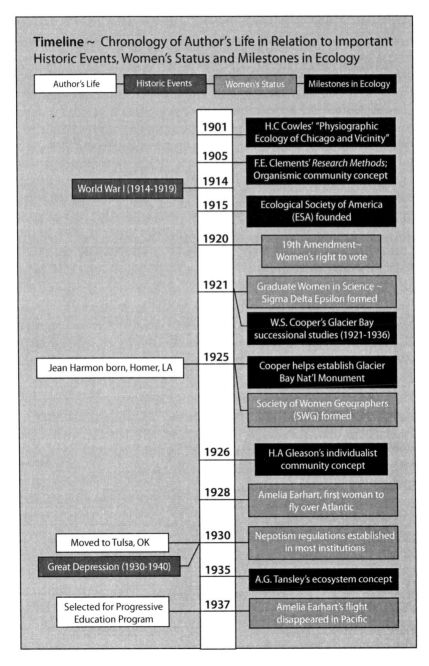

Timeline ~ Chronology of Author's Life in Relation to Important Historic Events, Women's Status and Milestones in Ecology

Author's Life	Historic Events	Women's Status	Milestones in Ecology

Author's Life		Historic Events / Women's Status / Milestones in Ecology
	1901	H.C Cowles' "Physiographic Ecology of Chicago and Vicinity"
	1905	F.E. Clements' *Research Methods*; Organismic community concept
World War I (1914-1919)	**1914**	
	1915	Ecological Society of America (ESA) founded
	1920	19th Amendment~ Women's right to vote
	1921	Graduate Women in Science ~ Sigma Delta Epsilon formed
		W.S. Cooper's Glacier Bay successional studies (1921-1936)
Jean Harmon born, Homer, LA	**1925**	Cooper helps establish Glacier Bay Nat'l Monument
		Society of Women Geographers (SWG) formed
	1926	H.A Gleason's individualist community concept
	1928	Amelia Earhart, first woman to fly over Atlantic
Moved to Tulsa, OK	**1930**	Nepotism regulations established in most institutions
Great Depression (1930-1940)	**1935**	A.G. Tansley's ecosystem concept
Selected for Progressive Education Program	**1937**	Amelia Earhart's flight disappeared in Pacific

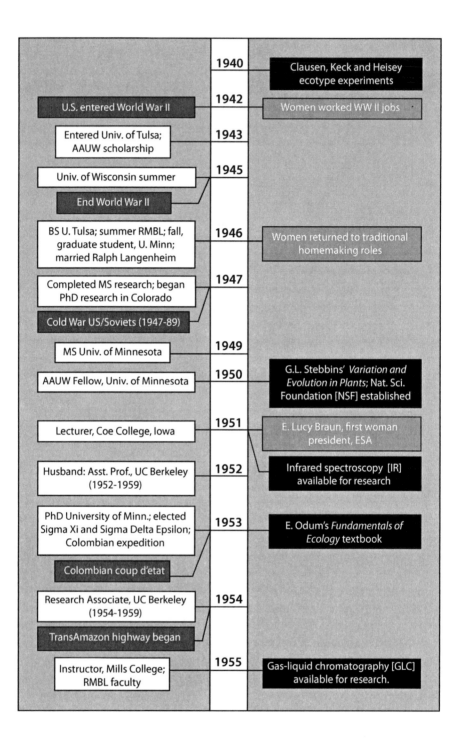

	1940	Clausen, Keck and Heisey ecotype experiments
U.S. entered World War II	1942	Women worked WW II jobs
Entered Univ. of Tulsa; AAUW scholarship	1943	
Univ. of Wisconsin summer	1945	
End World War II		
BS U. Tulsa; summer RMBL; fall, graduate student, U. Minn; married Ralph Langenheim	1946	Women returned to traditional homemaking roles
Completed MS research; began PhD research in Colorado	1947	
Cold War US/Soviets (1947-89)		
MS Univ. of Minnesota	1949	
AAUW Fellow, Univ. of Minnesota	1950	G.L. Stebbins' *Variation and Evolution in Plants*; Nat. Sci. Foundation [NSF] established
Lecturer, Coe College, Iowa	1951	E. Lucy Braun, first woman president, ESA
Husband: Asst. Prof., UC Berkeley (1952-1959)	1952	Infrared spectroscopy [IR] available for research
PhD University of Minn.; elected Sigma Xi and Sigma Delta Epsilon; Colombian expedition	1953	E. Odum's *Fundamentals of Ecology* textbook
Colombian coup d'etat		
Research Associate, UC Berkeley (1954-1959)	1954	
TransAmazon highway began		
Instructor, Mills College; RMBL faculty	1955	Gas-liquid chromatography [GLC] available for research.

	1956	R.H. Whittaker's gradient analysis concept
Instructor, San Francisco College for Women [SFCW]		
Asst. Professor, SFCW (1957-1959)	1957	
Research in Sierra & other California projects	1958	Recognition of Natural Selection in Ecology
Moved to Univ. of Illinois, Urbana; RMBL faculty	1959	J.T. Curtis' continuum concept; G.S. Fraenkels' "Raison d'etre of secondary products"
Research/Teaching Associate, U. of Illinois (1960-1962)	1960	'60's- 'The Pill' available; many women enter the workforce again
Mexican amber expedition	1961	Radcliffe Institute for Independent Study established
Divorce; RMBL faculty; moved to Harvard as Research Fellow (1962-1966): AAUW Fellow	1962	Continental drift theory accepted
Radcliffe Institute Scholar; Mexico research & meeting	1963	Betty Friedan's *The Feminine Mystique*
US involved in Vietnam war (1963-1975)		Organization for Tropical Studies [OTS]; Association for Tropical Biology [ATB] formed
Amber research in Europe	1964	P. Ehrlich & P. Raven's "Co-evolution mediated by secondary chemicals"
UC Berkeley Free Speech Movement; Civil Rights Act		
OTS research, Mexico & Costa Rica	1965	
UC Santa Cruz founded		
Amazonian trip; moved to UCSC as Assistant Professor	1966	National Organization of Women (NOW) founded
Chinese Cultural Revolution (1966-1976)		P.W. Richards' *Tropical Rainforest*
Elected AAAS Fellow	1967	

Year	Personal/Career	Context/Events
1968	Associate Professor, UCSC African research	Ecology participation in IBP (1968-1974)
	Martin Luther King assassinated	Mildred Mathias, President, OTS Board of Directors (1968-71)
1969	Brazilian research (1969-1989)	Journal *Biotropica* founded
1971	Organization for Tropical Studies Board (1971-1987)	
1972		Landsat- remote sensing available for mapping landscape
		Equal Rights Amendment vote; Title IX; UC Nepotism exceptions
1973	Professor, UCSC; elected fellow, Cal. Acad. of Sciences & SWG	Journal *Biochemical Systematics and Ecology* founded
1974	U. Pará/INPA Brazil botany course; Chair, UCSC Biology	
1975	Soviet Union/Yugoslavia meetings	*Journal of Chemical Ecol* founded
1976	NAS/CNPq Chair; research in Venezuela & Brazil (1976-1977)	First burst of women obtaining PhDs in ecology
1978	OTS Executive Comm. Vice President; mother died	Tree climbing technique developed for canopy research
	Wide use of word processing	
1979	Univ. of Tulsa Distinguished Alumna	D. Mckey/D. Rhoades contribute to optimal defense theory
1980	Thailand meeting, China visit	Glacier Bay becomes National Park
	China opens to visitors	
1981	Research Fellow, Australian National Univ.; ESA Vice Pres.	80s- agroecology recognized
1982	*Botany: Plant biology in its Relation to Humans* published	

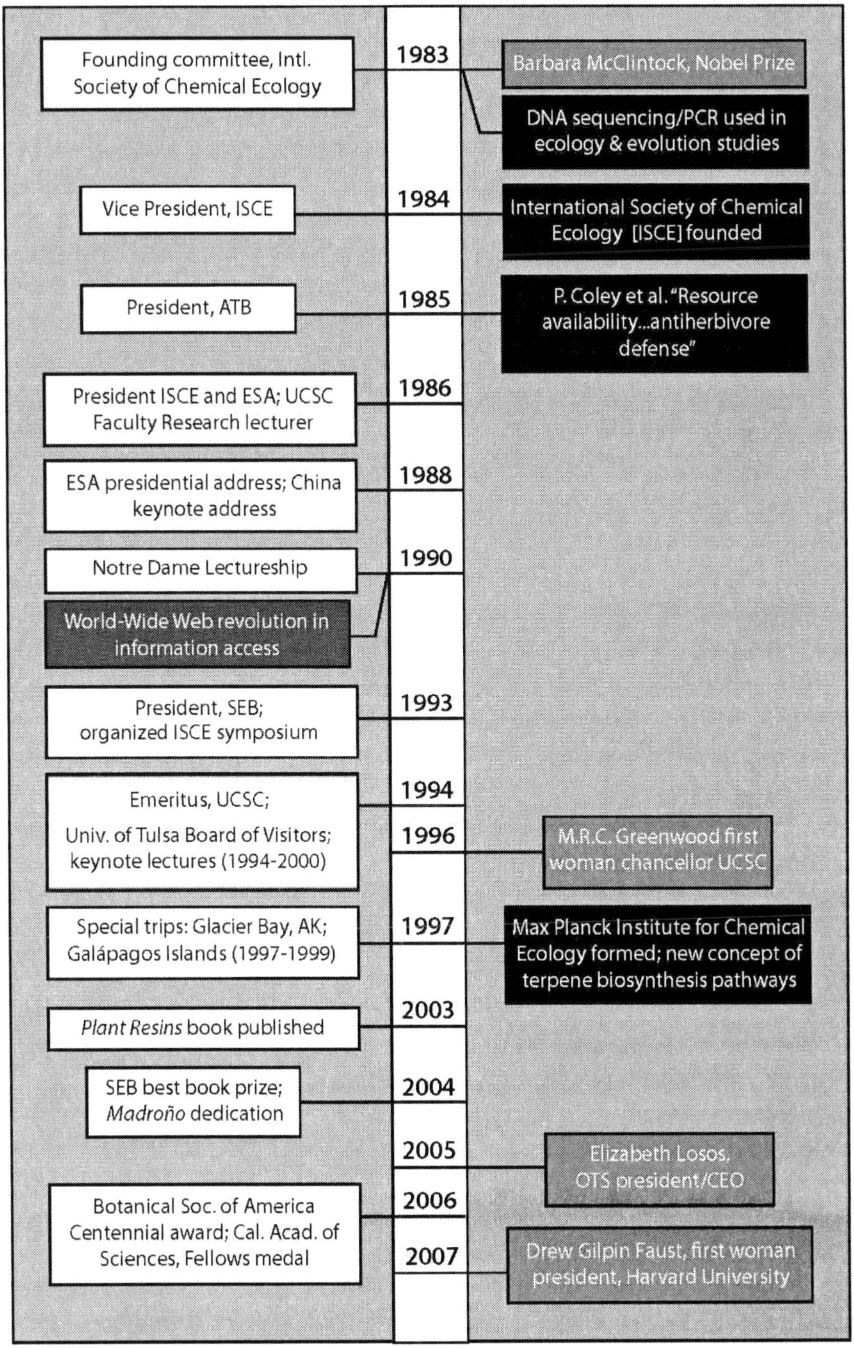

Left column	Year	Right column
Founding committee, Intl. Society of Chemical Ecology	1983	Barbara McClintock, Nobel Prize
		DNA sequencing/PCR used in ecology & evolution studies
Vice President, ISCE	1984	International Society of Chemical Ecology [ISCE] founded
President, ATB	1985	P. Coley et al. "Resource availability...antiherbivore defense"
President ISCE and ESA; UCSC Faculty Research lecturer	1986	
ESA presidential address; China keynote address	1988	
Notre Dame Lectureship	1990	
World-Wide Web revolution in information access		
President, SEB; organized ISCE symposium	1993	
Emeritus, UCSC;	1994	
Univ. of Tulsa Board of Visitors; keynote lectures (1994-2000)	1996	M.R.C. Greenwood first woman chancellor UCSC
Special trips: Glacier Bay, AK; Galápagos Islands (1997-1999)	1997	Max Planck Institute for Chemical Ecology formed; new concept of terpene biosynthesis pathways
Plant Resins book published	2003	
SEB best book prize; Madroño dedication	2004	
	2005	Elizabeth Losos, OTS president/CEO
Botanical Soc. of America Centennial award; Cal. Acad. of Sciences, Fellows medal	2006	
	2007	Drew Gilpin Faust, first woman president, Harvard University

PART I

BEGINNINGS

*As Girl Scout campaigning for leadership program
of Tulsa Community Fund*

About 3 years old, already investigating plants

Ever-avid traveler at Atlantic City, NJ at around 4 years old

EARLY YEARS

1925-1943

Faster than fairies, faster than witches, . . .
All of the sights of the hill and the plain
Fly as thick as driving rain . . . .

From a Railway Carriage,
—Robert Louis Stevenson

Some of my earliest recollections are of having my eyes glued to train windows, especially fascinated with the plants in the different landscapes as they moved by, and wanting to get out to investigate them. This early opportunity for travel came by way of my father who worked for a railroad and my mother who took me on many train trips to visit her family. From these early days of riding in trains across the landscapes of North America, my travels eventually took me, along with some surprising adventures, to five continents.

My mother, Jeanette Smith, grew up in upstate New York and met my father, Virgil Wilson Harmon, in 1919 in New York City, where he was stationed in World War I. My father came from a southern family that had moved to Arkansas, and after his graduation from high school there he attended Chillecothe Business College in Missouri. My mother was very much a Yankee, whereas my father was a southern man to the core—cultural differences that ultimately affected my relationship with each of them. Following their marriage in 1920, my parents moved to Homer, Louisiana, where Father had taken a job as an accountant with Louisiana and North West (L&NW) Railroad—a connecting freight line to Union Pacific. I was born in Homer on September 5, 1925; it was Labor Day, which my mother thought most appropriate.

We were able to pay reduced fare for train travel, and my mother and I took long train trips to New York and other parts of the eastern seaboard to visit her family. Mother told stories about how I always loved the trains (especially the big steam locomotives of these days) as well as my excitement of accompanying her on trips. She also often recounted how, as a three-year-old, I insisted that a neighbor child walk with me several blocks to the station to see the trains that took me to faraway places. When my father found us there my little companion, now in tears, was not as enthusiastic about the adventures these trains seemed to signify for me.

In the early 1930s, because of Great Depression economics, my father's job with the railroad was terminated and we moved to Tulsa, Oklahoma, where he had found a job as an accountant with a truck line. Trucks became important in Tulsa during the Great Depression, with the construction of Route 66, the transcontinental highway from Chicago to Los Angeles, which went through the city. This highway presaged the country's greater utilization of trucks to transport freight, and my father continued to work with this developing industry. Because of the presence of the oil and gas industries, the effects of the Great Depression were less felt in Tulsa than in so many places; nonetheless, it had an impact that influenced my family for many years. A lifestyle of thriftiness and finding ingenious ways of achieving goals—including happiness—that did not require large sums of money became permanent parts of my character, traits that have stayed me throughout my life.

Tulsa was known as the Oil Capital of the World, and many people were employed by oil companies and related industries (forty-five major companies and more than 500 smaller ones had offices there). A number of these employees had been moved to Tulsa from eastern states, and their presence made for an invigorating mix with the Indian (Native American) and "Sooner" (nickname for early pioneers) populations. Before Oklahoma became a state, it was Indian Territory—the area where the Five Civilized Tribes of the southeastern US had been forced to relocate.

I was captivated by the Indian history of Tulsa. It was first a Creek town—*Tulsa* means "town" in the Creek language—and the town's development was particularly influenced by these Indians. The Cherokee Indians were so advanced as to have a written language, and the Osage Indians, who had been displaced from Missouri, were wealthy because of their excellent range land, which contained oil as well. I was very interested in the cultures of these Indians and how they differed from mine. I admired them, especially the ones with whom I had some contact, and as a youngster I sometimes wished my heritage was some part Indian. This admiration was certainly a part of my nascent interest in different cultures.

Our house was full of books, especially as I was constantly lugging home so many from the public library. I treasured my library card—it provided a free way to enjoy myself and expand my horizons. Mother and I went to the library frequently and roamed the shelves, and we found that we had a lot of common interests to discuss together. I was fascinated with natural history and spent hours poring over *National Geographic*. I also very much wanted to know about people in other countries—how they lived and how their cultures differed from ours. I loved *Heidi* and had my heart set on visiting the mountains in Switzerland early in my life. Later in high school I began delving into biographies—being especially interested in how influential people, such as Madame Curie, had overcome difficulties to attain their goals. Despite lots of reading, I got outdoors a great deal, taking walks with my dogs, playing tennis and softball, as well as ice skating. I successfully competed in city and regional tennis tournaments, but I had no coaching, and there were no organized softball teams for girls in those days.

My mother was the strongest influence on my life. We developed a deep bond that persisted until her death when I was 53-years-old. In a high school essay, I wrote "I am exceedingly thankful for the ideas she (Mother) instilled in me . . . expression of gratitude, looking on the sunny side of life . . . but one of the attributes I cherish most is the love of good books." Although Mother only finished high school, she was a truly educated woman with a great appreciation of learning. She always encouraged my insatiable reading habits and my enjoyment of school—in sharp contrast to my father, who felt a little disappointed that I wasn't more of a Southern Belle. Although there was no real enmity, my relationship with my father was never close. His ingrained racial prejudice about Negroes (correct name at that time) from his southern upbringing resulted in some heated arguments, but primarily I felt he just never really understood me or my interests, and thus he had little impact in the trajectory of my life.

Another difference between my mother and father was their politics—especially their views on racial issues. Mother simply could not support my father's ingrained attitudes toward segregation of Negroes. She was a Northern Republican (her older brother was prominent in New York Republican politics) and my father was a strong Southern Democrat. The right for women to vote had only come in 1920, the year when my parents married, and Mother definitely wanted to exercise that privilege. She did give in to voting for the Democrat, Franklin D. Roosevelt, because she thought he was helping to get the US through the Great Depression *(and* he was from upstate New York). Listening to discussions of both the Republican and Democratic views as a youth may have led in part to my having voted independently in most elections.

Mother enrolled me in a Christian Science Sunday School, which I attended through my youth. She had been influenced by its philosophy while growing up and attended church, although not as a member. Similarly, I neither became a member nor completely accepted all of its doctrines. I did gain a significant foundation in faith that a God of Love was ever-present, which gave me an attitude that dispelled fear and helped transcend difficulties. Further, I turned to Christian Science practitioners to help me spiritually in times of need throughout my life.

Life was much simpler while I was growing up than today. There was no TV; for entertainment, we listened to the radio or went to movies in the ornate Art Deco theaters. We laughed together at many comic shows on the radio. These comedians provided needed laughter during the stressful years of the Depression and World War II. Mother was a great music lover and regularly listened to the Metropolitan Opera on Saturdays, one of her New York traditions; she soon incorporated me into participating—initiating a long interest in opera. She also took me to any concerts that were available in Tulsa during those hard times.

Most of Mother's ancestry was English, and this had influenced her love of things English. Following the abdication of King Edward VIII in 1936, we got up at 3:00 AM Tulsa time to follow the pageantry of the coronation of King George VI over the radio. I was fascinated with Princess Elizabeth, often called royalty's Shirley Temple (the child movie marvel of the time), who was just my age. After her ascension to the throne in 1952, I have continued to follow her activities. Like my mother, I have maintained a strong interest in England's history, literature, and her people. Some of my closest personal and professional associations have been with English men and women.

Mother had some of the British "stiff upper lip attitude," but not in the extreme. Although times were tough financially for us during the Depression, I never remember her dwelling on it. She was imbued with the importance of duty in doing one's job well and in bearing any difficulty with dignity and little complaint.

Another experience that spurred my interest in people from other countries was having pen pals. Especially important was my correspondence with Mirko Feric, a Yugoslavian boy whose wealthy Zagreb family had a summer home near Dubrovnik. His letters, written in wonderfully poetic English, often included a little bouquet of forest violets that he had collected along the Adriatic. He wrote so lovingly of his home that I fell in love with it—and with him, a little bit. We exchanged letters for four years, but after

World War II had begun and he had become a pilot, he wrote to me that he could not continue our correspondence. Thirty years later I visited Zagreb and Dubrovnik, still wishing I could finally meet him.

I remained fascinated with all possibilities of travel, which, during the mid-1930s, expanded from trains to include flights. As it was for many girls of my age, Amelia Earhart was my heroine. Her solo flights captured my imagination for adventure, and I was a devastated twelve-year-old when her plane disappeared over the Pacific Ocean in 1937 while attempting to encircle the world at the equator. In French class I was enthralled by Antoine Saint Exupery's *Vol de Nuit* and later his *Wind, Sand, and Stars*. His poetic descriptions of flying over the Sahara and Andes made an indelible impression on me. I was so fascinated with flying that I pleaded for family trips to the airport to watch planes come and go. Tulsa was becoming an aviation center with the development of a leading institution to train civilian pilots and engineers. As a special birthday present one year, my parents gave me my first airplane ride. It was with a local pilot who included a few simple stunts in the ride. My father went with me but was terrified; he was tightly holding onto my hand, rather than the other way around. I loved it.

I did not have the pleasure and special benefits of knowing grandparents; I had only a few aunts, uncles, and cousins who all lived far away. Since I had no siblings, my mother encouraged me to have pets as a source of companionship. I dearly loved my dogs and took them with me for long walks in the tall grass prairie and woodlands on the Osage Indian Reservation two blocks away. Together we wandered among the beautiful big bluestem grasses often waving in the wind—and purple cone flowers, penstemons, asters, and golden coreopsis. I frequently stopped to draw plants or bring some home to paint. During the War I collected the pods of milkweed—the floss was used as a substitute for kapok in life jackets. These walks not only enlivened my appreciation of the beauty of the natural world, but also were a part of my ever-increasing interest in understanding it. Recognition of the area where I once walked, known as Osage Hills, has come recently in a 216-acre site which is being selected for the Oklahoma Centennial Garden and Research Center. Over 400 native plants have been found there, an unusually rich local flora for Oklahoma.

I had a beautiful collie whom I had named Lassie after the dog in Eric Knight and Lilian Oligado's book, *Lassie Come Home* (later to become a much-loved TV program). My wonderful dog companion met a horrible death that greatly affected me. She was lured to eat poisoned meat by a neighbor who feared dogs. She died a painful death to which the neighbor admitted. It was the first time I had ever felt an intense sense of hatred and my mother had a difficult time convincing me to let it go, as such hatred would only be a burden that would hurt me in the end. This unforgettable experience has led to a lifetime of activities to help all animals, and especially those that have suffered from either human neglect or cruelty.

Mother had a life-long love for animals as well. During the Depression years there were soup lines for humans, but Mother worried about the welfare of homeless animals. Even though we had little to spare, she fed neighborhood strays, even making space for some of them in our basement area. She was commended later by the local humane society for her efforts to help these animals.

As another antidote to my being an only child, Mother fostered a kind of sisterhood for me in Girl Scouts. Mother was the leader of the Forget-Me-Not Troop from my early years in junior high through high school. In this troop I developed some long-lasting friendships, which have survived to this day. Pursuing merit badges allowed me to satisfy many of my interests. Although several natural history projects influenced the direction my later education would take, one in particular had captivated me. I made an extensive collection of rocks and minerals and began to learn how they were formed, which inspired me to want to learn more about geology—and the earth's history. This was an area that also fascinated my father and a Girl Scout activity that he actively supported.

With father and mother discussing Girl Scout work

Scouting not only provided "sisters" for me, but also provided an inspirational mentor for the other girls. Mother was a beautiful woman who radiated warmth and friendliness. I never knew a person who disliked her. Although my "sister" scouts loved their own mothers, some openly told me that they were envious of mine. She was a feminist in her own way, encouraging me and other girls to explore our interests and go as far in our education as we wanted. She became highly respected in the entire Tulsa scouting community; she was, in fact, a quietly effective leader wherever she turned her hand.

Mother was particularly proud of my having been selected to join an academically elite group of junior high students who took special courses and then continued together in some other courses at high school. Robert Hutchins at the University of Chicago had designed some of the basic ideas of this program. In our case, students moved as rapidly as the group was able through certain subjects (I especially remember English, foreign languages—Latin and French—and history), and were encouraged to cross boundaries between them. Speed did not drive our learning, but rather indicated our ability to grasp information and then move on—not to be held back by any standard timetable. Moreover, we students and our teachers (who also had been selected for the program) enjoyed the intellectual excitement of sharing ideas, and discussing them in some depth. It was an early version of an honors program, referred to at the time as "progressive education." My association with intellectually-oriented boys in this program may have helped me later in my relationship with male faculty colleagues. I have always felt at ease with them—even with those brighter than myself—and confident that I could hold my own without needing to compete aggressively. Demonstrating that we could comprehend new kinds of material rapidly may also have given me the courage later to venture into new academic disciplines—especially in establishing interconnections between them necessary to understand complicated scientific questions.

Upon graduation from high school in 1943, I was well prepared for college. I had many interests but was leaning toward pursing some area in the natural sciences, having been tipped in that direction by my scouting activities, and these being reinforced by inspirational teachers. I still was not sure where I would go to college. Mother had always dreamed of my going to an eastern girl's college such as Vassar or Smith. But faced with problems posed by World War II, and some financial constraints, I decided to stay close to home at the University of Tulsa (TU).

LAYING THE FOUNDATION

1943-1946

What a large volume of adventures may be grasped within this little space of life by him who interests his heart in everything.
—Laurence Sterne

The University of Tulsa (TU) was founded in 1894 as Henry Kendall College, a Presbyterian Church school for Indian girls, and assumed its present name in 1921. Although the church relinquished strong control over the years, it is still one of their largest doctoral degree-granting institutions, and has grown with continuous generous endowments from wealthy oil people in particular. My financial concerns were ameliorated by scholarships from TU and the American Association of University Women (AAUW).

As a college student

I had finally decided that I wanted to major in geology, partly because a charismatic high school geology teacher had encouraged me to continue that interest. It was unusual for geology to be taught in high school, but the subject was fostered in Tulsa because of the large number of geologists employed there in the oil industry. Geology also was an especially strong field at TU because of its globally recognized petroleum engineering program. When I tried to enroll as a geology major, however, I was decidedly discouraged from doing so because women were not allowed to take a summer's required field course. This perceived inappropriateness of women living in the field with men posed problems for women wanting to study and become geologists not only at TU but also at universities across the country. (Marcia McNutt's 2009 appointment as the first woman director of the US Geological Survey is evidence of slow, but enormous change for women in the discipline of geology.)

Fortunately, during my freshman year I met a botany professor, Harriet Barclay, who suggested a way out of this impasse by combining geology with botany—a more acceptable outlet for my interests at this time. Harriet had taken her MS in plant ecology with W.S. Cooper at the University of Minnesota and her PhD from Henry Chandler Cowles at the University of Chicago, both of whom emphasized the role of geomorphology in ecological understanding of the succession of plant communities from originally bare areas. Cowles, a geologist turned ecologist by his own admission, had developed what was called the "physiographic school of ecology." With great enthusiasm, Harriet persuaded me that this was the direction for me to go. I enrolled in both botany and geology courses.

Field trips were what I most enjoyed in botany courses with the Barclays and they were the beginning of the strong thread representing my passion for field research. Harriet and her morphologist husband comprised the botanists in the biology department. Both were often present on field trips. I took their courses, Flora of Oklahoma during the summer of 1944, and Plant Ecology during the next spring. Despite rationing during the war years, the Barclays somehow managed to obtain gasoline and cars with sufficiently decent tires for field trips around Oklahoma. Importantly for me, during these trips I became well acquainted with these two botanists, and I began to learn how informal interactions on field trips could help establish relationships between students and faculty—something I later tried to develop in my own courses.

As we surveyed the flora and vegetation in Oklahoma, I was also introduced to thinking from an ecological perspective. Harriet used the first American textbook in plant ecology, by John Weaver and Frederic E. Clements, in which the authors presented it predominantly as a field subject. They emphasized climate and soil in understanding the distribution of vegetation, and discussed in detail prairie and dry deciduous forest communities—the major vegetation types in Oklahoma. Tulsa is at the edge of the tall grass prairie with post and blackjack oaks forming a characteristic scrubby forest on the ridges and uplands. Our ecology course trip to the Ouachita Mountains in southeastern Oklahoma and neighboring Arkansas was an outstanding event for me because here we observed not only oak-hickory forest but also a relict forest that comprised other kinds of deciduous trees and especially large cypress trees. This relict forest led me to wonder what kind of deciduous forest might have existed in this and other areas in Oklahoma before the Ice Ages.

In western Oklahoma, we saw many abandoned farmhouses almost engulfed by drifts of sand, which had led to the vast emigration of farmers from this region. I was particularly impressed by the sand dunes built up along the Cimarron River in the Oklahoma panhandle. This area, along with the red desert of neighboring Kansas, had been the source of much of the red sandy dust that had sometimes turned the sky red, and that I had continually swept from our porch during Dust Bowl times. We also discussed Paul Sears' book *Deserts on the March* while observing some of the devastation that he described. Sears had experienced the drought of the 1930s while a professor at the University of Oklahoma, and had effectively highlighted the catastrophic effects of allowing excessive plowing of soil, overgrazing, and cultivation of margin lands in removing plant cover.

In addition to academic life, I had an active social life as a member of the Delta Delta Delta (Tri Delt) sorority, which several of my longtime girl friends had also joined. Campus social life was much simpler then. Alcohol was rarely available because Oklahoma was still a "dry state" (alcoholic beverages being illegal). Drugs were not on the scene yet. Smoking, however, was considered sophisticated, in part because glamorous women in the movies smoked. In my case, however, my first try was my last simply because I disliked it. We were well-mannered, having been taught social graces as part of being brought up as well-bred young ladies. Our femininity focused on our appearance. We were nattily dressed—no pants or sweat shirts except for field trips—dressing fashionably for parties with carefully coifed hair. Our revolts against tradition were expressed mildly by wearing a special cashmere sweater backwards or scuffing up a new pair of saddle oxfords. We accepted society's expectation that we would be virgins until we married.

Because of the war, there were fewer full-time male students at TU than usual, but numerous servicemen regularly visited from nearby army camps. We felt entertaining these men was one of our wartime responsibilities, and they were happy to be our dates for parties at the Tri Delt house, at football games (an important part of southwest culture), and dances where we jitterbugged to bands that played hits by Glenn Miller, Count Basie, and Benny Goodman.

Richard (Dick) Zahner

At one of these dances, I met a young Yale man who was studying to be a translator at Camp Gruber near Muskogee, just southeast of Tulsa. Richard (Dick) Zahner started coming to Tulsa with friends on weekends and we went to various functions together. Our friendship continued with more than a two-year correspondence. (I received letters I had written to Dick in an extraordinary manner. His children had found a packet of 30 of them in the attic following his death. They found my e-mail address and asked me if I would like to have them!) These letters were lively intellectual exchanges about literature and politics, and Dick even wrote one letter to me in French—but they also detailed what an active academic and social life I led. I not only took my science (geology, biology, and chemistry) classes, but also philosophy, world literature, and history. At the same time, even with scholarships, I also worked in the library, graded English papers, and was a lab assistant in botany to bring in extra money. In one of these letters to Dick I made a prophetic statement. In discussing my feeling of inadequacy in being a teaching assistant in a botany class, I wrote, "Teachers are, of course, still students who have gained more knowledge . . . I like that idea because I somehow feel that I will be a student (a teacher?) all of my life."

During the summer of 1945 I had a wonderful time taking courses in plant physiology and history of civilization at the University of Wisconsin in Madison. I relished my first exposure to plant physiological experiments, which were considered so important for explanations in many ecological studies.I also was enthralled with a civilization course that emphasized the history of eastern cultures, in contrast to a TU course I had taken about western civilization. It was the TU professor who taught this course who suggested that I could combine my interests in botany and the humanities by taking courses at the University of Wisconsin during the summer. It also was my first experience in a northern glacial lake country and beautiful mixed conifer-hardwood forests, and I enjoyed learning to canoe and sail on Lake Mendota. Moreover, I celebrated the excitement and sheer jubilation of V-J Day, the end of World War II, in Madison. Having spent most of my high school and college years while the US was at war, it took some time for me truly to realize that it was finally over in both Europe and the South Pacific.

Plant physiology experiments

Another favorite professor at TU, Nels Bailkey, was a charismatic historian and political scientist, who was also very active in student politics. In 1942, he led efforts to establish a campus community government with representation of faculty and students on a council. Previous student governments had existed in several forms but along typical student council lines—student members with a faculty sponsor. However, the Community Council was founded upon the idea of giving both students and faculty representation. Having faculty representation rather than sponsorship was designed to strengthen relationships between faculty and students—an idea well in advance of the later 1960s campus "revolutions" I witnessed in California. The president was a student elected by the entire community and held accountable for the success or failure of all school activities (other than academics, of course). Called a "Laboratory for Democracy," the council was meant to foster the democratic habit of civic participation as well as to train leaders.

In the spring of 1945, as a junior, I was elected president of the Community Council and was the first woman president in the history of TU student government. Some doubters suggested I was chosen only because so many good male competitors were still in the armed forces at the time of the election! I had previously represented my sorority on the council, had served as its secretary and as chairman of the assemblies committee, and felt ready to be at the helm. And apparently the campus community thought I was as well.

The success of the council under my leadership led Bailkey to suggest enlarging the scope of our influence to include a Conference on Campus

Taking oath as president of TU Community Council

Government and Leadership Training and invite student body presidents from various universities to come to TU to discuss these issues. In addition to good campus governance I was concerned about training leaders to preserve peace and strive to solve global problems following the end of World War

II. There was an enthusiastic response to our Laboratory for Democracy idea, and in the spring of 1946, twenty-seven colleges and universities were represented from eight southwestern states at the TU meeting. We had a spirited exchange of ideas and students vowed to return to their campuses to try to increase the role of student government in training future leaders.

By taking summer college courses I finished my studies at TU in three years. In 1946 I graduated in a blaze of glory with more honors than any other senior. One award was from the Panhellenic Council, which voted me the most outstanding senior woman. I also was elected to Phi Gamma Mu, the social sciences honor society, as the most outstanding student in the social sciences, quite a feat for a natural science major. Of course, my leadership activities associated with the Community Council were instrumental in this recognition.

I had applied to the Universities of Minnesota, Illinois, Wisconsin, Nebraska, and Pennsylvania (the institutions with the leading figures in plant ecology at that time) to do my graduate studies. I was happily surprised to be accepted by all of them, with offers of financial support. I accepted Minnesota as I wanted to work with Harriet Barclay's mentor, W.S. Cooper, with whom I would be able to combine my interests in geology and botany.

Harriet Barclay was to be the only professional female role model I would have. She had obtained her PhD from the University of Chicago in a botany department, which was a leader in granting PhDs to women in botany during the 1920s. She also was one of the first active women plant ecologists with a doctorate at that time. Only E. Lucy Braun had preceded her in 1914. However, after women got degrees they were usually unable to find jobs, especially if they married. Harriet found a way to work and have a family by teaching in the same university department as her husband—an unusual situation for a wife, as most institutions had strict nepotism regulations during and for some time following the Great Depression. She was a very energetic person and an enthusiastic teacher who inspired interest in ecology among numerous students both at TU and at Rocky Mountain Biology Laboratory (RMBL). Although she participated in various research projects, notoriously she did not bring the work to publication. She told me later that, although she finished her PhD dissertation, she never really got over the severity of Cooper's criticism in writing her MS thesis. Probably because she did not publish her limited research, but was heralded as an outstanding teacher, I never heard her talk about careers for women in ecology other than teaching. I was the only woman of her many students who went on for doctoral studies.

Later in life, following her husband's death she displayed her adventurous side—collecting plants in the Colombian, Venezuelan, and Ecuadorian Andes as well as in Africa and other parts of the world. Her collections finally reached over 30,000 alpine plants, but she did not publish articles about them. Ultimately our perspectives diverged because I became associated with institutions that emphasized research and publications. She had remained focused on teaching, local conservation activities, painting, and giving beautifully illustrated lectures to civic groups. She certainly received much recognition in these areas—even becoming a member of Oklahoma's Hall of Fame.

SURPRISE ENGAGEMENT

In the spring of 1946, I met Ralph Langenheim, Jr., the son of the dean of the Petroleum Engineering School, at a TU dance. Ralph had a BS in geological engineering from TU and had graduated from midshipman's school at Annapolis. He had been the commanding officer of a LST (landing ship tank) in England, France, Alaska, and the South Pacific, thus encompassing both theaters of the war. Immediately following the war, he had enrolled in a master's program in geology at the University of Colorado, and visited Tulsa for only a few weeks during his spring vacation. We were introduced at a dance and followed it by playing tennis and going on fossil-collecting trips together. He surprised me, before returning to Colorado, by offering me his fraternity pin followed by an engagement ring. He also gave me a geology hammer as an engagement present—to be symbolic of a partnership to work together.

I was completely swept off my feet by this handsome, dashing young geologist. The Barclays were so enthusiastic, as were both my and Ralph's parents (whom I liked very much), that I seemed compelled to accept the engagement. It was as though some force was leading me in a certain direction. I had been in continuous correspondence with George Bowen, my high school beau, who had spent the war at Cal Tech, studying physics under a special Navy program that enabled him to continue as a student. He had been looking forward to seeing me soon in Tulsa, and been more or less assuming that we would probably marry after he finished his education. George was extremely bright and a "great guy," but did not have an adventurous spirit that Ralph displayed. Also, in his post-war letters to me, Dick Zahner had asked a few leading questions—he was thinking about marriage, to which I had replied noncommittally, focusing instead on my plans for an advanced degree. Dick was a delightful, very kind and thoughtful person whose company I greatly enjoyed. But he too lacked the sense of excitement that Ralph had created. Writing to tell both George and Richard of my decision to marry Ralph was no easy thing. Although both of these fine men appreciated my intellectual leanings, my life would probably have been much more traditional if I had married either one of them—certainly would not have involved the adventures of joint field studies in various parts of the world.

In the 1940s and into the 1950s it was assumed that following a girl's college education, she married and settled down to have a family. All of my close girl friends accepted this traditional pattern of family commitment and becoming a housewife. Moreover, in 1946 the men were back from war, eager to marry and to use the GI bill to further their education. Ralph intended to obtain an MS in geology by the end of the summer of 1947 at the University of Colorado and then continue for a PhD at a still undetermined university. With a certain amount of naiveté, I just assumed that we would marry and both continue our graduate studies. Ralph too, unlike most men of his generation, considered that a possibility. How it all happened I think amazed friends and parents.

RMBL

With Harriet's encouragement, I had signed up to attend the 1946 summer session at Rocky Mountain Biological Laboratory (RMBL) in Colorado, and then I would proceed to graduate studies in the Botany Department at the University of Minnesota. RMBL is located in the ghost town of Gothic, Colorado. Gothic had been a mining town in the 1880s and after large finds of high grade silver led to an influx of prospectors, it became a thriving community of five thousand people, with two hotels, many dance halls, and even more saloons. However, when the silver yield did not live up to expectations, the town declined and had essentially died by the Panic of 1893.

At RMBL, Gothic saloon in background

In 1928, John C. Johnson, a professor at Western State College in Gunnison, Colorado, held the first RMBL classes in one of the old hotels. In 1930 he bought the whole town for $200 in back taxes and set up the lab permanently, remaining its director for thirty years. During the early years many faculty came from Oklahoma, including the well-known animal ecologist A.O. Weese, from the University of Oklahoma. He encouraged Harriet Barclay and the geologist Arthur Murray from TU to become Gothic community members. Other TU faculty and administrators, including the Langenheim family, had become acquainted with Gothic and enjoyed summer vacations there. Thus my future husband had already been introduced to the beauty of the area, as well as its interesting geology, by Professor Murray.

Following A.O. Weese and Harriet Barclay on field trip

The courses during the summer of 1946 were the first offered by RMBL following the end of World War II. I took Field Botany, taught by Harriet Barclay, and Field Ecology taught jointly by Harriet and Weese, who had been a Victor Shelford student at the University of Illinois. They used the text *Bioecology,* by Clements and Shelford, which integrated plant and animal ecology. With the use of Weaver and Clements's *Plant Ecology* and now *Bioecology*, I had been grounded in the ideas of Frederick Clements. Clements was early recognized as the first formulator of a logical hierarchical system of vegetation, but his ideas were controversial. He formulated ideas about the holistic nature of communities as complex super organisms that develop to a climax state controlled by climate. Clementsian organismic views have an orderly neatness, which made them useful pedagogically—especially displayed in his textbooks. However, these views were criticized at the research level, and his overly detailed terminology was roundly decried as bringing ecological studies into discredit. Clementsian concepts were ones that I too would soon be discarding in my research.

The Gothic area is not only an incredibly beautiful environment, but also an exhilarating place to study and do research. There was no end to fascinating discoveries in these mountains, expedited by knowledgeable people who also loved the area. I enjoyed the comradeship of the students, who were a mixture of friends from TU and others from Harvard, Syracuse, Georgia, and Oregon State. It was the first time for all of us to live in such primitive conditions. We shared in good humor the jobs of hauling water for bathing and wood and coal for heat, taking care of kerosene lamps for light, and so on.

The flora, plant communities, and high Rocky Mountain environment had been entirely new to me, and the RMBL field botany and ecology courses provided background about them for my MS research. I had obtained Cooper's permission to investigate, for my master's thesis, the physiography and succession of plants from the bare areas on the Gothic Earthflow, a prominent feature along East River Valley seen along the one-lane road into Gothic. I had begun the study of this earthflow (similar to a landslide, but in which the earth flows) with a class project and learned about some of the rigors of doing research there. Nonetheless, I was enthusiastic that this successional study of an earthflow would fit into the tradition of the classic analyses of primary plant succession done by Henry Cowles on the Lake Michigan dunes and by his student and my soon-to-be mentor, W.S. Cooper, on glaciers, dunes, and various other initially bare areas.

Ralph and his family visited at the end of the summer, and we returned to Tulsa together to plan our December wedding before Ralph and I headed off to our respective universities. Plans unfolded rapidly in the seemingly endless tasks involved in organizing this large event. I reaped the benefits of the sisterhood Mother had created for me in that several of these girls were to be my bridesmaids, and Mother had been such an inspiration for them that they were happy to help her finish details for the wedding in my absence.

I took the train to Minneapolis in the fall to begin my professional life, but returned to Tulsa during Christmas vacation to start a different personal life as a married woman. After a beautiful and joyful wedding among many friends and a short honeymoon in the Ozark Mountains, Ralph headed back

Marriage to Ralph L. Langenheim, Jr

to Colorado and I to Minnesota to await reunion during spring vacation in Boulder and the summer at Gothic. We wrote many letters; long distance telephone conversations at that time tended to be restricted to either urgent situations or special occasions. Nonetheless, we managed to keep in communication, although it would be considered very limited by today's standards. Perhaps our ability to endure such separation as a young married couple traces to our just having lived through World War II, when people had to accept periods of separation as routine. At least now it was no longer under the threat of war.

PART II
DUAL CAREERS

Husband-wife team for doctoral research in Colorado

GRADUATE-STUDENT YEARS

1946-1952

The alpine tundra is a place of infinite enchantment . . .
—Ann Zwinger and Beatrice Wood

In the fall of 1946, I arrived at the University of Minnesota's Botany Department eager to begin my graduate studies. I was impressed with the number of professors, the variety of courses, and the research being done in the department. I was part of a large group of ecology graduate students who were studying succession and analyzing communities (with W.S. Cooper) or investigating the physiological ecology of individual organisms (with D.B. Lawrence). Although I joined Cooper's group, I also wanted to emphasize paleobotany, which Harlan Banks taught. Banks was an enthusiastic proponent of plant evolution displayed by plant fossils, and our interests soon intermeshed.

William S. Cooper

In addition, inspired by Cooper's hallmark studies of plant succession in relation to geomorphic (physiographic) conditions and relevant geological history, I declared a minor in geology. With Cooper's encouragement I took more geology courses than needed for a minor—I almost felt that I was back as a freshman at TU, when I had hoped to major in the subject. Robert Sharpe, a glaciologist, was my geology advisor. A charismatic teacher, he spellbound students in his course on the geomorphology of North America by delivering a fascinating lecture while simultaneously drawing landforms on the board by hand. He also gave generously of his time in discussing projects with Cooper's students. I felt fortunate to have the guidance of Cooper in plant ecology, Sharpe in geomorphology, and Banks in paleobotany—all superb teachers as well as leaders in their fields. Truly they were an extraordinary match for my interests, helping me interweave the geological and botanical threads that would diverge and reemerge over the course of my career.

The Botany building was a square, four-story structure bordering a bluff along a gorge in the Mississippi River. Cooper considered it an architectural monstrosity, but graduate students liked the roof house (the top floor) where we had offices with fine views of the river. For us from warmer climes, we watched with interest as the ice formed on the river, and were especially impressed with its breaking up into massive chunks in the spring, followed by the river again becoming filled with activity. One large room in the roof house had a refrigerator and a big table where graduate students ate various meals, and every month we celebrated birthdays in the department. We went together to football games and took canoeing trips along the Wisconsin River; I remember several memorable jaunts to see the magnificent northern lights. In sharing social activities as well as academic travails we became fast friends, and I count among my lifelong friends several people I met during that time in Minnesota.

THE COOPER INFLUENCE

I was happily consumed with increasing my botanical background by taking courses that had not been available at TU, but it was two of Cooper's courses, Field Ecology and Ecological Plant Geography, that most influenced me. In Field Ecology, Cooper used continental glaciation, which characterizes the Minneapolis-Saint Paul landscape, to demonstrate the interrelation of geomorphic and successional processes in plant communities. He could speak in detail from his own studies of glacial drift, glacial lake bogs, and sand dunes developed from glacial outwash as well as make comparisons with his continuing well-known research on tidal glaciers in Alaska and dune systems along the Pacific Coast. His monograph on the late glacial and postglacial environment of the Upper Mississippi Basin is considered a classic, and later as a Teaching Assistant in Field Ecology I got a bird's eye view of this landscape in a small plane flight over much of the area (he thought all of us teaching in this course should have this aerial perspective). He helped to clearly establish such relationships in our thinking, much as he had been influenced as a student at the University of Chicago by the physiographic ecologist H.C. Cowles, along with a glaciologist and a geographic geologist.

Cooper's geobotanical approach focused on careful description of relationships and historical explanations. He encouraged us to learn to use other techniques, such as palynology (study of fossil pollen) and dendrochronology (analysis of tree rings), to amplify the history. His inductive procedure was based on facts but he used these to test and reject "multiple working hypotheses." We were required to write an extensive report on our field work for each trip, which Cooper thoroughly edited, indicating the importance he gave to presenting research results effectively. My only disappointment with this course was that Cooper did not accompany us on any of the field trips. In fact, I never had the opportunity to be in the field with him.

Cooper emphasized unceasing change as a unifying concept throughout his teaching and research about plant succession. This idea was first expressed in "Fundamentals of Vegetational Change" (1926), which came from his seventeen-year study of permanent quadrats that he had established in the forest on Isle Royale in Lake Superior during work for his 1913 PhD dissertation. He had departed from Frederick Clements' generally accepted concept of linear succession and presented a more complex analysis, using the metaphor of a braided stream. To bolster his arguments, he mapped the trees on sampled stands and aged them by ring counts. In contrast to the then-common image of an essentially homogeneous community, Cooper described the forest as a mosaic, or patchwork of different ages, that was in a state of constant change. Cooper's exposition of the importance of small-scale disturbance in the community has gone largely unrecognized—attention having been given instead to A.S. Watt's 1947 *gap-phase* description of this phenomenon. (Robert McIntosh, an historian of ecology, has noted that long-term recognition often follows the presentation of a descriptive term, which seems to have happened in this case.)

In Cooper's course in Ecological Plant Geography of North America and ecological seminars, I began to be fascinated by the historical development of ecological concepts, which later became a prominent thread in both my teaching and research. He discussed the impact of the great German plant geographers, starting with Alexander von Humboldt's recognition of an "association" based on plant growth forms, which gave any vegetative "community" the distinctive appearance, or physiognomy, by which it could be recognized. Clements' philosophical orientation had been toward this German geographical tradition, especially that of Oscar Drude (with an organismic orientation) and August Grisebach, and their great treatises on the world's vegetation. Although Cooper discussed such plant geographers and recognized the important role of regional climates in determining major vegetation types, he avoided the organismal community concept as well as the complex hierarchical classification system and terminology formulated by Clements. Rather, he emphasized Andreas Schimper's *Plant Geography on a Physiological Basis*, which was based on the "marriage" of physiology and ecology. Cowles and Cooper also followed the more individualistic philosophical position of the Dane Eugenius Warming, who was critical of applying causes to any higher-level units, although he is celebrated for basing his geographical studies on the plant community. Warming was the author of the first textbook in ecology, *Plantesamfund (Oecology of Plants)* and its German translation *Lehrbuch der Okologischen Pflanzengeographie* led to wide development of courses called "Ecological Plant Geography." Here he created a new perspective regarding plant distribution. Warming shifted plant geography from largely descriptive and floristic studies to ones considering plant adaptation to the environment, and thus he hoped for more explanation of plant distribution.

In his Plant Geography course, Cooper displayed his flair for photography and demonstrated its utility in describing the composition of plant communities and the environmental factors that control their distribution. In this, he may have been influenced by Humboldt, who had incorporated aesthetic elements in his popular publications. Cooper felt that contemplating nature was an awe-inspiring pleasure, similar to that of seeing a great work of art. I have followed Cooper's path with great pleasure, photographing the vegetation in areas wherever I was doing research around the world, always thinking with a geographic and geomorphic perspective, while appreciating and recording its beauty.

The group of plant ecologists, often with visitors from other departments, met for weekly seminars at Cooper's spacious home. These meetings were characterized by stimulating discussions recognized later by numerous former students as influencing their work. For example, Raymond Lindeman, author on the classic paper on energy flow—"trophic-dynamic concept in ecology" indicated in a letter to Cooper: "Many of the good parts of the paper were due to the stimuli given by yourself and spirited discussions out at your home . . ."

Cooper enjoyed teaching and especially *training* graduate students. His meticulously prepared and presented courses in Field Ecology and Plant Geography were not only attended by botany department students, but by those in applied fields at the University of Minnesota. Foresters, wildlife students, and educators, among others, flocked to his courses, often overflowing the classroom. Although Cooper never wrote a textbook, six of his graduate students did later (R.F. Daubenmire, H.J. Oosting, J. Kittredge,

R. Humphrey, F.E. Egler, and P.C. Lemon). These textbooks spanned basic and applied areas such as forestry and range management. Although the Oosting and Daubenmire texts, on synecology and autecology respectively, were widely used for courses in plant ecology during the post-war years, Egler, a heretic among Cooper's students, strongly criticized both texts for just presenting traditional dogma. He did, however, laud Kittredge's *Forest Influences*, which is the first book in which effects of vegetation on environment are discussed. Egler did not direct his critique against Cooper but his former students, hoping to provoke reexamination of ecology, especially during its rapid growth in the 1950s. In the process, he unfortunately irritated many ecologists.

In addition to his teaching, Cooper continued to keep his hand in analyses at Glacier Bay, Alaska, through the field work of his associate D.B. Lawrence, but he was more actively involved in researching the formation of sand dunes. He had written papers on the vegetation of the Pacific Coast dune system of North America, but he wanted to better understand the factors controlling the development of different kinds of dunes. He was doing this experimentally by simulating the effect of different wind conditions using smoke bombs in the field and fans blowing on sand in his lab. He later (1958) received the Penrose Medal from the Geological Society of America (GSA)—the society's highest award and an unusual honor for a botanist—for "Coastal Sand Dunes of Washington and Oregon," published as a *GSA Memoir*.

ESTABLISHING A HUSBAND-WIFE TEAM

Following my marriage during Christmas vacation and subsequent separation from my husband, Cooper convinced Sharpe (without my urging) to talk with the stratigrapher and invertebrate paleontologist in the geology department about accepting Ralph as a PhD student once he had completed his MS at Colorado. Ralph was accepted and offered a fellowship in Minnesota's excellent geology department for his PhD, and we agreed that this was where we would continue our graduate studies. I feel that I should give Ralph special credit for my PhD because during these times it was unusual for a husband to let his wife's position determine where he would complete his training. I didn't even have to try to convince him. He said since we both loved Gothic, this would provide the opportunity to work together there.

I was the only woman PhD student Cooper ever accepted. I did not think much about being the *only woman*, but focused on the opportunity to continue my education. Cooper often said that he did not want to spend

Gothic Earthflow near Crested Butte, Colorado

time supervising a PhD for a woman when most of them got married and would never use more than a master's degree professionally (in most cases teaching in high school). This was a predominant assumption during the late 1940s and 1950s and even in some cases into the early 1970s. Although Cooper had taken me on initially as an MS student, by bringing Ralph to Minnesota, he was willing to support us as a doctoral team, especially as it meant combining botanical and geological research in the Colorado Rocky Mountains—one of his favorite areas.

The plan for our PhD dissertations was for Ralph to map the rocks and their complex structural relationships, ranging in age from very old Precambrian to very young Pleistocene, while I mapped the distribution of the vegetation, in the Crested Butte Quadrangle in which Gothic is located. He, however, would focus his research on a study of the stratigraphy and fossils of the Pennsylvanian-Permian (ca 300-290 ma) redbed sediments (ones composed of sandstones and shales that are red in color due to iron oxides). Part of these redbeds make up the Maroon Bells so prominent in tourist photos taken around Aspen, Colorado. He would reassess their age via the fossils and describe the environmental conditions when they were deposited from carefully-collected rock samples. I would describe the composition of the plant communities over the same area by using various sampling techniques. We would assist each other with our respective tasks.

COMPLETION OF MY MS RESEARCH

First, however, I had to complete my masters degree research on the Gothic Earthflow. During the summer of 1947, I described the physiographic conditions and the combination of topographic and structural conditions that favored movement of the earthflow. I also dated the movement, partly by using ring counts of trees bent over by the mass of earth as it flowed. I used line transects across the flow as a first basis for describing the plant community patterns. After Ralph had completed his master's degree that summer, he came to Gothic to help me map the earthflow in detail, using surveying equipment, and establish permanent quadrats (plots of a prescribed size). We also fenced a weather station, which I was using to assess some of the microclimate conditions. I had learned how destructive cattle could be when they wandered over from neighboring meadows.

Establishing permanent quadrats to monitor change had been an important part of Cooper's approach to the study of plant succession on Isle

Royale and in southeastern Alaska. At Glacier Bay he used them to follow the establishment and mortality of individual plants through the entire process of vegetation development from bare ground at the glacier front to forest cover. Through such means he could understand not only the path of succession but also its absolute rate. Similarly, I had carefully mapped the vegetation, topography, and location of line transects and quadrats of the Gothic Earthflow. With some refurbishing since then, these quadrats have enabled continuous monitoring of the slow successional changes on the earthflow.

With our masters degree research completed and the course of action for our PhD research laid out, Ralph and I knew our field headquarters would be located at Gothic for a number of summers. We decided to lease land from RMBL in Gothic and build some sort of cabin. We leased a plot in a trembling aspen (*Populus tremuloides*) grove on the hill immediately above the Mess Hall, where an access road could be made. I was delighted with the site. The understory was lush, with an abundance of blue columbine (*Aquilegia coerulea*—the Colorado state flower), and I had become especially fond of aspen trees—I loved their beautiful white bark, their leaves trembling in the wind and turning various colors of gold and bronze in the autumn. I made it one of my research goals to better understand the communities in which these trees dominate.

Also that summer Ralph purchased a used Chevrolet two-door sedan that he named "Zulabelle Clapsaddle." She served us loyally; I learned to drive over winding mountain roads with Zulabelle. She also took us back and forth across the plains between Minnesota and Colorado, as well as slipping and sliding on icy roads in the roundtrips to Tulsa for Christmas vacation.

MARRIED LIFE IN MINNESOTA
In the fall of 1947, the beginning of our first long period of living together, we naively rented a winterized cottage on Lake Minnetonka. Having both grown up where snow was considered a special event, we were eager to experience Minnesota winters. During the autumn we appreciated living where we could daily witness the brilliant colors of the fall foliage. Later, we were fascinated to see the architecture of the deciduous and coniferous trees silhouetted against a background of snow and a sun hung low in the sky. We enjoyed occasionally ice skating on the lake, but it was so cold in the cottage that we had to sleep in our double down sleeping bags on top of the bed. In the spring, however, it was again such a pleasure to witness

the changes in the forest, especially the understory flowers such as Bleeding Heart (*Hepatica*), *Cypripedium* orchids, and *Trillium* emerging from the heavy brown leaf litter. Spring was my only opportunity to see northern forest plants flowering because we spent our summers in Colorado. Despite enjoying the beauty of the different seasons in a northern forest, the rigors of living in the cold cottage sent us fleeing back to city dwelling the following year.

Cooper was extremely demanding in the writing of my master's thesis, preparing me for a PhD dissertation under his aegis. As Harriet Barclay had warned me, he was notorious for his

Ice skating on Lake Minnetonka

perfectionism—both in the execution of the research and in writing the results. Cooper abhorred the unwieldy terminology and labyrinthine logic with which he thought Clements had burdened ecology and emphasized simplicity and directness in ecological exposition. He admitted later that he had been testing me at the master's level to see if I could take criticism in stride. He told me that learning to use criticism to my advantage was a significant skill I could gain for my professional career. He certainly helped me to attain it! This was a point I later tried to communicate to my students, not only in dealing with writing their dissertations, but also in facing reviewers of manuscripts and grants.

The Botany Department had intensive PhD qualifying exams. Written questions from every member of the department were supposed to ensure that you had a well-rounded botanical background. Students also had to pass written exams in French and German. Ralph and I studied together for these intimidating language exams. Our high school French got us through that exam successfully but we had to take a course in scientific German to be ready for the exam in that language. Ralph also helped me in studying for my minor field of geology. He supported me throughout this period with unwavering confidence that I would excel.

The Botany Department's oral exam provided some of my most vivid (and traumatic) memories of graduate school. The Orals Committee was assigned by the Graduate Division, so the student did not know who would be on the committee until he or she walked into the exam room. There was no preparing for particular faculty as can be done by many graduate students today. I can remember the awful anticipation I felt wondering who my inquisitors would be. When I entered the room, Dr. Cooper was there, of course, and I will never forget the first question he asked: "Define art and discuss the relationship between art and writing a PhD dissertation in science." What a shock! I was so flabbergasted that today I don't remember how I answered other than something about art being an expression of beauty, which could be transferred to producing a dissertation. I do remember that Cooper smiled and said, "Think about it." Cooper was very involved in fine arts, having written plays and even operatic librettos—one of his closest friends was the conductor of the Minneapolis symphony. Both he and Ernst Abbe, a morphologist who also sat on my exam committee, held the opinion that the PhD, after all, was a Doctor of Philosophy degree and therefore should reflect a broad educational background. One of the questions that Abbe asked me was what Goethe's impact had been on both biology and philosophy. What a difference from the kind of knowledge expected from PhD candidates today, in the age of exploding scientific data and progressively newer technological and molecular advances.

After I passed my oral exam, Dr. Cooper gave me a special congratulatory gift that I treasured—a seedling of *Metasequoia*, the dawn redwood, which had recently been recognized as a living fossil. Kwei-ling Chu, one of Cooper's students, had done an ecological reconnaissance of the small, remote area in central China where it still occurs and brought back seed, from which Cooper had grown seedlings in the botany department greenhouse.

DOCTORAL RESEARCH IN TANDEM

Ralph and I had limited finances to support our field studies so we couldn't afford to build a log cabin on our RMBL site, as faculty and some researchers had done. Neither grants (the National Science Foundation was not formed until 1950), nor assistance from faculty in our departments were available at that time. So during the winter of 1948 we ordered a prefabricated farm building from a catalog—actually a domed chicken coop with a wooden floor that came in pieces we could assemble. It cost $200. We also ordered a bunk bed that would fit across the back wall and a sheepherder's stove.

The coop, our Gothic living quarters

The pieces of the coop and other building supplies were shipped via the narrow gauge railroad that came to the mining community of Crested Butte, then the small town where we bought groceries and received mail. A truck from the town's hardware store and gas station carried supplies up the one-lane dirt road from Crested Butte to Gothic. Thus in mid-June 1948, when much of the ground was still covered with snow and the road was very slippery, we jubilantly welcomed the slowly progressing, slipping and sliding truck bearing our prefab cabin.

We assembled the coop very quickly, built a table that would fit under one front window and fashioned stools with aspen branches for legs. We installed the sheepherder's stove, routing the stovepipe through the roof. Shelves and some homemade curtains completed the furnishings. We also set up the all-important outhouse close by (indoor plumbing didn't come to Gothic until the 1960s). The weather had been cold and wet, and we were happy to have our warm, snug shelter to return to as we started our field studies. Many other students have also relied on the coop in the decades since then. Over the years I have received postcards from students who stayed there, and others have approached me at scientific meetings to say that they had been happy occupants of that small and sturdy space.

The geological diversity of the Crested Butte area contributes to the occurrence of a rich flora and accounts for some of the differences in vegetation patterns. Ninety percent of the rock is sedimentary, from fine shales to coarse sandstones, with the remainder consisting of different kinds of igneous intrusions. Almost half of the sedimentary rocks comprise the redbeds on which Ralph was focusing his dissertation. They contrast dramatically with the white igneous rocks, which add to the striking beauty of these mountains. The topography is rugged, with glaciers having carved numerous cirques (natural amphitheaters) out of the sediments, often with glacial lakes occupying their floors. The diversity, size, character, and orientation of these cirques, often separated by narrow ridges, provided a variety of interesting habitats for high subalpine and alpine plant communities. The shale substrates resulted in broad glacial valleys, often filled with moraine (the accumulation of rocky debris carried and deposited by the glacier), that are threaded with meandering streams and vegetated by forest and grassland communities. The vegetation had been little disturbed by humans since the Gunnison National Forest had been established in 1909, so there were amazingly few adventive plants. The area's fire history, however, was coincident with the peak of mining activity from 1880 to 1900.

*Queens Basin, a glacial cirque with prominent ridges surrounding it
that provide a variety of high altitude plant habitats. Timberline
of spruce-fir forest and extension as krummholz evident*

Describing plant communities, determining their successional status, and classifying them constituted mainline research during the 1940s and 1950s. The vegetation of many areas of our large country, especially the western areas, had not been described. These descriptions of the pristine vegetation were considered valuable in helping to determine management over vast areas of forest and grazing land that was being increasingly utilized, as well as for later comparisons. Inherent in these studies for plant ecologists were questions regarding the nature of the community, how best to define its boundaries, and the best methods to quantify its floristic composition. These were issues with which I grappled—starting with establishing boundaries in mapping the plant communities. I depended on field observation as the fundamental source of data in determining their boundaries, which were based primarily upon discontinuities in physiognomy—that is, the dominant form of plant growth.

As early as the 1890s, C. Hart Merriam had identified zonal belts of vegetation in western North America, primarily in arid mountains where moisture and temperature gradients are strongly correlated with elevation. Merriam based his zones on temperature, but in the 1940s Rexford Daubenmire and others defined zones in the Rocky Mountains strictly by the vegetation itself. Cooper had suggested that I get an aerial view of the Crested Butte area if possible, and in the summer of 1948 I took a small plane flight, which gave me a bird's eye view of the vegetation of the Crested Butte area and reinforced observations I'd made from the ground. I could see five well-defined vegetation zones—Sagebrush, Aspen, Spruce-Fir, Upland Herb, and Alpine—along an altitudinal gradient from 8,500 to 13,500 feet. It was these vegetation zones that I planned to map and relate to mappable environmental parameters. I would then analyze the floristic composition of the zones quantitatively by counting the plants along transects and in associated quadrats.

I loved the striking colors of plants characterizing the vegetative zones, which only added to the color backdrop of the area's rocks. Their interplay seemed to me like the brilliant contrasts and light effects rendered by late nineteenth century Impressionists such as Monet, Pissarro, and Gauguin. And if landscape color was not enough, the abundance and array of colorful individual plants also enchanted me. Simply put, it is an exceptionally beautiful place to do research.

The many strikingly beautiful plants that had adapted to harsh alpine conditions particularly fascinated me. I replaced the plant drawings and paintings of my younger years with photographs and continually took portraits of these alpine plants. They have become a lifelong thread of interest and a love affair, so to speak, that exceeds even my feeling about aspen.

Although the Alpine Zone is well demarcated from approximately 12,500 to 13,500 feet in the Crested Butte area, plant aggregations form a mosaic that is more closely related to the diversity of the geologic substrate than in any other vegetation zone. An abundance of perennials—occurring as cushions or polsters, rosettes, or leafy stemmed plants—occupy the rocky fell fields, boulder fields, and talus slopes with different species characterizing different sites. I was enamored with the intensity of pink moss campion (*Silene*), reddish clover, and deep blue dwarf forget-me-not (*Eritrichium*) flowers as well as the size and color of single-stemmed violet gentians and

In my favorite mountain habitat

yellow gold fields (*Rydbergia*). In the melting snowbanks, yellow buttercups and glacier lilies (*Erythronium*) displayed unique adaptations of rapid growth in a matter of a week or two, and there was growth in profusion of fuchsia shooting stars (*Dodecatheon*) and *Epilobium*.

top left Claytonia megarhiza *(alpine spring beauty) in rocky areas*

top right Dryas octapetala *(mountain dryad) forming ground cover*

bottom left Rydbergia grandiflora *(alpine gold flower) in fell fields*

The extraordinarily lush meadows comprising the Upland Herb Zone are characteristic of the Crested Butte area between 10,500 and 12,500 feet, interdigitate with some lower parts of the Alpine Zone on slope exposures where snow maintains moisture late in the summer. These dense, luxuriant meadows—knee-deep in paintbrushes of varying colors from cream to magenta, blue columbines, lupines, and delphiniums, yellow senecios, and mule's ear (*Helianthella*), as well as subalpine daisies (*Erigeron*), bistort (*Polygonum*), and many others—are a major reason that this area was officially designated as "the wildflower capital of Colorado" by the state legislature.

Below the Alpine and Upland Herb Zones is the belt of dense, dark green conifer forest dominated by spruce (*Picea engelmannii*) and fir (*Abies lasiocarpa*), which comprises three-quarters of the vegetation in the Crested Butte area between 10,500 and 11,500 feet. Timberline generally occurs around 11,500 feet, with krummholz (patches of dwarfed trees) appearing as isolated outposts of the forest up to 12,500 feet.

Below the Spruce-Fir Zone, at about 9,500 feet, aspens form an open, pale green zonal forest. Because aspen is the most widely distributed broadleaf tree in North America, it has been differentiated into physiological races with different understory species and community relationships in different localities. In the zonal community in the Crested Butte area, aspen trees can reach an age of at least 130 years and have a much larger diameter than the successional trees that replace burned Spruce-Fir forest. This more mature community, like the one in which we set up our chicken coop, has a luxuriant but variable understory assemblage that includes several umbellifers as well as geranium, columbine, delphinium, and many others. In areas where aspen are expanding by root suckers, the understory reflects the fescue bunch grassland it is overtaking, but progressively this changes to the more lush, colorful understory of older zonal stands of trees.

At the drier, lower elevations between 8,500 and 9,500 feet, even the zonal Sagebrush (*Artemisia tridentata*) and associated Fescue (*Festuca thurberi*) bunch grassland communities have massive showy displays. They are visually set apart by domination either by gray-colored sagebrush or fescue bunch grasses that turn brown after fruiting, but, usually contiguous, they share a number of colorful species, such as the scarlet gilias (*Ipomopsis*), blue wild flax (*Linum*), and yellow cinquefoil (*Potentilla*), which often form a patchwork of color.

The summers of 1948, 1949, and 1950 passed quickly as we traversed one hundred square miles of the diverse geology and vegetation between 8,500 and almost 13,000 feet over most of the Crested Butte Quadrangle. Cooper had pioneered the use of aerial reconnaissance photography in geobotanical studies and our mapping would have been easier if we could have used it. But only a few photos were available over a small part of our area, so we relied instead on the 1894 USGS topographic map of the Crested Butte Quadrangle. With this as our base, we used Brunton compass techniques in determining the complex faults and other structural relationships, but used plane table, alidade, and surveying rod for detailed mapping. Frequently I was the one holding the surveying rod and I was nearly blown off more than a few alpine ridges. I also had a few literally hair-raising experiences, holding what could have easily become a lightning rod during approaching thunderstorms. We were always more concerned about finishing a bit of mapping before the heavy downpour occurred than my being struck by lightning! Our rashness, however, was abetted by the excitement of seeing the outlines of the geology and vegetation appearing on the topographic base map. The striking color contrasts of the rocks and plants dominating the zonal communities often aided our drawing their boundaries on the map. We measured the thickness of the rock formations with a tape and collected rock samples and fossils for laboratory examination to determine the conditions of their deposition. I was collecting plants to document those we were counting in transects and quadrats. We often had a heavy load to carry back to the coop.

*Demonstrating use of plane table and alidade in a
meadow amid aspens near our coop*

Doing field work across such a wide area and altitudinal range necessitated camping out for days at a time. We carried our food, sleeping bags, and fossil and rock samples in Trapper Nelson backpacks (made of balsa wood and canvas—the ultimate in mountain technology at the time) along with surveying equipment, a vasculum and a press for plant collections, and cameras dangling from our shoulders. Although it was a heavy load, especially noticeable returning from long periods at the highest elevations, carrying it ourselves seemed better than trying to deal with mules or burros. We felt like pack animals ourselves with all we carried, and sometimes we wearily wished for help. We slept in a little alpine tent in army-issue double sleeping bags; we usually needed both bags in alpine and some subalpine areas, as temperatures were frequently well below freezing. We used fir boughs from nearby conifers in lieu of air mattresses. We often camped on cirque floors where we melted snow for water or got it from springs and streams flowing from snow patches. We rarely saw other humans and thus were not concerned about polluted water. Our food was mostly army-issue dehydrated meals (soups and stews) or cereal cooked over an open fire; these were accompanied by hot tea and some dried fruit, or chunks of cheese or squares of Dot chocolate. We also savored eating the abundant wild strawberries, huckleberries, and gooseberries in the understory of the Spruce-Fir forest. Meals were definitely minimal but we both had endured the Depression and World War II, which meant we were not fussy about simple food. It was sufficiently nutritious that we stayed in good thin, muscular shape. As was true with my academic hurdles, Ralph never questioned whether I'd be able to withstand any of the rigors of our field work. I have to admit there were times when I wished he would suggest we go back to camp for a while, but he was unrelenting and I fell into agreement.

We enjoyed watching the activities of animals as we worked. Because our eyes were focused groundward in fossil collection and counting and collecting plants, we did not notice as many birds as mammals. Throughout our work, we were aware of the busy activities of spruce squirrels and chipmunks, as well as marmots on the talus slopes and the occasional porcupine. We saw mule deer more often than elk, despite the Crested Butte area being in the Elk Mountains. In the alpine areas, we caught glimpses of ptarmigan (the high mountain grouse), sometimes with young and always well camouflaged in the tundra fell and boulder fields, and we watched the small rabbit-allied pikas building their hay nests amid the rocky talus, making their presence known with their characteristic shrill alarm calls.

The coop always seemed luxurious when we returned to it with our loads of rocks, fossils, and plants. It was cozily warm and we could get thoroughly dry as well as have meals with some fresh meat and vegetables cooked in the pressure cooker (how I depended on that piece of equipment at our high altitude). On special occasions we loved having freshly caught rainbow trout from nearby Copper Creek with biscuits baked in the little sheepherder's stove. We hauled our water in buckets from the spring near the Mess Hall and cut wood for the stove. As we did our chores, we occasionally saw members of a weasel family that had taken up residence under the coop. A Coleman lantern and kerosene lamps provided light at nights—though we usually went to bed early after very physically active days.

It rained often and we endured being damp much of the time—except for our feet. If they remained wet, we became cold all over. Dry socks were at a premium, and when one of a pair wore out we'd keep the good one and continue to use it, which meant that sometimes we wore mixed pairs. When Ralph's parents visited one summer, they were shocked to see us wearing unmatched socks and asked if they could help us a bit financially so we didn't appear to be so desperate for decent clothing. We laughed a good deal over their offer as we were only finding an easy way to have enough socks available to keep our feet warm and dry. We appreciated Ralph's parents' kindness, even though their concern for our appearance at Gothic was misplaced. At other times of year, when we saw Gothic researchers at meetings or their home universities, we often joked about how different they (and we) looked in more respectable clothing.

Back at Minnesota during the 1949-50 academic year, both Ralph and I needed time to concentrate on analyzing data and writing up the last three years of field research. I had been awarded a fellowship to aid in completion of my doctorate, which was rare for a woman at that time. With this support from the American Association of University Women (AAUW), I was able to focus on my research. Having received three AAUW scholarships as an undergraduate, I now proudly became part of the AAUW tradition of helping their undergraduate awardees obtain doctorate degrees.

DISSERTATION WRITING WHILE AT COE COLLEGE
Because both Ralph and I were now focusing on writing our dissertations, and Ralph's GI funding had run out in the spring of 1950, he applied for a position teaching geology at Coe College in Cedar Rapids, Iowa, for the 1950-51 academic year. This would provide us with more income and the opportunity to see if a small liberal arts college was where we would like

to locate permanently. We both had such fond memories of the stimulating undergraduate education we had experienced at TU. Cedar Rapids also was close enough to Minneapolis that we could return during the year to use the library and confer with our advisors about dissertation progress. Teaching new courses in geology took more time than anticipated, of course, and even with my help, it took Ralph two years to complete his dissertation. He had to type all of the drafts on a big, old black typewriter, using carbon paper for copies and lots of "white out" to correct errors, as well cutting and pasting larger changes with scissors and tape. It meant that after editing, it was necessary to retype the entire draft. I not only helped to edit but also helped to draft all of his maps, graphs, and tables by hand. Without word processors and photocopy machines now available, it took much longer than it does now to prepare a dissertation for review.

Although my fellowship the previous year had enabled me to begin to analyze and organize data, I only had drafts of part of my dissertation. I was using a slide rule to make my computations. At Coe I spent most of my time assisting Ralph with his dissertation, as it was assumed that he would be the breadwinner hunting for a job. Dr. Cooper retired in the spring of 1951 and moved to Boulder, Colorado. Dr. Lawrence was his backup for the final formalities in completing my PhD, but Cooper wanted me to finish writing my dissertation as his student. It was an honor to be his only woman doctoral student, but during the agonies of his demanding perfectionism in writing, I sometimes didn't feel quite so lucky.

In general, the Coe years were not a good time for me. The faculty in the natural sciences were friendly, but some of their wives were less welcoming. They openly questioned why I should bother to complete a PhD; why did I not settle down and have a family, as they had done. It was the same refrain I had heard in graduate school about even allowing a woman to take a PhD. What I found difficult to reconcile was that these *women* did not allow for any possibilities other than what was the norm for our gender at that time—the traditional housewife. I found myself developing an uncharacteristically defiant attitude toward them. Ralph, on the other hand, encouraged me to finish my degree, saying that it was the best insurance policy he could give me. We enjoyed working together, especially in the field, and neither of us felt psychologically ready to start a family. And no complaints about our lifestyle had come from either of our families.

During the academic year of 1951-52, I became a lecturer at Coe, teaching a course in geography for high school teachers. Although these women (they were all women) appeared to be devoted to teaching, I was puzzled that most of them were not interested in geographic knowledge beyond the states surrounding Iowa. I found a similarly insular perspective among some other educated women. Because I had benefited from AAUW fellowships, I offered to help raise funds for fellowships, and suggested the possibility of bringing a foreign girl to Iowa University. I was unprepared for the response that the award had to go to an Iowa girl.

Our visits back to the University of Minnesota convinced us that we preferred a more stimulating intellectual atmosphere than we had at Coe College; it was time to move on. After Ralph graduated with his PhD in June 1952, he accepted an assistant professorship in the Department of Paleontology at UC Berkeley and we left the Midwest behind—for the time being.

WESTWARD TO CALIFORNIA
1952-1953

In the summer of 1952, after I checked the quadrats on the Gothic Earthflow and we collected fossils in western Colorado, we headed for California. Traveling with us was the little dawn redwood that Cooper had given me. It had withstood the trip across the plains and a period at high elevation at Gothic, and now it had to survive the high summer temperatures and dry environment of the Great Basin. Survive it did, and this little *Metasequoia* finally reached the place where the paleobotanist Ralph Chaney, who had first recognized *Metasequoia* as a living fossil, was working. In 1952 dawn redwood plants were still rare, as this was well before the time when they would be planted in various areas in the United States.

NEW ECOLOGICAL AND EVOLUTIONARY IDEAS

UC Berkeley provided a heady intellectual atmosphere—so different from the one at Coe College. For both of us UC Berkeley was exciting, as it had become one of the premier research universities following World War II. Moreover, Ralph was starting his career as an assistant professor in the only paleontology department in the country and one well endowed with its own research funds.

The botanists Herbert Mason and Lincoln Constance, along with the herbarium staff, formed a friendly, welcoming group and immediately invited me to attend field trips, work in the herbarium, and so on. Having spent four years enduring Minnesota winters, I clearly remember being startled by discussions in the herbarium about field trips in January to see the vernal flora. "Vernal"—didn't this mean spring? We were soon exploring the redwood understory plants followed later by incredible floral displays in Death Valley and the striking floral patterns around vernal pools; we later visited the coastal pigmy conifer forest, and looked at fire succession in different types of chaparral. I was intrigued with the research inspired by Herbert Mason on the relationship between narrowly restricted endemic plants and soils, especially on serpentine (rocks high in iron and magnesium) outcrops. This included the work at UC Berkeley of Hans Jenny on the physiological basis for serpentine tolerances and Art Kruckeberg on the genetic basis for a plant's tolerance of these soils. This was my introduction to another kind of geobotany, as I was learning about what Kruckeberg today refers to as the "kooky soils" that have shaped much of the rich California flora. I was not only observing the amazing diversity of this flora but also being apprised of experimental research into the environmental conditions controlling the evolution of the species populations.

William Hiesey (left) and Jens Clausen at Sierra Nevada study garden

I was particularly stimulated in visiting the common garden sites in the Sierra Nevada where the Carnegie Institution of Washington (CIW) team of Jens Clausen, David Keck, and William Hiesey at Stanford had launched the first large-scale interdisciplinary field experiment to understand evolution in plants by integrating systematic, genetic, and physiological studies of widespread species along a mountain transect. Although their research was directed toward understanding the nature of species, by generalizing on how genotypes are selected by local environment (called ecotypes), they provided essential understanding for much ecological research. I had heard about their research while at Minnesota, but it had not been given the emphasis it deserved. My "discovery" of it in California added significantly to my understanding of the distribution of several dominant, widespread species, such as aspen and sagebrush, that were part of my dissertation research. The emphases of these field trips in California contrasted with those in the Midwest, where research describing the plant communities, the impact of continental glaciation, and bog and riparian succession received prime attention. Experiments were used in plant life history and some physiologically-oriented (then called autecology) research but were not discussed in the field. California initiated a shift for me, broadening my thinking about a different flora in different environments and introducing me to botanists with different approaches to studying them. I was also incorporating a different paleobotanical perspective—a more long term ecological/evolutionary one, based on the research of Mason and Chaney, relating the history of current Pacific Coast vegetation to fossil leaves through Tertiary time, starting 65 million years ago (or even earlier in the Cretaceous). Previously, I had only thought about vegetational history through pollen records left during glacial time, a timescale of merely thousands of years ago.

The interdisciplinary synthesis of plant evolution—that is, the integration of systematics, population genetics, plant geography, and paleobotany—that I was witnessing had been greatly influenced by the Biosystematists, an elite organization that had formed in the San Francisco Bay Area in 1936. Among its botanical founders were a group at UC Berkeley, including Constance, Mason, and Chaney as well as Ledyard Stebbins at UC Davis, and the CIW team of Clausen, Keck, and Heisey at Stanford. An important aspect of the Biosystematists for the botanists was that it created a collegial atmosphere of sharing insights regarding the incredible array of variation provided by the California flora for the study of plant evolution from an interdisciplinary perspective.

Although the Biosystematists invited women to attend particular meetings, they did not invite them to become members of the organization until 1971, thirty-five years after the group was founded—at which time several members implied that this omission was more a matter of neglect than gender bias! (This was not the opinion of some excluded women.) There were two requirements for membership: having a PhD, and having an established, independent research program in some aspect of evolutionary biology. Several women met the first requirement, but even in my day, none could meet the second. There is evidence that some members objected *in principle* to opening membership to women. Ira Wiggins, a plant systematist from Stanford, had noted in a letter that "he had been opposed because founders of Biosystematics in the east, before we set up our group in business, included females and within five years infighting had wrecked the group and it ceased to function." The women "licked their wounds," so to speak, with membership in the San Francisco Bay chapter of the Society of Women Geographers. This organization had been established in 1925 in New York and Washington, DC when women had been excluded from the Explorers' Club.

The founders of the Biosystematists in the San Francisco Bay Area, along with increasing numbers of other researchers working on the diverse California flora, were responsible for bringing plants into the mainstream of evolutionary thinking then promulgated by zoologists in the eastern United States, known as the "Modern Synthesis," or "Neodarwinism."

Theodosius Dobzansky's *Genetics and the Origin of Species* (1941) had integrated genetics with natural selection and Ernest Mayr's *Systematics and the Origin of Species* (1942) had defined a genetic basis for describing

species and presented a logical way to think about classification using the phylogenetic method. Also the paleontologist G. Gaylord Simpson, in *Tempo and Mode of Evolution* (1944), demonstrated that the fossil record was consistent with the ongoing evidence seen in living species. All three books were products of the Morris Jessup lectures at Columbia University and were published as a series by Columbia University Press. Botanical members of the Biosystematists such as Babcock, Mason, Stebbins, and Chaney met with

Herbert Mason (left) and Ledyard Stebbins on a field trip

members of this group of east coast evolutionists, whose work had focused on animals, to form a committee on common problems in genetics, paleontology, and systematics. This led to the formation of the Society for the Study of Evolution in 1946. The domination of the eastern evolutionists continued, however. This resulted in friction between Mayr, the first editor of the journal *Evolution,* and the botanists. In 1949 Stebbins heatedly reported to Mayr: "Many of us on the plant side are beginning to feel that *Evolution* is favoring animals too much, and our interest in the journal and society are beginning to decline." Although botanists in the Biosystematists had made numerous contributions to current thinking, it was only after Dobzansky suggested that Stebbins accept the invitation to give the Jessup Lectures on *Variation and Evolution of Plants,* which were subsequently published in the Columbia University series in 1950, that the active interdisciplinary thinking of the California botanists was brought to the fore for many biologists. In so doing,

Ledyard Stebbins became the principle architect of evolutionary synthesis in botany. Overall the Neodarwinian synthesis has been considered one of the great intellectual triumphs of the twentieth century.

With Peter Raven (left) and Don Stone (right) in 2006

In addition to being intellectually inspired by prominent members of the 1950s group of Biosystematists on field trips, at seminars, and in discussions at the Berkeley herbarium, I interacted with botany graduate students who became lifelong friends and colleagues, many of whom went on to become leaders in plant systematics and related areas. Included are Otto Solbrig (Harvard), Robert Ornduff (UC Berkeley), and Don Stone (Duke and the Organization for Tropical Studies). Peter Raven (later at Stanford and Missouri Botanical Garden) was an undergraduate at Berkeley during this time; he joined activities with this group of graduate students and maintained his Berkeley contacts while getting his PhD at UCLA. One woman, Mildred Mathias, who visited the herbarium periodically from UCLA, became another important longtime friend. Mildred had taken her PhD in 1929 at Washington University, married, and, like me, had held a variety of part-time positions. She became a lecturer in botany at UCLA, but had so proved herself that she was appointed assistant professor in 1955 as well as director of the botanical garden in 1956—positions that she held until her retirement in 1974. We interacted repeatedly on field trips, in the herbarium, and especially on numerous committees after I too finally gained a UC ladder appointment in 1966.

Mildred Mathias in 1993

The timing of my arrival and involvement in the intellectual ferment among the botanists in the Bay Area was propitious. It helped me think more deeply about the physiological tolerances of individual plants and the genetics of their populational variation within a community framework. It set me on the road to combining my ecological background with paleobotanical and evolutionary thinking rooted in systematics and population genetics. Ultimately, this perspective would prepare me to leap into the field of chemical ecology.

COMPLETION OF MY DOCTORAL DISSERTATION

Despite going on many field trips, learning about a new flora, and meeting so many exciting researchers with new perspectives, my primary job during this first year at Berkeley was to finish writing my dissertation. Doing so was a trial, partly because of organizational problems arising from the complexity and amount of data I had collected. I also was struggling with plant community concepts during this period of ferment regarding the very nature of a plant community. Recognition of vegetation zones based on physiognomy of the dominant plants had made mapping of the vegetation relatively easy, and I had been bolstered in using the concept of zonal communities by successful descriptions of them for other Rocky Mountain vegetation. On the other hand, discussions with Mason and other Berkeley botanists led me to ponder the differences between Henry Gleason's individualistic approach to describing and classifying communities and the one I had used in my dissertation.

Gleason had learned ecology as an undergraduate at the University of Illinois from Victor Shelford in the Zoology Department and Stephen Forbes, director of the Illinois State Natural History Agency. It was Forbes' keen insights and especially his far-sighted use of statistical methods that greatly influenced Gleason's thinking—rather than Shelford's promotion of the organismal concept of the community. Gleason's doctoral work at Columbia University centered on plant systematics, the field he pursued during most of his career at the New York Botanical Garden. Mathematics had always attracted him, however, and in his early career he spent several years doing quantitative studies (using probability statistics) of the prairie and forest associations of Illinois and Michigan. It was these studies published as, "The individualistic concept of the plant association" in 1926 and again in 1939, that led to the turmoil over what many ecologists considered his heretical "individualistic" interpretation of plant communities comprising species occurring together coincidentally, or worse, the misinterpretation that he thought species occur in random mixtures.

Cooper agreed with Gleason that individual plants were distributed according to their tolerance of environmental conditions. However, he felt Gleason, the systematist, was correct in his 1953 description of himself when he wrote "to ecologists I was an anathema . . . I was an ecological outlaw, sometimes referred to as a good man gone wrong" with regard to his ideas about plant communities. Gleason had followed Cooper's 1926 view in emphasizing the element of chance in seed migration and seedling establishment as well as different durations of similar successional stages in different localities. The two also agreed that different initial conditions and different histories of disturbance could lead to different "terminal" aggregations of species. But Cooper disagreed with Gleason's *apparent* idea that plant communities were to a large extent a *random assemblage* of adapted species. Cooper still followed the idea that the community was a natural unit—what Whittaker later named the community-unit concept—though he rejected the concept of a community being a closely integrated system with emergent properties analogous to a superorganism, as Clements and his followers proposed.

I recognized the individual plant's physiological tolerance of environmental conditions, and found the concept of ecotypic differentiation (formation of races adapted to local habitats) of great importance in my interpretation of several Crested Butte communities. Under Cooper's tutelage, I had accepted the community-unit concept as I mapped vegetative zones based on physiognomy determined by a few dominant plants along an altitudinal gradient. I then had sampled these zones. The individualistic proponents avoided sampling a predetermined unit, thinking that the best way to understand aggregations of plants was to sample them quantitatively and then establish community boundaries. In my dissertation, however, I largely avoided these philosophical issues, leaving that for later discussion in its publication.

Whatever community concept ecologists espoused, they were also evaluating quantitative methods that would increase rigor in accurately describing communities. After much thought, I chose to use pace transects, also called step point quadrats—counting a specified number of plants intersected while pacing a line through numerous stands of each zonal community type—as this had been reported to be effective in rapid vegetation surveys over extensive areas of different community types. In forest communities, large plots were located at random along the transects to determine the density, size, and age of the trees. I could quantify the composition (other than trees) of the communities according to their cover and constancy from the transect data collected in many stands of each zonal community.

I also presented relationships between mappable environmental patterns (altitude, slope exposure, and rock type) and distribution of the zonal community types. I assumed that cause-and-effect relationships could not be established between these three mappable environmental patterns and the distribution of communities. At the community level, such relations are summaries of population phenomena and hence provide only partial correlations or coincidences with environmental pattern. Changes in moisture and temperature along altitudinal gradients, as well as with slope exposure, have long been shown to influence plant distribution. The effect of slope exposure on the distribution of vegetation types is strongly evident in the Rocky Mountains, and is in some cases related to rock type (soil parent material). The importance of parent materials had recently been pointed out by Jack Major, who indicated that "only parent material of a soil is independent of other landscape or ecosystem properties which determine both vegetation and soil." Not having been able to find statistical techniques to express the correlation between vegetative and environmental patterns quantitatively, I finally devised my own quasi-quantitative "coincidence index" (percent area of a zonal community coincident with an environmental pattern was divided by the total area of that pattern.) Although not a rigorous analysis, this index revealed noteworthy relationships not immediately obvious from field observation.

I concluded that the vegetation zones of the Crested Butte area are unique for the Colorado Rockies but have more similarities to parts of the southwestern slope and mountainous Great Basin than the better-known eastern slope. I also conjectured that this unique zonal sequence in the Crested Butte area primarily results from the steep precipitation gradient between 8,000 and 10,000 feet (two-thirds of the area is dry and southwest-facing) but a combination of various sedimentary and igneous rock contributes to different kinds of soil as well. Although not a part of the conclusions in the dissertation, I also realized that the unique juxtaposition of colorful rocks and vegetation zones had contributed to its extraordinary beauty.

Cooper edited drafts of my dissertation by mail, and our voluminous correspondence seemed endless. I had become inured to Cooper's relentless perfectionism while writing my master's thesis, but my PhD dissertation was much more complex, containing as much data as it did and covering such a large area. Cooper constantly exhorted me to write with simplicity, conciseness, and clarity, although he admitted that he too struggled with curbing verbosity. "State the situation as directly as possible and avoid jargon" was his edict, with *jargon* referring particularly to Clements' excessive terminology. Cooper was sharp in his criticism of details, emphasizing that the fine points often made the difference between good and excellent writing.

Finally, as we neared the end, the reward came. He wrote, "Now that the job is done so far as I am concerned, I want to tell you that I greatly admire your patience and persistence throughout the long process. I suppose that I have been hard to please, but I can't let work go until it is as good as it can be. And your contribution is a valuable one and needs to be made as nearly perfect as possible. Do your damnedest to make the final copy perfect both in substance and in appearance." At this point I could, with firsthand knowledge, have discussed the relationship between art and writing a doctoral dissertation!

As we exchanged numerous drafts, Cooper began to intersperse personal and even humorous comments in his letters to me. He described his garden, problems in starting a Boulder Philharmonic, and having dinner before a roaring fire at his mountain retreat—named *Tapiola* for the symphonic poem of Jean Sibelius. Previously, he had seemed caring but distant and very formal. I was surprised but pleased that we were developing a personal friendship, which grew over the years I was in Berkeley. His publications on California redwoods and broad sclerophyll vegetation (which he only mentioned peripherally in his plant geography course at Minnesota) and his brief teaching stint at Stanford before going to Minnesota began to play into my relationship with him. We ultimately had the interweaving threads of plant ecology in Minnesota, Colorado, and California in common. These threads led to a friendship that Cooper established with few of his graduate students; it was one I cherished. He was a man of unusual accomplishments spanning science and the arts, and I am grateful for the role he played in mentoring my intellectual development during the formative years of my graduate studies. Moreover, he remained an inspiration and a friend until his death in 1978—the same year I lost Mother. The loss of these great influences in my life, only several months apart, was devastating.

In the 1950s, women were still defined exclusively by their relationship with men. Cooper always addressed his correspondence to me as "Mrs. Ralph Langenheim." Even after I obtained my PhD, he did not give me individual recognition as "Dr. Jean Langenheim," although occasionally he addressed letters to "Mrs. Dr. Ralph Langenheim." Recognizing my husband always came first, I did not think anything about it at the time, because working as a team with my husband was part of what had convinced Cooper to take me as a PhD student.

I returned to the University of Minnesota in the spring of 1953 for the oral dissertation defense, where all went well. The Botany Department recognized my research accomplishments by nominating me as a Full Member in Sigma Xi—the Scientific Research Society—which was a special honor since at that time each department was allowed only one such nominee a year (I had been taken in as an Associate Member in 1949 when I completed my master's degree). I was inducted as well into Sigma Delta Epsilon, now also known as Graduate Women in Science, a group that was founded in 1921 to advance the participation and recognition of women in the sciences.

After the struggle with writing the dissertation followed by Dr. Cooper's high praise for its "valuable contribution," I was a little deflated with Dr. Lawrence's comment that "it is a very *useful* piece of work." On the other hand, it has turned out to be just that. Over the years, many RMBL students and other Rocky Mountain researchers have made use of this research.

To celebrate successfully defending the dissertation, I took the trip westward to California on the legendary California Zephyr out of Chicago. This was a special ride for a train lover because it was and is still considered the greatest of all US trains. It was all first class with a dining car, elegantly appointed and famous for its food. Zepherettes (like airline stewardesses) were available to assist passengers. I savored the opportunity to relax and view from the domed lounge cars the ever-changing landscape and oft-changing light that enhanced its beauty. The train schedule was timed so that during daylight hours passengers passed through the most scenic country and slept through what most people considered more monotonous areas. I appreciated the variety of natural vegetation and agriculture—Midwestern deciduous forests were mixed with prosperous farms across prairie country until it was too dark, and in the early morning, I followed the changes in forests as we gained altitude on the eastern slope and then lost altitude on the western slope of the Rocky Mountains. I slept across much of the Great Basin cold desert, missing the arid landforms and vegetation, but ate breakfast while traversing the Sierra Nevada forests so different from the Rockies, then watched the appearance of the rich Central Valley agricultural areas, the savanna-like California Coast Ranges and finally glided into Oakland along the Pacific Coast. I was glued to the windows watching the passing landscape, much as I was reported to have done as a young child while traveling with my mother from Louisiana to the East Coast. Now, however, as a newly-minted PhD, I was recalling Cooper's beautiful photos, which had introduced me to the relationship between plant geography and geomorphology that I was now witnessing as we moved across the country. Darwin's words also came to mind: "A traveler should be a botanist, for in all views plants form the chief embellisher." Being fascinated with observing vegetation patterns in relation to landforms would be a strong continued thread in my later travels.

COLOMBIAN EXPEDITION
1953

*The test of an adventure is that when you're in the middle of
it, you say to yourself, "Oh now I've got myself into an awful
mess;
I wish I were sitting quietly at home."*
—Thornton Wilder

During our first year at UC Berkeley, Ralph and I were invited by the
Colombian National Geological Institute (Instituto Nacional Geológico de
Colombia) to study the stratigraphy and paleontology of the Girón Formation
in northern central Colombia. These redbeds are prominent among Paleozoic
and early Mesozoic rocks (300-200 ma) that form the core of many ranges in
the Cordillera Oriental of Colombia and Venezuela. Ralph was now considered
an authority on such sediments because of his dissertation on the redbeds
of the Colorado Maroon and Gothic Formations. The primary purpose of
our research was to better determine the age of the Girón Formation by
examining the invertebrate and plant fossils stratigraphically. I was hired as a
paleobotanista to study the plant fossils. I also became a botanical opportunist
on this trip, collecting plants in the areas where the geologists were making
stratigraphic measurements. This was still a time when "hit and miss" plant
collections from South America were highly valued.

So, a few days after my return to Berkeley from Minnesota, and Ralph
had finished teaching his spring courses, we embarked on our Colombian
adventure. It was our first international flight. We took a Pan American
(PanAm) plane to New York, where we transferred to a Colombian Avianca
plane to Bogotá that stopped in Jamaica. It was a wearily long flight as only
prop planes flew to Latin America in 1953 (PanAm's first jet flight didn't
come until 1958).

The flight from New York began at night and we were soon engulfed
in a turbulent storm with dramatic lightning. The plane was frighteningly
tossed about. Many people were sick and some of the Jamaicans were praying
loudly. After surviving the night's storm, most travelers seemed happy to
terminate their trip in Jamaica but we were eager to proceed. We were thrilled

to view the spectacular mountain scenery of the Andes in the daylight, and I remember thinking about how inspired I had been in high school French class in reading Saint Exupéry's accounts of his flights over the Andes. The sky was more or less clear until nearing Bogotá where the mountains were enshrouded in clouds. We disembarked in the cold and gloomy atmosphere of Bogotá, which frequently would be overcome, however, by the warm hospitality of the Colombian people.

We arrived the first of June and were soon initiated into the Latin culture of official wheels grinding very slowly. This inertia can be especially frustrating when one is on a limited time schedule, as most American researchers usually are. We had to learn that it is best to relax and take it as it comes—unless, of course, you know the right person in a position of power who can expedite matters. The upside is that if you have been invited to work there, you usually are being wined and dined and shown the tourist sites in the meantime. This was true for us in Bogotá for ten days after we arrived. We were taken by the Institute's geologists on several trips, including one to the famous Salta de Tequendama waterfall. Near the falls I saw for the first time tree ferns and poinsettia trees, which were growing around nearby houses. The falls drop 400 feet from the *sabana* on which Bogotá is located, at 8,000 feet. The *sabana*, an old lake bed, has rich soils used for farming; here agriculture occurs up to 12,000 feet—an elevation that, I marveled, would be above timberline in Colorado.

Another jaunt took us two-thirds of the way across the eastern cordillera, where the poorly-designed, largely unpaved roads and Colombian driving habits made for a hair-raising trip. Our drivers tended to dash around curves in the middle of the road while honking their horns. If they met another car on the other side, it could be a bit alarming—and exhilarating—especially if you were on the outside of the road with a thousand-foot drop off. *Campesinos*, and all their cows and sheep, were scattered over the road, leading to constant conversation about those who had been *aplastados* (hit and flattened). These drivers dramatically—often while hanging onto a Saint Christopher's medal dangling from the rearview mirror—pointed out many shrines where cars or buses had collided with people or animals or gone off the side of the mountain. In many Latin American countries, these shrines are considered the site where people made the transition from this world to a spiritual one. They both pay tribute to the deceased and warn of a dangerous spot in the road. There were entirely too many of them for our comfort! Although I was fascinated with the Andean vegetation, I couldn't look much at plants because my eyes were fastened on the road.

Another of our "tourist" experiences included an event that influenced our entire summer's research. A brother of the geologist who was going to assist us in the field was in the president's guard and had access to the president's box at the bullfight arena when *El Presidente* was not planning to attend. On such a day we were invited to see a bullfight. We had taken our seats and were being informed about the bullfight when army tanks entered the ring! Not a usual part of the program, we wondered? We were soon hustled out, being informed that a military coup had just occurred. Mayhem reigned in the streets. Dr. Enrique Hubach, the director of the geological institute, met us, saying that we needed to get into the field as soon as possible because this change in government could result in our contracts not being recognized. We never thought to ask him whether we should be returning to the United States rather than proceeding with our research. We just followed the lead of the persuasive Dr. Hubach.

The coup, led by the head of the army, Gustavo Rojas Pinilla, had overthrown Laureano Goméz, an arch conservative dictator, who had taken power as president in 1950. In 1953, various guerilla groups (some responsible for the civil war period of La Violencia from 1948 to 1953, which was particularly bad in rural areas) merged with Rojas Pinilla to depose this hated ultra-conservative president, who was collaborating with powerful clergy of the Catholic Church. Catholicism was the state religion, and one goal of the revolution was to secularize education and thereby diffuse some of the power of the church. It also was considered a social revolution to help the desperately poor people comprising the majority of Colombians. We really had no idea what was ahead of us by going into rural Colombia, still the center for guerilla activity. In retrospect, it was good that we were so naive; this naiveté assisted me in particular during several difficult situations.

RESEARCH IN TROPICAL GUERILLA COUNTRY

Soon after Rojas Pinilla took control of the government, Hubach told us to go immediately to our hotel to pack for the field and take our remaining luggage to the institute where it would be held for us. He managed to get an institute *camioneta* (van), collected necessary research equipment and soon our group left Bogotá for Bucaramanga in the province of Santander del Sur, where good exposures of the Girón Formation occur.

The group included Ralph and me, Hubach, a young Colombian geologist Alberto Ronderos, and an institute assistant, Daniel Valenzuela. We hadn't gone

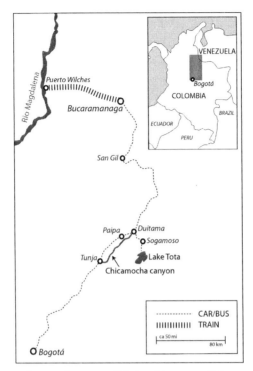

Research areas of Colombian expedition

far, however, before we discovered that the guerillas had blown up bridges on major highways to control movement of people across the country. When we reached the first big river, only a foot bridge was standing. The guerillas there confiscated our government *camioneta*; they made it clear that it was theirs to be had! Dr. Hubach was bemused by the whole affair; he calmly brought out a cloth bag with cheese, some large crackers, nuts, and several bottles of water for us to eat while we dealt with the situation.

Fortunately, the guerillas did not confiscate our belongings and scientific equipment. Dr. Hubach and Alberto negotiated vigorously with them to let Alberto, Daniel, Ralph, and me proceed to San Gil, where one of Alberto's brothers ran a cement plant—and for Dr. Hubach to return to Bogotá with the next available transportation. It was a tricky negotiation because we had national identification cards (*cédulas*) that showed we were affiliated with the ousted government. This was more serious for our Colombian companions than for Ralph or me, but the guerillas released all of us and, luckily, a truck loaded with potatoes on the other side of the river was going to San Gil. I swallowed my fear as we all walked across a rickety footbridge, which had been hastily assembled, over a roaring river in the dead of night. We were then hoisted up onto the truck. There we sat on a huge pile of potatoes amid our gear and in the company of other *campesinos* for the very bumpy ride to San Gil. We found lodging at a little pension along one side of the main plaza, which introduced us to our now tropical environment, with the church immediately opposite. We were awakened early the next morning by church bells, which sounded more like someone banging on old wash tubs, and a priest speaking loudly over a public address system. With our rudimentary knowledge of Spanish, we surmised that he was exhorting people to rid the area of Protestants. Our Colombian friends confirmed that the priest had suggested that Protestants should be threatened to leave Colombia. They thought he was probably referring to missionaries, who were siding with the guerrillas, wishing to free themselves from the grip of the Catholic Church. On the surface it appeared to be a *rouge et noir* situation of a dictatorial government working with the church to control the lives of the people—the powerful and the rich telling the poor that God had willed it so. The opulence displayed by priests and the rich ornamentation within the churches contrasted sharply with the extreme poverty of most *campesinos*.

Alberto's brother provided transportation for us to Bucaramanga where a garrison of soldiers was located. Dr. Hubach arranged for soldiers to protect us while working in the Magdalena River Valley, which was known to be inhabited by active guerillas (and still is today). Meanwhile our oil company friends in Bogotá, whom we had gotten to know because they had taken petroleum engineering degrees at TU,

View from pension window in San Gil plaza

thought we needed independent transportation. They sent a telegram to Bucaramanga informing us of the imminent arrival of another geologist in an International Petroleum Company (Intercol) jeep; however, he arrived before the telegram. This connection to TU and its petroleum engineering program, which was headed by Ralph's father, provided us with valuable assistance while we were in Colombia.

We spent six weeks in Santander del Sur, where I was introduced to South American tropical and subtropical vegetation amid fields of sugarcane and bananas. Because it is well vegetated mesa-canyon country, we could only find exposures of the Girón Formation along roads, railroad cuts, or streams. The most exciting and untoward event came along the railroad tracks, where we were usually escorted by soldiers in a railroad handcar. We had not encountered any previous trouble in working along the railroad, so the soldiers left us in the morning and would pick us up later in the afternoon to return to Bucaramanga.

As was often the case, when the geologists were not hunting for fossils, I wandered off to collect herbarium specimens. I was collecting plants along the tracks, and stopping intermittently to put them between newspapers in a plant press, because they quickly wilted in the heat. I had gone around a curve and was no longer in view of the others. I was not concerned about a group of men standing by the tracks, because the local people had been friendly. They seemed particularly curious about this young pith-helmeted American woman collecting what they considered weeds (*mala hierba*). They offered to help me collect, bringing me hard-to-reach plants high on the bank above the track. We all laughed when I tried to explain to them what I was doing in my fragmented Spanish. But then a distant rumble alerted them to the approaching train. Their demeanor changed; they whistled and other people began to emerge from the forest as the train rounded the curve. The group who had been collecting with me jumped in front of the train to stop it. The other guerillas boarded the train and began to take passengers forcibly into the forest. I rapidly retreated, running back as fast as I could to the small train station at Puerto Wilches where the railway men were already calling the soldiers in Bucaramanga. Ralph and the others in our group had realized that something was wrong when the train stopped. They could not see well around the curve in the train track but had also converged on the train station.

I don't remember all of the lurid details (which I purposely did not include in letters to my mother), but what remains vivid is that we had to carry a body bag with the cadaver of the train's engineer in the handcar with us on our return to Bucaramanga with the soldiers. The soldiers told us that he had been decapitated by the men—in fact, those who so jovially had helped me collect plants a short time before. Afterward, we wondered what happened to the body of the engineer or if the guerillas, who stopped the train, had been sought by the military. We never heard more about the incident from the soldiers who accompanied us—and we were very hesitant to ask. After all, the sympathy of the head of the army, now Colombian president, with the plight of the guerillas had led to the coup d'etat. Although Rojas Pinilla had allowed national scientific institutes, such as ours, to continue as before the revolution, the guerillas outside of Bogotá did not know anything about us beyond our *cédulas* issued by the former hated government. Thus because of this complex situation the director had arranged to have the military to protect us in case there were problems with the guerillas.

Following this incident, the army restricted our activities in the Magdalena Valley, and we did not go there without them. Because of the nature of the revolution, we North Americans were considered at less risk than our Colombian colleagues. Having me along also was deemed good protection, because the guerillas generally seemed mystified by this English-speaking woman collecting plants. They apparently thought that capturing or harming me would not help their cause. This was a case where being a woman on a scientific expedition was considered an extra value!

Civil upheaval and close calls notwithstanding, our measurement of stratigraphic sections and collections of fossil proceeded. Invertebrate fossils were much more abundant than plants. The plant fossils were such sparse and scrappy impressions or compressions that I was worried about identifying them—a problem that plagued me for a number of years afterwards.

At the end of July we returned somewhat wearily to Bogotá to reorganize for work in the high-altitude provinces of Boyacá and Cundinamarca (where Bogotá is located). Ralph drove the three hundred miles back in the jeep with the Intercol geologist. Because of limited space in the jeep, I flew in a small plane which, uncomfortably, did not appear to be in the best shape. The takeoff from a very short runway that ended over a small canyon only added to my apprehension, but all went well.

HIGH COUNTRY ADVENTURES

In August, our work was primarily centered between the small towns of Paipa, Sogamosa, and Duitama in alpine country where deep canyons cut into a *planalto* (high plain) were surrounded by high mountains. The cold, cloudy climate, *páramo* vegetation, and associated culture of the people contrasted sharply with the subtropical regions around Bucaramanga. The *páramo*—Neotropical vegetation that occurs between the upper forest line and permanent snow—is particularly characteristic of high elevations in Colombia. We had moved from a land of sugarcane and bananas to one of potatoes, from people thinly clad in light colors to ones in dark wool *ruanas* (poncho-like garments) and black hats. Importantly, however, we did not need military protection as there was much less guerilla activity here.

When we left Bogotá, we had shared an institute *camioneta* with two Dutch geologists. The driver first dropped us off to spend the day in Paipa. After he delivered the geologists to a meteorite they were investigating, he was supposed to return to us in Paipa and then take us to Lake Tota. This is a favorite retreat for oil company expatriates, where we had planned to spend some of a big holiday. Known locally as Boyacá Day, it is the celebration of the liberation of five South American countries from Spain by Simon Bolívar. When the driver didn't show up at the appointed time, we walked to an area of hot springs to take a dip and warm up. We had been shivering in the cold alpine climate despite purchasing our own heavy wool *ruanas* and other woolen items to keep warm. The owner of the hotel at the hot springs made temporary arrangements for us to stay there overnight. In the morning we went back to Paipa but still could not find the *camioneta*.

Our team in páramo near Paipa
(Ralph third from left and me far right)

The congestion surrounding the holiday had made things chaotic. Although we were having transport problems and trouble finding a place to stay, when we just relaxed, we realized that we had the opportunity to learn about the local people during these festivities. What could have been a trial became an illuminating experience—and strikingly different from staying with our expatriate friends.

We crammed onto an already-full bus bound for Sogamosa, which was as close as we could get to Lake Tota. Since the local people depend on bus transport, they will somehow make room for anyone wanting to get on, quite often with loads of their belongings, including farm animals. On this trip, an elderly woman on the seat next to me tried, with a partially toothless smile, to hand me the chicken she had on her lap. A gift? Surely not? I declined with many a *"Gracias."* The tops of the buses are packed with almost everything you could imagine a person might want to transport, which this time included our luggage and mapping equipment.

When we got to Sogamosa, we found that there was no telephone at Tota. It had never entered our heads that there would be no way to communicate with this resort. And all the hotels in Sogamosa were full. So we boarded another bus, with our mountain of gear, for Duitama, where we finally found crowded accommodations in a small *pensión* with a very raucous parrot reigning in the courtyard. Since we couldn't work, we joined the crowd of *campesinos* in boisterous Boyacá Day festivities, which included fireworks and enthusiastic shouting of *"Viva Presidente"*, now Rojas Pinilla, when he arrived to speak. The people here welcomed him joyously as a collaborator to help the Colombian downtrodden.

The next day the driver and the *camioneta* finally appeared. After getting three tires fixed (tires seemed to be worse here than even the synthetic ones we had during World War II in the US), we finally headed to Lake Tota. The large lake is at 9,000 feet, and the mountains that surround it are perpetually enshrouded in clouds. When we arrived, we saw our oil company friends, who looked like they were going on an Arctic expedition as they climbed into boats to fish for the huge trout (weighing as much as twenty-five pounds) that occur in the lake. That night, after eating luscious trout dinners fixed by the hotel cooks, we sat around a roaring fire with our Tulsa friends from Mobil Oil Company, other Americans from Texaco, and some British with Shell.

Because numerous English-speaking expatriates came to the hotel, magazines and books in English were available, which we devoured. We had only occasionally seen an old *Time* magazine or *Reader's Digest* in

English during our travels and had not received any news other than that of our local areas. Although we sent weekly letters home, we hadn't yet gotten any replies as they were all addressed to the geological institute in Bogotá. For the first time, I knew what it was like to be out of touch with the rest of the world—either because of language differences or the means of communication in a foreign country.

Following the festival we resumed our work, which continued to be plagued by transport problems—and the high mountain weather. The Intercol jeep had broken a spring on the rough roads and we couldn't find parts for it in any of the small towns where we were working. We even had trouble finding mules to take us into the Chicamocha River Canyon between Paipa and Duitama, where there were good exposures of the Girón Formation. It was so windy on the *páramo* that we had difficulty in mapping; it was hard to keep the surveying table on the ground, let alone hold the surveying rod erect. Even at much higher elevations in the Rockies, we had never faced such consistently high wind problems. We were forced to stop mapping when the winds were too strong and concentrate on collecting fossils. One such time, en route to a collection site, we went through a village on market day. We gathered a crowd wherever we went, and as we were buying a drink, Ralph counted the number of people watching us—fifteen children and ten adults stood wide-eyed and open-mouthed. He asked if anyone had seen any *caracoles* (shells) in the rocks nearby. No one answered, but such crowds would stand

In Chicamocha Canyon; Girón Formation displayed on canyon wall

staring until we left. I had the same experience later in other Latin American countries, as well as in urban China soon after it opened to the rest of the world in 1980. At that time, we were fascinatingly different.

To shake off the pervasive chill, we went to swim in the hot springs on several occasions and in the course of these visits made friends with the Hungarian owner of the Hotel Thermales. He was building a large house amid orchards of hundreds of fruit trees under which he was growing potatoes as a crop—an expatriate quite different from those with oil companies. They all, however, considered themselves to be helping to develop a "backward country." On the other hand, many of those who had fomented the revolution considered most expatriates to be imperialists and part of the problems created by the native rich.

TAKING LEAVE OF COLOMBIA
All was quiet in Bogotá with the military in control. We had been concerned that with the change in government Dr. Hubach might have been removed as director of the institute. Traditionally, new governments replace the administration in the national institutes. If this had happened, there was a possibility that our contract would have been in jeopardy. However, we had good news upon our return. Dr. Hubach was still the director and we were finally going to be paid. Furthermore, it would be in dollars, but only because Dr. Hubach's wife was a friend of the treasurer of Colombia!

Ralph needed to return to Berkeley before I did for the beginning of his classes at the university. With no time constraints facing me, I had planned to see some other Latin American countries en route home by getting a berth on a Grace Line freighter that went along the west coast of South and Central America to San Francisco. After many broken promises regarding my reservations over several weeks, I decided to fly, with brief stops in Panama, Costa Rica, and Mexico. Ralph flew home while I stayed in Bogotá for another week.

I did not meet another woman botanist (nor geologist) while I was in Colombia; however, the male botanists at the University of Colombia's herbarium in Bogotá treated me royally. During the week before my departure, we cemented relationships that lasted many years. First, they celebrated my birthday with a cake and a corsage of carnations. When they told me they were going to give me a corsage, I envisioned an orchid. Carnations reminded me of high school dances at home, but in Colombia they were prized for corsages because they were unusual, whereas orchids were common. Along with a typical Colombian *bizcocho* (sponge cake), they were proud of having peach *melbas* made with rubbery canned peaches (again a treat for them). It's the unusual that we seem to prize for special occasions, no matter where we live.

*In herbarium with director
Hernando Garcia-Barriga*

Very cold me collecting Espeletia plant

While I was working with my plant collections at the herbarium, Dr. Hubach kindly loaned me a *camioneta* to take some of my botanist friends, led by Jesus Idrobo, to *Páramo de la Siberica* to collect *frailejón* (*Espeletia*). A member of the composite (sunflower) family, *Espeletia* is a giant, tree-like rosette reaching six to eight feet in height with large yellow flowers and silvery pubescent leaves. It is a characteristic plant of the Colombian *páramo* and particularly rich in species at *Siberica*. Such tall plants, along with the tussock grasses and large shrubs, give this alpine vegetation quite a different appearance from that in the Colorado Rockies, where alpine plants commonly occur in small cushions, mats, or rosettes close to the ground or as isolated plants amid rocky areas. I was told that at higher elevations in rocky and more barren areas of the Colombian mountains I would see more prostrate alpine adaptations. Because it was a densely foggy day and very windy, we were so cold that we agreed *Siberica* was an appropriate name for this *páramo* area. We focused on only collecting *frailejónes* because of our extreme discomfort—plus we were worried about the condition of our *camioneta*. Soon after we had picked it up, oil began to pour out underneath. When we took it back to the institute garage, instead of giving us a different vehicle, the mechanics gave us an enormous can of oil. We had been pouring oil in the *camioneta* all day, hoping that it would be enough to get us back to Bogotá. We were happy with an uneventful return!

During this interval I again joined the company of the well-to-do oil company personnel. They were a cosmopolitan group. At one party, among five couples, seven nationalities were represented, and a bewildering number of languages were being spoken. In addition to mingling at parties, we also went to posh country clubs and trendy, expensive restaurants together. These people were living a stereotypical colonial lifestyle; they were bringing technical expertise to an undeveloped country, but they lived luxuriously apart from most Colombians, only associating with the wealthy or powerful who served their purposes. The only other Colombians they knew were their servants, chauffeurs, cooks, and gardeners. This was the only time in all the years I would do research in Latin America that I had close association with such a group of expatriates. It was an edifying experience.

VISITING OTHER LATIN AMERICAN COUNTRIES
Leaving Colombia was even more difficult than beginning to work there. It seemed to take a suitcase full of papers, all of which required standing in long lines to be officially stamped. Leaving by plane was also wait, wait, wait—in an unheated airport—with the men standing around in long black

coats drinking *tintos* (strong black coffee here laced with brandy) in an attempt to stay warm while waiting for delayed planes. Of course my plane was scheduled for late leaving, but Dr. Hubach, Alberto Ronderos from the geological institute, and Hernando Garcia-Barriga and Jesus Idrobo from the herbarium were there bearing gifts to send me off with a flourish.

After leaving the cold high country of Bogotá in the morning, it was quite a shock to arrive in the afternoon heat in the lowland tropics of Panama. I stopped there only for a day mainly to see the Panama Canal, which Ralph had talked so much about from his naval experience. Cultural contrasts between Panama and Colombia stood out. First, I noticed the prevalence of American culture in Panama City, which was bilingual—resulting from the building of the canal. Most signs were in both Spanish and English, and American-style food was advertised everywhere. In Bogotá, American cars seemed to be the primary evidence of American culture. There was a large number (70 percent) of people of Afro-Caribbean descent in Panama, but very few in Colombia. The houses in Panama were mainly frame, painted in bright colors, and often built on stilts, whereas in rural Colombia the houses were usually white stucco, and in Bogotá they were stone or brick.

My flight from Panama to Costa Rica left early in the morning to avoid the convection clouds created by heat rising from the ground and the ensuing turbulent storms over the mountains. On my flight, the weather was clear and the plane went directly along the Pacific Coast over sparkling beaches, traversed the well-vegetated mountains (which were not as dramatic as the snow-capped Andes but displayed different vegetation zones interspersed with farms), to the Caribbean coast, and then west to San José. When we arrived, one of my bags had not made the plane, a common experience, of course. The help offered by an experienced traveler, however, was the beginning of my learning how to travel alone on international trips (not so usual for women at that time), and how often friendly strangers help each other. My 1953 US passport was evidence that women international travelers were considered as adjuncts to their husbands. Following the bearer's name was the line "accompanied by *his* . . ." where one was meant to fill in the words "wife" or "minor children." My listed occupation was, of course, "housewife."

I stayed in the San José Inn, a beautiful old Costa Rican residence run by Americans who were UC graduates. They operated a papaya juice factory and ran the inn family-style. Some of the visitors and I drove to the active Volcan Irazu, which also took us through magnificent cloud forests and the *páramo* above—here occurring at much lower altitudes than in Colombia.

We passed numerous artistically painted oxcarts, so characteristic of Costa Rica, which I only had rare opportunities to see later as the country became more mechanized. In the evening on Sunday we went to the plaza in San José where I became enamored with marimba music. In fact, I had fallen in love with Costa Rica.

From Costa Rica my flight stopped briefly in Nicaragua, Honduras, El Salvador, and Guatemala, and, for the first time, I spent several days establishing my first contacts with botanists at the Mexican national university (Universidad Nacional Autónomo de México—UNAM) before arriving back in California. As usual on all my flights, I watched the changing geomorphology along with the vegetation, and in this trip I was enthralled with the spectacular Central American volcanoes jutting out of the still dense forests.

TEACHING DURING
BERKELEY YEARS
1955-1959

During my limited experience as a teaching assistant both as an undergraduate and graduate student and my brief stint as a lecturer at Coe College, I found interacting with students to be enjoyable and thought-provoking. Part-time (sometimes full-time) teaching, especially at women's colleges, was a major professional outlet for women with advanced degrees in the 1950s. I was fortunate to live in the San Francisco Bay Area with two good women's colleges where I was invited to teach. Additionally I was offered the opportunity to teach a summer field course at RMBL. Thus, although teaching would become an important part of my work while we were in Berkeley, it did not begin until three years after our arrival.

RMBL FIELD COURSE

The first such opportunity came in 1955, when the director of RMBL asked me to teach their Field Ecology course that summer. He thought I could provide a special perspective, since I had done both my MS and PhD research there. Ralph was doing research with graduate students in Nevada but planned to come to Gothic late in the summer for our usual vacation period there. I drove to Colorado in our new Chevrolet sedan, which I would use for field trips.

I had big shoes to fill in following Harriet Barclay, the inspirational teacher who had taught me and so many other students in this RMBL course over the years. She was teaching elsewhere this summer. My task was made easier because I began teaching the course when Bill Weber, the University of Colorado systematist who had published a *Handbook of Plants of the Front Range* and was working on a *Rocky Mountain Flora,* was teaching the Field Botany course. We had gotten to know each other when I had sought his aid in identifying some plants during my dissertation research, and now we decided to run some of our class field trips together. I had some concern about my limited field background for the animal part of my course, but those fears were allayed by David E. Davis, an animal ecologist from Johns

Hopkins University. Davis was teaching the Mammalogy and Ornithology courses at RMBL, and suggested that he and his students would benefit by joining some of the field trips with Weber and me. Because we were addressing the rich natural history of this area, it was great to have a plant taxonomist as well as plant and animal ecologists pooling their knowledge on field trips—and this interaction became a highlight of my summer.

Harriet Barclay had used ecology textbooks, but I found none that incorporated the evolutionary and ecological approach I was finding so exciting among the Berkeley botanists. I also had become aware of the impact of textbooks—how they could indoctrinate ideas rather than encourage critical thinking about issues. Because it was a small class of six students, I brought copies of reprints of relevant journal articles and books by Stebbins, Clausen, Keck, and Hiesey, among others. I planned to ponder community concepts in the context of my dissertation study of the Crested Butte vegetation. For discussing succession, I had now compiled data on changes in the vegetation from ten permanent quadrats on the Gothic Earthflow over seven years. Changes were much slower than I originally had thought they might be during the thirty years since the earthflow occurred. The earthflow provided an intriguing on-the-scene comparison with classical dune and glacial studies.

Discussing changes in Gothic Earthflow at
microclimate plot—me in hat at right

Changes were occurring rapidly in the Crested Butte area, some of which influenced RMBL. The town of Crested Butte had been essentially dormant after the closing of its coal mine, but was now being revived by the opening of a large lead mine. On the other hand, the tracks of the narrow gauge railroad that had transported coal were being removed—a sad sight for those of us who loved trains, as this one had seemed so much a part of the colorful history of these mountains. Rural electrification poles were being erected to bring electricity to Gothic, with the bill being paid by the National Science Foundation. The electricity at this time was limited to the research facilities and administration at RMBL. The building where courses had previously been taught was now the research lab, another sign that in the future more emphasis would be put on research at RMBL.

Our courses were to be held in the Ore House, a late 1800s building, which was in such poor shape that a new floor had hastily been laid to avert the possibility that we might fall into the old weighing pit during a lecture. Although living conditions at RMBL were improving, the students still had to live and work in a primitive setting. It was considered part of their mountain experience. The students often helped in hauling coal and wood to warm the Ore House and their dorms, which were located in other old mining town buildings. Plus, we took them on long hikes (often exceeding several thousand feet in elevation gain and ten to twelve miles one way), especially to get to some interesting alpine sites. Because RMBL did not own field vehicles, we had to use our private cars to get as close as we could to other areas of interest. Many roads were essentially one-way tracks, often rocky or filled with mud holes, which resulted in many flat tires, loose steering wheels, and other kinds of breakdowns. Thus we were frequently very late returning to Gothic, but the hungry and tired students were unfailingly good sports about it all.

Although heavy storms periodically made field work miserable, there were numerous days with when the sky was absolutely clear and intensely blue; the temperature was crisp, like October days in the Midwest. The particularly cool weather in 1955, with heavy frosts most nights, had kept the flowering season late. The Sagebrush and Fescue bunch grassland communities were unusually ablaze with color, and the lush Upland Herb meadows were spectacular. Although the flora is always lovely, it seemed particularly striking this year at the elevations immediately around RMBL.

For many years, field trips had culminated in taking the RMBL students on a three-day Circle Trip that traversed all the vegetation zones down the western slope, from Kebler Pass in the Spruce-Fir forest, through the extensive Aspen zone, into Oak Scrub and Pinyon-Juniper forest, and finally into Desert

Ringing dinner bell at RMBL mess hall

Shadscale and alkali flats. I particularly enjoyed this year's trip done jointly with Davis and his Ornithology and Mammalogy courses. This gave students a sense of geography in exploring the diversity of vegetation, birds, and mammals (where possible), and their environments other than in the Crested Butte area. Camping together amid the pinyon trees on the rim of the Black Canyon of the Gunnison River (then a monument, now a national park) led to more bonding amongst the students and insightful discussions around the evening campfires.

FLORISTIC AFFINITIES OF CRESTED BUTTE PLANTS

Working with Weber on courses at RMBL, I resumed our discussion of the geographic affinities of the flora in the Crested Butte vegetation, which we had begun to consider while I was doing my dissertation. I had written a section on this, but Cooper thought it was extraneous to the dissertation topic. I realized now this was probably because Cooper's community-based (ecological) geographic perspective differed from the floristic approaches of plant geographers who were oriented towards systematics.

On the other hand, Herbert Mason as editor of *Madroño,* had enthusiastically published my paper in April of 1955, in which I addressed the affinities of the Crested Butte flora and provided a list of voucher specimens for future study. The UC Berkeley systematists were pleased to see me publish data on voucher specimens, because they thought that the taxonomy was sloppily done in much ecological community research. Their attitude represented one side of a schism that existed at that time between many systematists and community ecologists, who had not yet seen common goals through an evolutionary perspective.

Using this publication, Weber and I continued to discuss floristic differences between the eastern and western slopes of the Colorado Rockies. The Crested Butte alpine species had their greatest affinity with circumboreal arctic species, and I was becoming more and more interested in comparing alpine and arctic flora and vegetation. Weber had a graduate student doing his PhD dissertation on Mount McKinley, which resulted in our making floristic comparisons of Crested Butte area with Alaska. Also, Bill Pruitt, a mammalogist working in Alaska, was spending the summer at Gothic comparing the Alaskan small mammals to those in the Crested Butte area. Knowing of my growing interest in seeing arctic tundra, Pruitt offered to assist me if I ever came to Alaska.

THE PRINCE OF BEASTS

On days that we weren't teaching, Weber often persuaded me to go collecting in remote areas. I not only soaked up the breadth of his botanical knowledge, but had several adventures with him as well. I especially remember a trip to Conundrum Pass on the Old Stage Coach route between Gothic and Aspen. This jaunt completely convinced me that Ralph and I had been right not to use pack animals for our dissertation research.

Weber and a Colorado University colleague who was joining us, Sam Shushan, were adamant about using a pack horse to carry our gear for the trip. I arranged for a horse from a Crested Butte tavern owner and with a couple of students went down to pick him up. It started to rain gently as we left, but by the time we got to Crested Butte, it was coming down in buckets. We struggled until late in the night walking the horse, named Prince, over the muddy roads in a driving rain from Crested Butte to a cowboy's stable near Gothic.

At 5:00 AM I turned out of bed to find the sky absolutely clear. Shushan and I went to the stables and got Prince, and the packing procedure began. We took guidance from a book entitled *Going Light with Backpack or Burro,* which Ralph had purchased when we were planning a trip to the Wind River Mountains. Two hours later we had everything tied down and were on our way.

Prince, Bill Weber and Sam Shushan (lying down)

Prince, however, only wanted to eat. We literally had to pull him along. Somehow in the attempt to keep Prince going, we missed the turnoff to Conundrum Pass and arrived with much panting at Copper Lake. We staggered back down the steep grade and finally found the turnoff but then had to pull and tug that animal for five miles up a very steep, narrow trail across talus. We had not brought a canteen, as we incorrectly thought we would cross a number of snow patches. We were soon acutely dehydrated. Then, a third of the way up, the pack saddle began to fall off. The exertion of unpacking and repacking at circa 12,000 feet was terrific. We finally reached the pass at 6:00 PM and decided to go to Conundrum Hot Springs to spend the night. On the map, it looked like a short distance, but it turned out to be another two-and-half miles and a 3,000-foot drop in elevation. We finally made it around 8:30 PM. We cooked a steak over an open fire, devoured it with some tea, and crept into our sleeping bags.

Unfortunately, sleeping was not an option. We were up most of the time trying to chase away animals eating our food, and making sure that the horse was okay. Finally we got up at 4:00 AM; we couldn't sleep, so we decided to get an early start collecting. We ate breakfast lethargically, then packed Prince. We were enormously proud of the job we had done. Now for the climb back up to the pass.

Prince of course wanted to eat every few feet, so we let him graze while we collected and took pictures. This went along fine for almost an hour, but then Prince suddenly took off galloping down the trail. We stood in amazement, watching as he disappeared from sight. Weber had even put our lunch on the horse, not wanting to carry anything extra. The three of us emptied our pockets; among us we had one chocolate bar, two ten-year-old malted milk tablets from a first aid kit, and a small package of lemon drops.

On the long trek back to Gothic it started to rain heavily and then came the final blow. We began to find evidence that Prince was progressively losing his load—we staggered back to camp carrying most of the equipment we found. Prince had been caught as he came through Gothic, but the next morning we had to go back up the trail to recover the remainder of our gear as well as the pack saddle. We found the panniers but the pack saddle had vanished; Prince somehow had gotten rid of it. We spent most of the afternoon trying to get arrangements straight with Prince's owner and returning him to Crested Butte. This adventure, except for a trip back to Copper Lake two days later with my class, closed my field season for the summer.

TEACHING AT MILLS COLLEGE AND FAMILY MATTERS
In the fall of 1955 I leapt at the opportunity to teach again as an instructor for the academic year at Mills College, an elite Bay Area women's school established in 1852 as the Young Ladies Seminary. A professor on sabbatical leave, who had built a strong program in botany there, needed a replacement during this period. Herbert Mason's wife, Lucile, taught there, and as a great supporter of women professionals, suggested me for the position. I was accepted and spent a pleasant year teaching general botany and systematics to bright girls, who were enthusiastic in learning about plants.

It was during this period that Ralph and I had decided to buy a house, and Lucile and Herbert alerted us to one being built across the street from them in the Berkeley Hills. The main part of the house, which was built on the uphill side of the street, was on the second floor, where the living room-dining room area and the master bedroom offered a magnificent view of San Francisco Bay. Its location provided us the opportunity to become even better acquainted with the Mason family both professionally and personally. We bought season tickets to the San Francisco Opera with them and we joined them on some weekends at their walnut ranch near Saint Helena in the Napa Valley. The Masons became among our closest personal friends in the Bay Area.

Our social life was greatly influenced by the amount of time on weekends we spent attending geology and botany field trips, often associated with research or courses given by colleagues. We both attended most of these, and they were a source of many happy memories. Ralph's summers were totally devoted to field research, either in Nevada, Alaska or Canada. When I could not join him, I too spent the summer in the field either in Colorado, Alaska or the Sierras in California.

With a new home I assumed that it was probably time to think about having children. However, strange as it may seem, we never discussed the matter! Ralph obviously was satisfied with our present situation and was not eager to change it. Although I was aware that my biological clock was ticking, I was increasingly concerned about Ralph's inability to express affection (as was my mother) as well as his discomfort around small children, and wondered just what kind of a father he might be. Without disparaging the important role of motherhood, I nevertheless was unwilling to take on the responsibility of essentially being a single parent. Ralph had even turned down my idea of having pets, which I had missed over the years, because of the "bother" of caring for them—especially in the field. So we just simply went along with a pleasant and interesting life without children. Remaining childless certainly did not hinge on my own professional ambitions. I felt fortunate during the 1950s to be able to participate in research, help my husband with his work, and do some part-time college teaching. Otherwise, our spousal arrangements were more or less typical of those in the 1950s.I did all of the cooking (he did help out when we were in the field) and house-keeping chores, whereas he handled the finances and took care of the car. We did so much together academically that this division was not noticed.

TEACHING AT SAN FRANCISCO COLLEGE FOR WOMEN
After my year's assignment as a substitute at Mills College, in the fall of 1956 I began to teach part-time, first as instructor and then as assistant professor, at San Francisco College for Women (SFCW), a Catholic school run by the Order of the Madames of the Sacred Heart. This gave me a different perspective from the one I had gained at Mills. Teaching at these two elite women's colleges, however, confirmed for me the valuable role such colleges have played in the history of educating women, not only in providing education for women unavailable elsewhere in their early years, but also in the encouraging atmosphere for education of women that they still foster today.

Above and beyond my teaching, being the only non-Catholic lay faculty member and ignorant of church rituals led to some interesting experiences at SFCW. My problems began on the first day. When I entered the classroom, the girls all stood up—and remained standing. When I asked them to please be seated, they looked horrified. Finally, one girl timidly informed me that the professor always led a prayer at the beginning of each class. I had no idea what kind of prayer to lead them in, so suggested a moment of silent prayer. In discussing this matter with the Mother Superior, she laughed and suggested that I inform the girls prayers would be dismissed for my classes, which surprised them no end. On the first Friday of the month, there was high mass and all of the faculty and students wore gowns for the occasion. After I had remained seated when everyone else was standing, and vice versa, several times, the Mother Superior suggested that I just remain quietly seated throughout mass—again viewing my naive missteps with amusement.

Most students were from upper-class families and many had been sent to the college from wealthy overseas families. As a result, SFCW had the overtones of a finishing school, and some emphasis was put upon producing a gracious lady. Nevertheless, the girls obtained a strong liberal arts education, and I think that some probably developed more intellectually than they would have in a coeducational environment. Moreover, they were constantly being urged to actively participate in their communities. During my time at the school, Rose Kennedy visited and gave a lecture on the importance of their role in society as educated Catholic women from well-to-do families. I was a little chilled by her emphasis on *Catholic* women, preferring it to be on *all* women; however, her point about the significant role that educated women could and should play in our society was well taken.

I carpooled from Berkeley to SFCW with a psychologist who taught a course on the subject at the college. He was a "good Catholic," as he put it, but was very concerned about the problems of birth control for Catholic women. Many women, mostly highly educated, in his practice emphatically did not want to have large families. He frequently heard that natural birth control was not working for them, and tensions were developing with their husbands over periods of abstinence. This psychologist, logically but naively, thought that the situation should be discussed openly by Catholics, and he organized a panel discussion to do just this. The Jesuit priests from the University of San Francisco, across the street from SFCW, were part of the panel and were adamant that no artificial means of birth control could be tolerated—women should subjugate their feelings to those of their husbands. I sat with my mouth open but did not let any words escape. Mother Hammock, the school nurse and biology teacher, was one of the few at the college, besides the psychologist and most of the students with whom I had contact, who seemed concerned about the issue. Driving back to Berkeley after the panel discussion, my psychologist colleague was very upset and predicted that most educated American Catholic women would ultimately revolt, especially when an easy, safe means of contraception became available. Indeed he was prophetic, as by the mid 1960s, the "pill" was available. (Many Catholic women hoped that the Pope would rescind restrictions to natural birth control. Despite his not doing so, it has been reported that by the 1980s over 80 percent of the US Catholic women were using some form of artificial birth control.)

The Madames of the Sacred Heart were cloistered in that they were not allowed to leave the college grounds. Mother Hammock, the other biology instructor, was very interested in my marine ecology course and wanted to join me and my students on one of our field trips to nearby intertidal areas. Finally, I persuaded the Mother Superior to allow her to come. The Madames wore long heavy robes, but I learned on this jaunt that they kept very large safety pins with them, to pin up their robes when they needed to. So Mother Hammock, with her robe tucked up, had a delightful time collecting starfish and algae, watching crabs and anemones open and close as she slipped and slid on the rocks along the shore. This trip gave her a taste of seeing plants and animals in their native habitats, which she said she would never forget.

I helped Mother Hammock break cloister on another occasion as well. She had always wanted to browse the shelves in the Biology Library at UC Berkeley, and Mother Superior consented if I served as Mother Hammock's chaperon. I made arrangements for her to enter the library stacks, where she was like the proverbial kid in the candy store. It was such a joy to witness her excitement. Her one day of freedom to browse the vast store of biological knowledge came to an end all too quickly, but she philosophically felt that she had satisfied a longing. Through all of my contacts with this wonderful woman I thought that she would have been more suited to a non-cloistered order where she could have better satisfied some of her natural curiosity.

The curiosity of one of my students resulted in discussion of different views regarding the relationship of religion and science. In class I had mentioned some of the ideas of the mid-twentieth century English biologist Julian Huxley, and afterwards this student asked me if scientists such as Huxley believed in God. I told her that Huxley's book *Religion Without Revelation* was a very readable exposition of his religious ideas. She wanted very much to read it, but was afraid that it was listed on the church's Index of Forbidden Books. When I brought up the subject to the Mother Superior, she replied that it was on the index, but added that in the future she thought it probably would be impossible to keep educated people from reading some of these books. (The official list was abandoned in 1966 as not having any force of law.) So several students read Huxley's book and we discussed it; they puzzled over his ideas, but their eyes were opened to a very different religious perspective.

I enjoyed the students and faculty while teaching as part of a liberal arts education in a small school environment at San Francisco College for Women. I was, however, a bit frustrated in not being able to intertwine teaching with the spirit of research in my own area of expertise—an opportunity I had exploited with undergraduate students at Rocky Mountain Biological Laboratory.

ALASKAN TREK

1956

The clearest way into the Universe is through a forest
wilderness.
—John Muir

Ralph had been invited by UC Berkeley colleagues to join them during the summer of 1956 to assist with a paleontological project on the Alaska Arctic Coastal Plain. I had not been invited to participate in the project, but I could drive up the Alaska Highway and meet Ralph in Fairbanks for his return to Berkeley. This was my chance to see vast expanses of northern forest (often referred to as boreal) and some of both the arctic and alpine flora and vegetation. What a fine opportunity, following all of my discussions about alpine and arctic flora with Bill Weber at Gothic the summer before. I would collect plants for the herbarium, but primarily would satisfy my curiosity in comparing the similarities and differences between the flora and vegetation in British Columbia, Yukon Territory, and Alaska with those that I had studied in the Colorado Rocky Mountains. The trip would also constitute a wilderness experience as well as provide historical and cultural experiences, different from previous ones.

It did not seem feasible, however, for me to make this long journey—much of it in uninhabited country—alone. Fortunately, a solution was at hand, thanks to our friendship with the Mason family. Their son David, who had just finished his freshman year at Reed College, was eager to see Alaska. He enjoyed collecting plants as he had grown up going on collection trips with his father when Herbert was surveying the California wetlands for his *Flora of the Marshes of California*. Because of our congenial relationship with the Masons, Ralph and I never questioned the idea of an eighteen-year-old college student traveling in remote areas over the summer with someone else's thirty-year-old wife. Perhaps some people in the 1950s did wonder about this arrangement, but we were oblivious. We planned to drive Auntie, our 1954 two-door Chevrolet sedan that had done yeoman service at Gothic the previous summer.

David Mason and me packing Auntie in Berkeley

Since we would have to be self-sufficient for most of the trip, David and I made lists of everything we thought we would need. Much to our dismay, when we assembled all of the items on our lists, they would not fit into Auntie. We had to remove the back seat to pack in an extra tire (in addition to the spare tire in the trunk), spare auto parts, a two-months' supply of dehydrated milk, fruit, and meals along with knapsacks, alpine tents, a Coleman stove and lantern, water can, refrigerator can, four cameras, a box of reference books, an umbrella, and much more.

We headed northward along the California coast for my first look at the old-growth redwoods (*Sequoia sempervirens*), which had not yet suffered the severe effects of lumbering that were soon to come. We traveled and camped in the lovely mixed conifer forests of Oregon and Washington—culminating in the Olympic National Park. Here we saw conifer trees with enormous girths (especially *Thuja plicata*)—reminiscent of the Big Tree (*Sequoiadendron giganteum*) in the Sierra Nevada. Soon after entering British Columbia, we joined Wayne Fry, an old grad student friend from Minnesota and now a paleobotanist with the Canadian Geological Survey, to collect plant fossils at the famous Princeton locality. Here we found astonishingly well-preserved Tertiary fossils of such plants as dawn redwood (*Metasequoia*), *Cercidophyllum,* and even the water fern *Azolla*.

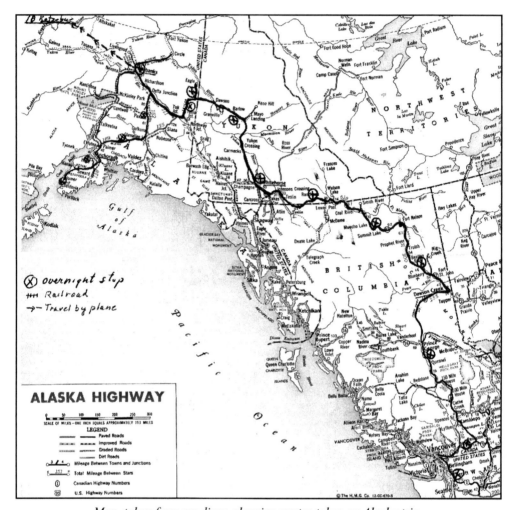

Map, taken from my diary, showing routes taken on Alaska trip.

From Princeton we proceeded northward past lakes nestled in the rolling hills, many so calm that the sky, clouds, and shoreline trees were reflected in sharp outlines. The intensity of the various shades of green and blue was impressive, and the farmhouses also had blue roofs that blended with their surroundings. The abundant clover along the roadsides was so fragrant it perfumed the air all afternoon—so much so that I still associate that aroma with central British Columbia. We frequently stopped to take pictures, which resulted in a 9:00 PM supper that night, but it was still so light that we read until 10:30. We began to select from our various books on the exciting history of this wilderness by authors such as the Scottish poet, Robert Service, and novelist, Jack

London, which we had brought along to read out loud during these long light evenings.

The next day we crept along dodging potholes at a maximum rate of 15 to 20 miles per hour. We were beginning to be discouraged by the slow pace and hoped that once we reached the Alaska Highway, the remaining 1,523 miles would go faster! Our spirits rose when we stopped in some mixed spruce-fir-birch forest with a luxuriant understory of ground orchids (*Calypso* and *Spiranthes*), ground dogwood (*Cornus canadensis*), lilies, Solomon's seal (*Polygonatum*), twin flower (*Linnaea borealis*), and coralroot (*Corallorhiza*)—a wonderful mixture of Rocky Mountain and North Woods flora. I had seldom seen such a flowering display of this type in one small place. Despite the beauty of our surroundings, we realized that we had only moved thirty miles in about two hours!

Nonetheless, the prospect of our transect across the great boreal forest to arctic tundra prevented me from being discouraged. This vast northern conifer forest, also known as taiga, encircles the globe from Siberia to Scandinavia as well as from Newfoundland to the interior of Alaska, and constitutes more than a quarter of the world's forests. Taiga plants must endure extremely cold temperatures; about two-thirds of the forests occur on permafrost (technically defined as any soil layer that has remained permanently frozen for two or more years). The most prominent trees here are aspen, black and white spruce (*Picea mariana* and *P. glauca*), and tamarack (*Larix laricina*). This forest is also a land of bogs, which can develop in any depression where water collects, and here are often called muskegs when the thick layers of decaying vegetation are covered with moss. I had enjoyed "bogging" around small glacial lakes while a student in Minnesota, and David was interested in freshwater systems because of his many excursions with his father (David later took his PhD in aquatic ecology). We thus inspected numerous boggy areas on this trip.

While we were having a refreshing swim near a river campsite one evening, a middle-aged couple drove up in a company car belonging to the Pacific Great Eastern Railway, which was building a railroad to Dawson Creek. They were British, and the husband had previously helped build railroads in Argentina. Following their traditions, they put up a card table, covered it with a white cloth, brought out a tea service, and invited us to join them. Interested in the purpose of our trip, they invited us to stay with them in Prince George on our return trip, laughingly saying that we would be ready for a hot bath by then.

DRIVING THE ALASKA HIGHWAY

We had been driving thus far on a British Columbian highway that connects to the Alaska Highway. When we arrived in Dawson Creek, we reached the zero milepost for the Alaska Highway, which was built in just eight months during World War II. It was completed in 1942 and, with some reconstruction, first opened for unrestricted travel in 1947. The Alaska Highway was constructed and paid for by the US Army Corp of Engineers, but because all but 302 of the 1,523 miles to Fairbanks ran through northern British Columbia and across the western Yukon Territory, it was originally called the Alaskan-Canadian Highway (shortened to Alcan). Although the US turned over the Canadian portion to the Canadian government after the war, today it is called the Alaska Highway and is still the only land route to Alaska.

Fortunately, the highway was much better leaving Dawson Creek than coming into it. We soon discovered, however, that the road would be good for a stretch and then it would change to huge chuck holes and teeth-shaking washboards, so we soon learned to curb our elation when we came to an improved stretch. Nonetheless, we were impressed with the construction of the road. The US Army Engineers had no map of the hundreds of miles of mountains and forest through which the highway passes and had never built a road through mushy muskegs or over permafrost. They were poorly equipped to work in these conditions, but were driven by knowledge that the Japanese had already taken one of the Aleutian Islands and a fear of their movement into Alaska. The lifeline of supplies this road would provide was desperately needed, and these engineers met the challenge.

There is no way to express the feeling of immensity of this area. In 1956, there were few signs of human habitation as far as the eye could see. Miles and miles of mixed conifer and deciduous forest with interspersed bogs appeared before us; sometimes westward we would get a glimpse of snow-capped peaks of coastal mountains. The main evidence of human activity was the fire-scarred, specter-like trees that often lined the road, remnants from fires caused primarily by the road's construction. Some sort of habitation, which usually consisted of a few tar-papered buildings or unpainted rough-hewn ones, occurred about every fifty miles or so. Sometimes there was a lone gas pump and a handmade sign announcing you could rent a room with meals. In this part of the highway there were no lodges or motels. When the road became drearily monotonous David started singing Gilbert and Sullivan operettas. He had quite a repertoire, being part of a group of singers who performed at Reed College. Nonetheless, by trip's end, I had had my fill of Gilbert and Sullivan. I long remembered some segments of the trip either by *The Pirates of Penzance*, *The Mikado*, or *HMS Pinafore*. This, however, was one of the few minor irritations in a very harmonious relationship with David during the entire summer. Sometimes we both were a little grumpy in mornings from lack of sleep as a result of our often reading out loud from our books on Alaska with the long hours of light.

Just prior to reaching Fort Nelson we moved into the northern tip of the Rockies with magnificent panoramas of angular, sedimentary, snow-capped peaks at every turn. We arrived in Fort Nelson in early afternoon hoping to have the car greased and the oil changed. However, there was a delay because the one Standard Oil station was overwhelmed with customers. This gave us time to look around Fort Nelson, a stereotypical western frontier town with Indians and bearded men in mackinaws and heavy boots standing around the several saloons or the Hudson Bay Trading Post.

Between Fort Nelson and Whitehorse we had a "tropical" experience at Laird Hot Springs. These springs are considered a phenomenon because they remain 115°F year-round. The vegetation surrounding them was luxuriant, appearing almost tropical, and the warm water of the springs had provided respite for workers during the highway construction, as it did for us. We dunked in it as though it were a hot tub. The experience reminded me of the reviving effects of the thermal springs in Colombia when we were working on the *páramo*. We didn't have time to explore the vegetation because Auntie had developed a thumping noise on the left side and we only hoped that she would make it to Whitehorse. She did, where we found that she had a broken spring.

Whitehorse was a town of about five thousand—half of all the people in the whole Yukon Territory. Bookstores, record shops, two movie theaters, and an interesting weekly newspaper mixed with the rough-and-tumble frontier activity. The town was booming because of a new hydroelectric plant. We enjoyed our stay in a waterfront hotel on the Yukon River, which had been constructed during the gold rush days, but we were in for a surprise when we picked up Auntie. Only heavy-duty springs were available; Auntie went in to the garage listing to the left with her broken spring and came out listing to the right because of the new spring.

After leaving Whitehorse, the countryside near the road was heavily burned. The density and extent (acres and acres) of the fuchsia-colored fireweed (*Epilobium angustifolium*) under the blackened trees was striking. The sight was beautiful when the contrasting colors were accentuated by the low-angle evening light. It was the first time I had ever found a burned area to be lovely. Of course, fires are often the principal agent of forest regeneration—releasing nutrients and clearing the way for a new cycle of plant succession—and a typical forest is apt to be consumed by fire every century or two, a pattern that has probably persisted for thousands of years. Here it had been accelerated at the hands of humans.

We more or less followed the Yukon River into Dawson City, which is at the mouth of the Klondike River and was in the heart of the Klondike gold rush of 1898. During the peak of the gold rush, an estimated 40,000 people swarmed over the Klondike area. The evidence of placer operations was everywhere around Dawson City with gold still being mined by giant dredges. We treated ourselves to a milkshake but discovered it was made with canned milk; in fact, we did not have any fresh milk on the entire trip. We filled our gas tank with "liquid gold," which cost 80¢ per gallon (compared to about 25¢ in the Lower Forty-Eight). We stopped to see Robert Service's cabin as we had been reading aloud his poems *Spell of the Yukon* and *The Shooting of Dan McGrew*, which epitomized the spirit of the glamorous days of the gold rush.

After crossing into Alaska Territory, we took a little detour off the highway. The highest elevations on the previous summit areas along the highway had had poor tundra vegetation. However, on the plateaus surrounding the old mining town of Eagle we found, on gravelly, rocky areas, carpets of *Dryas octopetala* (an old friend at Gothic) and *Arenaria arctica* (an arctic species of a common genus in the Rockies) as well as abundant *Campanula*. Finding such plants at less than 4,000 feet reminded us how far north we were.

Upon our return to the Alaska Highway we were on paved road. We could not speed up much, however, because undulations in the road, caused by permafrost, left us feeling whiplashed at higher speeds. Amazingly, after we hit paved road, all four tires, having lasted throughout the graveled and pot-holed roads without a flat, blew out. We had to buy four new ones.

We reached Fairbanks seventeen days after leaving Berkeley. We were not very impressed with our first view of the city; the streets were narrow and many were little more than badly rutted dirt tracks. Many homes were just tar-papered shacks and initially it seemed to us that saloons were the main business establishments. Perhaps we were being a little harsh in our judgment, as Alaska Territory was still primarily wilderness; it was not admitted as a state until three years later. We later discovered the more civilized parts of Fairbanks, which boasted of churches, a hospital, banks, and a radio station.

We headed to the outskirts of Fairbanks, where the University of Alaska is located in a town named College. Known as the "farthest north university," it was a collection of about ten architecturally undistinguished cement buildings, located on a small hill overlooking the attractive Tanana River Valley and surrounding plateaus. College was where Bill and Erna Pruitt, whom I had met in Gothic the year before, lived. They had invited

Pruitts and friend outside their cabin

us to visit them and offered to help me see the tundra with some of their Eskimo friends. They were away on a research trip when we reached the Fairbanks area, but, anticipating our arrival, they had asked a friend studying Eskimo culture to take care of us. He got us established in the Pruitt's snug log cabin and made dinner for us, and thus we were initiated into a network of people living and working in Alaska. Survival on the frontier dictated a close sense of interdependence—people had to be willing to lend a helping hand, share a meal and shelter, as well as offer their knowledge.

Bill Pruitt was studying the population fluctuations of small mammals as part of the Survival Project at Ladd Air Force Base. The Pruitts had built their cabin and used sled dogs for transportation during the winter. Housing prices were extremely high around Fairbanks because the scarcity of trees this far north meant there was little cheap timber. Living costs seemed astronomical (I wrote to Mother that it cost 75¢ for a small head of cabbage and 85¢ for a loaf of bread). The Pruitts had a small garden of leaf lettuce, rutabagas, and radishes and were planning to build a little greenhouse. Most of the better-built homes had their own greenhouses along with a cache house on stilts to stash any food that needed protection from wild animals.

VISITING MCKINLEY PARK AND SEVERAL COASTAL AREAS

Our next destination was McKinley (now known by its Athabascan name, Denali) National Park. Bill Weber had flown to Fairbanks from Colorado and we met him at the train station, where we put our car on the train that took passengers to

Bill Weber and me boarding train to McKinley Park

the entrance of the park; from there we drove a hundred-mile gravel track that went to Wonder Lake. We saw some of the snow-capped Alaska range from the train because of fair weather, although Mount McKinley, North America's highest peak, was under complete cloud cover. Weber's PhD student met us at the train at the park entrance, and took Weber with him to a cabin where he was staying on the flanks of Mount McKinley. David and I were to meet them there a day later.

David and I weren't able to leave the entrance to the park until late afternoon because we couldn't get Auntie off the flat car until the railroad company found the key to the car behind us. The delay actually served us well because, as we drove along the road to the Wonder Lake campground, the clouds began to lift over Mount McKinley and adjacent peaks in the Alaska range. By suppertime the entire snow-capped range was in full view, bathed in rosy alpen glow with a full moon rising. It was an unforgettable, awe-inspiring sight that few visitors have the privilege to see.

The next morning we packed sleeping bags and food in our knapsacks and headed for the cabin on the side of Mount McKinley where Weber and his student were staying. We had to cross the floodplains of numerous braided streams. From the Muldrow glacier, the outwash area alone was over a mile across. We were soon wading knee-deep in icy streams. The

Crossing outwash streams from Muldrow Glacier

water was so cold that our feet were cramped when we came out of one stream—only to face another a few feet beyond. As we topped a morainal ridge where we could be seen from the cabin, Weber and his student saw a grizzly bear appear on the next ridge opposite us and watched as we and the bear descended into the same gully between the two ridges. Struggling through the willows in the gully, I noticed bear dung and commented to

David about its freshness, but did not realize just how fresh it was! We appeared on the next ridge unaware of our proximity to the bear. When we arrived at the cabin, our friends excitedly informed us that from their vantage point it appeared that we would meet the bear head on. They were happy to see us emerge from the gully unfazed.

The following day we hiked to the ice front of the Muldrow Glacier, where we followed back over a moraine that had been deposited within the last few years and thus recently exposed for plant invasion. We then moved to successively older moraines where community development had begun about a hundred years ago. For me it was exciting to see Alaska glacial succession, although here succession was toward tundra, not the forest systems that Cooper and his students had studied at Glacier Bay. Weber's student had found that the moss *Hylocomium* occurred in the pioneer stage but was still abundant in the climax (terminal stage) tundra. Mats of several species of *Dryas*, with their nitrogen-fixing root nodules, occurred along with the legume locoweed (*Oxytropis)* and the low kinnikinnick (*Arctostaphylos uva-ursi*) familiar from the Rocky Mountain alpine areas, followed by dwarf willow (*Salix*) and dwarf birch (*Betula glandulosa*) thickets. Looking down through masses of willow branches we could see old Gothic friends *Silene acaulis* and *Papaver radicatum*. In older moraine shrubs of blueberry (*Vaccinium uglinosum*) and Labrador tea (*Ledum decumbens*) continued into the tundra climax with the characteristic cottongrass (*Eriophorum vaginatum*).

We next climbed the 6,000-foot Mount Eielson, which involved a long haul over talus with a wonderful display of arctic alpine plants in the crevices of the rocks. Seeing and collecting Alaskan species of *Saxifraga, Myosotis, Stellaria, Campanula*, and *Polemonium,* among others, and discussing their Rocky Mountain floristic affinities with Weber made this trip an extension of those during the previous summer at Gothic. As we arrived at the summit, a heavy cloud cover lifted to give a magnificent view over the Muldrow glacier and the entire sequence of plant succession that we had walked through the day before.

After a day of collecting near the McKinley River, David and I left for Camp Denali. We stayed in the nearby ghost mining village of Kantishna in a tar-papered shack where we could dry our soggy clothes. Here we had the good fortune to meet and talk with Olaus and Mardy Murie, who were also there at the time. They were very friendly and we soon felt as though we had known them for a long time. They spoke so lovingly of the wildlands of Alaska and hoped we were enjoying our taste of them. Two of the great pioneers of wildlands conservation in America, they would become instrumental in enacting the 1964 Wilderness Act and creating the Arctic National Wildlife Refuge. Olaus was president of the Wilderness Society and Mardy, the first woman graduate of the University of Alaska, wrote influential, award-winning books on conservation and is considered by many to be a matriarch of the conservation movement. (Her environmental leadership also earned her a Presidential Medal of Freedom in 2003.)

We put our car on the freight train to Anchorage and boarded the passenger train for an overnight trip to Anchorage. Anchorage was a pleasant, friendly town in a magnificent location facing Cook Inlet and surrounded by mountains. We bought groceries; feeling starved for fruit, I included some Washington apples at an exorbitant price of one dollar each as a special treat. This was the only time on the trip that the easy-going David was upset with me. He thought I was being ridiculously extravagant in buying those apples (we had a food budget in common). Soon after leaving Anchorage, we were stopped by a huge mudslide that was a result of heavy rain. But since it was no longer raining, we set up our Coleman stove by the side of the road, cooked our dinner, and then rolled out our sleeping bags. In those days, it seemed safe to sleep anywhere.

The next day we drove the entire length of the Kenai Peninsula to the quaint little fishing village of Homer, known as the "Shangri-La of Alaska." We camped near Hope, where gold was first discovered in Alaska. In the morning when we tried to get Auntie up a questionable road for some collecting on alpine tundra, we met a two-ton truck driven by a guide, Keith Specking, who had a hay field near timberline. He and his wife offered to take us to the tundra area around his hayfield and bring us back when the hay was loaded. All went well until his big truck got stuck in the mud. So we all walked to timberline, and I exchanged my knowledge about boreal forests and alpine plants for the guide's understanding of this interesting mountainous area with its many glaciers. As we walked back down to Auntie (the truck was still stuck), Keith and his wife invited us to have supper and spend the night with them. When we got to their two-story log cabin, Keith's mother already had dinner ready—fresh crab, large pieces of homemade bread, and low bush cranberry jelly. That night we slept comfortably in a warm dry house. In the morning, we were served an enormous breakfast of wild strawberries, sourdough pancakes, bacon, and very strong coffee; we left feeling grateful for extraordinary hospitality offered to complete strangers.

After leaving the Speckings we passed the fertile agricultural area of the Matanuska Valley with its farms started by the government as a New Deal agricultural experiment in 1935 to help destitute Depression farmers. The sight was strangely reminiscent of prosperous southern Minnesota farms but surrounded by rugged mountains and located in a valley with stunning glaciers flowing into it. After another very wet night of camping, we were so tired of being cold and damp that we headed back to the town of College.

A TUNDRA VISIT WITH ESKIMO FRIENDS
In College, we launched into preparations to visit the Eskimo friends of the Pruitts. We needed to take everything for living on the tundra at Kotzebue Sound. Kotzebue is north of the Arctic Circle and we were flying via Wien Airline, which advertised at that time as "the farthest-north scheduled airline in the world." We stuffed knapsacks, duffel bags, and a food kit. When we left for the airport we wore two pairs of trousers (the outer one being windproof) that had eight enormous pockets, all of which we also filled with canteens, hunting knives, notebooks, bird books, and more. We had on heavy alpaca-lined jackets with ponchos, rain hats, and heavy gloves. When we arrived at the airport, with all our gear and looking like pieces of luggage ourselves, we were told that the plane had to carry extra gasoline and could not take us and our equipment. David and I made such a convincing fuss about the importance of our trip that some tourists were unhappily bumped and we got on with the bulging pockets of our coats and trousers forcing us to squeeze down the aisle sideways.

It was cloudy from Fairbanks to just outside Kotzebue Sound, where the plane dipped down under the clouds. Then we could see the amazing patterned ground of frost polygons extending for miles in a sea of mottled brown and yellowish tundra, dotted by small lakes of tea-colored water. These frost polygons develop on flat, poorly-drained peat with a shallow frost table, which creates conditions for preservation of cracks surrounding them. Kotzebue, consisting of a few scattered frame buildings, some painted in bright colors, finally came into view. Along the edge of town were numerous canvas tents and tar-papered shacks, the summer homes of Eskimos. We could see their fish-drying racks in front and dogs tethered in the back. Maimie Beaver, Bill Pruitt's Eskimo friend, was at the airport to meet us and had arranged to take us to Sadie Creek to camp on the tundra.

We went in a twenty-foot-long boat with three of Maimie's cousins, who were accompanying us to collect greens and berries to store in seal oil for winter. In the very friendly fashion that we found throughout our visit, the Eskimo crew asked if they could call us by our first names and told us theirs. They carefully covered David and me with canvas so we wouldn't get wet from spray, though they seemed to delight in it. They smiled and laughed constantly; they had such a happy expression on their faces, and their black eyes snapped with merriment. Their English was broken but understandable. When we arrived at Sadie Creek our new friends suggested we put our little alpine tent inside a reindeer corral to get some protection from the sea breezes and where we could also be close to a muskeg lake for water. We set up our camp in a wonderful patch of cottongrass, so characteristic of the arctic tundra that we had first seen on the Muldrow Glacier moraine.

Sadie Creek campsite

The Eskimo women who accompanied us in the boat went off with sacks to collect sour dock (*Rumex crispus*), cranberries (*Vaccinium vitis-idea*), and crowberries (*Empetrum nigrum*). When they had finished collecting in this area, they invited us to join them in a picnic. They started a fire, suspended a kettle over it from an overhanging branch, and put on a pot of water to which they added big chunks of caribou and reindeer meat. They then brought out whole dried salmon, shee, and white fish as well as pieces of dried whale (*ookruk*) and pickled pieces of white beluga whale blubber (*muktuk*). We tried some of everything but were happy to accept their warning not to eat too much *muktuk* because it was all fat. After the picnic we rode on the glassy-surfaced, meandering Sadie Creek, stopping occasionally to disembark and collect more greens and berries. David and I were busily taking many photos but also helped our friends collect, which we all did with much laughter. I felt as though we had known these people for a long time.

Eskimo picnic

The next morning we awakened to the patter of rain on the tent. When we stuck our heads out, we saw our neighbors (two very old Eskimo women and a little girl) busily gathering firewood. They too were camping out, collecting greens and berries as well as trapping fish while the men in the family earned money helping to construct a nearby Air Force radar station.

The intensity of the women's efforts convinced us that we should make similar preparations. We rushed out to collect dry driftwood; the rain now seemed to be coming down more horizontally than vertically and soon had us drenched even through two pairs of trousers. Our noses and fingers were numb and our toes had long since passed that stage. We decided that we must start walking to increase circulation in our extremities. We put together some items to carry for lunch and started to walk the seven miles along the shore to Cape Blossom.

The most intriguing sight for me on our walk was an exposure of about twenty feet of frozen subsoil. Permafrost had become a topic of research during the building of the Alaska Highway and airfield landing strips during World War II, when ecologists began to consider its possible effects on succession in arctic tundra vegetation and how it also might affect alpine vegetation. Some ecologists questioned whether soil stability concepts could be applied where such frost activity occurs. Other researchers suggested that at least arctic vegetation is highly adapted to permafrost—that is, it is in equilibrium with the frost activity at each site, and therefore successional relationships of the vegetation could not be compared among sites.

Whether permafrost occurred at all in alpine areas was even more controversial. Thus I was fascinated to actually see a cross section of permafrost and its parent material. In keeping with other postwar studies of the physiological ecology of North American alpine areas, I had considered the possibility that frozen ground had produced some poorly formed polygons in the Crested Butte alpine vegetation. Later, well-developed polygons were found to be restricted to level tundra areas with poor drainage in the Rocky Mountains of Wyoming and Colorado.

We spent most of the heavily misty next day walking across tundra hummocks of sedges and grasses. We wobbled from one hummock to another, often falling in between them in water-soaked sphagnum moss; the unfrozen, mushy soil was about two feet deep. We primarily collected fruiting specimens, as flowering had occurred much earlier. The amount of sphagnum, and the predominance of shrubby plants such as Labrador tea, cranberries, blueberries, and crowberry were different from the Crested Butte alpine vegetation. We eagerly ate the berries to quench our thirst. There was the same circumboreal species of dwarf *Arctostaphylos,* but different species of dwarf willows than in the Crested Butte area. We were both delighted and amazed that the entire time we were on the tundra around

Kotzebue, we saw so few mosquitoes that our head nets remained in our packs—so different from what we had been told to expect. After dinner back in camp, we read aloud from the Eskimo novel *Top of the World*, sitting before a campfire, watching a golden midnight sun hanging at the horizon among intensely red clouds across the edge of Kotzebue Sound to the Chukchi Sea.

After three days on the tundra at Sadie Creek, Maimie's cousins returned in their boat to pick us up. Upon on our arrival in Kotzebue, Maimie and Jackson Beaver were still asleep so we stacked our gear near the door of their waterfront tar-papered house, filled our pockets with lunch items, and explored the town. Everyone was smiling and nodding, and children and Husky pups followed us everywhere. The bright-eyed children were delightful, seeming to be so happy, affectionate, and well-mannered. We stopped to chat with numerous people who were pegging out seal skins, making seal pokes (bags in which to store food in oil), catching and drying fish, and making *mukluks* (skin shoes).

While we were eating lunch near a fishing boat, an Eskimo with big bushy eyebrows began to ask questions of us, and invited us into his tent to meet his family. They lived in Norvik during the winter and for twenty-six years had come to Kotzebue for the summer. Most of the families who lived farther north in the winter, migrated here for the summer. Kotzebue had become sort of a summer resort for them while they fished, hunted, and collected plants for their winter stores. They made us coffee and we watched them mend their fish nets while they told us

Eskimo children in Kotzebue

about their concerns for the disappearance of Eskimo culture. Although they wanted to know what "White Man's" culture had to offer them, they decried the loss of their legends, their skills, and their language (which is unwritten and thus has to be handed down from generation to generation). In Alaska Territory, Eskimo language was not used in schools, so children were growing up primarily knowing only English. The wife spoke good English but was holding classes in her village to teach Bible lessons in Eskimo in order to preserve some of her native tongue. This was my first direct contact with such cultural losses, but I would meet them again in other parts of the world.

That evening we went with Maimie and Jackson to an Eskimo dance. Emphasis in these dances was upon expression of feeling, focusing upon happy events in life and the importance of sharing and generosity. There was little music but rather chanting with a very strong rhythm (reminiscent for me of Southwest Indians). Some dances were reserved for the old and wise ones while others were a free for all when anyone who wished could get up and dance. Both David and I were entranced but felt a little too shy to join in the dancing.

After the dance we crawled into our sleeping bags on the floor of the Maimie and Jackson's hut, but it was difficult to get to sleep. Sadie Creek had been so quiet with only the sounds of water lapping on the beach. In Kotzebue, people were active essentially around the clock. With the almost perpetual light, kids played in the streets at 2:00 AM. Most people had no schedule, just going with the flow and sleeping when they got tired. We could hear people walking on the graveled streets and dogs howling throughout what we considered to be night. We finally drifted off to sleep from sheer exhaustion.

We awoke to another bright day with everyone in Kotzebue discussing the unusually good weather. David and I took another long walk to observe and collect more tundra plants. Upon our return, we snacked on Eskimo "ice cream" made with whipped seal oil and blueberries. It was quite good. For dinner Maimie made a stew from fresh reindeer shank and spinach they had grown in a little garden by their house. We devoured it with gusto, eating from a table about a foot from the floor. We talked about the effects of "White Man's" culture on their life. Jackson's immediate family had all contracted tuberculosis from prospectors, and he had spent part of his childhood with his mother in a TB sanitarium in Seattle. He ruefully reported that he had seen his first polar bear in the Seattle zoo.

Maimie and Jackson Beaver beside
their house and spinach patch

Maimie sat chewing skins for *mukluks* and I praised some beautiful ones she had made. Generosity and giving are deeply ingrained in Eskimo culture, and she insisted that they were now mine. I protested, not realizing that I was committing the gravest faux pas in not readily accepting this gift as an expression of generosity to a visitor. I learned this lesson here and fortunately so, as I would face similar issues in other cultures I later visited.

David and I could have happily stayed longer in Kotzebue. We had quickly become fond of these Eskimo people and would have appreciated spending more time on the arctic tundra as well. But we had to return to Fairbanks to meet Ralph for our return to California. The weather for our flight gave us a good bird's eye view of the tundra on the Seward Peninsula. The colors were striking from the air—all shades of brown and gold, with patterns of deep green and dull red around muskegs and lakes, along sluggish streams, and amid large, prominent frost polygons. The mighty Yukon River was especially impressive with its many meandering tributaries, each producing sinuous designs of vegetation along their banks. We also had a good areal view this time of the Alaska Range as we flew toward Fairbanks.

Ralph and I had planned before we left Berkeley to return by taking ferries from Anchorage down the Inside Passage to Vancouver. David would fly back as we had taken out the back seat for needed storage space at the beginning of the trip. Just before the time for our return, however, the ferry workers went on strike, and the ferries stopped running. We were on a tight schedule and could not wait, so Ralph and I drove back down the Alaska Highway. This time, we traveled long days, not stopping for photos or to collect as David and I had on our way up. The only exception to our hasty overnight camps (we did not even bother to set up tents) was the night we spent occupying beds and taking hot baths in Prince George at the home of the nice British couple David and I had met. The main goal was to get to Berkeley as quickly as we could to meet Ralph's teaching commitments at the university. Fortunately our faithful Auntie did not develop any troubles and our Alaskan adventure came to a close.

As I reflect on that summer's adventure, I feel fortunate to have traveled the highway and seen parts of Alaska and its people during the mid-1950s, when it was still a frontier territory. I saw large tracts of intact natural forest, whereas now the vast northern forest is under siege. For many, its habitat is worthless—difficult to farm because of poor soils and harsh climatic conditions, its trees only useful for making newsprint and toilet paper. The forest and tundra are cut with roads built for resource extraction as well as hydroelectric megaprojects. The effects of the gold rush pale by comparison. I had the luxury of making this trip to satisfy my intellectual interests, but it was rich in learning from scientists as well as meeting local people and experiencing the frontier spirit in Alaska Territory. It was an experience I have treasured all my life.

EXPANDING HORIZONS WITH COLLABORATIVE RESEARCH

1953-1959

Because of nepotism regulations established during the Depression, educated women whose husbands worked at the university could not themselves have a paid position there. Lincoln Constance, patriarch of UC Berkeley botany, as Chair of the Botany Department in 1954, was instrumental in my appointment as a Research Associate. This position provided no salary but offered my first official recognition as a researcher. Appointees were assured of space in which to work and most importantly, for me and other women like me, it was an acknowledgment of the significance of our work. Fortunately, my place to work in the herbarium was next to that of Constance, which led to a fruitful professional friendship that continued throughout my career.

During the 1950s, there was little reason to expect much expansion in the status of women in science, though there had been some glimmer of recognizing women's potential in the UC Berkeley Botany Department—three women had obtained PhDs as early as the 1930s, and one of these, Katherine Esau, had become a distinguished professor of plant anatomy at UC Davis. She was a rare exception, however, and had to make her way to professorship from the UC Agricultural Experiment Station.

From 1954 to 1959, along with part-time teaching, assisting Ralph, and going on numerous field trips, I pursued a hodgepodge of research, mainly characterized by sporadic opportunities that arose, without any clear-cut projects of my own design. Nonetheless, I participated enthusiastically, and expanded my horizons through various collaborative activities. This was a time when several important conceptual changes in both ecology and geology were in the offing. Much of my research during this period was in association with Herbert Mason, with whom I had begun to interact during the fall of 1953. Although Mason considered himself a systematist, his greatest interests were past and present causes underlying the distribution and evolution of plants. He had done his PhD research with Ralph Chaney on western American Tertiary paleobotany, and he had spent a summer during his graduate student days with Frederick Clements on Pikes Peak when the Carnegie Institution of Washington ecotype transplant study was located there. During this time Mason became opposed to Clements' NeoLamarckian views of plant adaptation as only being molded by the environment, and to the idea of the plant community as a superorganism.

Moreover, in describing Tertiary plant assemblages, Mason had criticized Chaney's acceptance of Clements' organismal and climatic climax concepts of communities. He concluded that in accepting these concepts, Chaney had made taxonomic errors by assuming that component species in an assemblage remained together as a unit through time. Mason's study of the evolution of certain floristic associations in western North America had, in fact, convincingly demonstrated the divergent and reticulate patterns of species occurrence across different associations from the Tertiary to the present. His results clearly supported the individualistic concept of the community and his idea that lack of recognition of such variation in species occurrence could result in false taxonomic assumptions, especially with poorly preserved plant fossils.

Because Mason's views challenged what seemed to be well-established and often-cherished ecological tenets, he had become defensive about them. He admitted to me that he felt insecure in talking with formally trained ecologists. To him, "formally trained" meant having accepted some of Clements' more extreme concepts—which, of course, was not true for some prominent ecologists (including Cooper). This situation opened my eyes to how one man's pervading influence (such as that of Clements) could, in the eyes of some, taint an entire discipline.

I found Mason affable personally, extremely stimulating intellectually, and we had common interests in the role that paleobotany could play in understanding plant geography. Mason invited me to attend his lectures in plant geography, where he expressed his ecological views, clearly distinguishing them from Clementsian ideas. Typical of the Biosystematists' evolutionary perspective, Mason's plant geography course was more conceptual and integrative than Cooper's course, which had been a beautifully illustrated description of the vegetation of North America and discussion of its relationship to climate and geomorphology. The essence of Mason's approach was that what happens to plant populations and communities is, in the last analysis, what happens to individual plants. Thus his was a more reductionist approach, emphasizing the need for ecologists to understand the genetics and physiology of the individual plant and then aggregate these individuals into classes of populations and communities based upon characteristics that they deemed significant to answer questions in their research. This approach did not deny interaction among individuals comprising populations or in communities—it just made it clear that the operational unit, i.e., that selected by the environment, was the individual. His ideas inspired me to think even more deeply about the nature of communities and their classification.

Mason's ideas, which Stanley Cain had been exposed to during a sabbatical leave, had also impacted the organization and content of Cain's influential 1944 book *Foundations of Plant Geography*. Cain was an important figure in ecology at that time and I had been impressed with his book while a student at Minnesota. I had not realized Mason's influence on Cain's book until I attended his course (although Cain had given credit to him).

FIELD WORK WITH PALEONTOLOGISTS

During part of the summers of 1954 and 1958, I joined Ralph and a group of his graduate students collecting Paleozoic invertebrate fossils in stratigraphic sequences in Nevada. I was a stereotypical educated wife-helpmate, but I did not feel put upon—I just enjoyed the field experience. I served various functions, from ferrying food to the campsites (including having bears attack cartons of *canned* goods in the back of my truck) to helping find and collect fossils (something I seemed to have a special eye for, perhaps because I considered it like a special treasure hunt). In assisting with stratigraphic measurements, I led with the tape, which meant that I was the first one to encounter the rattlesnakes sunning on ledges, but also the first one to be thrilled by a fleeting glimpse of majestic desert mountain sheep as they quickly scampered off among the higher rocky areas.

Although in the 1950s women still were turned away from majoring in geology because they were not allowed to take a required course that put them into field with male students and faculty, I never felt uncomfortable camped out amid Ralph's all-male grad students. My experience on the Colombian expedition and here in Nevada helped me to feel at ease living in the field with men. Though I did not plan it this way, these experiences prepared me for future work on my own in various parts of the world in the company of men from different cultures.

While helping the paleontologists, I increased my familiarity with the flora and vegetation of the Great Basin high desert and my appreciation of its beauty—the pastel coloring of the mountains in late afternoons, followed by spectacular sunsets that heightened the rugged arid features of the landscape—and the smell of the sagebrush vegetation, especially after a rain shower. At the same time, I learned to tolerate living there—to endure the heat, rationing of every drop of water, the ever-present dust, wondering what might be inhabiting my sleeping bag (having once been surprised by a scorpion!) as I crawled in, awakening to the high winds blowing so hard that our small tent seemed about to roll away like a tumbleweed. It was a totally different experience from that in the high elevations of the Rocky Mountains, in northern Canada and Alaska, and in the subtropics and high country of Colombia. Although I did no research of my own, these experiences enhanced my appreciation for the adaptation of desert plants to harsh conditions, increasing my perspectives for teaching in ways that were not quantifiable with publications.

I also took some especially interesting geology field trips with Ralph and his associates, such as flying to the Grand Canyon with a vertebrate paleontologist colleague who owned his own airplane. Flying low over the canyon, we got a bird's eye view of this display of geologic history. We walked to the bottom of the canyon discussing the different periods of this amazing record of the earth's story from the combined perspective of invertebrate, vertebrate, and plant paleontologists—a very special experience. We also flew home over the Utah canyon country—viewing it in a way not common at that time.

During 1958, the invertebrate paleontologist J. Wyatt Durham discovered a travertine (limestone deposited by a hot springs) outcrop with incorporated plant fossils in a coastal area near Little Sur, California. I joined him later to collect these fossils and analyze the neighboring present-day vegetation. The fossils indicated that a closed-cone pine forest of Monterey pine (*Pinus radiata*) and Gowen cypress (*Cupressus goveniana*) with typical understory trees of silk-tassel bush (*Garrya*), California lilac (*Ceanothus*), and oak (*Quercus*) had existed along the canyon near the hot springs. Horsetails, sedges, and rushes characterized the stream side. The hot springs where the travertine was deposited were thought to be 10,000 or more years old, based on amino acid dating of gastropod shells. The composition of the fossil forest was strikingly different from the present-day coastal sage scrub, but documented a more extensive distribution of a closed-cone pine forests during Quaternary times, which was close to the endemic forests that still exist on the Monterey Peninsula. Our findings are consistent with Axelrod's evidence that the closed-cone pine forests shifted north and south along the outer coasts in alternating glacial and interglacial climates, but were broken into their highly discontinuous modern-day moist patches during the hot, dry interglacial periods.

*Malcolm McKenna's plane from which we surveyed
Grand Canyon and neighboring canyon parks*

On Supai Trail in Grand Canyon. Me, far left, and the McKennas in middle

With this research my paleobotanical thread had appeared again but this thread was different from that initiated in Colombia—my own research that combined paleobotany with ecology.

BOTANICAL FIELD ACTVITIES

During the summer of 1957, Ralph was doing research with the Canadian Geological Survey. The survey did not invite me to accompany him because one of the survey's paleobotanists was working on the project. Being free for the summer, Mason asked me (along with Robert Ornduff as a Teaching Assistant) to assist him with a Field Botany course, but I would focus on research about the bogs at Sagehen Creek Field Station (SCFS). I was sort of a "handyman," which provided me with an opportunity to absorb some of Mason's vast knowledge of the Sierra Nevada flora. Part of a reserve established by UC Berkeley and the USDA Forest Service in 1951, SCFS is located at 6,400 feet near Truckee on the eastern slope of the central Sierra Nevada. We camped in tents and we cooked our own food, but when we got tired of camp cuisine, we'd get into our rumpled "good clothes" and take off for dinner in one of the casinos in Reno. We agreed that each of us would spend only five dollars on the slot machines, but anyone who made a big haul would host the group to drinks. On our last trip to Reno, Herbert hit the jackpot on the silver dollar machine. When he met up with the rest of the group, the large number of silver dollars in the pockets of his pants made them sag so much that it looked as though they might soon be around his ankles. He hosted us all to an unforgettable dinner and still had silver dollars left over!

Robert Ornduff and Herbert Mason at Sagehen Creek vernal pool

I helped to establish a reference herbarium at the station using our class plant collections, and directed the mapping, using surveying instruments, of the wet, mossy areas near Sagehen Creek, which Mason had called "hanging bogs" (using a generic definition of "bog" that still is the one presented in most dictionaries). One of the bogs was increasing in size by invading the neighboring lodgepole pine forest and our carefully constructed map, expanded during 1958, was to provide the basis for future studies of this invasion. In the 1970s, studies by researchers at

UC Davis first showed that the dominant mosses, which Mason had assumed to be the common sphagnum that occurs under acid conditions, actually were brown mosses (*Drepanocladus* and *Cratoneuera*), which are characteristic of alkaline—or at least calcium-rich systems. It seemed strange that Mason, the meticulous taxonomist of higher plants, had never bothered to carefully identify the Sagehen moss. With the discovery of these alkaline conditions and their associated mosses as well as free-flowing water from a spring, the UC Davis researchers changed the name of these features from "bog" to "fen", and named the one we studied "Mason Fen." The clarification helped explain why these "bogs" were so different from the ones I had known, loaded with sphagnum mosses and exhibiting a characteristic zonal plant succession, around glacial ponds in the Midwest and in northern forests of British Columbia and Alaska. Subsequently, these researchers found that Mason fen had extended down slope beyond the 1957-58 map and killed numerous lodgepole pines by peat encroachment.

One of the most thought-provoking parts of the summer for me resulted from the class traversing the central Sierra Nevada. I had the chance to compare more carefully Sierra forest communities with those in the Colorado Rockies. Although I had noted some differences previously, now I could observe and think more deeply about them. On the western slope of this portion of the Sierra, a few dominant species do not demarcate zonal forest communities in the way Engelmann Spruce-Subalpine Fir and Ponderosa Pine-Douglas Fir forests do on the eastern slope of the Colorado Rockies, and certainly not like the Spruce-Fir forest, with vast aspen forests below, on the Rockies' western slope. In the Sierra Nevada, the montane and subalpine forests are essentially a continuum of overlapping conifer species. The conifer forests begin at about 2,000 feet above an oak woodland. Ponderosa pine is perhaps the most common and conspicuous species, with incense cedar (*Calocedrus decurrens*), white fir (*Abies concolor*), sugar pine (*P. lambertiana*), and Douglas fir (*Pseudotsuga menziesii*) accompanying it. This group of species has been called the mixed conifer forest by some and montane forest by others. The upper, cooler forest areas are sometimes referred to as a subalpine forest; it is characterized by an abundance of red fir (*A. magnifica*), along with jeffrey pine (*P. jeffreyi*), and lodgepole pine (*P. contorta* var. *murryana*). These species may intergrade with lower altitude conifers.

Aspen (*Populus tremuloides* var. *aurea*) sometimes occurs abundantly but replaces other forests in disturbed areas rather than forming a major forest type. Western white pine (*P. monticola*) and mountain hemlock (*Tsuga mertensiana*) occur at even higher altitudes. The scattered timberline pines, such as white bark (*P. albicaulis*), limber pine (*P. flexilis*), and foxtail pine (*P. balfouriana*) at around 9,500 feet give way to alpine fell fields—a timberline that is much lower than in the Colorado Rockies. This complex, overlapping distribution of conifers, with lack of a few clearly dominant species, along an altitudinal gradient made Robert Whittaker's individualistic gradient model seem to be an excellent way to describe, and classify the conifer communities in the Sierra Nevada, as he had done for the complex distribution of eastern deciduous trees in the Smoky Mountains.

Because the eastern, desert facing slope of the Sierra Nevada is within a rain shadow region, the forests are different from the western slope. In the area we visited, *Pinus jeffreyi* was the dominant species in a mixed conifer forest, with some intrusions of aspen, and below it a sagebrush-dominated vegetation from the adjacent Great Basin high cold desert. Having spent part of the last two summers comparing Alaskan arctic and Colorado Rocky Mountain alpine vegetation, seeing some "arctic-alpine friends" as well as the unique presence of desert annual plants in the alpine vegetation of the Sierra Nevada was a delightful experience. A majority of these desert annual species are invaders from lower elevations in the Great Basin.

In the following summer of 1958, again at Mason's instigation, I joined a group of volunteers at the Boundary Hill Biotic Succession Research Area in Yosemite National Park. The Yosemite Field School of Natural History also used the area to train ranger naturalists. In 1933, volunteers had established permanent quadrats with a plan to reanalyze them, take comparative photos, and publish the data every twenty years. The goal of these studies was to provide a descriptive record of the changes in the vegetation of the park, which could serve for the southern Sierra Nevada as well. These constitute precious records of what the vegetation was like—especially before heavy human impact. Mason had been involved with training ranger naturalists and the related study for many years, and was trying to energize the group to synthesize the first set of twenty-year data for publication.

Herbert Mason, center, and volunteers
at Boundary Hill camp, Yosemite

Mason was, characteristically, thinking ahead of his time in advocating and implementing such long-term studies. It wasn't until 1976 that the University of California established a system of natural reserves (called living laboratories) throughout the state to enable long-term studies of California's great natural diversity and provide background records for researchers (there are now 36 sites and the system continues to expand). A national network of long-term ecological research (LTER) sites, sponsored by NSF, was not established until 1980.

At 7,000 to 9,000 feet, most of the Boundary Hill reserve is low rounded hills and glacial valleys replete with marshy areas and good stands of lodgepole pine, red fir, and jeffrey pine along the streams. It was the marshy areas that interested Mason and me. In particular, we were intrigued with plant succession on logs and the way they merged to form floating islands on Swamp Lake. We used the Swamp Lake succession as an example of the Boundary Hill studies in a presentation at the 1959 meeting of Ecological Society of America. We hoped that this paper, "Long Range Vegetation Studies in Yosemite National Park," would lead to other presentations from the Boundary Hill Studies done so devotedly by loyal volunteers over so many years. Otherwise, valuable data would disappear in file drawers. Although Jack Major at UC Davis espoused interest and made some initial attempts, unfortunately, no further data have been published.

SCIENTIFIC PHILOSOPHY: LANGUAGE ANALYSIS WITH MASON

Apart from the continued field studies and interesting field jaunts, my enthusiastic response in 1954 to the ideas Mason presented in his geography course, led to my joining his efforts to clarify ambiguities in the use of some important terms and their underlying concepts in ecology. The highly complex nature of the relations between the environment and organisms and the aggregate nature of vegetation can often frustrate researchers trying to interpret them and lead to confusion in generalizations about them. Mason convinced me that confusion in understanding perennial questions in ecology—such as "Do communities really exist or are they abstractions?", "Should the fundamental unit of study be the individual, species populations, or the community, (ecosystem not commonly used then)?" and "How can we analyze the complexities of the environment?" often can be traced to how knowledge is organized and the language in which the issue is expressed.

I think that it is helpful to understand Mason's quest for linguistic clarity in the context of the 1950s. Semantics was a popular topic in the mid-1950s and had been promoted by such writers as S.I. Hayakawa, who emphasized the psychological impact that language has. There is no doubt that people become emotionally attached to certain terms, which can perpetuate confusion. On the other hand, some physicists, led by Einstein, had discovered that a scientific philosophical approach to semantics was useful in resolving some of their controversies. The physicists' success encouraged Mason and me to enlist the help of scientific philosophers in the Berkeley philosophy department to learn more about the semantics of science, which involved logical reasoning and what was called language analysis.

Mason and I then attended philosophy classes at UC Berkeley and conferences at the Center for Advanced Study in Menlo Park concerned with language analysis. I found these experiences fascinating, and dived into them with enthusiasm. Basically we were learning a set of logical rules to make operational definitions by sorting out empirical relations from our abstractions about them. We discussed the language problems that produced confusion in ecology with various philosophers, and then organized a group of ecologically-oriented UC Berkeley biologists to discuss how important language analysis might be for them. Our first step was to point out that many authors used terms without making clear their definitions and with little regard for how others used them.

We picked fundamental terms such as "plant succession" and "environment" and went around the room asking for each person's definition.

Everyone was surprised, except for Mason and me, at the lack of agreement on even necessary criteria for understanding such commonly used terms. Historians of ecology, such as Robert McIntosh, have declared that ecologists have the tendency "to use terms like Lewis Carroll's Humpty Dumpty" (As Humpty Dumpty told Alice in *Through the Looking Glass*, "when I use a word, it means just what I choose it to mean . . . neither more or less."), and this became clear in our discussions.

By 1955, we had received sufficient encouragement to think of publishing some of our semantic approaches. We also were prodded by Einstein's exhortations to physicists to undertake the "laborious process . . . in achieving more precise definitions of concepts and conclusions." We decided to start with a paper on the concept of environment, a hot topic at the time, which we would preface with language analysis that emphasized logic and recognition of the distinction between empirical conditions and abstraction (class concepts) about them.

We attempted to circumvent the unwieldy complexity (what Egler called the "nebulous unlimitedness") of ecological thinking by reducing the concept of environment to only those empirical conditions (phenomena) that could be confirmed as directly entering a reaction with an individual organism. The environment, thus conceived, had to be operationally significant during the life of the organism as ordered by its ontogeny and hence was organism-directed-timed and spaced. This was a different way of viewing the "unlimitedness" of the environment by sorting out the empirical relations instead of referring to factors comprising an incredible complex of interactions, not all of which were significant to the organism at specific times in its ontogeny. In so doing, it helped reassure other scientists, particularly plant physiologists, that despite the complex nature of the environment and its relation to the complex aggregation of plants in communities, testable ecological experiments could be designed. In some disagreement with our perspective, the paper achieved a certain notoriety in discussion in numerous graduate seminars across the country.

Today, with the availability of computers to assist in analysis, study of not only the environment but also ecosystems is often based on the "science of complexity," which describes such systems with many strongly interacting parts. However, researchers are still faced with fundamental problems in knowing what complexity is, with authors stating that "defining complexity is frustrating"—with no agreed definition and drawing different lines of demarcation with the "field of chaos." There seems to be agreement that the science of complexity currently is an "unfinished mosaic."

The perpetual existence of semantic problems also is exasperatingly evident in statements from a current plant ecology text: "A very confusing array of terms has developed to describe communities. Sometimes the same term is used in different ways by different ecologists, while in other cases different terms are given to the same concept." Recognition of such problems with commonly used terms has brought semantics again to the forefront of thinking, particularly since the late 1990s. There has been a strong movement to standardize meaning of terms that are important in aiding non-scientists and policy makers to understand ecological research. In some cases there also has been a plea for more "operationalized" definitions, which physicists generally still adhere to. The idea of standardization, however, has resulted in a backlash by some, who indicate that reviews of terminology "often make unwarranted assumptions about language, meaning, and how language interacts with scientific progress." I'm sure that at least recognition of "why semantics matters" (part of title of a recent paper) would warm the heart of Herbert Mason.

SEMANTICS AND NATURAL SELECTION

Back in 1958 on another front, Mason was concerned that in the centenary celebration at the Zoological Congress of Darwin and Wallace's presentation of the doctrine of natural selection to the Linnean Society in London, discussions were devoted solely to evolutionary theory concerned with the origin of species. There was no mention of its ecological relevance. Therefore, I joined Mason in organizing a symposium, "Natural Selection as an Ecological Concept," for the western section meetings of the Ecological Society of America. We presented language analysis as a means to clarify confusion surrounding the concept of natural selection, and researchers such as Harlan Lewis and Art Kruckeberg discussed specific cases of what they considered to be natural selection in their ecological studies. It elicited lively discussion, with some attendees admitting that they had never thought of Darwin's concept of natural selection in an ecological context. This was probably due in part to their focus on communities with only those researchers beginning to think in terms of populations seeing its relevance. (To show the change in recognition of natural selection as an ecological concept—the current renowned evolutionists, Peter and Rosemary Grant wrote in 2008 that "nothing in evolutionary biology makes sense except in the light of ecology.")

Our concern about an ecological perspective on natural selection arose again a year later during the 1959 worldwide centennial celebration of the publication of Darwin's *Origin of Species*. Numerous researchers reviewed the role of natural selection in evolutionary theory, but none even alluded to its importance in ecological thinking. As we had discovered at our symposium the year before, most ecologists at the time were not seeing the direct relation of natural selection to their investigations. We reasoned that this lack of recognition both by evolutionists and ecologists during the late 1950s resulted from Darwin having presented his theory as an *evolutionary* explanation of the origin of species, much of which became incorporated into the concept of natural selection.

Mason strongly felt there was so much confusion surrounding the concepts of species, evolution, and natural selection that the relation of the latter to ecology had been left unrecognized. Therefore, building on the 1958 ESA symposium, Mason and I began to prepare a manuscript for the journal *Ecology*, where we earlier had used language analysis to try untangling the complexities of the concept of environment. We wanted to reiterate that some of the confusion regarding natural selection might stem from problems in expressing and organizing knowledge about the process. A central concern was to clarify for ecologists that natural selection was basically an ecological concept as well as an evolutionary one.

In our 1961 paper we concluded that Darwin's conception of natural selection came from both the assessment of the variation of different properties within an organism and the selective role of the environment in determining which individuals would survive. He had abstracted only those changed and useful properties that were meaningful to his motive of explaining the origin of species. This led to ambiguity as to whether it was the properties or the individuals that were being selected and hence the precise locus of the operation. Furthermore, it built selection and evolution into a single idea that combined the empirical and environmental relations of the individual organism with the abstractions of continuity in the variations of properties in the succession of organisms. We thought that the subsequent history of the theory had amplified these ambiguities in language.

Fundamentally, what Mason and I were trying to clarify for plant ecologists was a 1950s individualistic approach—that each and every individual plant is selected by environmental conditions. With this understanding, the problems of the ecologist then shift from the fundamental biological operation to dealing with conceptual knowledge derived, for example, from properties of individuals, species populations, and communities. Despite this paper on natural selection as an ecological concept being earlier than most commonly cited papers that recognize this view, it has been generally overlooked. Why? There may be several reasons, but I suspect that it may have been neglected primarily because of the emphasis on the philosophical tools of language analysis, rather than research examples, as well as, *ironically*, the exposition style. Mason probed ecological concepts deeply but he did not have the ability to express his ideas with the simplicity and clarity that graced, for example, Cooper's writing (in fact, after Cooper saw the first paper, he wrote me that "he longed to get his claws into it and put it into simple language").

Six years later, in 1967, the plant population ecologist John Harper, in his presidential address to the British Ecological Society, framed natural selection as an ecological concept in a way that impacted ecologists' thinking. He claimed that "the theory of evolution by natural selection is an ecological theory—founded on ecological observations by perhaps the greatest of all ecologists." He added that natural selection "has been adopted by and brought up by the science of genetics, and ecologists, being modest people, are apt to forget their distinguished parenthood. Indeed, Darwinian plant ecology has been largely neglected and a changeling child nourished and brought to adulthood by Schimper and Warming who asked geographic questions about vegetation, and answered questions by demonstrating correlations between climate and soils on the one hand and comparative physiology on the other. By contrast . . . Darwin's ecological observations and the questions he asked were based on a consideration of individuals and populations." Harper concluded his lecture by referring to a range of ecological thought and stimulus to modern experimental plant ecology (replete with examples), all of which, he said, had a "highly respectable origin in the ecological thinking of Darwin."

It was not until Richard Lewontin's 1970s review article on units of selection, however, that evolutionary ecologists accepted that natural selection operates primarily at the level of the individual. The merger of ecological and evolutionary thinking so common today, in which natural selection is automatically incorporated into population analysis, finally occurred. This would come clearly into focus for me, and I would begin to apply these principles, when I moved into the emerging subfield of chemical ecology. Nonetheless, even today, controversy still exists in contemporary evolutionary biology over units of selection, whether selection operates exclusively on individual organisms, and just how it operates.

CONTINENTAL DRIFT CONTROVERSY

It was an especially exciting time in that I was witnessing controversy not just over fundamental ecological concepts, but geological ones as well. Among the many interesting research seminars and meetings I attended at UC Berkeley, one stands out in which the prevailing view of the geologists would soon be overturned. During the mid to late 1950s (I don't recall the exact date), the Biosystematists and members of the Paleontology Department at UC Berkeley planned this meeting with members of the Geology Department at Berkeley and Stanford to discuss the validity of the concept of continental drift. Biologists and paleontologists for many years had been intrigued with Alfred Wegener's 1920 theory, which offered an explanation for the history of the distribution of many taxa. If continents that seemed to fit together like puzzle pieces had indeed drifted apart, that would help explain situations such as the same or similar fossils being found in South America and Africa. However, Wegener's mechanisms for continental drift had been rejected as insufficient to move continents and even ridiculed by geologists.

Arthur Holmes later elaborated on Wegener's many hypotheses regarding mechanisms for drift and concluded that thermal convection could produce a sufficient current to cause continents to move. It could act like a conveyor belt, and upwelling pressure could break apart a continent, forcing the continent in opposite directions carried by the convection currents. Holmes' ideas also were being given little credence by geologists. After heated discussion at the Berkeley meeting, a vote was taken. As I remember it, the results were essentially split between the biologically-oriented group's "yes" for continental drift, based on compelling circumstantial evidence, and the geologist group's "no" because of insufficient evidence for a mechanism to explain its occurrence.

Less than a decade later in 1961, however, Holmes' explanation of convection received support, in fact, moved from ridicule to general acceptance. Greater understanding of geomagnetic anomalies parallel to mid-oceanic ridges, and the association of island arcs and oceanic trenches near continental margins, suggested that convection—now known as sea floor spreading—could move continents. It is difficult today to imagine and understand our world without reference to plate tectonics—one of the most far-ranging geological theories of all times. Its consequences for geology have been immense and it has helped evolutionary biologists and biogeographers explain the patterns of distribution of many plants and animals as well.

BACK TO THE MIDWEST

1959-1961

It's not the strongest of the species that survive nor the most intelligent, but the one most responsive to change.
—Charles Darwin

The University of California's policy is "seven years up to tenure, or out." Ralph's teaching and research were sufficient for tenure, but by the critical sixth year of assessment Ralph had hopelessly irritated the chairman of the department of paleontology, whom he had frequently criticized. Ralph's brash personality had resulted in his often being misunderstood or even disliked, a problem I had to deal with over the years—but in this case the chairman had vowed that he should not remain in the department. On the other hand, there were those who strongly supported Ralph, thinking his many contributions as a very active scientist outweighed his brashness. This controversy divided the department into pro-and con-Langenheim camps. The Dean of the Letters and Sciences College, and Academic Senate committees reviewing his tenure promotion finally decided that to maintain harmony in the paleontology department it was necessary for Ralph to leave.

Those who backed Ralph, especially the highly respected invertebrate paleontologist J. Wyatt Durham, began to actively help him find another position. Thus, later in the spring of 1959, an offer came from the outstanding Geology Department at the University of Illinois at Urbana. We were glad for this opportunity, but it would be a difficult move for both of us. The Paleontology Department at Berkeley was unique and Ralph had a good group of students. I had gotten well established as a Research Associate in the Botany Department, and was enjoying my part-time teaching at SFCW. Although there appeared to be little chance of further professional advancement, I lived a comfortable and interesting life, for which I was grateful. We loved our home in the Berkeley Hills and the San Francisco Bay Area was a magnificent place to live. I am not prone to cry much, but tears rolled down my face when we left for Ralph's summer field work in Nevada, knowing we would not be returning to Berkeley. Ralph had been both grim and furiously angry over his dismissal, and I tried to avoid discussing it and emphasized making the best of the situation.

While Ralph was working in Nevada, I taught Field Ecology at RMBL again. I had gained considerable confidence from teaching the course in 1955 and proceeded with similar lectures and field trips. This group of students, however, lacked the enthusiastic interest displayed by those in my previous class. It may have partly been my fault as I was still somewhat depressed about leaving Berkeley and apprehensive about what lay ahead in Urbana. In some ways my despondent feelings were exacerbated by a visit from the Masons. Although Herbert participated in some of our class discussions and attended several field trips, both of us realized that our collaboration would never be the same. In many ways, most of that summer's activities with the Masons had the atmosphere of a wake.

Mother and Herbert Mason (far left),
Lucile Mason (far right) on RMBL field trip

Mother also came for her first visit to Gothic during the time the Masons were there. She and Lucile had become good friends when Mother had visited in Berkeley. Mother enjoyed seeing places in the Crested Butte area that she had heard about for over a decade, and she also met several long-term RMBL friends whom I had written about in letters. Mother most enjoyed meeting the MacFarlanes at the University of Kentucky geology camp; they offered her a sumptuous meal of southern fried chicken and all the fixings, just as they had so many times for Ralph and me. Mother stayed in touch with both the MacFarlanes and the Masons for many years. It was such a pleasure to see Mother so easily become good friends with those who meant much to me.

Other memorable moments included a trip to the opera in Aspen. For a number of years at RMBL, there had been talk about hiking the old stagecoach trail to Aspen—especially to attend the opera there. Since both the Masons and Mother were great opera fans, we hatched a plan for a small group of us to hike, while the Masons and other interested persons would drive around and bring us home the next day. It was a rigorous thirteen-mile hike, and as we went over Conundrum Pass I recalled the travails of the 1955 trip with the pack horse Prince! We barely made Aspen in time for the opera (Madame Butterfly, as I remember) and were very happy indeed to have a ride back to Gothic, but we were proud of having made the trek.

After the course was finished and the Masons and Mother had left, Ralph and I headed for Illinois. Although still a bit dispirited, I was consoled that we were not being consigned to outer oblivion. Both the geology and botany departments at the University of Illinois at Urbana were excellent. On the other hand, Ralph still felt belligerent about his dismissal.

After living in the San Francisco Bay Area, however, the environs were a shock. The main quadrangle had once been a lovely sight, with huge arching American elms that had essentially enclosed the area. I could envision what it must have been like because in Tulsa I had grown up along the elm-lined "shady Cheyenne Street," as it was often called. Dutch elm disease, caused by a fungus spread by the elm bark beetle, however, had decimated the university elms and the quad looked barren. This disease had been brought into New England and spread southward and westward, completely destroying trees in many cities such as it had in Urbana. Recently planted honey locust trees would eventually mitigate the loss but they were never going to produce the grand impression the elms had. Along residential streets some elms had survived, but the older homes where they had been removed appeared a bit dowdy. The overall scene stood in strong contrast to the beauty of the Berkeley campus and the Berkeley Hills where our home had had such beautiful views of San Francisco Bay.

The Illinois period was a dreary one for me professionally as I continued to face nepotism regulations. Some exceptions were made; for example, a wife could be paid for a temporary and menial job if no qualified man was available. I wondered if this qualified man would be able to support a family on the salary offered? Otherwise, was the regulation more gender discrimination than prevention of nepotism? Even with a PhD the only paying job I was allowed to have was supervising teaching assistants in the labs for Introductory Botany. The course, with its required lab, was very large because it served all of the students needing botanical background, including those in agriculture. Although the lab was somewhat demanding, it was basic information, routinely presented—not very thought-provoking for either the students or me. However, this job did enable me to save a little money, and I became acquainted with most of the graduate students in the department, since nearly all of them did a stint as teaching assistants in this large course. I enjoyed my interaction with the grad students, and again made some lifelong friends among them.

SURMOUNTING CHALLENGES

Two of the strengths of the University of Illinois botany department were plant ecology and paleobotany, with each discipline being recognized for its outstanding faculty and large number of graduate students. These were bright spots that enabled me to continue to learn from researchers in my two primary fields of interest. The friendship and support of these people helped me surmount professional and increasing personal problems.

I had not completed my part of the Colombian Girón Formation research project because I needed assistance in describing the old Paleozoic and Mesozoic plant fossils. The paleobotanists at UC Berkeley had been focused on younger Cretaceous and Tertiary fossils in the context of evolution of forest communities. At Illinois, the paleobotanists Wilson Stewart and Ted Delyvoras and their graduate students studied the anatomy and developmental evolution of plants from older ages, most of which were now extinct. With their assistance, I completed the publication "Late Paleozoic and Early Mesozoic Plant Fossils from the Cordillera Oriental of Colombia and Correlation of the Girón Formation." Although plant fossils were much less abundant and more poorly preserved than invertebrate fossils in the Girón Formation, I was able to determine genera from the Late Carboniferous to the Jurassic in different stratigraphic sections. The assemblages of fern and fern-like foliage from extinct seed ferns, in particular, provided a better indication of Jurassic age (for most people known as the age of the dinosaurs) in some strata than the invertebrates. In working with the Illinois paleobotanists I discovered that such seed-fern foliage assemblages had been successfully used to identify particular time stratigraphic units in other parts of the world. Since controversy over the age of the formation was the central problem that the Colombian Geological Institute had wanted our team to solve, these scrappy plant fossils made an unexpectedly important contribution to understanding some parts of the Girón Formation in Colombia. Controversy persists regards the age of this formation with Colombian geologists continuing to search for more clear evidence for the span of time in which these extensively occurring terrestrial sediments were deposited.

I felt very much at home with the department's plant ecologist, Larry Bliss, as he was part of the W.S. Cooper lineage. His PhD advisor, Dwight Billings, was a student of H.J. Oosting, who in turn had been a Cooper student. Larry was a physiological ecologist who studied arctic-alpine plants; the experiments he and his students were conducting increased my persistent interest in understanding how these plants adapt physiologically to the harsh environmental conditions in which they exist. The small mobile laboratories they were taking into alpine areas enabled them to measure various physiological parameters such as rates of photosynthesis, thus moving field experiments to a new level.

Since farmlands clothed most of central Illinois, Bliss had to take the students in his ecology class along railroad right of ways to see original grasslands. Railroads—a prime cause of human disturbance in grasslands—had now become a chief means by which samples of original prairie were being preserved in Illinois. I joined several trips out of the corn fields to such places as the Lake Michigan dunes, where Cowles originally set forth his seminal ideas regarding primary plant succession, and the famous glacial lake bogs at Warren Woods in Wisconsin, which provide a traditional example of this kind of zonal succession. These are classic Midwest examples of primary succession commonly presented in ecology textbooks, and I enjoyed revisiting them.

*Larry Bliss (center) with Illinois Field Ecology
course at Lake Michigan dunes*

MORE ON PLANT COMMUNITY CONCEPTS

These Midwestern trips strengthened my thread of interest in the history of ecological concepts. The historic importance of the Universities of Chicago, Minnesota, Illinois, and, later, Wisconsin in the development of American ecology in the early to mid-twentieth century became clear to me. I reflected, too, about how some of the traditional community-unit concepts I had learned at the University of Minnesota had been altered during my Berkeley experience, which had played into my thinking favorably about the individualistic concept of communities espoused by Henry Gleason.

During my time at the University of Illinois, the very active research being done by John Curtis, Grant Cottam, and their students at the University of Wisconsin was providing strong support for Gleason's individualistic concept of communities. (Curtis died in 1961 having had 36 doctoral students and Cottam continued with 27 more). Although Curtis did not begin his description of Wisconsin vegetation with the intention of overthrowing Clementsian ideas, the first stirring of change came with his innovations in quantitative methods of sampling and data analysis. Curtis and Cottam developed the first non-areal sampling technique for analyzing variation in vegetation. They were convinced that to understand the puzzling variation in Wisconsin vegetation, it was necessary to do intensive analysis over large areas, which their ordination techniques would enable. Curtis drew the analogy with an increasingly used approach in studying the variation of many individuals within populations of a species (a viewpoint that had influenced me in association with California Bay Area systematists). Curtis' analysis of many stands of vegetation, without an *a priori* idea of what their characteristics should be, avoided the circularity of reasoning that had plagued ecology from its outset. It was a radically different approach to vegetation analysis in the late 1940s and probably the most important contribution of the Wisconsin school of ecology.

Curtis' quantitative results showed that plant communities, such as those in Wisconsin deciduous forests, did not have discrete boundaries. Rather, there were gradual or continuous changes in species comprising the vegetation over a given region, and this continuum of species could be described by overlapping bell-shaped (Gaussian-type) curves. Curtis also thought that human impact had blurred boundaries, decreased the complexity and level of organization, as well as introduced randomness into communities. His 1959 book, *The Vegetation of Wisconsin,* is still one of the best works on regional vegetation in the United States—receiving accolades similar to those of for E. Lucy Braun's book on the eastern deciduous forest.

Unknown to Curtis and his students until 1950, Robert Whittaker at the University of Illinois, was developing strikingly similar approaches, terminology, and ideas. Whittaker had begun his dissertation studies in 1946 on foliage insects in the Smoky Mountains, but to do this he needed knowledge of the plant communities. Whittaker had two advisors—the Clementsian-oriented zoologist Charles Kendeigh, a Shelford student, and the Gleasonian-oriented botanist Arthur Vestal. Thus, Whittaker found himself, as he expressed it, in the "exciting confusion" of a crossfire of views regarding community concepts. This was similar to, although less divergent than, my situation with Cooper and Mason.

Whittaker rejected the usual practice of subjectively choosing samples to represent associations in analyzing and describing deciduous forest communities in the Smoky Mountains. Like the Curtis group, he thought that natural units would become evident by sampling through the complex mixture of deciduous trees. He discovered that each species had a bell-shaped distribution and that he could group them along a topographic moisture gradient. Thus, these different kinds of tree aggregations intergraded continuously. He referred to his analytic approach as gradient analysis, because patterns of intergrading combinations of species corresponded to patterns in the environment. Although Whittaker initially had difficulty in getting his Smoky Mountain research published, Curtis, better established in the ecological community, and Mason, the ecological heretic, were those who helped him succeed.

The considerable impact of the continuum studies of Wisconsin school of ecologists along with Whittaker's gradient analysis research, sealed a shift for many ecologists from the traditional community-unit concept to the individualistic community concept. Some of these ecologists even suggested that this change in paradigms constituted a Kuhnsian scientific revolution in American ecology.

This shift, however, was not universal. In California, both paradigms were being espoused by researchers during the 1950s. I had seen the overturn of the community-unit view in support of the individualistic perspective among the plant systematists. Some paleobotanists and animal ecologists, however, still held the extreme view of the community being an integrated system analogous to a superorganism. At the University of Illinois, too, there had been a history of parallel existence of the two paradigms. The rich tradition of the Clementsian organism concept, established by Victor Shelford, was still strong among the zoologists during my stay there from 1959 to 1962. Nor was Bliss an enthusiastic follower of the individualistic ideas, as Vestal had been before him. In his ecology courses, Bliss acknowledged the research of ecologists following either view.

Having gained a more in-depth understanding of community concepts following discussions over the years at Berkeley and now at Illinois, as well as thinking about my own research while teaching at RMBL, I finally returned to preparing my dissertation for publication. It was long overdue. I had remained firmly convinced that my use of the vegetation zone as a relatively stable community type based on physiognomy, which occurred in an environmentally ordered serial sequence, had been the best means to map the vegetation of the Crested Butte area. Furthermore, the mapping allowed comparison of the zones to altitude, slope exposure, and soil parent material. I also could accept Whittaker's viewpoint that discontinuity of the total aggregation of the species comprising the community type is essentially a segmentation of a fundamental vegetation continuum along mountain environmental gradients (i.e., recognizing the individualistic distribution of the component species' populations). This reconciliation was clear to me in recognizing that it is we ecologists who choose to set boundaries and classify communities based on characteristics that fit our particular objectives.

I still faced an arduous job of cutting the extensive analyses of floristic composition of the vegetation zones and their relation to various mapped environmental parameters. I was gratified that the editor of *Ecological Monographs*, Henry Oosting, acknowledged the importance of the vegetation map of the Crested Butte area by endorsing a foldout sheet of it for publication. Distinct from the dissertation, I also discussed concepts of the community, focusing on varied use of vegetative zones (particularly common in the western US mountains), and changed from the dissertation title of "Plant Ecological Reconaissance of the Crested Butte Area, Gunnison County, Colorado" to "Vegetative and Environmental Patterns in the Crested Butte Area, Gunnison County, Colorado."

McIntosh in 1993 pointed out that over the years ecologists have been "looking for unity of the continuity-discontinuity poles—or at least a range of possibilities of 'classification-ability' between them." Nonetheless, difference of opinion persists today regarding the nature of communities as well as methods to describe and classify them. In the United States, some progress has been achieved in recognizing that it is necessary to understand the process of classification and for the researcher to establish the objectives for classifying the vegetation under study. In 1995, ESA constituted a Panel for Vegetation Classification to support and facilitate the creation of a standardized, scientifically credible North American vegetation classification system. Four years later the panel formed a partnership with The Nature Conservancy, United States Geological Survey-National Park Service (USGS-NPS) and others to further this goal. They recognize that a physiogonomic classification enables identification of vegetation patterns where little is known about an area and more detailed analysis is impractical; importantly it also facilitates mapping of discrete patterns. On the other hand, floristic classifications are most useful for detailed site analyses of environmental gradients, succession and floristic assemblages (which tend to display continuous distribution of species).

PLANT GEOGRAPHY FIELD TRIPS

Bliss taught an Ecological Plant Geography course in the Cooperian tradition, which had been followed at Duke University by Oosting and Billings. He led extensive spring field trips associated with the course, and I participated in several of these. The Illinois students eagerly looked forward to seeing more than just patches of natural vegetation among corn fields, and I increased my understanding of the vegetation of the southeastern United States—a region I had not seen previously.

One trip focused on the Smoky Mountains. I was particularly excited to see and discuss the deciduous forest of these mountains, which E. Lucy Braun had described as a center of diversity in her 1950 classic book *Deciduous Forests of Eastern North America*. This was also where Whittaker had arrived at the idea of gradient analysis. No other area in the eastern United States can boast of such a large variety of plants—1,300 flowering plants alone. In the lower-mid altitudes there are almost as many kinds of native trees as in all of Europe. The most common canopy trees are sugar maple (*Acer saccharum*), beech (*Fagus grandiflora*), tulip tree (*Liriodendron tuliperum*), basswood (*Tilia heterophylla*), buckeye (*Aesculus octandra*), and white oak (*Quercus alba*). I was amazed by the size—both height and girth—of many of them; I had never seen deciduous trees this large. Lower layers of trees include magnolia, redbud (*Cercis canadensis*), dogwood (*Cornus florida*), hornbeam (*Ostrya virginiana*), and ironwood (*Carpinus caroliniana*), among many others. Braun became the most prominent woman ecologist of the time for her extensive studies of the eastern deciduous forest. Highly praised for her research, she was elected the first woman president of the Ecological Society of America. Her book was lauded in a review by Fosberg "as a definitive work and that it has reached a level of excellence seldom or never before attained in American ecology or vegetation science, at least in any work of comparable importance."

Braun focused on undisturbed "pristine" forests and recognized regional climax communities based on climate, but often extrapolated these regions so that their boundaries coincided with the physiography. Despite differences today in community concepts and methodologies for analysis used by the US Forest Service, as well as their including forests at all levels of human disturbance, a recent report states that "to this day,

Big deciduous tree in Smoky Mountains

Braun's maps of forest regions remain one of the most widely referenced classifications of eastern forest."

Nonetheless, Braun's basic community-unit approach has led to erroneous conclusions regarding the geological history of these forest communities. Braun argued that refugia near the ice front during the Pleistocene made it possible for eastern deciduous tree species to maintain their distribution patterns since the close of the Tertiary two million years ago. Recent fossil pollen evidence, however, suggests that prominent genera, such as beech (*Fagus*) and sugar maple (*Acer*), illustrate an individualistic response to post-Pleistocene climate. Although today they are common associates in the Great Lakes region and New England, fossil pollen indicates that after the glacial maximum beech occurred primarily in the southern Appalachian mountains and coastal plains and then migrated rapidly up the eastern seaboard. Sugar maple appeared west of the Appalachians following the glacial retreat, migrating into its current range from there. This paleobotanical evidence demonstrates the pitfalls of using the community-unit concept to understand the development of eastern deciduous forest communities on an evolutionary scale. This is similar to Mason demonstrating the individualistic distribution of Pacific coast trees in forests from the Tertiary to the present—the redwood forest, for example, did not migrate as a unit; characteristic components migrated independently, based on their physiological tolerance of environmental conditions. Even today, not a single associated species approximates a complete coincidence of geographic area with that occupied by coastal redwood (*Sequoia sempervirens*).

In addition to the major contribution of E. Lucy Braun, it is the research of two other women (Catherine Keever and Elsie Quarterman), extending through the late 1930s until the early 1950s, that stands out in analysis and description of the eastern deciduous forest. And, they faced many hurdles to overcome. First, although the Eighteenth Amendment (Prohibition) had been repealed in 1933, its effects, as well as those of the Great Depression, lingered in the southern mountains. Moonshiners were ever-present in remote forest areas, and doing field work alone was a major challenge for women. Braun solved the problem by bringing along her entomologist sister Annette, and stories abound about their skill in dealing with these "outlaws."

Keever and Quarterman did field work together and credit the encouragement and support of Henry Oosting in being able to do their PhD dissertations during the mid 1940s at Duke University. Only later, when these women were teaching in colleges, did they have help from their students. A humorous aside regarding their later field work is documented in Keever's memoir, *Moving On*. She says when she and Quarterman applied

Annette and E. Lucy Braun, at right

for an NSF grant in 1956, they answered why they needed financial support, that "we have run out of relatives to support us." One of the reviewers' comments was "that if two fool women were willing to work in the snake, chigger, and mosquito infested woods of the south, that they [NSF] should give them the money." They were given $8,000 for two field seasons. These two women are highly respected for both their perseverance and insightful research in the southeastern forests, and I have enjoyed comparing experiences with them over the years at national meetings. I never had the privilege of meeting E. Lucy Braun.

After exploring the incredible diversity of deciduous trees in the Smoky Mountain forests, we followed the vegetation in a transect from the North Carolina coast back to Illinois. Across the Piedmont area, a gently rolling foothill region of the Appalachians still forested with a mosaic of oak-hickory and pine forests, we witnessed progressive stages of classic secondary succession in old fields of the sort often pictured in ecology textbooks. Unlike the large farms of the Midwest and West, here many farms comprise but a few acres—generally planted with corn and cash crops such as cotton and tobacco. Diversity in land utilization in this area has enabled an old-field succession to be well documented from abandoned fields, through various herbs and grasses, to different kinds of pine forest, to oak-hickory forest.

GREAT BASIN ADVENTURES
I also continued to broaden my background of the Great Basin vegetation while in the field with Ralph and his students. They were expanding their paleontological research from the Spring Mountains of southwestern Nevada into northeastern areas of the state. Although Mount Charleston reached 11,000 feet, Ralph's work was primarily at much lower elevations, whereas the work around Ely reached into elevations up to 13,000 feet. We had bought a jeep truck which gave me more freedom to use our car for ecological exploration when Ralph and his students did not need my assistance. We overwintered this truck in a garage in Ely. At Wheeler Peak, which later became part of Great Basin National Park, I had an opportunity to survey the high subalpine and alpine vegetation—and to stand in awe of the 4,000-year-old bristlecone pines (*Pinus aristata*). Before, I had only briefly seen them in the White Mountains of California.

Ralph in our jeep truck in Spring Mountains

During Christmas vacation in 1960, we visited the Masons and other friends in Berkeley. It was the last time that I saw Herbert in person. We had finished our natural selection paper, which was published early in 1961. Herbert retired from UC Berkley in 1963, and he and Lucile moved to Bellingham, Washington, to be with David at Western Washington University.

Ralph and I spent Christmas eve and day in the Spring Mountains. Although it seemed strange to camp in the desert for Christmas, I reminded myself that this was an environment much closer to the one in which Christ was born than the northern European atmosphere that we usually associate with Christmas. We decorated a small pinyon pine with various desert plant fruits and strung together some shadscale leaves in a garland—actually not bad when viewed sitting around a big bonfire. Moreover, I shall never forget the end of this stay.

On this trip, Ralph thought that the most efficient way to terminate his work was for me to drive the jeep back to Ely. I could make arrangements for its storage until summer and he would follow me later. It had snowed lightly in the Spring Mountains but the day I left was bright and sunny. So off I went, on an infrequently used state highway. The farther north I got, the more snow there was on the ground, and then it began to snow heavily. I continued onward, singing Christmas carols as I took in the beauty of the countryside laden with snow, periodically stamping my numb feet as there was no heater in the truck. I was soon essentially plowing the road in four-wheel drive. I wondered why I hadn't seen any snowplows, or, for that matter, *any* other vehicle! It was a long drive (more than 250 miles) through largely unoccupied country that reminded me of driving the Alaska Highway. There were no towns and just a few scattered ranches. The absence of anyone else on the road went on for entirely too many miles for comfort. When I finally reached the outskirts of Ely, over five hours later, I saw a sign indicating that the road was closed because of blizzard conditions! I had been entirely alone, isolated from help if I had needed it. At the garage, when I stopped the truck, it would not start again because the accelerator was frozen. I was almost in a state of hypothermia, and the people at the garage marveled that I had made it through.

Typical of Ralph when he got to Ely two days later, his only comment was,·"Oh well, you always seem to muddle through somehow." I guess this was his vote of confidence. Despite my mother's considering it another example of his apparent lack of concern for my welfare, his letting me muddle through on many occasions did help prepare me for future field work when I was on my own.

NEW DIRECTIONS: AMBER AND DIVORCE

1961-1962

Fortune may have a better success in reserve for you,
and those who lose today may win tomorrow.
—Cervantes

During the summer of 1961, while I was still at the University of Illinois, Ralph and I participated in a UC Berkeley expedition to collect amber in Chiapas, Mexico. This expedition changed the direction of research for the rest of my career. Amber, which today is a term generally used interchangeably with fossil resin, preserves insects in great detail, thus providing excellent material for the study of their evolution. Entomologists, Ray Smith and Paul Herd, and paleontologist, J. Wyatt Durham had started the project five years earlier, after they had obtained abundant tropical insects from samples of Mexican amber. The entomologists' interests had especially been piqued because the Chiapas deposits were one of the first large sources of New World tropical amber from mid-Tertiary times. Durham had secured NSF funds to collect additional amber specimens and study the paleontology and stratigraphy of the amber-bearing sediments to more precisely determine their age. Six of us would comprise the amber team—Durham and Ralph, three graduate students, and me. As the lone botanist, it was my job to oversee an investigation of the botanical source of the amber. With the exception of Baltic amber, the trees that produced the resin and the forests in which the insects lived were poorly studied. And, this would be the first Neotropical amber to be studied botanically.

Upon our arrival in Mexico City, I met Faustino Miranda, the Spanish botanist at the University of Mexico (UNAM) Herbarium and Botanical Garden. Prior to the trip, I had had pleasant correspondence with him about Chiapas amber, but in person I found him to be an even more charming Old World gentleman, as well as a store of information about Chiapas plants. He had immigrated to Mexico during the civil war in Spain and become a faculty member of the Institute of Biology of UNAM. He also assumed the directorship of the Botanical Institute of Chiapas, during which time he wrote *La Vegetación de Chiapas.* He became a close friend and great supporter of my research in Mexico.

We drove from Mexico City to Chiapas, and between Tuxtla Gutiérrez and the colonial town of San Cristobal de Las Casas the road was clogged with Mayan Indians flocking into Las Casas. We were to stay there in the home of Frans Blom, which was often the headquarters for archaeologists and anthropologists studying the Mayans. Blom informed us that these Indians were coming in droves to Las Casas because the usual rains had not come after they had planted their corn, not even after they had made incense pleas to their gods. They were now making an appeal to the White Man's god and saints by lighting candles in Las Casas, a town famous for its cathedral and numerous Catholic churches. We later saw other instances of this mixture of the Indians' own religion with elements of Christianity.

Expedition team at Frans Blom house;
J. Wyatt Durham center with Ralph and me at ends

The Indians (primarily Tzeltales and Tzotziles) and local people recovered most of the amber from landslides or small mines, but Blom warned us that they were often very protective about other people collecting from their mines. We needed to see and obtain amber in situ, and to collect fossils in their enclosing and neighboring sediments to determine the age of the amber, so we collected primarily from outcrops exposed by landslides, along streams, and in road cuts. The landslides were particularly good for stratigraphic study, because we could easily measure sediments and describe them. We were interested not only in the age that the fossils from these sediments revealed, but also in determining the marine and estuarine conditions in which the plant-produced amber was deposited.

Collecting amber along banks of a river

We found that the amber occurred in marine calcareous sandstones but was concentrated in lenses of lignite (early stages of coal, often still containing the woody remains), which might provide pollen evidence that we could then use to better understand and describe the vegetation at the site of the amber's deposition. This information also could contribute to our understanding of the amber-producing tree. For example, was it a tree that typically occurred along estuaries in coastal areas? I also collected resin from present-day trees growing at the sites and began to learn about the variety of tropical angiosperm resin producers—not only as potential sources of amber, but also as plants whose products are useful to humans today. Thus began my ethnobotanical thread of interest in resins. To a certain extent I had, as usual, to be an opportunist in my collecting, because I was mainly restricted to the areas where the geologists were working. On the other hand, we stayed at several *fincas* (farms), where I learned much about trees that produced resin and how it was used by talking with farmhands, Indian laborers, and our muleteers.

We established our headquarters in the small town of Simojovel, a center of amber-collecting in the Chiapas highlands. At first we stayed in a little hotel there, but sanitation was terrible and the food was lousy; the living conditions were worse than any Ralph and I had encountered in Colombia.

Doing geological field work with my husband, I had become accustomed to roughing it, but conditions in Chiapas were a real test for our entire group! We all fell victim to various intestinal problems, and decided to rent an empty house in Simojovel where we could have more control over our living conditions when we returned from field work in more remote areas.

Except for a few outcrops along the roadcuts, most of the sites that contained amber—the landslides and stream beds—were sufficiently inaccessible that we had to travel by mule team. Our muleteers loaded our equipment and collections of rock, fossils, and amber on the mules and gave us small Spanish horses to ride.

Ralph on horse with muleteers

Being the only woman among five men made for some interesting situations. I wore a blue work shirt, which emphasized the color of my eyes. Since most of the Indians apparently had not seen blue eyes, they would gather around staring at me when we rode into the villages. I became known as "*La Señora Ojos Azules.*" As we passed from one village to the next, they were waiting for this *señora* with blue eyes and always presented me with a *regalito* (gift) of a piece of amber. I felt I had the right to keep these *regalitos* separate from the scientific collection, which would go to the UC Berkeley Paleontology Museum. I had been told that a woman in Simojovel made amber jewelry, and I wanted her to make a necklace of these gifts.

On a return to Simojovel from several collection sites, I visited this jewelry maker. I left some of my *regalitos*, expecting her to make beads from these pieces in the somewhat rough form and style in which local women wore them. Alas, when I returned from another trip, eagerly awaiting my necklace, I found that she had, with great effort, sorted through all of the pieces of amber she had for perfectly clear yellow specimens. Furthermore, she had made them as round as possible. When I saw my string of beads, I apparently showed my disappointment and the woman who had made them was devastated. We were in a peculiar cultural dilemma. I had wanted her to use the amber *regalitos*, as they were significant to me, and also wanted her to make a necklace like the Chiapas women had. On the other hand, she wanted to produce something that she thought would please a *gringa*, that is, something she visualized might be sold in a store in the United States. With my general store friend, who spoke some English, acting as go-between, we reached a solution. I would happily take the beautiful yellow amber necklace, plus another one made from my *regalitos*, though the jewelry maker insisted that she be allowed to make the individual beads as round as she could with her equipment. A compromise, and to this day I enjoy thinking about this cultural situation as I choose which amber necklace to wear for different occasions.

Another more startling experience of cultural misunderstanding was being castigated by a visiting priest from the pulpit of the Simojovel Catholic church. Since our team often divided into groups to do different tasks, I stayed with different men, not necessarily including my husband, on some nights. Because the idea of a woman scientist was not common here (although Franz Blom's wife had done anthropological work in the area), the supposition of this priest was that I was present to "service" the men. He decried me as a loose woman. My woman friend at the general store was furious; she warned me that such a pronouncement put me in jeopardy of being considered as an available woman by the local men. She told our three muleteers to watch over me carefully while we were doing our field research. She so convinced them to keep me in sight that it was difficult for me to secrete myself in the bushes to take care of bodily functions.

We faced other unexpected events as we traveled in the low country. Itinerant doctors and dentists also traveled in these remote areas periodically to take care of people's various ailments.

Because our group included several *doctores*, the people in the villages thought we were medical doctors. In the previous villages we passed through there had not been any serious medical conditions, although we had given out our entire aspirin supply to people asking for relief from apparently nonthreatening aches and pains. Our luck ran out in a village where an older man had a terrible toothache and wanted us to extract the tooth. We faced two problems: we did not have any tools adequate for the task, and the gum surrounding the tooth was badly infected. So we were indeed hesitant, which infuriated a group of villagers, who accused us of being unwilling to help the old man! They offered rusty pliers to pull the tooth and *pulque* to anesthetize the man. We elected Wyatt Durham, the leader of our team as well as the biggest and most imposing man, to do the job. He accepted reluctantly! The old man's family and friends sedated him with the *pulque* and Wyatt yanked. The tooth came out readily, but the pus from the infection horrified us. Wyatt emptied some capsules of penicillin (meant for internal use) into the wound, and we left the village post haste. We did not return by way of this village and never heard how the man fared.

We stayed at several *fincas*, whose main crop, in the pine highlands, was coffee and, in the lowlands, tobacco. We did not get to know the families and their lifestyles, however. We ate and slept in rooms apart from the families. Most often we were so tired from traveling in the heat and clambering over outcrops that we ate our simple meal of tortillas, beans and rice and crept into bed. On the trail, we carried pineapples to eat while working and for lunch spread avocado on bread with cheese, and ate "sweet lemons" to quench our thirst.

Expedition team in mangas in pine highlands; me in back at left

At one point along the trail, one of the muleteers shouted "*tzotze, tzotze,*" and the three muleteers immediately rushed to a large-trunked tree that had a shimmering black mass slowly moving up it. They had soon bagged what turned out to be many black, hairy caterpillars, which they informed us would provide gourmet fare. That evening they fried the caterpillars and ate them with gusto while we *gringos* had difficulty even attempting to eat them. The center was a repulsive green goo; I tried unsuccessfully to swallow a small one whole. Ants were commonly fried and salted; eaten as a snack, like peanuts, they were tasty. One night our slow progress on the trail landed us in an Indian village at suppertime where we were offered a *caldo* (soup) by candle light. It had a strange flavor that none of us recognized, and pieces of meat with skin that had an unusual patterning, which turned out to be armadillo.

We missed an opportunity to eat iguana in an area where I was looking for resin-producing plants. While everyone else was occupied, I started hacking away at the underbrush with a machete. Suddenly in front of me there was rustling and I soon was face to face with what looked like a prehistoric creature—a very large iguana. We were surprised to see each other and simultaneously fled in opposite directions. When our muleteers heard my story, they were disgusted that I had not let them know about it, as they would have tried to kill it. "Good eating," they said. I was glad that I had inadvertently saved the creature's life, even though it would have been interesting to taste it.

END OF AN EXPEDITION—AND A MARRIAGE

When our field work finished, Ralph went back immediately to Urbana for classes at the university. Our relationship had not been the same since his dismissal from UC Berkeley. Ralph was bitterly holding onto anger over being denied tenure and he had vowed revenge. I found this attitude intolerable, as I did not believe in harboring hateful thoughts and plotting how to take action against your enemies. Ralph felt that in my attitude, I failed to support him.

I knew he had been in constant contact with a former graduate student in Berkeley who gave him psychological support by agreeing with his ideas. I had put up with this until he could get established and achieve tenure at the University of Illinois, which he did in 1961, just before we left for Chiapas. I had hoped that tenure would solve some of our problems but, quite to the contrary, we became more estranged during the Chiapas trip. I was not sure why at the time. After he left, I stopped in Mexico City en route home to process my plant collections. Tensions reached a peak just after my return from Mexico, and I now had my answer to the increased estrangement. He announced that this former student had moved to a nearby town and that he would be at least spending weekends with her.

Wyatt Durham came to Urbana a little later to try to help us work things out. Ralph was becoming increasingly focused on his revenge idea and more and more sought solace in the affair with his former student, each of which I could not abide. Both Wyatt and I felt that Ralph needed to seek psychological guidance (uncommon in those days), but he refused. Following Wyatt's visit, it became very clear that separation and probably divorce were imminent. Finally, one weekend, the Blisses helped me take my possessions from our apartment and store them. I moved into the Women's Faculty Club on the Illinois campus. The Blisses were particularly supportive throughout this personally difficult period, and other members of the botany department were thoughtfully helpful. I felt fortunate for their kindness.

During this very sad time, I sought the assistance of a Christian Science practitioner whom I had met fortuitously. In this I was leaning on precepts I had learned as a child in Christian Science Sunday School. Although Mother always provided comfort, the practitioner's support was especially valuable because she daily sustained my spirits, and helped me over any fear of what the future might bring. When divorce became inevitable, she directed me to an excellent lawyer for assistance through those difficult proceedings. At this time I also became grateful that we had not had children who would have been entangled in this breakup.

I did not know what my next steps would be. At Durham's urging, I had submitted an NSF proposal to study the pollen in Chiapas amber. If it had been funded, I would have stayed in the Illinois Botany Department as a Research Associate. Fortunately, it was not funded, which freed me to leave Urbana, where Ralph would be. Friends at the UC Berkeley herbarium suggested that I return there, where some sort of a position probably could be found. But this seemed unwise too, even though I loved the Bay Area. My practitioner friend was convinced that my place was elsewhere and counseled me to wait calmly for appropriate plans to unfold.

Soon a door of opportunity opened. One of the Illinois paleobotany graduate students, who was a Radcliffe graduate, had just received word about the newly organized Radcliffe Institute for Independent Study. The new president of Radcliffe, Polly Bunting, had established this institute to address the discrepancy between the number of American women with advanced college education, and those engaged in professional activity and holding positions of influence and responsibility. She thought that this disparity might partially be explained by a "climate of nonexpectation"—the assumption that women would not use their educations (which was certainly the attitude I had encountered during and after my graduate school years). Bunting established this experimental program to "harness the talents of these collectively displaced women." The institute's aim was to open new opportunities for highly educated women, especially those with doctorates who lacked a professional outlet for their talent.

I contacted the director, who immediately told me to apply, especially since Elso Barghoorn at Harvard was already interested in my research on amber. I also contacted the AAUW who had given me undergraduate scholarships and a graduate fellowship. AAUW's postdoctoral deadline had passed but they too told me to apply because they emphasized helping former fellows at a critical time in their careers. I can't say enough about this organization, which has provided assistance for women's education since 1863 and especially during many years when funds were not available elsewhere. They had given me extraordinary support at every juncture—I benefited at each step forward when I was in need. Because responses had been positive from both the Radcliffe Institute and AAUW, I was assured that Harvard would be in my immediate future (and incidentally fulfilling my mother's dream of my attending an Ivy League college).

The institute suggested that I accept the somewhat limited funding provided by the AAUW fellowship for the first year. They would help with additional funds as a visiting research scholar in the institute, but then would back me up with a full appointment as a scholar any succeeding year that I needed it. This was the kind of strong support that the institute provided during my Harvard tenure. Moreover, the divorce lawyer, knowing my whole story and the small size of my fellowship, decided not to charge a fee for the divorce, asking me only to pay court costs. His only request was that I let him know about the progress of my new life in Cambridge! I was grateful beyond words for the love and caring that had seen me through this traumatic period in my life.

The divorce was finalized in March 1962, and in April I celebrated my release from this agonizing time by joining Larry Bliss' Plant Geography field trip to Mexico. We observed vegetation along the west side of the Mississippi River, the Gulf Coast of Louisiana and Texas, and en route to Mexico, where our explorations complemented my previous botanical experiences in the tropical lowlands and temperate highlands of Mexico's southernmost state of Chiapas.

We spent much time in the vegetation on the volcano Popocateptl. The high-altitude pine and fir forests are the southernmost extension of the boreal forests of the Rocky Mountains, which form the backbone of the North American continent—extending from Alaska and the Yukon to the Mexican volcanoes. The alpine zone, beginning at very high elevations of almost 14,000 feet, was of special interest to both Bliss and me. Alpine vegetation occurs on all of the eleven Mexican volcanoes, and many genera here are also common in alpine areas in the United States—making it floristically different from the Andean *páramo*. On Popocateptl, the most prominent plants we saw were shrubby junipers and mats of the ericaceous *Pernettya* amid patches of grasses and snow, as we were too early for herbaceous species. The dry vegetation of northern Mexico, such as mesquite grassland, was new to me. We proceeded through the northern Mexican shrub and cactus vegetation back to Texas and thence to Urbana.

Back at Urbana, I bought a VW bug, which gave me a wonderful sense of independence, having been without my own transportation since fall. I also completed several manuscripts from the California period and prepared Chiapas specimens to take to Harvard. I had been asked to teach Field Ecology at RMBL again over the summer.

A FINAL SUMMER AT RMBL

I drove to Colorado realizing that this was the beginning of a new era in my life. It was with sadness and nostalgia that I began this transition at RMBL in Gothic, because Ralph and I had spent so many happy and productive years in the Crested Butte area. We had done all of our PhD research there together—for me, even being allowed to do a PhD with Cooper had depended on our joint studies. And I thought back to Coe College, where some faculty wives questioned my completing my doctorate because I was married, and Ralph had staunchly supported me, maintaining that the degree was the best insurance policy he could give me. I am quite sure, however, that divorce was not what he had in mind! Since our parting, Ralph and I have not had contact. Ralph remained at the University of Illinois throughout his career and married again three times.

Teaching the Field Ecology course again, however, was a joy. The contingent of students and faculty from Yale, Swarthmore, Wellesley, and Amherst—several of whom I later interacted with while at Harvard—helped me to project my thoughts forward rather than backwards. My students were all well prepared and eager to learn, which led to thought-provoking discussions and enthusiastic field trips. I again did not use a textbook but went directly to research papers, and put even more emphasis on independent projects than I had in 1955 and 1959. Discussing different viewpoints, especially where we could observe and sometimes test their validity, seemed appropriate for such a motivated group of students. I suggested projects from unanswered questions in my own research—I had further refined my ideas regarding the Crested Butte vegetation from my dissertation research, which fortuitously had just been published in *Ecological Monographs*. My discussion in this paper provided a basis for understanding different community concepts and quantitative techniques in sampling.

Without getting mired in the complex history of vegetation analysis, I compared Robert Whittaker's research in two mountainous areas, which was garnering considerable attention from plant ecologists, with mine. I focused on Whittaker's research for several reasons. The first was because of Sears' (1956) suggestion that plant ecologists' ideas are conditioned by the vegetation in which they find themselves. Whittaker had encountered a bewildering mixture of intergrading species in the deciduous forests of the Smoky Mountains (1956) and conifer forests of the Siskiyou Mountains (1960). His goal of describing such complex vegetation led him to analyze the distribution of each plant species and then relate their populations to environmental gradients along an elevational cline. He only determined boundaries and hence classified the community types following these analyses. These analytical approaches prohibited mapping according to community types over any sizable area.

In contrast, we were viewing my work in a mountain area where physiognomy, determined by a few dominants, made it easy to determine boundaries of community types altitudinally and classify them as vegetative zones. Defining these boundaries before analyzing the composition of the community types had been essential to my goal of mapping them, especially as I was doing it concurrently with mapping the geology. The value of having such a map was evident from its constant use by the RMBL community for various purposes, such as planning projects and trips. (This, of course, was before even the development of Landsat in the early 1970s and subsequent common use of maps created by global satellite imaging. Now the many photos we took while we were mapping are probably of greatest value in providing a view of change in relation to the current detail available in satellite-created maps.)

Spirited discussion of these comparisons helped the students realize that recognition of community types results from the human process of classification, in which different defining properties and associated techniques of analysis are used to best fit the purpose of the researcher in vegetation of particular areas.

The extremely slow rate of plant succession on the Gothic Earthflow intrigued the students. Very little change was evident, in fact, since my last course at RMBL three years before and my publication of "Plant Succession on a Subalpine Earthflow in Colorado" in 1956. Because my thinking had been influenced by the Glacier Bay successional studies, I had assumed that lack of nitrogen-producing plants and negligible soil profile development were probably the primary cause of the earthflow's slow rate of change. Aware of the extremes of the microclimate on the flow, I had also tried to establish instruments there to measure them, but found the project infeasible. So we were left wondering . . .

Actually, interest in this puzzle has continued through the years since 1962. RMBL students have continued to study the Gothic Earthflow, and in 1994, C. G. Curtin, a University of Wisconsin student, published his MS thesis on observations covering forty-five years since its occurrence seventy years ago. Little change had occurred in the density of the species and their diversity had reached a plateau over the last twenty years. Neither facilitation of conditions for succeeding plants by the pioneers nor inhibition by others was evident. Curtin's soil translocation studies did not support my ideas about soil development. He proposed, without supporting data, that during the short growing season, the exceptionally hot and dry microclimate of the earthflow may be the major factor prohibiting these aggregations from achieving the composition of the surrounding fescue grassland and sagebrush communities. He further concluded that the natural recovery process would likely require hundreds of years. Other studies of the earthflow have continued.

(In 2008, it was used as a part of a project to analyze the effect of community assembly and primary succession on the species-area relationship (SAR). S. Carey and associates reported a space-for-time study of the earthflow in which temporal trends were approximated by assuming that different locations along a disturbance gradient represented different points in successional time. They concluded that observed changes in SAR properties raise questions about the appropriateness of using present-day SARs to predict future levels of richness in successional communities.)

Back in 1962, I thought that it would be instructive for the class to compare the Gothic Earthflow with the famous large and much older Slumgullion Earthflow (also called the Slumgullion Mudslide) in the San Juan Mountains between the towns of Creede and Lake City. It originated about 800 years ago when Tertiary volcanic rock, lubricated by heavy rains, slumped over two miles down the steep sides of a high mesa. This flow was so large that it blocked the Lake Fork of the Gunnison River, creating Lake San Cristobal, Colorado's second largest lake. Although causes and rates of movement of the Slumgullion Earthflow have been studied long-term in some detail by the US Geological Survey, the successional changes in open stands of Engelmann spruce and aspen on it have not been analyzed as the vegetation has on the Gothic Earthflow.

On the trip to the San Juan Mountains we also observed the extensive zone of aspen forests on the western slope outside the Crested Butte area. Since the late nineteenth century aspen forests have been reported to cover extensive areas between 9,000 and 10,500 feet in southwestern Colorado, and to form an altitudinal belt in central Utah. Some students became entranced, as I had been, with these aspen forests and did class projects on them. By sampling aspen at various sites, they tested the hypothesis from my doctoral research that the western slope zonal aspen forests were mature forests rather than primarily being populations that follow disturbance,which occur in most areas of the Rocky Mountains. Their summer studies at least agreed with my assessments!

Such trips were part of an effort to give students a larger picture of Colorado ecosystems, especially as compared to the unique zonation in the Crested Butte area. Traditionally, we had accomplished this by taking the Circle Trip, in which my 1955 and 1959 classes had both participated. This year, in addition to the San Juan jaunt, we spent three days at the University of Colorado Science Lodge field station. Here we compared the higher-elevation communities on the eastern slope with those in the Crested Butte area. My long-time colleague and friend Bill Weber joined us for a day, and we reminisced about our Gothic and Alaska experiences in the context of the vegetation at hand. We saw rolling alpine summit areas with relatively stable sedge and grass meadow communities, which were not common in the Crested Butte area, with its mosaic of diverse alpine habitats. We observed some "fossil" stone polygons, evidence of soil frost action so abundant in the arctic, but only characteristic of these relatively level alpine sites in the Rocky Mountains. We did not see, however, an altitudinally defined zone of lush upland herb meadows so characteristic of areas around Crested Butte. Although many of the same plants occur in other high Rocky Mountain areas, the Wasatch Plateau and the Uinta Mountains are the only other areas in which such a belt of upland herb vegetation has been reported. Furthermore, on the eastern slope, aspen only occurred following disturbance of conifer forests, which is typical of other areas in the western United States. Below the spruce-fir forest we visited the prominent belt of ponderosa pine-Douglas fir, which is strikingly absent in the Crested Butte area. Thus our trips to both the eastern slope and other areas of the western slope of the Colorado Rockies made the uniqueness of the vegetation around RMBL stand out.

On field trips in the Crested Butte area, I emphasized the alpine vegetation and the plants' special adaptations—such as rapid shoot growth in a matter of weeks after snow melt, predominantly vegetative means of reproduction despite many active pollinating butterflies and bees, and narrowly restricted endemic plants. A professor from the University of Glasgow, G. Pontecorvo, who was at RMBL that summer, enlivened our trips to see plants with restricted distributions. He was interested in comparing Crested Butte alpine plants, especially ones restricted to calcareous rocks, with those he knew in Switzerland. Professor Pontecorvo later invited me to visit his summer home in Valais, Switzerland, where we could see alpine endemics on the chalks around the Zinal Glacier—an invitation that I looked forward to accepting. We also spent time analyzing the adaptation of the conifers (as krummholz) at their upper limits bordering the alpine zone.

My RMBL class taking samples to age krummholz

After my course was completed, I left Gothic in my little VW bug for the American Institute for Biological Sciences (AIBS) meetings at Oregon State University. I served on the RMBL Board of Directors from 1962 to 1966 and as vice president from 1965 to 1966, but since then have only returned to Gothic for short, nostalgic visits. The publication of my dissertation in 1962 further closed the door on my high mountain vegetation research. I subsequently turned to the tropics, although my favorite habitat has remained high mountains and its vegetation.

On the trip to the West Coast I had an RMBL student companion, but I drove alone from Oregon to the East Coast. The trip was for the most part uneventful, with one exception. In Idaho, along one stretch of road, north winds were very strong and I had been holding on to the steering wheel with all my might. I went through a long road cut that provided protection from the wind, but when I came out the other side, the wind literally lifted the little car off the road and into a grassy ditch. The big pink Cadillac from Texas that was immediately behind me pulled over, and a man yelled "Honey, you *flew* into that ditch. We saw it all." I pushed open the door amid tall grasses and climbed out. It was soon evident that the car had not been visibly damaged. The Texan was still exclaiming to a number of drivers, who had subsequently stopped, that the little car had been lifted by the wind and then let down gently in the ditch. The problem now was how to get it out of the ditch? Everyone was convinced that it would be impossible to drive the car up the relatively steep side of the ditch. In the end, eight men just lifted it to the road; after much laughter and my profuse thanks, I was on my way again! The kindly Texans continued to follow me and we stayed in the same motel that night. They couldn't get over what they had witnessed and repeatedly said that obviously "someone above" was watching over me.

It had taken me five full days of driving from coast to coast. Except for being lifted off the road, all went well until I arrived in Cambridge and was hunting for the Cronkite Center, where I was going to live. At Brattle Street, a main thoroughfare in Cambridge, I lawfully stopped at a stop sign. A man crashed into the rear of my car, and got out of his car shouting "You *auslander* (I had Illinois license plates), no one in Cambridge stops at Brattle Street!" I found out from the police later that people in the Boston area are notorious for driving through stop signs, and that this area had one of the highest incidences in the country of rear-end crashes. I had been officially "welcomed" to the area. I also was about to begin an especially happy period in my career.

PART III

SOLO CAREER

Adding chemistry to botany and geology at Harvard

BEGINNING A NEW CAREER

1962-1964

No longer forward nor behind
I look in hope or fear;
But, grateful, take the good I find,
The best of now and here.

My Psalm,
—John Greenleaf Whittier

I immediately felt at home in my Harvard community. I lived for several years in a nice suite at the Cronkite Center, a lovely facility for women scholars, visiting faculty, and advanced graduate students, especially from foreign countries. I immediately met and made friends with women in fields spanning the arts and sciences from around the world. I fell in with the great group of scholars at the Radcliffe Institute for Independent Studies as well as the botanists at the Harvard Biological Laboratories and the Botanical Museum. Interacting with people in the social sciences and humanities as well as those from the natural sciences harkened back to my undergraduate days, and had been largely missing at UC Berkeley and Illinois. I was never lonely or bored.

I was grateful that no one asked about my immediate past. I left behind the nastiness associated with the divorce without resentment and did not want to relive it anyway. My summer at Gothic had left me with a sense of gratitude for the good years of the marriage, rather than any bitterness, and helped me recognize how much Ralph had aided in my professional training as well. Now, embarking on exhilarating new phases of activity, I did not know where they would ultimately lead, but I was headed in the right direction. (Little did I realize how much the biology professor Kenneth Thimann, who sat next to me at the institute's dinner party to introduce new scholars in my first week in Cambridge, would be part of my long-term future!)

Harvard had a Biology Department, which was different for me since I had previously been associated with Botany Departments at Minnesota, UC Berkeley, and Illinois. My official Harvard sponsor, the paleobotanist

Elso Barghoorn in his Harvard office

and geochemist Elso Barghoorn, was the leading researcher on fossil evidence of early life on earth. He was an extraordinary intellect, his research having encompassed microfossils in the Precambrian, woods in the Mesozoic, seeds in the Tertiary, and pollen in the Pleistocene. And, he immediately became a strong supporter of my amber research. His office and lab were on the floor below the Harvard Herbarium and office of the Arnold Arboretum, across the street from the Botanical Museum, which led to lots of casual contact with numerous faculty and students studying plants. Many of these plant-oriented faculty and researchers interacted closely. I also had connections back to Berkeley with Reed Rollins, director of the herbarium, and Otto Solbrig, a professor in the biology department—both former students of Lincoln Constance. Through them, I was buffered from the turmoil of the "molecular revolution" at Harvard, which had been initiated by the arrival of James Watson—the pugnacious codiscoverer of the structure of DNA.

Traditionally, the group associated with Barghoorn ate lunch together around a big table in the laboratory. These noontime conversations were known to have inspired many a student and visiting researcher. Our group included "Father of Plant Anatomy," I.W. Bailey (then long-retired and approaching age ninety, but amazingly sharp and intellectually active), a visiting paleobotanical researcher from Stanford, a post-doctoral fellow from India, as well as three graduate students (two who went on to become preeminent researchers—both faculty within the UC system), and a Radcliffe senior thesis student. Like those who had come before us, we all found these lunch meetings, in which we probed our own and "wave-of-the-future" research, to be both fun and thought-provoking.

Later, I also became a part of the Thimann-Wetmore lab group, which added new physiological/developmental perspectives to my thinking about plants. And, I gained new insights from the seminars of the Evolutionary Biology Group that E.O. Wilson had instigated to balance the pervading influence of the molecularist James Watson, who viewed any study involving natural history as "stamp collecting." Although Harvard at this time was still a male bastion (women even had to enter and eat in a side room at the Faculty Club and women professors were almost nonexistent), these botanical and evolutionary groups, along with the Radcliffe Institute, provided great professional and personal support to pursue my ambitious goals of cross-disciplinary research.

CHEMICAL AND POLLEN STUDIES OF MEXICAN AMBER

During my first year, I began to explore how chemical analysis of Chiapas amber could help determine its botanical source. I was convinced that the amber was derived from resin produced by trees in the genus *Hymenaea* (a member of the legume or pea family but in a subfamily of tropical trees), especially after smelling both this resin and amber being burned as incense by the Mayan Indians. But I needed definitive evidence. I had not done chemical analyses in my previous research but, having been interested in chemistry since high school days, I was amenable to learning relevant analytical techniques. I soon discovered that the amber was extremely difficult to dissolve, so I was forced into using solid state techniques. After discussing the problem with a Harvard chemist, we tried infrared (IR) spectroscopy, a technique that can allow identification of materials by comparison to a known material. Much to our amazement, we got spectra of Chiapas amber in which the fingerprint area was very similar to spectra from *Hymenaea* resin.

The word "resin" is often used in a general way to refer to several quite different chemical substances, often characterized as being "sticky."

However, I use the shorthand term "resin" in this memoir to refer only to a specific chemical group called "terpenoid resins." These resins are based on five-carbon units, which can attach together, then structurally rearrange to form classes of compounds composed, respectively, of ten (monoterpenes), fifteen (sesquiterpenes), twenty (diterpenes), or even greater number of units. Collectively, compounds with such carbon skeletons are called "terpenes" or "terpenoids." Monoterpenes and some sesquiterpenes volatilize relatively easily, producing aroma, leading to them being called "essential oils." Diterpenes, by contrast, are viscous and nonvolatile. Amber is comprised primarily of a mixture of diterpenes that polymerize to form the very durable fossilized material. Sometimes it also contains a few volatile terpenes as well. Because the IR technique is usually used to identify a single compound, the IR evidence for amber's mixture was much clearer than the chemist had expected. These IR analyses were the beginning of a chemical thread in my paleobotanical studies, and would also lead to a new approach in my ecological research.

I also planned to investigate the pollen found in the lignites in which the Chiapas amber was deposited for hints regarding the vegetation at its depositional site. This information could provide corroborative evidence for *Hymenaea* being the source of the amber as well as forest conditions of interest to the entomologists. Fortunately, the Radcliffe student in Barghoorn's lab was interested in analyzing this pollen for her senior thesis, and one of Barghoorn's graduate students, who was investigating pollen in sediments from Panama for her PhD, could assist the Radcliffe student in identifying the Chiapas pollen. Barghoorn generously and enthusiastically supported their involvement in my project. This study worked out better than we could ever have anticipated, as we found that species of mangrove comprised the primary pollen in the lignites where the amber occurred, thus supporting the idea that Chiapas amber was deposited from trees growing near mangrove swamps. In fact, the stilt roots of the mangroves were ideal to trap the resin and ensure its deposition. Our publication, "Mangrove Pollen at the Depositional Site of Oligo-Miocene Amber from Chiapas, Mexico," has become a highly cited paper, useful not only for paleoecologists but also for researchers studying the ecology and management of mangroves along tropical coastlines throughout the world.

Initial successes with the chemical and pollen studies encouraged Barghoorn to endorse a proposal for an NSF grant, which we obtained initially for 1963-1964 but was later extended to provide funding through 1966. Barghoorn provided continual and significant assistance, but he suggested that his name be omitted as an author on publications. He wanted it to be clear that this research was based on my ideas, not his, which he suggested might position me better for a job. He thought that often women were not given their due credit. I greatly appreciated his support and kind concern for my future.

I had heard that American Cyanamid Company in Stamford, Connecticut, used IR for chemical identification of synthetic resins. I found a helpful and supportive ally there, and we together became art sleuths. Our sidelight activities began at an elite jewelry shop in Atlantic City that was selling as rare Burmese amber, at a very high price, a large Chinese carving of a red bird. I felt certain that this bird was not amber, let alone Burmese amber, and asked the manager to give me a few milligrams for IR analysis. At first I received a rather stiff and even hostile response to my request, as in "Just who do you think you are?" Finally I convinced him, however, and the spectrum I made definitively demonstrated that the bird was not amber. The Cyanamid chemist was then able to match it with bakelite, an early red synthetic resin. The manager of the jewelry store, who had bought the piece in China, was amazed and thankful for our joint endeavor! This experience led to numerous requests from various institutions, such as the Smithsonian, to verify the validity of many kinds of amber art.

In October 1963, I presented my chemical results supporting *Hymenaea* as the botanical source of Chiapas amber at a meeting of the Mexican Botanical Society in San Luis Potosí. This was the first report of an angiosperm being the source of amber. The meeting was held in Spanish. Harvard professor Otto Solbrig, an Argentinean, helped me write my paper in Spanish and practice presenting it. I could recite it forward and backward. My presentation went well, although afterward the Mexican botanists were questioning me about where I had learned Argentinean pronunciation of Spanish!

When I arrived at the meeting, however, I was horrified to discover that I had also been made chairman of the session and would be expected to comment on papers. It was here that I made my most dramatic Spanish-language blunder. I somehow bungled my way through chairing the session but afterwards petulantly sought out the honorary president of the congress, my friend Faustino Miranda, to express my embarrassment in leading the discussion using such poor Spanish. He was sitting with a group of distinguished Mexican botanists, including the president of the Mexican Botanical Society, Efraim Hernandez-Xolocotzi. I rushed up, spouting out "*Yo estoy tan embarazada.*" When Miranda gently replied,

"*Creo que no*," I vehemently replied, "*Creo que sí!*" At this point everyone at the table was laughing, and finally someone explained my faux pas in English. I knew there was a verb *embarazar*, and had naively assumed that it only meant "to be embarrassed." Although it can mean this, at least in most Latin American countries, the colloquial meaning "to be pregnant" is more commonly used. This, to me, conclusively emphasized the basic problem about which I was complaining—that sometimes a little knowledge of a language can lead you into trouble. I became notorious at the meeting for this blunder, but it was all in good fun. The shared laughter was worth the small price of embarrassment.

Following the congress, Miranda arranged a trip for me to collect more resin-producing plants than had been possible on the amber-collecting expedition in 1961. This was my first time making arrangements for field research on my own in Latin America. From my previous expeditions with Ralph in Colombia and Chiapas, however, I had learned the necessity of working closely with personnel at institutes, field stations, or universities. The itinerary for this trip included going down the Pacific Coast to Oaxaca, on to Chiapas, eastward across the Isthmus of Tehuantepec to Veracruz, Yucatan, and Quintana Roo along the Gulf Coast in Mexico and finally to Belize (then British Honduras). Miranda provided a UNAM Botanical Garden camioneta and a young botanist, Arturo Gomez-Pompa, to help identify the plants.

We collected a variety of resin-producing plants (e.g., *Bursera*, *Pistacia*, *Pinus*, and *Hymenaea*) in areas ranging from the open, dry lowland forests to the upland pine forests in southern Mexico. I was especially amazed at the diversity of *Bursera;* Mexico is the center of its distribution and its resins would later receive much phylogenetic and ecological research. Certain groups of *Bursera* species have the remarkable ability to store leaf resin under pressure and with a consistency that allows the plant to squirt it at insects that attempt to eat the leaves. Another of our goals was to find *Tapirira* because its flower had been found in Chiapas amber. I therefore wanted to examine *Tapirira* resin chemically to be sure that it was not the source of a resin, other than *Hymenaea,* that might have formed some of the Chiapas amber.

Soon after we entered British Honduras, we stopped to collect from a small tree that Arturo thought was *Tapirira*. We collected many branches from this small tree and made gashes in the trunk to obtain resin. I had the fluid resin all over my hands and on my face. The resin started to turn black where it touched my skin. When we stopped at a small store to get some cold drinks, the woman there began shouting *"chichin, chichin"* and took me to the back of the store where she vigorously scrubbed my stained hands. She was particularly worried about my face, repeatedly stressing that blindness could result from getting the resin in one's eyes. *Chichin* is *Metopium*, a relative of poison oak and poison ivy in the Anacardiaceae. Also known as poison wood, its resin is extremely toxic. Since I had never reacted allergically to poison oak or poison ivy, I hoped that I would not be sensitive to poison wood. About a week later, however, when we were riding horseback on a mountain trip in a forest preserve, my hands became red and began to swell so much that they looked like boxing gloves. I could hardly hold on to the rough rope reins. More alarming was the areas where the resin had touched my face—they had also become red and swollen.

It was evening when we finally got back to the town of Belize, where we rushed around trying to find some medical assistance (no emergency rooms there!). We ultimately found a doctor at his home, and he immediately started giving me antihistamine shots at random—not knowing what would work. Most importantly, he told me to get a plane to Mexico City the next day to see a dermatologist as soon as possible. We telexed Miranda in Mexico City to make an appointment with a physician, and I managed to get a seat on a plane the next day.

By the time I was en route, the antihistamines had begun to work and the swelling was subsiding, although my hands and face were extremely light-sensitive. As soon as I arrived in Mexico City I was whisked off to the waiting doctor, who said I was extremely lucky the antihistamines had been successful. Progressively I got better, but I had layers of skin peeling off for weeks. I dodged a bullet, but Arturo could not talk about the incident for a number of years, since he was the botanist who was supposed to help me avoid such problems.

I returned to Cambridge with specimens of most potential resin sources of Chiapas amber, ready to analyze them with IR spectroscopy. By serendipity I had discovered that a chemistry professor at Vassar College, Curt Beck, was using IR to determine the provenance of amber art objects. The director of the Harvard Botanical Museum, Paul Mangelsdorf, had met Beck while giving a lecture at Vassar, and put me in contact with him. We soon began to collaborate on a paper for the journal *Science* on the use of IR as corroborative evidence in determining the botanical source of amber. We followed our paper with a catalog of IR spectra of North and South American ambers, made from samples from the Harvard, New York Botanical Garden, and Smithsonian Institution collections. (Infrared analysis only requires a few milligrams of material, and museums were willing to allow me to take shavings from their samples.) Historically, amber had been analyzed chemically as a mineral to describe it as a gem. Our analyses were some of the first that described amber as an organic product of trees, and they created much interest among amber researchers Years later more sophisticated geochemical techniques became available, such as pyrolysis gas chromatography coupled with mass spectrometry, which have enabled geochemists to identify and elucidate the structures of the amber polymer constituents. IR, however, remains the chemical technique most commonly used by amber researchers wanting some idea of the plant source and who do not have more complicated means of chemical analysis available.

STUDIES OF POLLEN TRAPPED IN CONIFEROUS AMBER

In addition to the study of pollen in the Chiapas amber-bearing lignites, I was interested in understanding more about whether the abundance of different kinds of pollen in amber could help in interpreting the nature of the forest in which amber-producing trees occurred. Other researchers' attempts in the past to reconstruct the Baltic amber forest using inclusions of insects and plant parts, other than pollen, had been inconclusive. Thus in spring 1964, again with the assistance of students from Barghoorn's lab, I set up a field project in the pine-hardwood forest at Drumlin Farms Sanctuary in Lincoln, Massachusetts. We studied pollen trapped in present-day coniferous resin to see if this would assist in interpreting pollen in amber. Results from this study would not be directly applicable to the leguminous Chiapas amber; its interest centered around the fact that the greatest abundance of amber is derived from conifers.

Our experiment consisted of gashing coniferous trees every two weeks for a year in a pine-oak forest that also contained a diversity of other trees, to determine what kinds of pollen got trapped in the resin. We also assessed the relative proportion of trees producing pollen in the area. We found that viscosity and rapidity of hardening of the resins, which varied with the taxa, were important in determining the surface area and length of time the resin was receptive to pollen, and hence could be significant in influencing the presence and quantity of pollen in amber.

Moreover, we discovered that the kinds and relative amounts of pollen found in the resin were not strongly influenced by the vegetation immediately surrounding the resin-producing trees. Some kinds of pollen, such as oak and birch, were over-represented whereas others, such as pine, maple, and hickory, were underrepresented. Although the proportions of the kinds of pollen in the resin did not give accurate quantitative representation of forest composition, they did indicate qualitatively the most common tree components. Thus, this study put the role of pollen in reconstructing ancient pinaceous amber forests into a perspective that had never been available. During the course of this work we also had discovered another caveat regarding investigating pollen in amber—that the diterpene resin acids often destroyed the exine (outer surface) of some pollen, which made them difficult to identify.

SOCIAL LIFE AT HARVARD

I also led a very active and diversified social life in Cambridge, which I welcomed after the dearth of such pleasures in Illinois, and even Berkeley, where our social life had centered so much around both botanical and geological field trips.

Ralph Wetmores (left) and Irving Baileys (right)
at Bailey's summer home

The families of illustrious Harvard botanists, Ralph Wetmore and I.W. Bailey, played important roles in expanding my social activities—in quite different ways. The Wetmores helped me obtain hard-to-get tickets to the Boston Symphony, which I greatly enjoyed as an interesting switch from the opera in San Francisco. They also introduced me to a wide array of art museums and included me in many dinners at their home with distinguished visitors. They, in many ways, were personal mentors and later became very involved in decisions regarding my future.

The Baileys introduced me to an amazing woman in her mid-eighties who collected amber art, and was a great supporter of young artists. Marnie Chamberlain had been bedridden for several years as a result of injuries from a car accident. She had finally managed to walk again with a cane when I met her, but her disabilities were overcome by her spirit which showed through sparkling eyes. Extremely active intellectually even during her convalescence, she learned Arabic and played chess with boys in the Harvard chess club. She became for me an

Marnie Chamberlain at later still active 95

inspirational example of a female octogenarian who lived life to its fullest. As a woman of means she had a summer home on Monhegan Island where she often entertained young artists. I enjoyed meeting some of these artist friends when I visited her there. I could understand why artists found inspiration on this small island ten miles off the Maine coast. Just a one-mile square of land, two-thirds of the island, including the highest cliffs of the New England coast, has been set aside as wildlife sanctuary. There is no electricity, no cars, just many hiking paths among the spruce and balsam fir trees. I also spent several weekends with Marnie in the Berkshire Hills of western Massachusetts to attend Tanglewood concerts of the Boston Symphony Orchestra. Again we kept company with young aspiring artists. My own interest in art had begun during my youth, making drawings and paintings of plants as I hiked—and had continued with photography in more recent years. It constituted a thread that would be interwoven in various ways as I traveled.

During the spring of 1963, I was introduced to the flora of Mount Washington, in New Hampshire, on an annual trip there of botanists from Harvard, Yale, and Brown universities. I was excited to see so many shrubby plants (e.g., *Vaccinium, Rhododendron, Loiseleuria, Empetrum,* and others) that resembled Alaskan arctic tundra, rather than the alpine vegetation of the Crested Butte area. I was interested, too, because my ecologist friend from University of Illinois, Larry Bliss, had just published a paper on the alpine plant communities of the Presidential Range, of which Mount Washington is a part. He had concluded that both the flora and vegetation there were more closely related to the arctic and alpine communities of Scandinavia and central Europe than those of the Rocky Mountains or the Sierra Nevada.

My appetite was whetted for more exploration of this alpine flora, which I did with Appalachian Mountain Club (AMC) members during the summer. Miriam Underhill, who was chairing the committee to write an AMC book, *New England Mountain Flowers*, persuaded me to write the chapter on lichens and mosses. I acquiesced as I had always been fascinated with lichens in particular. I also spent many wonderful winter weekends climbing on snowshoes in New Hampshire with Miriam and other AMC members. She convinced me to buy handmade "bear paw" snowshoes with attached crampons (spiked plates fixed to boots) for mountain climbing. With them we could navigate rocky areas that would have been inaccessible on skis or regular snowshoes, and we had some exhilarating winter adventures. These trips also provided the opportunity for me to think more about adaptations of the alpine plants during their dormant season. Although I would never again do formal research on alpine vegetation, I continued throughout the remainder of my life, to take every opportunity to get into alpine (and arctic) areas to see and photograph the flora and think about the adaptation of these plants to their rigorous environment.

Snowshoeing in New England White Mountains

I continued these winter mountain activities throughout my stay at Harvard. Later ones, however, became misadventures. As a result of climbing steep cliffs of Mount Washington with an AMC group in subzero temperatures, with what I thought was just a slight cold, I developed viral pneumonia. I discovered how many wonderful friends I had in Cambridge during a several weeks' stay in the Harvard Health Center. To try to expedite my recovery, these friends advised me to seek a balmier climate than in Boston, so I made my first ocean voyage from New York to Bermuda. Unfortunately, an Atlantic storm blew in just as we were leaving New York and it was a very rough trip with cold winds and high waves sweeping over the deck. When we reached Bermuda I finally felt the warm recuperative atmosphere I had been seeking in the lovely pink-hued beaches, turquoise waters, and beautiful gardens.

This misadventure, however, did not deter me from snow-shoeing the following winter—until another disaster struck. With AMC friends I climbed Mount Monadnock in New Hampshire, which the Sierra Club reports is "the most climbed summit in the world." Although only a little over 3,000 feet, on clear days all six New England states are visible from the top. We had climbed along snowy trails through dense spruce and maple forest but the bare, rocky summit was coated with ice and little snow. We decided to take off our snowshoes to avoid breaching them. I took one shoe off but then stepped into a crevice, leaving the snowshoe on my other foot twisting in the air, which badly twisted my knee. The incident was a bit embarrassing, as I had already done the difficult climbing and ended up injuring my knee while just trying to take off a snowshoe! Against the better judgment of the AMC group, I limped painfully down the mountain with assistance from my companions. The Harvard physicians thought I had damaged a ligament, but arthroscopic surgery did not exist in those days. So I limped for months with no good suggestions for a remedy from the medical world, and it would terminate my active participation in this sport for good.

Another change in my social life involved moving from the Cronkite Center, after several years, into a pleasant third-story apartment in a large house next to the Wetmores on Francis Street, just a block from the biology labs. Many interesting people lived or had lived in the stately homes on this lovely little street lined with large old trees. The famed liberal economist John Galbraith lived several houses away, and Julia Child was immediately next door. She had already premiered her PBS television series, *The French Chef* in 1963, in which she demystified French cooking for home cooks. Little did I know that the woman I could see from my kitchen window hanging out her washing on the line in her backyard would become the *grande dame* of gastronomy! Here I had the great pleasure to invite and entertain my growing group of friends. These included not only single women from the institute but also numerous married ones—including those from foreign countries visiting the various Harvard botanical facilities. I would later visit a number of these friends in their home countries. I did not meet any eligible men in my age range—at that time women in their late thirties didn't often find "Mr. Right."

I made a number of trips to the New York Botanical Garden (NYBG) to obtain resin and amber specimens from their collections. Beyond my collecting, I enjoyed seeing NYBG's magnificent gardens, of course, as well as reading and being told about the garden's historic role in the early twentieth century as a premier US institution in botany particularly fascinated me. Such information intensified my growing interest in the history of ecology and changing scientific concepts. NYBG's early research-oriented program was broad, embracing traditional studies in systematics and natural history and also integrating new subjects that involved laboratory and experimental studies. The botanical garden helped Andrew Carnegie establish the Carnegie Institution of Washington (CIW) laboratories in Arizona, Colorado, and California, which fostered fundamental ecological studies at the turn of the twentieth century in the western United States—some of which continue today under CIW's auspices.

One of my most memorable amber collection trips to Washington, DC, was the day that John F. Kennedy was assassinated. I was standing in one of the towers of the Smithsonian Institution when his death was announced on a public address system. I watched, still stunned like those around me, as people poured out of the buildings surrounding the mall. Soon after I left to return to my hotel, Washington fell eerily silent. As for most Americans, it was for me an unfathomable event on an unforgettable day.

COLLECTING AMBER
FROM EUROPEAN MUSEUMS
1964

Amber is produced from the marrow discharged
by trees belonging to the pine genus, like gum from the
cherry and resin from an ordinary pine.
—Pliny the Elder

As background for an analysis of the botanical origin of all ambers through geological time, I had written a paper, "Present Status of Botanical Studies of Amber," using the excellent literature available from the Harvard libraries. And I had obtained amber samples for IR analysis from the Harvard collections as well as those of the New York Botanical Garden and the Smithsonian Institution in Washington, DC. To continue my work, I needed to obtain samples from the major European museums, where more specimens were available from widespread locations and of different ages—going back to plants' first production of resins. Gathering these samples would give me some of the evolutionary background for a question that had begun to form in my mind: "Why did plants begin to produce this complex mixture of terpenes sequestered in specialized secretory structures soon after trees had evolved?" Could it not be involved in defense of the plant?

I had been corresponding with amber researchers in Europe about collecting specimens for IR analysis. I also had been discussing with them the controversial botanical origin and forest environment of Baltic amber, which is the world's largest and most intensively studied amber. Deposits were so huge on the Samland Peninsula along the Baltic Sea that it was still being recovered from open pit mines during the mid-later twentieth century. Because of the importance of this amber from throughout European history, the term "amber" is often synonymous with Baltic amber in the older European literature. I also wanted to use this opportunity learn more about the history of fabled Baltic amber art. I obtained sponsorship from the American Philosophical Society to

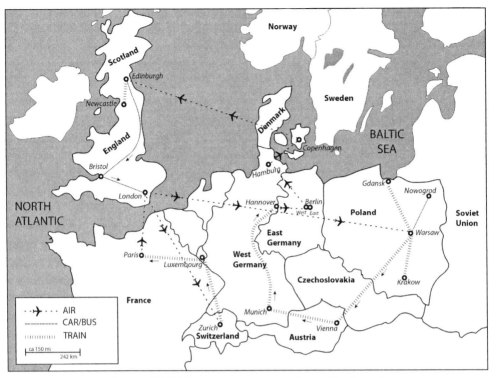

Route of 1964 European museum amber-collecting trip

spend most of the summer of 1964 collecting from museums in England, Poland, Austria, Germany, and Denmark. With a grant from the Botanical Society of America, I also planned to attend the X International Botanical Congress in Edinburgh, Scotland, and participate in a paleobotany field trip to classic fossil sites across England. The trip also educated me about the terrible effects of World War II and the impact of the Cold War on relationships among scientists.

The venerable British Museum in London was the first stop on my European itinerary. After I obtained specimens from their large collections of rare red Burmese amber, I planned to proceed to Warsaw, Poland, where I would meet with Madame Czeczott, a researcher who had compiled the most recent list of plants enclosed in Baltic amber. I was taking a Harvard charter flight to London, but just before my departure my passport, with an enclosed visa for Poland, had not arrived from the Polish Embassy in Washington, DC. The Harvard travel office wangled an emergency temporary passport to get me to England and gained assurances from the

Polish Embassy that my visa for Poland in my passport would be ready for me at their embassy in London.

At the Polish Embassy in London I was told that my visa would only be available close to the time for my flight to Warsaw. Colleagues at the British Museum tried to convince me to bypass Poland, because they thought all of the delays were designed to warn me not to go. They were particularly concerned that my visa problems might be related to Elso Barghoorn's brother, a Yale professor in charge of their foreign relations program, who had been recently jailed in Moscow—ostensibly as an American spy. Elso and his brother had been classmates of John F. Kennedy and, as president, Kennedy had convinced Nikita Kruschev to free Barghoorn. During this entire period I had been corresponding with Polish paleobotanists and sending greetings from "Professor Barghoorn." Had I somehow become confused in being associated with the Yale Barghoorn? We would never know, of course, if my problems had anything to do with the scenario surrounding Elso's brother—or even why he was taken into custody. In any event, my British friends strongly suggested that I should try to retrieve my passport and proceed directly to Vienna, the next stop in my itinerary. I was stubbornly determined, nevertheless, to go to Poland, because I thought that there was just too much to be learned about amber there. But it was also becoming evident to me that I would be witnessing the impact of the Cold War while traveling in Eastern Europe.

The embassy finally made my passport, with visa, available just a few hours before my flight to Warsaw was due to depart. My skeptical British Museum friends kindly rushed me to the airport and reluctantly said good-bye as I literally ran to board the plane just as the door was being closed.

Again my passport was taken upon entry in Poland, and was unavailable to me during my stay there. Thus, I did not have official identification while I was traveling alone on trains around Poland. Because I didn't know Polish, I had my pockets full of Polish phrases that my researcher friends had written down for me. In letters following my visit, these friends told me that they had been terrified when I was traveling alone, without a passport, and unable to speak the language. Unbeknown to me they had heaved a huge sigh of relief each time I returned safely to Warsaw. As in Colombia, I had no doubts about being able, as Ralph had put it, "to somehow muddle through." My mother also often had said that she had never really seen me fearful throughout my childhood.

I spent my first few days in Warsaw collecting from the large array of Baltic amber samples at the Museum Ziemi and discussing Madame Czeczott's recent compilation of plant inclusions in this amber. I was particularly interested in the large number of angiosperms she had reported, and that almost a quarter of the flora had affinities with the tropics. She too had been surprised by these data but offered no possible explanation.

I was taken on sightseeing trips around the city, and was horrified to see incredible devastation from World War II still evident almost twenty years after its conclusion. Poland was now a member of the Soviet Bloc and the new, dull gray, massive, and uninteresting Soviet-style buildings created a depressing atmosphere. The Poles, however, were doggedly reconstructing the old city, where they could reassert some of their unique cultural charm in the architecture. This area had been completely destroyed by the Germans during the Warsaw Uprising—while the Russians stood on the other side of the Volga River, refusing to come to their rescue.

I clearly remember a dinner party at Madame Czeczott's house. Potatoes dominated the meal. I did not eat all of the mountain of mashed potatoes on my plate, and the people around the table sat waiting and waiting before someone politely said, "We were starving during the war and potatoes often saved us. So we can't bear to see any go to waste." I then ate up promptly! After dinner Madame Czeczott showed me her library, in which most of the books were badly burned. The burning was part of the German retribution following the Warsaw Uprising. They took books and other valuables from people's homes and threw them into huge bonfires in the streets. When the soldiers moved from Madame Czeczott's street to plunder homes elsewhere, she had frantically pulled out whatever books she could from the fire. Of course, this act of burning peoples' belongings was almost trivial considering the enormous atrocities the Germans committed against the Polish people themselves—especially those of Jewish background. This trip to Poland was my first direct contact with how civilians had suffered during World War II, and it greatly affected me. More than ever it reinforced my tendency to be a pacifist.

I took the train south to Krakow to meet Professor Szafer, Poland's most famous paleobotanist and a friend of Elso Barghoorn. Krakow, the cultural center of Poland, is a beautiful ancient city (the first capital of the country) with a very old university. Krakow escaped the devastation that engulfed Warsaw and its people, which raised my spirits a little regarding the awful effects of the war. Although the largest deposits of Baltic amber occur along the Baltic Sea from Estonia to Denmark, amber eroded from marine sediments near sea level were washed ashore during storms, and subsequently carried by water and Pleistocene glaciers to secondary deposits across much of northern and eastern Europe. Most of the amber samples in the Krakow University's collections were from such glacial deposits in southern Poland.

Upon my return to Warsaw, Madame Czezcott had arranged for a car to drive to an outdoor regional folk museum at Nowogrod in northern Poland, which had extensive amber art work and a reconstruction of what researchers there thought the amber forests were like. In planning the trip, Madame Czeczott thought that we would take a picnic lunch and had asked me what kind of sandwiches I would like. I said anything would be fine but then had an inspiration—"Polish ham would be lovely," I said. When it was time to leave for our trip, Madame Czezcott had not appeared. We waited and waited, worrying what could be wrong, but finally she arrived looking very harried. Since Polish ham was a valuable export item, it was almost impossible for Poles to obtain any for themselves. She had somehow managed to find a small piece just for me. It was another case of my inadvertently causing a problem because I was ignorant of difficulties faced by the people I was visiting, who were trying so hard to be hospitable!

Madame Czecott and the Chetniks at museum

The Chetniks, who were in charge of the outdoor museum at Nowogrod, also went to great lengths to be helpful. Because the soil on the glacial outwash in this Baltic Sea area is poor, suitable only for growing potatoes and rye, the trade of a precious commodity such as amber was important through its human history—especially during Roman times, and the museum had displays showing details of trade routes from this area to the Mediterranean. Pliny the Elder has even recorded that "the price of an amber figurine, however small, exceeded that of a living, healthy slave." Polish authors on amber have often stated that this demand for amber has made Poland's history inseparable from the cultural history of the Baltic region. The Chetniks generously gave me numerous historical photographs of traditional Polish folk amber art. We also discussed their reconstruction of the amber forest—a pine and spruce forest with palms in a subtropical swamp—suggesting similarities to Florida today. However, their suggestion did not help explain the large number of plant remains with even more tropical affinities.

Amber occurs all along Poland's Baltic coast, but the town of Gdansk is famous for the abundance of amber that has been collected along its coast through the centuries and was a starting point near the Vistula River for major trade routes to the south. I took the train to Gdansk where I was hosted by a physician who had graduated from Harvard Medical School. He said that belief in the healing power of amber was still prevalent among people of the area. Often his patients, who had serious illnesses that were not responding to conventional medicine, would ask if he could help them obtain oil of amber to treat their ailments.

Baltic amber provided material for all kinds of art objects. In the thirteenth century, paternoster beads were the mainstay of the amber economy and guilds of *paternostermacher*s produced rosaries for the entire Christian church. In the seventeenth and nineteenth centuries, great master craftsmen with sophisticated skills made large art objects, including chandeliers, inlaid cabinets and paneling, and much else. Today, most Polish jewelry consists only of polished pieces of amber, because there are few artisans who have the skill to cut facets and intricately carve amber as was done in earlier times. We visited the Gdansk State Jewelry Factory, where we saw jewelry being created. At this factory, the jewelers also complained that the Soviets took the best pieces of amber for making jewelry and other items because they had become such a lucrative item in the Soviet tourist trade.

Making amber jewelry in Gdansk factory

When I returned from Gdansk, we were surprised by my hotel having been taken over by Tito and his entourage from Yugoslavia. Hotel reservations in Soviet countries were made by an agency (Intourist) and the traveler neither had the choice of hotels nor the freedom to move from one to another. Furthermore, I was not allowed to stay with my friends. All the hotel guests displaced by Tito's visit were told that we would either have to sit up or try to sleep in the hotel's lobby that night. Among them were an American couple, a man from Rotterdam, and another from Berlin—all in Warsaw for business.

The hotel, however, had not faced the fury of the amazingly vigorous Madame Czeczott—despite her advanced age. She and some university people whom she had marshaled made quite a ruckus over my situation, which actually helped all those displaced that night. Finally the hotel informed us that they were asking people in some rooms (all from Communist countries) if they would double up, so as to accommodate us. When they asked the Dutchman from Rotterdam if he would room with the Berliner, he was furious. He told me that "there was no way he was going to share a room with a Goddamn German after what the Germans did to Rotterdam during the war." He even went so far as to ask me if I would share the room with him. Shortly thereafter I was told that a Bulgarian woman engineer from Sofia was willing to share her room with me.

That was fine with me, but when I got to the room I was surprised to find my roommate was terrified of me. I had been told that she spoke excellent English, but she wouldn't utter a word—only nod yes or no. Her fear was so obvious that I simply washed up and went to bed. The next morning she had turned on the radio, and there were some excerpts in English about President Kennedy. Again I tried to engage her in conversation, to no avail. So I packed up quickly and left, thanking her for kindly giving me the privilege of staying with her. As I was walking down the long hallway, she came rushing after me and thrust two small, hand-painted vases, made in typical Sofia craft style, into my hands. She said that she had very much wanted to be friendly but when they asked her to let me stay in her room, she became afraid that the room was bugged. She emphasized that Bulgarians were constantly warned not to be friendly with Americans when they traveled. I indeed was being educated in the effects of the Cold War.

Throughout the later parts of my European trip to collect amber specimens I was treated in a friendly and helpful manner, but nowhere with the exceptional warmth and hospitality I experienced in Poland. When Madame Czeczott and others from the Museum Ziemi came to see me depart on the train to Vienna, I was almost brought to tears. She had brought an amber necklace to give to me that had been in her family for generations. The faceted beads were worn from constant use over the many years. I started to decline, but then remembered my faux pas in Alaska with the *mukluks*. Madame Czeczott wanted me to remember the long Polish history of esteem for amber when I wore them. I am still touched by the gesture when I look at the necklace. I have certainly never forgotten this incredible woman—an indomitable spirit like that of Marnie Chamberlain in Cambridge. What models they provided of living life to its fullest—each in her own way!

I had been particularly looking forward to visiting Vienna, to see the large Bachofen-Echt amber collection, which was beautifully illustrated in a 1949 book *Der Bernstein und Seine Einschlusse*. After my arrival, the researchers at the Paleontology Institute of the University of Vienna seemed overly anxious to show me tourist sights—we looked at castles, the Vienna Woods, and famous Viennese coffeehouses, but not the amber I had come to see. As the days of my stay in Vienna were waning, I reminded my kind hosts about the amber. Then the awful truth emerged; they could not find the Bachofen-Echt collection! It had been packed up during the war and they had thought it was still in the basement. However, they had not been able to find it anywhere and ultimately had given up hope of discovering its whereabouts. They were afraid the Germans had either taken the collection as spoils of war, or possibly that the Bachofen-Echt heirs had it. If sold, they wondered if it might now be in Russia. Whatever the explanation, the collection was no longer in Vienna.

My train departure from Vienna was the most dramatic I've ever had. I was leaving on an early afternoon train but had been taken out for a lively farewell lunch that lasted too long. By the time we arrived at the platform, the train was already pulling out of the station. I only managed to board with the help of a Viennese fellow who literally picked me up, carried me as he ran, and somehow managed to deposit me on the steps of the moving train. He shouted to me as the train lurched forward that he knew we'd make it because he had been on the Austrian Olympic track team!

My next stop was Munich, and when I arrived at the Geological Institute there, I recognized pieces of amber among their specimens that had been prominent in photos in the Bachofen-Echt book. When I questioned the Munchners, some said that it had been sold to them. Others thought that the specimens had been obtained as spoils of war and were unapologetic about their right to have them as such. I asked myself if I should let the Viennese researchers know? I decided not to do so but later wondered if this was the right decision.

I enjoyed examining the many flower parts enclosed in this amber and discussed the history of their study with my hosts. We compared the detailed drawings, done in magnificent quarto volumes, by renowned nineteenth century botanists H.A. Conwentz and H.G. Goeppert. This led to discussions of the botanical origin of Baltic amber centering around the abundant coniferous remains in the amber. Goeppert designated the amber tree as *Pinites succinifer* from amber associated with wood. He used the ending —*ites* to confer an affinity but not an identity of the fossil wood with any living pine. Although Conwentz recognized that the anatomy of the wood was unlike any living pine, he included several species of pine and perhaps spruce under a single name, *Pinus succinifera*. His use of the genus *Pinus* is probably the source of considerable subsequent confusion about whether a modern species of pine is the source of Baltic amber. Conwentz also pointed out that pines today do not naturally produce the massive amounts of resin necessary to account for the huge accumulations of Baltic amber. He proposed that trees suffered from a unique pathological condition so pervasive that the entire amber-producing forest was affected—"Das pathologische war die Regel, das Normale die Ausnahme"—the pathological was the rule, the normal the exception. I wondered if this was an early insight into the protective role of resins. On the other hand, there was so much focus on temperate zone pine forests that botanists such as Conwentz did not give attention to the enormous amount of resin produced today by certain conifers and angiosperms in subtropical and tropical environments. I have wondered if he was aware of this copious production of resin by tropical trees, or, if so, why he did not think it was applicable to the Baltic region?

While visiting the University of Munich I got my first opportunity to see European alpine flora. Herman Merxmüller, Professor of Systematics at University of Munich, who had revised Hegi's *Alpen Flora* took me on several good trips into alpine vegetation around Garmish Partenkirchen. The campanulas and gentians were especially spectacular and I saw my first edelweiss (*Leontopodium alpinum*) here. Later in the summer I also got to visit the high tundra and lush meadows adjacent to a glacier in the Valois area of Switzerland with Professor Pontecorvo, with whom I had explored alpine areas at Gothic in 1962. We renewed our discussions of highly restricted alpine plants on calcareous rocks—a diversion from my main research goal of this trip that I thoroughly enjoyed.

From Munich en route to West Berlin I made a brief stop in Hannover, to meet with a plant anatomist whose studies of the wood and bark found in Baltic amber strongly supported Conwentz's conclusion that the amber was not produced by any present-day pines. European travel by train was always pleasant but I found it especially efficient in Germany. These train trips brought home to me the small size of most European countries compared to the United States. Although I was able to observe the countryside, here it was more the farms, villages, and architectural differences among the countries that fascinated me. What a different experience from crossing the vast areas of the western United States where I focused so much on changes in the vegetation and their relationships to the geomorphology.

In West Berlin I stayed with Else Hecht, a friend from the Radcliffe Institute. Else was originally from Leipzig, where her father had been killed by the Nazis because he had helped a Jewish professor during the Hitler era. After the war she had remained in Leipzig, where she became a professor at the university, though she

Else Hecht
at afternoon coffee

abhorred the communist rule in East Germany. Through the West German underground of academics, she fled from Leipzig to West Berlin where she had been offered a professorship at the Frei University. As a result of this harrowing escape, she feared retribution if the Soviets were to discover her in West Berlin. Because of this, Else was extremely uncomfortable about my going through Checkpoint Charlie to get to one of the famous German museums in the Unter der Linden area of East Berlin. She was very concerned that if I got into trouble in East Berlin, she could not help me. I naively assured her not to worry; there would be no problem.

The contrast between East and West Berlin was striking. West Berlin was already a bustling city that had mostly been reconstructed, probably in good measure due to the Marshall Plan. On the other hand, where I entered East Berlin, bombed-out areas still remained amid dreary Soviet-style buildings like the ones I had seen in Warsaw. Though I found the environs bleak, I had no problems until I reached the Museum für Naturkunde, where I was to meet the paleobotanists who had arranged my visit. The receptionist would not allow me to enter and even accused me of having false papers. He had information about the visit of a "Dr. Professor Jean Langenheim," *not a woman*. He assumed that a "Dr. Professor" would be male! I did not have my passport to show who I was, as it had been kept at Checkpoint Charlie. Eventually, since I had not appeared, the paleobotanists came to the reception area to see what might have happened, and rescued me from what was developing into an unpleasant situation.

The paleobotanists were excited about my chemical studies of amber and helped me obtain numerous specimens. These included many of Baltic amber, but also ambers of different ages and probably different botanical origin from other European areas such as Sicily, France, Austria, and Romania. They were eager to hear about my future results, but warned me to be guarded in my correspondence with them and *never* to send any personal greetings such as Christmas cards. When I tried to leave Checkpoint Charlie on the second day, the authorities wanted to see my notebook, which contained all of my information about the samples I had taken from other institutions during my trip. I definitely did not want to lose it and apparently showed some concern about them having it. After hours of waiting, they informed me that they were keeping the notebook until the next day, when I could obtain it. It was now long hours after the time that Else had expected me to return, and I knew that she would be worried. To top off the disastrous situation, I had missed the last trolley that went directly to her area. With transfers it took even more time and I could not find a taxi. When I eventually arrived, Else was frantic. Fortunately, we both survived the night, and the next day I was able to retrieve my notebook. But I think Else was glad when I left for Hamburg!

The Hamburg Geological Institute did not have the large collections of amber that had been available in Munich and East Berlin. However, researchers there, who worked on fossil soils, kindly gave me an unusual necklace made of amber pieces containing soil particles. This necklace probably would not attract most people interested in amber jewelry, but I was delighted with its unique beauty and meaning. After all, falling into soil is a significant way in which resin becomes deposited to form amber.

In Copenhagen I visited the Danish amber researcher S. G. Larsson, at the University of Copenhagen's Mineralogical Museum and Zoological Institute where I collected numerous samples. Larsson was writing a book on both the plant and insect inclusions in Baltic amber and we began our long-term discussions about the possible role of tropical conditions in explaining the enormous deposits of it. Although in *Baltic Amber—A Paleontological Study* Larsson pointed out the intermingling of plants (and insects) representing different climates, he like Czeczott, was interested in the strong element of tropical plants. In fact Larsson concluded that European amber trees grew over a large area as long as subtropical and tropical conditions prevailed during early Tertiary times. He was a proponent of my view of the role of the tropics in trees producing large quantities of resin.

The hospitable Larsson family took me to the *Nationalmuseet* (National Museum) to see the superb amber art collections spanning a long history of the region, beginning with charming amulets of animals and sun wheels related to sun worship in the Stone Age and culminating with magnificently crafted nineteenth century tankards and chandeliers, among others. We also went to a beach where local people came to collect amber that is washed onto shore during winter storms—that is, we visited a site where amber was still collected in the way early amber collectors had all along the Baltic Sea shores. During this visit I established a warm relationship with the Larssons and would return to accept their kind hospitality on other occasions.

While in Copenhagen, I stayed with relatives of a Danish friend I had known in Berkeley, and again learned more about the cultural impact of World War II. To get to the museum for my visits with Professor Larsson,

I needed to transfer from one streetcar to another. I had been told to ask for a transfer, or *omstignes*, in Danish. Having just been in Germany and where I had often used streetcars, I inadvertently used the somewhat similar-sounding German *umsteiger*, and added "*bitte*." It seemed as if every eye in the streetcar turned toward me, and the conductor said in English, "Why did you ask for the transfer in German? Since the war, we definitely do not like to hear German in Copenhagen." The German occupation had been such an unpleasant period that Danes did not want any reminder of it.

I ended the amber collection part of this European trip in Copenhagen. The specimens I had gathered became, in large measure, the basis for what became a classic publication, "Amber: A Botanical Inquiry", in which I discussed amber evidence for the first resin-producing trees in the Carboniferous (300 million years ago), and followed the kinds of trees that produced amber to the present day. By this time, I had become convinced that many trees utilized these resins as a defense against enemies such as herbivores and pathogens—an idea not generally accepted at that time.

OTHER ACTIVITIES WHILE IN EUROPE

After Copenhagen, I proceeded to Edinburgh for the International Botanical Congress. My dominant recollection of those meetings was the unpleasant problem of attempting to be friendly with the people who had been my hosts in Poland. Although I had experienced the Bulgarian woman and East German paleobotanists' extreme fear of interacting with Americans, I nevertheless was not prepared for my Polish friends refusing to have *any* contact with me at an international meeting. My every approach was met with frigid, unfriendly rebuffs. Finally, I accidentally met one of them in a women's restroom and across a stall she told me that they knew they were being watched, especially when they were visiting a western country. Furthermore, they were not allowed to go on the paleobotany field trip across Scotland and England to see classic plant fossil sites, because of the continual casual association with westerners.

Midway through the congress I took a train from Edinburgh to Durham, England, to meet with a leading coal researcher at the University of Newcastle upon Tyne. He had used infrared spectroscopy to study resin in Carboniferous English coals, which provided some of the first evidence of resin being produced by early conifers. His evidence gave me additional confidence that I was on the right track in using IR as a means of determining the botanic source of ambers.

Harlan Banks (front) and Edna Plumstead (back)
collecting fossils along Yorkshire coast

I then joined paleobotanists for a tour of important English plant fossil localities. The group was primarily European, with only a few Americans (among them Harlan Banks, who had introduced me to paleobotany at the University of Minnesota) and just two women (one, Edna Plumstead, I would later see in South Africa). The trip was led by an English paleobotanist from Reading University who was a leading researcher on Jurassic plants and had concentrated his studies at sites along the beautiful Yorkshire coast. The fossils here reminded me of my struggles to identify those in the Colombian Girón Formation, the genera of which had first been described in Yorkshire. If only I had been able to put my questions then to such a Jurassic plant authority! We went southwest across England and terminated the trip at the tropical Tertiary London Clay deposits. I was particularly eager to see some of these famous fossils that had been considered to have elements of flora similar to Southeast Asia—supporting the potential importance of the tropical environment in the Baltic amber forests.

Following an alpine plant trek in Switzerland with Pontecorvo, and a brief visit in Luxembourg with a friend, my last stop was in Paris for a few days. Here I stayed in a "romantic" little pension (as advertised) along the Seine River, and saw the usual highlights of the city, with special emphasis on a visit to the Louvre. For the first time in this entire European trip, however, I felt lonely. I realized I had not been alone, except on the train, bus, or plane, throughout the trip. Instead I had been "passed along" to various scientists at different stops or been among colleagues at the congress and on its field trip. I began to appreciate how as a scientist I had become a citizen of the world, with a ready-made circle of friends with common interests around the globe. I saw that traveling professionally also gave one the opportunity to learn directly about a country's culture from people who lived there, rather than being dependent on canned tours. My experiences off the tourist-trodden path created unique memories, the ones that I most remembered, and wrote about most intensely in letters and diaries.

My last day in Paris was my birthday and I was having a drink alone at an outdoor table when a friendly French college student came over to me wanting to practice his English, and we ended up having a lovely meal together. It was a perfect, unexpected gift of the moment. I returned to my little pension the happiest I had been in Paris, but quite ready to leave for home.

FAR-REACHING
HARVARD ACTIVITIES

1964-1966

It appears to me that nothing can be more improving to a
young naturalist than a journey in distant countries.
— Charles Darwin

By the fall of 1964 I was a full scholar at the Radcliffe Institute, and in that capacity I taught in the Radcliffe Seminar program. These were special seminars directed primarily to women college graduates or those with comparable interests or experience who sought intellectual stimulus. The age of the students ranged from early twenties to over eighty. Although seminar topics were concentrated in the humanities, I was asked to teach one that would provide biological background for understanding conservation and other environmental issues. My students were mostly highly intelligent senior citizens who plied me with penetrating and thought-provoking questions. Indeed it was the octogenarians who kept me on my toes! Like Marnie Chamberlain and her friends, these women further opened my eyes to the lively intellectual activities of elderly women in the Cambridge area. Theirs was a spirit I found particularly pronounced in the Cambridge community, and I have wondered over the years how much it resulted from the activities of Radcliffe in fostering lifelong learning for women. Certainly these women remain an inspiration, especially now that I am an octogenarian!

EARLY 1960S FEMINISM

I had participated in many lively discussions over several years in the community of women scholars at the institute, but I don't remember any discussions of Betty Friedan's book, *The Feminine Mystique*, which was published in 1963 and achieved worldwide fame in 1964. Commenting on "a sense of dissatisfaction, a yearning that women suffered in the middle of the twentieth century in the United States," Friedan stated that education wasn't the problem but rather the narrow definition of the role of women.

Friedan's outcry started a new consciousness that became the second wave of feminism—the first wave having achieved goals regarding voting and legal rights as well as education. The institute consisted of a group of women who should have been primed to embrace Friedan's message, which ultimately permanently transformed the social fabric of so many parts of the world. Could we possibly have been so busy utilizing our opportunity to expand our role as educated women that we did not stop to recognize this chief architect of what would become a sweeping upheaval that hearkened back to the suffragettes? Or were Friedan's ideas being discussed while I was away on my travels? I am still unsure today.

Ellen Goodman of the *Boston Globe* has written that the year Friedan's book was published Adlai Stevenson told Goodman's graduating class at Radcliffe "how important our education would be in raising our children." His apparent assumption was that this was the only role for a good Radcliffe education. Although this still may have been the typical view in 1963, Goodman strongly disagreed with him. Nevertheless, she wrote that in 1964 she worked "in the sex-segregated research pool at *Newsweek* magazine—and thought I was lucky to have a job."

Goodman's comments made me wonder about the viewpoint of Radcliffe undergraduates before Friedan's book came out. A survey of 1952, 1953, and 1958 alumnae, conducted by the Radcliffe Murray Research Center, shows that these women initially pursued traditional patterns of work and family commitments. Nonetheless, with social changes begun in the sixties, "this was the first generation of women that made inroads into traditionally male professions, but it was only accomplished at midlife."

Ann Shapiro is an interesting example of a 1958 Radcliffe graduate. She has written that nothing in her privileged education prepared her "for any of the realities confronting a young woman who came of age in the 1950s. The only published information about our options (for the future) appeared in the Radcliffe Yearbook of 1958"—and those possibilities were "washing diapers, typing an employer's dull letters, or tackling graduate work." Although the last was most attractive to Shapiro, who by this time had married a Harvard man, she stated that "access to graduate school was by no means assured." By the time her third child was born, Shapiro wrote that "she had become the woman Friedan had written about in *The Feminine Mystique*, vaguely longing for something beyond the confines of my pink kitchen." Twenty-five years after her Radcliffe graduation she got a divorce, completed a PhD, and now teaches women's studies to undergraduates as Distinguished Professor of English at State University of New York at Farmingdale.

Although I was fortunate to do my doctoral studies in the late 1940s and early 1950s, I did not pursue a career of my own until I reached midlife, in the 1960s. And, I was aided by the visionary foresight of Polly Bunting, the then-president of Radcliffe College, in establishing the Radcliffe Institute for Independent Study. In the early sixties she designed this institute to help educated women surmount the restricted opportunities for them to establish a reputation of their own. Nevertheless, there was so little sympathy for its goals at the time that the institute had to be fiscally independent from Radcliffe, separately financed from corporate and individual sources. The change in attitudes of Radcliffe/Harvard today is clear, with the evolution of the Radcliffe Institute for Independent Studies into the world-renowned think-tank, now called the Radcliffe Institute for Advanced Studies. Furthermore, the last director of this institute, Drew Gilpin Faust, was elected in 2007 as the first woman president of Harvard University!

STUDIES OF MEXICAN AND COSTA RICAN RESIN-PRODUCING PLANTS

The National Science Foundation had funded a two-year continuation of my amber research in 1964, and during the summer of 1965 I dived into research on *Hymenaea* as a tropical resin-producing tree, primarily with logistic support and some funding from the Organization of Tropical Studies (OTS) in Costa Rica. This consortium of universities had recently formed to advance tropical education and research. Harvard had been actively involved in its formation, as the university had had to cancel its training and research programs at the Atkins Gardens in Cuba with Castro's takeover in 1959. Reed Rollins, director of the herbarium, became the first president of the organization during 1964-5, and a large group of Harvard botanists participated in OTS activities that summer.

I had previously planned a Mexican trip, in collaboration with personnel from the University of Mexico's botanical garden, to collect from resin-producing trees along the Oaxaca coast and in parts of Chiapas. My primary goal, however, was to see if estuarine areas along the Acapulco coast might represent conditions under which the Chiapas amber was deposited. Dan Janzen, the coordinator of OTS-sponsored research, accepted my proposed OTS project, but permitted me to begin my research in Mexico and then continue in Costa Rica for the month of July and first two weeks of August. It was the beginning of what would become prominent and persistent threads in my research—systematic, ecological, and chemical studies of *Hymenaea*—as well as my close association with OTS. Janzen, who became a premier tropical ecologist noted for his provocative ideas, shared my interest in *H. courbaril,* his focus being on how resin protected the pods against rhinochinid weevils. Additionally, both of us were simply fond of this handsome tropical tree.

On my trip to Oaxaca, male botanist traveling companions and I passed through the small town of Juchitán, where Zapoteca Indian women were having a fiesta. They were part of a relatively wealthy matriarchal society of women traders. Despite the society espousing equal rights for men and women, this party was exclusively for women. When we looked in the room, several of them came out and pulled me into a dancing group of women in brightly colored dresses and headgear, reminiscent of Carmen Miranda. Everyone seemed inebriated. They had a barrel of *pulque* and shouted insistently for me to drink some. I refused and struggled to retreat. What might have been a most intriguing event involving a fascinating women's group began to seem like a nightmare. When I finally broke free, my male traveling companions on the outside were relieved to see me get out. The men in the village were standing around outside the party venue, having been refused admittance, and were laughing as we left town in a hurry. The remainder of this trip was quietly focused on collecting plants.

Arturo Gomez-Pompa, who had been my botanical guide for the fateful trip to Belize, again assisted my investigation in the Acapulco area in Guerrero. I had forgiven him for the poison wood episode, and since that time we had interacted while he was on a fellowship at the Harvard Forest. He would later go on to become one of Mexico's most prominent ecologists. On the Acapulco trip we excitedly found *Hymenaea courbaril* trees growing on the slopes above or lining mangrove-dominated estuaries and swamps, as Faustino Miranda had predicted. These observations supported conclusions from our pollen analyses of the Chiapas lignites, which indicated that most of the amber had been deposited in brackish estuaries or back swamps dominated by mangroves such as *Rhizophora mangle.*

Additionally, in Guerrero and later in Costa Rica I collected pieces of *Hymenaea* trunk and large roots to determine the nature and location of the resin secretory structures. I collected seeds to grow plants in the Harvard greenhouse to study young plants under experimental conditions. We dug out the roots and saw that they produced resin copiously, which supported our predictions that resin found in the soil had not only fallen from the trunk of the tree but accumulated from the roots. I assumed that this resin in the soil had been washed into the mangrove swamps, where it was probably trapped by the mangrove stilt roots, and over time could be incorporated into sediments as amber.

In Costa Rica I set up a field experiment on *Hymenaea courbaril* trees growing under different moisture conditions on the coffee *finca* of Luis Fournier, a University of Costa Rica professor. His *finca* was close to San José, and thus I could gash the trees and easily return at intervals to observe differences in resin production under wet and dry conditions within the same forest community. I was continuing the idea I had initiated at the Drumlin Farms in Massachusetts, of doing field experimentation on resins from modern trees to try to understand fossil resin. At the end of this experiment I obtained wood samples from the cut trunks to analyze the anatomy of the resin secretory tissue. With this work I established a long-term friendship with Fournier, which was similar in its continued support to that of Rafael Rodiguez, whom I had met on my very first trip to Costa Rica.

Supporters of my research, Rafael Rodriguez and Luis Fournier,
professors at University of Costa Rica, with Gunnera
(umbrella plant)

Only one species of *Hymenaea, H. courbaril,* grows in Mexico and Central America. It is restricted to the Pacific side of Costa Rica, but spans from the driest to the wettest forests. With the assistance of the vegetation and tropical tree identification expert at the Tropical Science Center, I visited this *H. courbaril* in vastly different habitats. In doing so I was reawakened to ecological thinking, after having been submerged in the chemical and paleobotanical worlds of establishing *Hymenaea* as the source of Mexican amber and obtaining evidence for the evolution of resin-producing trees. I was beginning to think about comparing resin production under a wide range of tropical conditions. If the resin was protecting the tree against herbivores and pathogens, how did these properties vary in different habitats? I now was not just collecting seed and resins but was beginning to learn about different tropical environments in which the resin-producing trees grew. I also began to think about how abiotic conditions could influence the fluidity and abundance of trunk resin as well as how injuries from biotic activities could determine the exposure of the resin to the outside of the tree.

I collected from the northwestern dry forests in Guanacaste province. I then flew to the moist tropical enivronment of the Osa Peninsula in southern Costa Rica, where I was introduced to four-storied rain forest. I saw huge *Hymenaea* trees producing massive amounts of resin—large sheets of resin on the trunks and long stalactites hanging from branches. I thought that these trees of an undescribed *Hymenaea* species (it was impossible to collect flower or fruit when I was there) might have produced abundant amber, and seeing them reinforced my growing ecological thinking about the different tropical environmental conditions that could result in variation in resin production.

Throughout my *Hymenaea* research in Costa Rica that summer, I encountered an array of interesting animals—howler monkeys calling their troops with loud, peculiar sounds, long-armed spider monkeys springing amazing distances from one tree to another in the canopy; strikingly colored tree frogs (still common at that time!) and was startled by small green snakes among the branches of *Hymenaea* that I was collecting. There was camouflage, such as a lichen-camouflaged moth that I disturbed when I leaned against what I thought was lichen on the trunk of a tree. When leaning on other trees, I was surprised to see them come alive with ants that lived inside. Leaf-cutter ants busily carried pieces of leaves they had cut much larger than themselves. It puzzled me they did not seem to cut many *Hymenaea* leaves—later I would find out why.

Upon returning to Harvard, I wanted to begin investigation of the secretory structures in which *Hymenaea* resin is produced. Again, assistance appeared at just the right time. Margaret McCully and Terry O'Brien, two students in the Thimann/Wetmore lab, helped with embedding, sectioning, and photographing the secretory tissue in *H. courbaril* that I had obtained in Guerrero, Mexico, and from seedlings now growing in the greenhouse. Their expertise enabled development of a special embedding technique that produced excellent sections for the microscope from very difficult material. Their fine photographs of the *Hymenaea* secretory tissue appeared in several publications, including one of their books—*Plant Structure and Development: A Pictorial and Physiological Approach.* Although *Hymenaea* secretory structures are being further studied today, these *Hymenaea* photos are still being used as examples of this kind of tissue.

INTRODUCTION TO AMAZONIA

During the spring of 1966 I made my first trip to Amazonia. I had decided that if I were to continue research as a plant ecologist within the framework of my amber research, I should choose a relevant model system to study. *Hymenaea* was the obvious choice, but the center of its distribution was Amazonia. Was it possible to continue there with *Hymenaea*—especially as a woman? I sought advice from the celebrated Amazonian researcher, Richard Schultes, in the botanical museum. He had spent twelve years (from 1941-1953) in Amazonia, and because seeking the sources of wild rubber had been one of Schultes' great quests there, he enthusiastically endorsed my research on resin—another tropical tree exudate.

Several weeks later Schultes came rushing into Barghoorn's lab with good news. A meeting on the biota of the Amazon was to be held in Belém, Brazil in June. I could accompany him and he would introduce me to researchers and administrators in the Brazilian institutions who could help me initiate my research there. Serendipity had entered again in providing the way for me.

Shortly thereafter, Schultes and I, with two Harvard students as field assistants, left for Belém, and several weeks of adventure. It was quite an introduction to Amazonia! Belém is located on the Amazon delta in the Bay of Marajó in the very large state of Pará. This delta is a most impressive sight from the air, seemingly endless. The island Marajó, in the middle of the delta is nearly the size of Switzerland. The muddy plume that flows from the river reaches some one hundred miles out into the Atlantic. (Sometime later, flying over the Mississippi delta and its surrounding areas, which I once had thought were huge, I found myself muttering, "It's nothing.")

The first night of the meeting, a reception was held at the Museu Paraense Emilio Goeldi, where the Botanical Garden and Zoo of Amazonia were also located. We were staying in a hotel in downtown Belém, which had the look of an old, weary town ravished by the equatorial climate. We took a similarly weary-looking taxi to the museum, but en route two of its tires blew out, so it was necessary to walk the remaining distance. Since it was a formal occasion, we had worn our dress shoes. Unfortunately, our feet had swollen from the long plane trip and the very hot, humid weather in Belém and, after hobbling painfully along for a few blocks, Schultes declared we should take off our shoes and walk in our stocking feet. We thus arrived at the large, formal reception with our shoes in our hands because they would no longer fit on our feet. It seemed to me that the men did not stand out as much in their stocking feet as I did in my dirty nylon stockings amid the elegantly attired Brazilian women—but no one questioned why. Besides, Schultes, a large, imposing person, was garnering much attention as one of the still-living pioneer Amazonian botanical explorers. He gathered a crowd around him wherever we went.

During the reception I asked if any researcher at the museum used formaldehyde as a preservative, because I needed some to preserve floral parts of *Hymenaea* for chromosome analysis. (I could not bring such chemicals with me because they are forbidden on planes.) A researcher took me to a lab near to the reception area of the museum where we filled an empty wine bottle with formaldehyde. Following the reception, Schultes wanted to introduce me to a "club," built to somewhat imitate an Amazonian Indian hut similar to some he had lived in during his ethnobotanical studies in the rain forest. Inside the club, there was a bar at one end, and small tables situated around the other walls with a central area for dancing. I put my bottle of formaldehyde under the table where we were seated while we awaited our order of *capirinhas* (a potent drink of *cachaça*—Brazilian liquor made from sugar cane—and various fruit juices). By this time people were beginning to samba with vigor, and someone inadvertently knocked over the bottle of formaldehyde under our table and broke it. The relatively small hut immediately filled with formaldehyde fumes, which quickly emptied the building of coughing, choking people. We fled rapidly from the scene with Schultes laughing with gusto. Schultes declared that I now had been officially introduced to Amazonia, and this evening's episodes became well known in ethnobotanical circles as Schultes repeated the story gleefully (with some embellishments) at various gatherings. He had a well-developed sense of humor and always enjoyed a good story that would elicit lots of laughter.

Immediately following the conference, I obtained another bottle of formaldehyde and then had my first opportunity to collect Amazonian species of *Hymenaea* in the newly established Guamá Ecological Research Area (APEG) on the grounds of the Instituto de Pesquisas e Experimentaçao Agropecurias do Norte (IPEAN). The botanists were mapping and laboriously identifying all the trees in several hectare plots. Although I had seen rain forest on the Osa Peninsula in Costa Rica, my first experience in an Amazonian upland *terra firma* forest overwhelmed me. It not only created a stately impression, but where it was possible to look up through it, I could discern four strata of trees *plus* emergent trees (including *Hymenaea*) towering above the canopy. It became painfully clear how difficult it was going to be just to find *Hymenaea* trees, let alone collect from these emergents—and how dependent I would be on knowledgeable assistance! I had not felt so overwhelmed in the rain forests in Mexico or even on the Osa Peninsula in Costa Rica.

IPEAN researchers were comparing root adaptations, such as the huge buttress bases of tree trunks in upland *terra firma* forest contrasted with stilt roots in the flooded (*varzea*) areas. Here I saw my first *Hymenaea* species other than *H. courbaril* and collected different species occupying these differing habitats. I also saw my first Brazil nut tree (*Bertholettia*) and other members of the Lethcyidaceae, such as *Couroupita* with its cannonball fruits. These are representatives of the phenomenon of cauliflory, that is, flowers emerging from the thin bark of the trunk or large branches. The understory was amazingly open except for palms.

My continued contact with Schultes, who is known as the Father of Modern Ethnobotany, led to the merger of ecology and ethnobotany in my thinking. I had begun to consider more deeply the role of resin not only for the plant but also for humans. Having collected different Mexican resin-producing plants with their human uses in mind, I here became interested, despite my focus on *Hymenaea*, in the abundant burseraceous *Protium* and *Trattinickia* that were so heavily used by the Amazonian Indians for their resins. This combined thinking was useful when later I chaired US/Brazilian committees concerned with sustainable utilization of non-timber products such as resins. Recently I've seen several researchers refer to their work as "ethnoecology"—so others now are officially merging the two fields.

After this first bit of collecting at APEG, we flew to Manaus, which had faded from its past days of glory during the Amazonian rubber boom.

During that period the town had been resplendent with mansions built by the "rubber barons," and opera troupes from Europe had been brought up the river by steamer to perform at the elegant Teatro Amazonas. When we arrived in 1965, the airport had only one paved runway, used primarily by military planes, and a single iron-roofed building. Schultes introduced me to Instituto Nacional de Pesquisas da Amazonia (INPA) staff who would assist our research on *Hymenaea* in central Amazonia. INPA maintained the Ducke Reserve, where researchers could work, and it was here that Schultes left me with the two Harvard students, to collect *Hymenaea* species while he returned to Cambridge.

After successfully collecting several species of *Hymenaea* at the reserve and neighboring areas, the two students and I took a commercial Brazilian airline (VASP) flight back to Belém. Our plane had almost gotten to Santarém and the huge Tapanjóz tributary, when we heard a terrible thumping and one of the twin prop engines began to sputter and finally died. After a seemingly interminable time, the pilot announced that the plane had lost one of the engines and that it was necessary to land, but not to worry. I peered out the window and all I could see was either uninterrupted forest or vast areas of water! We flew for a while longer, until a group of huts appeared along the river. Behind them, a fairly long field was cut out of the forest. We circled and circled and finally came down in a spiral to land, bumping along over the field with the pilot managing to stop close to the forest edge. Apparently, small planes doing work in this part of Amazonia used this area when in need.

People from the village excitedly came running as about thirty passengers and airlines staff climbed out of the plane on a small, shaky ladder. I was alarmed when a passenger dressed in a suit (and looking very much like a businessman) accompanied the pilot to examine the plane's engine. I told my Harvard companions I had no intention of flying again in that plane if its engine was going to be repaired with rubber bands and paper clips, so to speak. I preferred to try some sort of boat transport! The pilot returned, saying that the "businessman" with him was a vacationing mechanic from VARIG airline, who reported that major repair was needed. We were not going anywhere in that plane at this time. He would radio, which was still working in the plane, for another plane to pick us up. The kind people in the village offered us food and lodging, probably with some enticement of money from the airline. The size of the plane and number of people it contained obviously was a big event in this village, and the children were especially excited.

*Two Harvard assistants, a Peace Corp worker and
me awaiting help for our plane*

I shared a room in one of the villager's huts with an American girl who had recently joined the Peace Corps. She had stopped in Manaus to see some of Amazonia en route to the area in central Brazil where she had been assigned. Our beds consisted of boards placed over stools made from cut tree trunks. These were put in a room with no windows and replete with buzzing insects. The first night, this girl started to recite in a wavering, frightened voice all of the dangerous Brazilian disease-bearing insects she had learned about in the Peace Corps manual. Sweltering in the heat, exhausted, and very uncomfortable on my boards, I finally shouted for her to be quiet. She broke into tears followed by almost nonstop whimpering. Despite feeling guilty about my harshness, I managed to doze off and sleep fitfully for several hours. I finally got up and sat in the doorway, where it was much cooler, until others began to arise.

While we were served a breakfast of much-needed strong coffee, flat bread made from manioc flour, and an unfamiliar native fruit whose family I couldn't even venture, the VASP pilot told us he had heard over the plane's radio that we would soon be rescued. Late that morning a plane circled several times but did not attempt to land. Most flights in the lowland tropics are in the morning, before the daily turbulent convectional storms that occur around noon or in the early afternoon. So we had another fitful night on the boards, but the next morning we heard the welcome sounds of a plane again. It was smaller than the previous day's, but it still made several attempts before managing to land. The airline had decided that trying to land another large plane was too risky and so had flown in a mechanic with some special equipment in a small plane.

Our plane was one of the old Douglas DC3s, built originally for American Airlines, which became World War II workhorses because they were amazingly adaptable to poor conditions. I thought we were lucky that these durable planes were still available. After working on the plane for some time, finally the mechanic assured the pilot and passengers that he had corrected the problem. We held our breath (and said a little prayer) at takeoff, hoping we would make it into the air with such a short runway. The pilot roared the engines, we literally bounced across the field, and took off at a steep angle toward the river. We scraped over the tops of the trees, picking up a long vine that trailed after us like an advertisement banner. We were in the air and on our way to Belém.

Mechanic repairing our plane

The Harvard students left me in Belém to return to Cambridge; my next destination was Rio de Janeiro, with a stop at the Federal University of Ceará in Forteleza. My most vivid memory of the visit there was a dinner in the home of one of the botany professors, where I observed the traditional role of at least some wives of Brazilian college professors. When I arrived, the wife was introduced but then disappeared until we were seated at the table. She was not doing the cooking because she had a cook and someone who served the meal. Although she did not speak English, the conversation at the table was mixed Portuguese and English. Nonetheless, she didn't say anything, and after the meal she disappeared again. On another trip, I had a similar experience in Campinas in São Paulo state, when several couples were present and after dinner the wives left me in the company of the men who were drinking *cafezinhos* and smoking. I felt very uncomfortable but possibly not as uncomfortable as the wives did with me, a *professora* who fit in better with the *professoros* than with them.

(In later years, however, I had the good fortune to meet in Rio and São Paulo several influential women botanists, thus learning that not all Brazilian women were so restricted as some wives I had encountered. I was the guest of a highly respected and beloved woman botanist, Doña Graziella Barrosa, at the Jardim Botanico do Rio de Janeiro. At the Instituto de Botanica in São Paulo, I met Professora Berta Lang de Morretes, Brazil's most distinguished plant anatomist. I had delightful visits with these two prominent women botanists, who were equally delighted to meet an American woman botanist doing fieldwork in Brazil.)

From Forteleza I went to Rio where I met with Luis de Mello Filho, director of the herbarium at the National Museum, whom I had gotten to know during the OTS program in Costa Rica. Luis was also a professor at the Federal University of Rio de Janeiro, because in those days, unless you were wealthy, it was necessary for an academic to hold two jobs to make ends meet. This situation was a holdover from the times when only the highly educated from wealthy families became professors. It was not until sometime later that most Latin American universities began to pay professors a living salary. Despite his busy schedule, Luis was extremely hospitable and helpful in planning my future study of *Hymenaea* in Brazil. He became one in my network of persistently enthusiastic supporters, and I continued to appreciate and utilize his extensive knowledge over the years. From Rio, I returned to Boston, feeling grateful for my introduction to doing research in Brazil.

A PERMANENT POSITION

During the 1965-66 academic year, I was being supported by a Marie Moors Cabot Fellowship, NSF research funds, and my work as a research associate in the botanical museum. Although support would probably continue to be available, it was time for me to begin to think about a permanent position. Paul Mangelsdorf, director of the museum, and Schultes (supported by Barghoorn) wanted me to become an employee of the museum, because of my research on amber and growing interest in ethnobotany. However, Ralph Wetmore thought that I should seek a professorial rather than a museum appointment. Because of the turmoil in the Harvard Biology Department being wrought by

Paul Mangelsdorf, Director of Harvard Botanical Museum (left) and Richard Schultes ready for commencement

molecularist James Watson over the future of "classical biology" (as he put it), Wetmore protectively did not want to see me relegated to Watson's "stamp collector status" in the botanical museum. He also saw how I enjoyed interacting with students and was convinced that I should be teaching as well as doing research.

Even during the mid-1960s, a logical place to look for an academic appointment where women would receive appropriate recognition, that is, not to be relegated to low-paying, subordinate positions, was a women's college, and there soon would be openings at both Wellesley and Mount Holyoke. I had enjoyed my part-time stints during the 1950s at Mills and San Francisco College for Women, and appreciated how well they often served women. Bob Enders, with whom I was associated at RMBL, also had mentioned a possible position at the fine liberal arts co-ed Swarthmore College. I had not been actively pursuing these jobs, however. Just like my coming to Harvard, I was hoping that the right position would appear on the scene at the right time, and, amazingly, it did.

Kenneth Thimann had decided to retire early from Harvard and take on the challenge of establishing the natural sciences on the new campus of the University of California at Santa Cruz (UCSC). He had shocked some of his Harvard colleagues in leaving the endowed Higgins Professorship to go to a new campus. In addition to being devoted to his world-renowned plant physiology research, Thimann was deeply interested in undergraduate education and enthusiastically accepted the challenge of helping to establish an innovative educational experiment at this new UC campus. He was particularly intrigued with the idea of residential colleges within the matrix of a research university because, as master of one of the Radcliffe/ Harvard Houses, he knew what a valuable experience they provided for undergraduates. Moreover, as an Englishman, he knew about the Oxford/ Cambridge approach, although he was a graduate of Imperial College of the University of London.

After attending meetings of the American Association for the Advancement of Science (AAAS) in December 1965 in San Francisco, I visited the Thimanns who were already in Santa Cruz. Ralph Wetmore had suggested to Thimann that he might want to consider me for one of the ecology positions at UCSC, knowing that Thimann was receptive to aiding women find positions appropriate to their qualifications. Thimann had three talented daughters, who he hoped would be able to find opportunities for expression of their talents—this is part of what had led him to play an advisory role for the Radcliffe Institute. Although he had known me through the institute and some research in his lab, he was unaware of my current interest in an academic teaching position. During my visit, Thimann encouraged me to apply for the plant ecology position at UCSC and invited me to meet the chancellor.

The idea of returning to central California, which I had previously grown to love, was very attractive to me. My visit on a clear day only heightened the idyllic beauty of the 2,000-acre campus on a hill overlooking Monterey Bay. Cattle were grazing in the lower meadow, and the new university's structures were being built near the beginning of a redwood forest fringed with oaks and madrone. I was almost overwhelmed with the prospects of becoming a faculty member there. What a marvelous place to live and teach ecology! I would also be close to friends at UC Berkeley and Stanford but would not be returning directly to the place that I had left with such sorrow. I was enticed by the pioneering experiment in university education as well. The founding chancellor, Dean McHenry, described it this way in the preface to the first UCSC catalog: "The Santa Cruz campus . . . will seek to organize teaching in such a way that advantages of the small college—particularly opportunity for discourse—are combined with those of a large university—great scholars, excellent libraries and laboratories, and a rich cultural life. We hope to overcome the too common separation of inquiry from teaching, of one discipline from others, of faculty from students."

I applied for the position and was accepted as an assistant professor—without tenure but at least "on the ladder." Later, Chancellor McHenry told me that not only the strong support of the Harvard biologists, but also that of the Radcliffe Institute was important in my acceptance for a tenure ladder position in UC as an "older woman." At that time only a few women faculty in the natural sciences, such as Katherine Esau and Mildred Mathias, were on the ladder throughout the UC system. Interestingly, Mildred also had started as an "older woman." In some sense, we both exemplified the findings of the Radcliffe survey—only achieving full professional recognition in midlife, once social conditions had opened up enough to permit us this success.

I had been so happy at Harvard that it was hard to think of leaving. On the bright side, however, I knew I would be able to maintain my broad and deep Harvard connections over the years. Furthermore, I would be returning to northern California, where I had so many friends that I also had found difficult to leave, and I was going to participate in an exciting educational experiment in the company of one of my Harvard mentors.

In addition to my position as a biology professor, I was appointed a fellow of Adlai E. Stevenson College and I accepted a faculty preceptorship, which meant I would be living in an apartment in one of the houses (a small dormitory) within the college. Since the buildings were still being finished, I did not have to arrive much before the opening of the term in late September. With ample time for my journey to California, I made plans to take the train that traversed Canada from Montreal to Vancouver.

I had decided to part with my faithful little VW bug because I could not think of driving it across the continent one more time. I sold it to some Harvard grad students and then watched, over the years, as that little bug was passed along to other Harvard students. I heard about it at scientific meetings for years—much like people staying in the chicken coop at RMBL. I bought a new VW station wagon that could carry my belongings to my new home and found a student to drive my new vehicle to San Francisco as a means of getting free transportation to California.

With my interest in trains, I had long wanted to take the transcontinental trip across Canada. Just as a transcontinental system of trains was considered vital to opening the western United States, so it was in Canada. The final rail linking the east with the west, was laid in British Columbia in 1885. Through the Rockies, it had been built in true wilderness, with land surveys taking place at the same time as construction of the tracks. Known as "Canadian Pacific," this railroad became synonymous with transportation in Canada because it also owned hotels and an airline, all of which were heavily advertised to tourists.

A friend from the Radcliffe Institute joined me for the trip. We boarded in Montreal, hoping we would make it across the country before a threatened railway strike, but this was not to be. We were well out into prairie country when the strike occurred, and passengers were put onto a series of buses that finally got us to Banff National Park, the oldest of Canada's parks. At least we were able to stay at the incredible, castle-like Banff Springs Hotel there. At last the strike was resolved and we were able to board the train again and enjoy the spectacular mountainous scenery from Banff to Vancouver. This magnificent glaciated area of striking sedimentary peaks, lakes, and glaciers reminded me of the deep interest in glaciation I had developed when studying with W.S. Cooper and glaciologist Robert Sharpe at the University of Minnesota. From Vancouver I flew to San Francisco to pick up my station wagon, and then headed for Santa Cruz to begin my long tenure at the University of California there.

RETURN TO CALIFORNIA—
UCSC RESIDENTIAL COLLEGES

1966-1976

We hope to overcome the too common separation of inquiry from teaching, of one discipline from others and faculty from students.
—Dean McHenry

The Harvard years had been a wonderful transition period that had led to my beginning a tenure-track professorial appointment at a major university. I was accepting the challenge in midlife (I had turned forty in early September). The low expectations for women professionals in the 1940s and 1950s had resulted in my being a "late bloomer" in the 1960s. Although it was a period of change in the recognition of women, as part of the newly ignited feminist movement, there were few women among the UC faculty in 1966. I was the only woman in the natural sciences faculty at UCSC for seven years, until a chemist and a marine scientist were hired in 1973. Because the UC system began in 1971 to allow exceptions to nepotism regulations, the chemist was the wife of another chemistry faculty member.

So just how different would the second half of my life be? I felt fortunate to be returning to Northern California—a place that I had been so sad to leave. My return was in part a testament to my resilience, and to my persistence in continuing to expand my professional horizons. Also, I had broad experience at small liberal arts colleges (as a student at TU, teaching at Coe, Mills, San Francisco College for Women, and Radcliffe), and at large research-oriented universities (as a graduate student at Minnesota, Research Associate at UC Berkeley and Illinois, and Research Fellow at Harvard). And, finally, I had a network of California colleagues from my stay in Berkeley throughout most of the 1950s. In essence, my previous experiences fitted me exceptionally well to accept the challenge of helping to implement the experiment of establishing undergraduate residential colleges within the context of the University of California. What I was not prepared for was how it would totally consume my life. I would literally become a workaholic, with life becoming almost entirely university-centered. The demands of this new campus also brought out my upbringing, in which I had been inculcated with a strong sense of altruism and the importance of duty in always trying to help out.

LIFE IN A RESIDENTIAL COLLEGE

There is an old Chinese saying—"May you live in interesting times." Starting a new and different campus was a heady, once in a lifetime venture. I certainly had landed in an interesting place to go along with the interesting times. During the 1960s students began to question the role of universities, such as UC, in their lives as well as in national and world affairs. Students developed a new political consciousness, resulting in a youthful rebellion that had an effect on universities across the nation. Although the Free Speech Movement at UC Berkeley in 1964 began as a political issue over rights of students to assemble on campus to discuss political and social action, this revolt soon escalated into a debate about the function of the university. Emphasis began to focus on the poor quality of education of undergraduate students, which many decried as being the result of faculty members giving priority to research rather than teaching. Students complained about indifferent faculty—as Mario Savio wrote, "we only meet the secretaries." The idea for the new UC campus at Santa Cruz was to mitigate lack of contact with faculty and institute an intimate intellectual community within a large research-oriented university by dividing the undergraduate population into a cluster of small residential colleges. All faculty College Fellows, except for the natural scientists, would have their offices in the colleges, and some faculty would live in college houses (small dorms).

I had been designated a fellow of the second college, which happened to have a social science emphasis—thus supporting an interest I had developed at TU, reignited during the Harvard years, and would continue here. As a founding fellow of Adlai E. Stevenson College, I jumped into the spirit of the endeavor with both feet, becoming one of the college's faculty preceptors. In that role I lived in one of the college's eight houses, with forty students. I ate most lunches and dinners with them in the dining commons. Someone had to be on hand in case of emergency, but a preceptor's primary role was to interact with undergraduate students. As a faculty member in the natural sciences, this arrangement also had practical benefits for me. Because our offices and labs were located in the natural sciences building, across the campus from the first colleges, living at Stevenson College gave me more contact with college activities and with the faculty in the social sciences and humanities, who had their offices in the college. From a personal and practical perspective, it saved money on rent and food, which I used later to buy a townhouse.

Stevenson College upper quadrangle (my first house in center)

It was clear upon my arrival at UCSC that this was going to be another pioneer adventure. The furniture for the preceptors' apartments had not arrived, and I couldn't retreat to my assigned biology office because a Cowell College economics professor still occupied it. The previous year, the first one for the campus, all faculty offices were in the Natural Sciences I building while Cowell College was being built. My research laboratory was completely empty except for benches and a few stools. I had to start from scratch and order everything. And, when I was finally able to move into my college apartment, I went from bare space to completely filled space. The bedroom was wall-to-wall mattress; the living room was so jammed with bulky furniture that I had to walk sideways to get through the room. We preceptors lived around it as best we could until more appropriate furniture had been delivered. We all were so occupied in this barn-raising experience that the many inconveniences were taken in stride and mostly with good humor.

I also considered living in Stevenson College a blessing because, as a single woman in a new location, it provided me with a family sense of belonging. There was never a question of being lonely, as many single faculty women have felt—even today with so few women in most departments in universities across the country. There were not only students (and their loud rock music!) always around me, but also my preceptor colleagues. One of them was the biologist with whom I taught ecology; he has been a postdoctoral fellow at Oxford University and already appreciated the residential college idea. Dinner conversations were seldom dull since the students were enthusiastic about their participation in this experiment and the preceptors were experts in different fields—anthropology, Russian literature, philosophy, and psychology among others. Topics might range from a Russian novel of particular interest to the latest evidence for the origin of humans. The diversity of expertise and interests, of course, was even greater among the faculty fellows of the entire college, who saw each other at the sherry hour for faculty before the monthly College Night dinner with students. For me, it continued the intellectual stimulation and personal pleasure I had enjoyed in knowing scholars from various disciplines at the Radcliffe Institute and living at the Cronkite Center at Harvard. On the other hand, living with undergraduate students in the 1960s provided a scenario different from any I had experienced before.

Stevenson Provost Willson

The first provost of Stevenson College was a gregarious free spirit, who helped create a vibrant sense of congeniality along with a spirit of shared responsibility to get the college established. When he left, an Englishman with Oxford credentials, F.M. Glenn Willson, succeeded him. Willson's previous post had been as dean of social sciences at University College of Rhodesia (now Zimbabwe). An important part of Willson's provostship was his and his wife's ability to build a real community of faculty and students around a friendly atmosphere and shared activities. The sense of community that we were all in this educational endeavor together was a hallmark of Stevenson College, and one that I will never forget.

In addition to the comradeship provided by my colleagues and students in the college, I would soon have feline companions as well, establishing a long, continuous line up to the present day. The first cat was a gorgeous long-haired male ginger tabby. He showed up at my apartment one day, appearing to be homeless though he was well socialized and extremely affectionate. He just settled in, not only with me, but with the girls in my house who loved him, and he adored all their attention. He often followed them to the Stevenson library and would cuddle up with them while they studied. Because of his affectionate ways, we named him Snuggles and he became a mascot of the house and, in fact, of the whole college.

Especially in these early years, wild animals were common on campus—deer, raccoons, coyotes, fox families, even an occasional cougar or bobcat. One of Snuggles' most alarming encounters was with a skunk that came into my apartment via his cat door. Fortunately, Snuggles let me know about the skunk's presence and we both retreated outside until it left peaceably. Snuggles disappeared one day, and everyone in the college as well as the campus police searched for several weeks. Newspaper notices, posted signs—nothing produced results. The girls were devastated by the loss of their special friend and mascot.

Snuggles, college mascot

Snuggles was not the only pet that became very much a part of the Stevenson College community. The Willsons had rescued a young German shepherd found on campus. Although restricted to the provost's house, Zelda became a friend of numerous frequent visitors there. Snuggles, the cat, and Zelda, the big dog, were beloved by so many Stevenson students and emblematic of the sense of family and community fostered by the Willsons.

THE TURBULENT SIXTIES

The period that I lived in Stevenson College (1966-1973) spanned a cultural revolution in which I had many interesting, exciting, and sometimes alarming interactions with students. For the students, this period included experimentation with hallucinatory drugs, use of the pill and attendant views regarding sex, the women's liberation movement, and revolt against authority and the establishment as well as against the Vietnam War. Of course, some of this change in young people's social consciousness was expressed in rock music, and its sounds were ever-present. These profound cultural events, so different from my own college years and upbringing, initially were difficult for me to absorb.

I was like many parents who felt themselves caught on one side of "the generation gap." Enjoying my interactions with the students and trying to understand their concerns kept me so busy that I was swept along with the milieu.

In 1966, the four houses in the upper quadrangle of Stevenson College were all female while the lower quad was all male, with hours of visitation strictly regulated, in keeping with the *in loco parentis* atmosphere standard in dormitories at most universities. The students, however, were intent upon overthrowing the idea of parental authority—demanding to be treated as adults. Within two years the houses in the quads were alternately male and female. Soon thereafter the houses became co-ed, with the floors within each house alternating between men and women. As Provost Willson so aptly summarized, the demands for change went from "unmixed quads to mixed quads, then from unmixed houses to mixed houses, then from mixed houses to mixed floors, and then the eventual demand, to mixed bathrooms." Furthermore, different sexes were allowed in the rooms most of the day, which went along with a developing philosophy that more normal contact between the sexes could lead to good friendships that didn't always have to involve sex. In dealing with the "intervisitation problem," as it had been dubbed, Chancellor McHenry had not been convinced that mixed floors (let alone bathrooms!) were desirable, so he spent a night in a room in a Stevenson house with men and women students on the same floor. I was one of the preceptors there that night. Even though McHenry was obviously very uncomfortable with the arrangement, he did not try to revoke it, which would have led to student revolt. I have often wondered just what he was thinking that night.

The increasingly common use of contraceptives, especially the pill, was leading to more casual sex. The impact it was having on the behavior of the women students was startlingly brought home to me when a delegation of girls in my house paid me a visit. They had wondered if I might enjoy the sexual freedom that the pill provided. They questioned me as to whether I had held back in asking for a prescription for the pill. (Apparently, at this time, some doctors hesitated to prescribe it.) If so, they would be happy to supply me, as they were encouraged to get the pills from the Health Service. As I managed to overcome my astonishment, I thanked them for their concern and generosity, but stated that I hadn't met anyone with whom I was seriously involved, so did not need them at this time. But they proclaimed that this was the beauty of the pill, that you would be protected from pregnancy while enjoying sex. They were polite when I explained that I had been brought up with the idea that you saved sexual intercourse for a special relationship. They undoubtedly thought me to be hopelessly old-fashioned and that I was missing out on some of life's pleasures. Such major changes in mores, or even morals, seemed to have occurred so quickly, once freedom from fear of pregnancy was provided! I found myself thinking back to the 1950s and the panel discussion on birth control at San Francisco College for Women. I wondered how Catholic girls were adjusting to this very real sexual revolution for women. I hoped (and assumed) that the girls in my house were more circumspect than their discussions of casual sex suggested.

Certainly some parents did not accept what they considered such promiscuous behavior. This was strikingly so for parents from some cultures. A Chinese-American girl in my house did become pregnant, creating a very difficult situation for her and her family. Her case was perhaps a bit unusual, in that she had not been allowed to have sex education and did not even realize that she was pregnant until she was months along. Wearing baggy clothes, she was able to hide the pregnancy right up to the end. I did not know about it until I received a telephone call at 2:00 A.M. asking me to take her to the hospital. She was in labor en route but we managed to get to the hospital, where they took over immediately. By the time I had parked the car and taken care of her paperwork the baby had arrived! The hospital contacted her parents in Sacramento, who forbid her to see the baby because they had already put it up for adoption to a Korean couple. They especially did not want her to see the child because the non-Chinese father had offered to marry their daughter. Carlos Noreno, Senior Preceptor in Stevenson College, and I were the only persons other than her parents allowed to see her. (Preceptors often relied on the advice of Carlos in difficult situations, such as this one.) The parents emphatically proclaimed that she was a ruined girl now and probably would never be able to marry a respectable Chinese boy. It was a tragically emotional time for the girl, and I spent as much time at the hospital with her as I could u'ntil her parents came and took her home. She dropped out of UCSC but I later heard that she enrolled at UC Davis the next year. I have wondered about her life in this world of changed norms and whether she continued to abide by her family's traditional Chinese views.

With Carlos Noreno in more pleasant situation than that of the Chinese student

In 1968, with so much turmoil concerning race following the assassination of Martin Luther King, Jr., many students wanted to join in protest marches. This terrible event had been preceded by riots across the United States, but the one in Watts (1965) got etched into the minds of Californians. I had grown up in racially segregated Tulsa, and I had lived with a difference in opinion between my northern mother and southern father over race—he favored segregation. I followed the battles against segregation, the bus boycotts of the mid-1950s and, of course, King's famous "I have a dream" speech in Washington, DC in 1963. If I had not been at a critical transition in my own life, I probably would have joined these protestors in Washington. In 1966, I still had never participated in a protest, but I sympathized with the students' desire to express their ire, and I shared their hope that group insistence would initiate change.

It was also the peak period of the anti-Vietnam War demonstrations, and associated anti-draft attitudes among students. Anti-war demonstrations were another stark contrast with my college years during World War II. Everyone I knew in college in 1943-1945 completely supported World War II and worked diligently to contribute to this fight for the survival of democracy and freedom against Hitler's fascist expansion. When we entered the war in 1942 there was no guarantee whatever that the Nazi war machine could even be stopped in Europe, and we had to contend with the "infamy" of Japanese bombing ships in our own Pearl Harbor. Practically every family had some male in the armed forces, which ultimately included sixteen million people, and the war's terrible death toll was counted in the millions. Women who had been stay-at-home moms went into factories to produce materials to support the war.

On the other hand, after the war in 1945, most people, including students, did not want another war like the one we had just been through. For example, an impetus for the leadership conference of college student body presidents I helped organize at TU was to train leaders who could help to maintain peace. In 1945, I was also president of the TU Forum, in which a fearful concern for the future was reflected in such topics as "Is Civilization Doomed?" Thus, maybe having endured but supported a terrible, long war, I had been prepared to support the 1960s peace movement. Even though I had witnessed unsettling aspects of communism during the Cold War era in my European travels, I could not condone the Vietnam War. I participated in numerous teach-ins and dinnertime discussions with UCSC students, but was troubled by the treatment of those who had patriotically served their country during this war. Living in the college and participating in so many discussions with the students probably forced me to think through these issues even more.

Along with students' desire to be treated as adults personally, they also wanted to break down authoritarianism within the university. The students not only wanted more contact but also wanted greater familiarity with faculty. They no longer wanted to refer to us as "Doctor" or "Professor," but by our first names. I felt this denied recognition of the depth of knowledge and often extensive experience of their professors—something that was completely alien to my background of admiring educational mentors with whom I had felt privileged to show respect. Furthermore, deference to elders was deeply ingrained in me by a father from the South. I had been taught that good manners demanded that I refer to all adult women as "ma'am" and men as "sir." I referred to our neighbors of many years in Tulsa as Mrs. and Mr.—never by their first names. I no longer was chained to these restrictive customs, but it took some adaptation on my part to accept the students' attitudes and what in some cases seemed to be an absence of manners.

Another difference to which I had to adjust was a personal revolt shown in purposeful sloppiness in dress. Dresses for the girls were relegated to the back of the closet. New jeans were made as ragged as possible with knees exposed through cuts. Tops were generally oversized T-shirts. I had arrived with suits and dresses I thought appropriate for a college professor but was soon asked when I was going to wear pants in the classroom. I gradually adapted to wearing pant suits for teaching but still reserved jeans for field trips. Men were frequently wearing their hair in ponytails and the girls' hair was often unkempt. Again, how different from my previous collegiate experiences!

COLLEGE COURSES
In addition to the proximity that living and office arrangements provided, college courses were conducted in a way that also gave students more access to faculty. These courses were restricted to around fifteen students, with the expectation that students would actively contribute to discussions and develop their skills in critical thinking. I enthusiastically taught three Stevenson College sophomores seminar courses. Starting in 1968, I gave a lecture/discussion course on Natural History and Conservation, addressing environmental concerns, which were becoming prominent issues. One of my big coups was to bring Ansel Adams, the great landscape photographer and ardent conservationist, whom I had met while he was photographing the campus, to speak. He discussed the magnificence of all of our national parks, and brought many of his Yosemite photographs to show the students. He also waxed eloquent about the environmental splendors of the UCSC campus and the importance of the students' appreciating their privilege to be there. Adams became so interested in talking with the students about such topics that at my suggestion he was made an Honorary Fellow of Stevenson College. He enthusiastically attended various college functions for a number of years.

Having discovered my great enjoyment in teaching during the Berkeley years, I relished the opportunities provided by these small college courses. Also, I was convinced from field courses I had taught at RMBL, that the informal atmosphere of learning in the field and the relationships students and faculty shared there often inspired life-long environmental interests. Therefore, I gave two courses—Ecology of Redwoods and Agriculture and Ecology in which students committed a number of their weekends to either camping out in different redwood state parks or staying at UC agricultural experiment stations.

In the redwoods course the students learned about the basic ecology of the redwood forest as well as considering how to manage these forests in parks for the public's enjoyment. We spent the most time in nearby Big Basin, California's first state park. In addition to our field projects in the parks, I invited members of the local family that owned a lumber company to talk to our students one evening in the college. They had been pioneers in timbering redwood, having homesteaded in the Santa Cruz area in 1860. Several generations of the family came, and discussed how redwood lumber from the Santa Cruz area had helped rebuild San Francisco following the 1906 earthquake, and how loggers at that time were considered heroes. They gave the students an historical perspective in pointing out the change in attitude toward timbering operations over the years and how their company was now directed toward balancing conservation and sustainable harvesting of redwoods.

In the agriculture course, students were exposed to the way the university actively addressed issues to improve environmental concerns in conventional agriculture, such as wasteful irrigation techniques, overuse use of fertilizer and pesticides, among others. We spent several weekends at the Kearney Horticultural Field Station in the San Joaquin Valley. Kearney lies at the heart of one of the most productive and diverse agricultural regions in the world, but where numerous environmental challenges were evident. With organic food being provided in the college cafeteria, the students wondered about expanded development of organic agriculture in California and if any UC research was being directed toward this goal. (Agroecology was not established on our campus until 1980).

The students became increasingly inquisitive and forthright in their questions and discussions in both of these courses—showing what they were thinking in some depth about the issues—which was just what we had hoped to achieve from close interactions. They wrote extensive reports in which they reflected on what they had learned. These courses had not only encouraged active discussion of important issues among the students and myself, but expanded *my* thinking, especially as I began teaching a class called Plants and Human Affairs in the Biology Board of Studies.

Four years later, I cosponsored a more sophisticated and expensive interdisciplinary college course, International Interactions in Science and Technology. The design of the course made it expensive, and it was only made possible by funding from the Sloan Foundation. It was offered at Merrill College because of that college's international focus, which included a Science and Society program. The idea for this course had come to George Hammond, dean of natural sciences, who, as the foreign secretary of the US National Academy, had realized how often science attachés were ill-prepared for their jobs. These special appointees by an ambassador often either had little foreign cultural background or little knowledge about science and technology. Merrill College was an excellent site to address the needs for potential foreign service employees as well as for others doing work in foreign countries. Furthermore, the colleges were a place within the university where cross-disciplinary courses were emphasized. Hammond asked me to cosponsor this course with him because we had discussed my interests in the culture and politics of the Latin American countries in which I was currently doing my scientific research. Furthermore, I was a member of the UC Standing Committee on Latin American Ecology, and had served on an American International Development (AID) committee regarding contributions of individual scientists to developing countries. Both of these groups were concerned about understanding the culture of such countries while doing scientific studies in them.

Within the broad scope of the International Interactions in Science and Technology course, which ran from 1976 to 1978, various smaller topics were chosen in each of the three years. The twenty students in the course came from a variety of majors such as international relations, economics, politics, Latin American studies, literature, history of science, and social ethics as well as biology and chemistry. Because of the generous funding from the Sloan Foundation, during the first two years the course consisted of seminars led by visiting authorities, who also gave public lectures. Each lived in a Merrill College apartment from four to five days, and was hosted by the students for meals and other events during which time they could continue discussions informally outside the classroom environment. We were pleased with the interest and willingness of many distinguished experts to devote so much time to our courses. They strongly supported our ideas regarding the values of this kind of education. Visiting authorities came from, among other places, Yale, Harvard, the Smithsonian Institution, Cal Tech, University of Illinois, and NASA as well as foreign countries such as Venezuela and Yugoslavia. Their public lectures frequently drew a standing-room-only audience in a large hall.

George Hammond and me standing behind visiting
Yale professor, Derek de Solla Price, amid some students in our college course

The topics for each year varied from interactions between developed and developing countries—with an emphasis on agriculture and industrialization—to interactions across cultural and political boundaries, especially between the United States and communist countries. The class discussions with our visitors further convinced me of the importance I had always placed on some understanding of the culture as well as political and related economic situations of the countries in which I and my students were doing scientific research. Moreover, the public lectures provided me an opportunity to emphasize to others my strong feelings about the need for such understanding.

UNIVERSITY SERVICE

Most universities impose a triad of responsibilities—teaching, research, and service—on their faculty and judge a faculty member on all three when considering promotions. I had been exempted from such service in my previous, part-time appointments at various institutions, but requests for service hit hard once I had a full-time professorial position at UCSC—for two obvious reasons. First, UCSC was a new campus with much to be accomplished and a limited number of faculty. Second, it was the time when the women's movement was opening consciousness to the lack of women in decision-making positions, and some organizations were beginning to require a woman member on committees and boards. Hence, for a number of years I was a "token woman" or the only qualified woman available, on numerous committees and boards on campus and within the UC system.

For Stevenson College, I served in multiple capacities. In addition to the major time commitment of being a faculty preceptor, I was asked to be a member of the heavy-duty personnel policies and the curriculum committees, as well as being the environmental studies advisor for the college. Chancellor McHenry was strongly committed to preservation of the natural beauty of the campus, and as the plant ecologist on campus I was asked to participate in its stewardship and to serve on a committee to establish the arboretum as well as the UCSC committee of the UC Natural Land and Water Reserves System—later known as the Natural Reserve System (NRS).

During these early days at UCSC everyone attended Academic Senate meetings, where faculty decisions regarding the development of the campus were hashed out (on most UC campuses, senate attendance tended to be dominated by senior faculty of long-standing experience). The role of the faculty in determining much campus policy through shared governance is zealously held in the University of California and executed through various senate committees with results being transmitted to the university administration. These meetings were extremely important, especially concerning the role of the residential colleges and the controversial evaluation grading system, in the early years of the UCSC campus and were characterized by many long sessions and spirited discussions. Overall, I found these senate meetings to be fascinating academic experiences involving a range of opinions from faculty across many fields of learning.

Although I loyally served on many Senate committees over the years, later I was appalled to learn, as an elected member of the senate's Committee on Committees, that some faculty members had never served on a senate committee. I realized that only a concerned group, often duty-driven like myself, had carried these important jobs to maintain hard-won faculty input to the administration. The persistence of my hard work resulted in part from the continual goad that women must make a good showing, not just for ourselves but for the sake of women who would follow us.

BOARDS OF STUDIES AND
GRADUATE PROGRAM
1966-1993

Publicity about educational "reform" on the UCSC campus had focused on the residential colleges, but all faculty had joint appointments in a college and a board of studies (the British name used for a group of disciplinary studies). The "board of studies" terminology was emblematic of Chancellor McHenry's crusade against discipline-dominated undergraduate education. He wanted to avoid the rigidity of traditional departments in crossing boundaries between them, and to encourage innovative approaches for undergraduate teaching of disciplinary subjects in the boards of studies. Because the graduate program did not become established for several years, faculty was expected to teach in five undergraduate courses a year, spread between the college and board of studies. For the biology board, I taught a lecture course in plant ecology, shared a field/laboratory ecology course with an animal ecologist, and also shared teaching general botany.

ECOLOGY COURSES
Because my thoughts had been primarily directed toward paleobotany while at Harvard, I had to catch up with rapidly changing perspectives in ecology. While at UC Berkeley I had been influenced by Herbert Mason's reductionist view of putting the individual plant and its selection by the environment at the center of importance, not only for thinking about its physiological tolerances but also as the basis of understanding the genetics of populations and the structure and dynamics of communities. I also had become imbued with the modern evolutionary synthesis expressed by the Biosystematists. This dual approach had been very well received by a stellar group of students in my RMBL course in 1962. At UCSC we not only had an exceptional group of students, who had been attracted to this new campus' innovative approaches, but its location allowed me to use many of the California examples to which I had previously been introduced. A new trend was developing in ecology during the mid-to late-1960s, however, that emphasized the ecosystem and system ecology concepts. Eugene Odum's

textbook *Fundamentals of Ecology*, in which the ecosystem concept was espoused, was being widely adopted. In addition, Odum predicted that the period approximately from 1968 to 1978 would be the era of emerging systems ecology. Some ecologists, however, were confused about the implied merging of ecosystem and systems ecology. The study of the structure and function of ecosystems, which involved understanding the connection of all organisms with their environment through energy flow and nutrient cycling, had been around for a long time. Systems ecology, on the other hand, was introducing new terms, techniques, types of training, and, most crucially, a new philosophy. Ecologists, such as Odum, were indicating that attributes of ecosystems demanded knowledge of physics, chemistry, among other disciplines, which required skills in instrumentation and computation that had become available in the post-war years. One of the hallmarks of systems ecology was the use of mathematical models. Most difficult for many ecologists to accept was the attitude of systems ecologists toward natural history-oriented studies, which, according to an historian of ecology, Robert McIntosh, they "equated with lack of rigor, intellectual softness and low status." They described systems ecology as an attempt to convert "soft" science into "hard" science.

Neither my marine mammal ecologist colleague nor I were interested in directly pursuing either ecosystem or systems approaches, although we would apprise students of these ideas. We preferred not to use the popular new textbooks but to go directly to research papers and focus on studies of some of the rich plant and animal diversity in the Santa Cruz area. On the campus alone, we had two thousand acres of varied vegetation, ranging from redwood forest through chaparral to grassy meadows with their associated animals, as well as Monterey Bay and its marine habitats, to study. In an innovative spirit for biology courses, we established a unique lecture/laboratory program in which I taught a lecture course in plant ecology and my colleague taught one in animal ecology. Then a selected group of students took a field/laboratory course we taught jointly. This arrangement allowed us to take long, several-day trips around California from high mountains to desert and various coastline sites and thereby to further the students' ecological experience and perspectives, including their understanding of human disturbance and the need for research to support preservation of this beauty and diversity. We bridled at the suggestion that our unabashedly scientific natural history studies, which included experimentation and quantification, lacked rigor. Our ideas were close to those of an emerging group of population ecologists interested in biodiversity and integrating evolutionary theory into ecology, who would later counterbalance the ecosystem ecologists. (Interestingly, recent increasing concern over how loss of species diversity, and ensuing changes in species composition will alter ecosystem properties and functions, has now led to an effort to find operational ways to integrate the dichotomous approaches of individualistic evolutionary and ecosystem ecology).

The three-course approach offered opportunity and time enough for thoughtful independent research projects, which a number of students expanded into senior theses. Some of these theses were of sufficiently high quality, incorporating both field and laboratory experiments, to be published in respected journals. Moreover, this research experience convinced some students to proceed to graduate studies. I continue to hear from students who took this sequence of courses; they enthusiastically report what an influence it had on their thinking and future careers.

I taught in this ecology sequence for six years with three teaching partners. One was a temporary appointment, but the death of one and the departure of another resulted in some troubling times. With the departure of the third animal ecologist, I took on his two graduate students, who were well along with their doctoral research on the ecology of bees. One of them was the wife of one of *my* graduate students! Under my sponsorship, Pat Lincoln and Jack Neff completed their dissertations on different aspects of bee phylogeny in a group of honeybees in one case, and on the community ecology of solitary bees in the other.

In recruiting another ecologist, the Biology Board of Studies—I was chair at this time (1974)—thought we had made a breakthrough for women. We hired a husband (marine ecologist) and wife (plant/herbivore specialist) who split the appointment. They each were given offices and labs, and they planned to obtain research grants that would pay the other half of their salaries. (Even more progress has been made since the early 1990s by allowing units to make full appointments for couples where there are appropriate openings for both their expertises.)

The development of molecular biology, and its concomitant recognition of molecular commonality, was leading to the breakdown in divisions between the study of plants and animals, and our new plant/herbivore specialist wanted to replace plant and animal ecology courses with ones in population and community ecology. I was a bit sad to see the demise of the special research emphasis and depth that the three-quarter set of courses provided, but I accepted this change. Later a similar idea (called Field Quarter) was taken up in the Environmental Studies Board of Studies.

NEW APPROACH TO TEACHING GENERAL BOTANY

I felt comfortable teaching a traditional General Botany course, as I had been a botany teaching assistant in Minnesota, had given botany lectures at Mills College, and had supervised the graduate student assistants for botany labs at Illinois. On the other hand, this traditional course, which I was coteaching in 1967, was not stimulating students' interests in plants at a time when relevance was deemed so important.

Kenneth Thimann could not imagine anyone lacking interest in plants, but he nonetheless gave thought of how to captivate the current students. He remembered a very successful course at Harvard, called Plants and Human Affairs, which had focused on the role of plants in peoples' lives, and he suggested that he and I join forces to design such a course for UCSC students.

Working with Thimann provided me an opportunity to become better acquainted with this distinguished plant physiologist. At Harvard, Thimann had invited me to use his lab for some of my research, but I did not get to know him well at that time. He was recognized worldwide for his chemical isolation of the first known plant hormone, indole-3-acetic acid (called auxin). His further discovery, that synthetic auxins with the same properties as the natural hormone could be made by substituting other chemical structures for the indole, opened the door to practical applications around the world. Likewise, his later discovery (with Frits Went) that auxin can induce plants to grow roots meant it could be used to promote plant cuttings. Having learned that it could inhibit growth as well as promote it, agriculturalists found that spraying auxin on fruit prevented it from falling before it was ready to be harvested. The importance of Thimann's contributions to plant physiological research led the Italian government in 1983 to give him the Balzan Prize, considered the equivalent of the Nobel Prize for a biological field other than medicine. The widespread agricultural use of his plant physiological research helped promote his interest in teaching plants and human affairs and fostered our approach of relating the history of the development of basic plant science with that of its utilization.

In 1971, Thimann and I began to coteach this upper division general botany course, built upon the introduction to plants given in general biology and requiring a chemistry background as well. Although we pirated the name "Plants and Human Affairs," the content of our course differed from that of Harvard's as well as from the Economic Botany and Plants and Civilization courses at other universities. We put plants and humans into context through presenting the long history of plant evolution, the much shorter history of plants' interrelationship with humans, and the very short history of plant science. We presented a more in-depth and integrated background of taxonomy, anatomy, physiology, genetics, and ecology as prerequisite to understanding how native plants influence human lives as well as how humans have modified plants and vegetation for their own use. In this kind of integration we had developed a new kind of General Botany course.

It was a privilege to teach with Thimann, as he was not just a preeminent plant physiologist but genuinely enjoyed teaching undergraduate students about plants. He was a man of culture, typifying the image of a scholar and gentleman. A superb lecturer (formal in style which might be expected from an urbane Englishman), he commanded respect (no calling him "Kenneth"). On the other hand, he loved to share his great depth of knowledge in discussions with students to whom he gave generously of his time, despite his ever-frenetic administrative, research, and travel schedule.

We often had the front of the lecture room filled with plants, plus we used many slides from both Thimann's and my world travels. We continually increased our slide collections by making special side trips during our travels just to photograph ethnobotanical material that we thought would enlighten our students in some way. We were convinced that our own photos had more appeal as they usually came with some illuminating story, and students constantly expressed their appreciation of our illustrative material. Both Thimann and I attended all-day Saturday field trips with the class to hear about such topics as selective cutting of redwood with a local lumber company and, with the aid of UC Extension, comparison of organic farming with large, conventional Salinas Valley crops of strawberries, carrots, and broccoli. My previous college courses in Redwood Ecology as well as Agriculture and Ecology had provided important contacts and background for these field trips. The quite different approaches to teaching in the college and the disciplinary board of studies were melding together in an unexpectedly useful way.

Thimann and I wrote a note for the *Plant Science Bulletin* of the Botanical Society of America about introducing students to plants through their relations to humans, and as word spread about the student interest in our course, publishers began courting us to write a textbook. We finally gave in, selected John Wiley as a publisher and started to transform our lecture notes into chapters. This was a bit ironic for me as I had refused to use a text in most of my previous teaching.

Plants and Human Affairs class field trip to see conventional
Salinas Valley agriculture; Thimann, center, in white coat

ENVIRONMENTAL STUDIES BOARD OF STUDIES

Starting in 1970 I was a member not only of the Board of Studies in Biology, but also of Environmental Studies. The chancellor's avid interest in providing opportunities for interdisciplinary cooperation was made explicit in the formation of the Environmental Studies Board of Studies. The formation of this new board resulted from activities surrounding Earth Day during the spring of 1970, just one of the many groups that were an outgrowth of Senator Gaylord Nelson's inspiration for this worldwide event.

Chancellor McHenry was greatly concerned about environmental protection and had hired Stanley Cain, a prominent ecologist who had been the first president of The Nature Conservancy and an assistant secretary at the Department of the Interior, to help plan the development of the campus in an environmentally sensitive manner. As a political scientist, however, the chancellor was convinced that environmental problems would only be solved through societal action, so the Environmental Studies Board of Studies was put in the Division of Social Sciences, and in the beginning natural scientists such as biologists, geologists, and chemists, were "borrowed" from their respective boards of studies. Full dual memberships in two boards lasted only for a short time because faculty became overwhelmed with the extra load (in addition to duties in their colleges and the graduate programs that had begun to develop). I continued, however, to serve on board recruitment committees, especially for the hiring of two agroecologists, Steve Gliessman and Deborah Letourneau, in the early 1980s, and later cosponsored graduate students with them. I have maintained close relationships with environmental studies colleagues and students throughout my career at UCSC. Over the years the faculty has become even more balanced between the natural and social sciences, training students to recognize that, along with dealing with the social issues involved in implementing environmental solutions, many problems in the domain of the natural sciences are yet to be resolved. From the beginning, majors in environmental studies were considered interdisciplinary.

BEGINNINGS OF THE UCSC GRADUATE PROGRAM
While McHenry labored to break down walls between the disciplines, Thimann was anxious to get the campus graduate program off to a good start. Graduate studies were a rare source of tension between Thimann and McHenry. Although the 1965 UCSC plan had stressed the importance of undergraduate education, it also indicated that "the graduate function was of equal importance in the final development of the campus." McHenry, however, did not want attention to be directed away from undergraduate education in the colleges too soon. On the other hand, Thimann knew that graduate students were essential in attracting talented scientists to UCSC—graduate student assistance would be necessary for the young faculty to establish active research programs. This meant that graduate education in the boards of studies had to be fostered along with their undergraduate disciplinary courses as well as the special undergraduate education in the colleges. Although Thimann wanted to incorporate graduate students into the life of the colleges, McHenry adamantly rejected it.

As Dean of the Division of Natural Sciences, Thimann asked me to assist with establishing the graduate programs by being a member of several UC system graduate committees, including the Standing Committee on New Graduate Programs, which I served on from 1967 through 1971. Once the UCSC program had begun, I chaired the Graduate Council in 1969 and remained a member for four years. I also represented the campus on a special committee at the All-University Conference on Graduate Affairs in 1970.

Although a few faculty members had brought graduate students with them from their previous universities, the UCSC graduate program did not officially begin until 1968. The arrival of four graduate students and a postdoctoral fellow in my lab during the program's first year was the beginning of a new research era for me. The first UCSC graduate commencement was in 1969.

Congratulating graduate students in first UCSC commencement, 1969, in my role as Chair of Graduate Council; Chancellor McHenry to left, handing out degrees

Thimann had continued his Harvard tradition of creating a means for botanically-oriented faculty and graduate students to congregate. This began in 1966. Every Thursday afternoon he invited the plant faculty and a few graduate students they had brought with them from their previous institutions to come to his office for tea and to discuss plant research. As the number of UCSC botanists grew, a larger venue than his office was needed, but the meeting always included tea, a habit maintained by this staunch Englishman. This weekly meeting of the botanists soon became known as the "Botany Tea," and the learning and fellowship we shared have remained fond memories for most of the graduate students, postdoctoral fellows, and faculty who participated. We trouped as a group to some seminars at Stanford, including those at the Carnegie Institution of Washington (CIW), which were wonderful in combining experimental aspects of plant physiology in the lab with field studies of ecological importance. Spring field trips were also a unifying activity for the growing number of graduate students and faculty studying plants.

Trips to Death Valley to see the spectacular spring flora had been a long-standing tradition among botanists at California colleges and universities. Kenneth Thimann and Frits Went had gone on such trips when they were working together on auxins at Cal Tech in the 1930s. I also had made such jaunts from UC Berkeley in the 1950s and Thimann suggested that I arrange similar trips for the Botany Tea group. We planned to not only enjoy the beauty of the floral displays but also do some rudimentary experiments, which would provide a learning experience as how plants adapt to severe desert conditions. Thus Thimann asked Went to bring his mobile laboratory from the University of Nevada Desert Institute where he was then working. Went did experiments in this mobile laboratory in desert areas such as Death Valley and the Mojave Desert, where we would be going. He was not only an authority on the physiology and ecology of desert plants, but also a pioneer in the concept of a multivariant environmental laboratory, the Climatron, at the Missouri Botanical Garden. His ever-innovative approaches were designed to provide better opportunities to simulate natural conditions in physiological experiments with plants.

Our Botany Tea group's desert trip took place for a week during spring break, two years in a row. In 1969, graduate and a few undergraduate senior thesis students went on the trip. We emphasized assessing the germination and survival of low-growing annuals, known as "belly plants," and the importance of fungi such as mycorrhiza to various desert plants in adapting to the harsh desert conditions. We discussed various factors (including allelopathy—when chemicals from the plant inhibit its own seedlings) that limit the distribution of the creosote bush, *Larrea tridentata*, which dominates the landscape in Death Valley. The next year, it was graduate students, postdoctoral fellows and visiting professors from Germany and South Africa who went on the trip. The Germans were particularly excited because it was their first time in a desert. We intensified observations of fungi in the soil, and their connections between living root systems and decaying organic material—important to mineral cycling under such dry conditions. Some of the biochemists also dug out roots to great depths to observe how characteristic shrubs such as salt bush (*Atriplex*) obtained water. Among experiments we carried out in the mobile laboratory were measurements of relative transpiration rates and water tension of some of these shrubs.

Doing experiments using Went's mobile laboratory;
Thimann on far right

The bonding that took place sitting around the campfire at night, and the sheer fun of examining these biological questions together in the field provided some of the most memorable aspects of these desert trips. What a sight, to see two of the world's most distinguished plant physiologists, Thimann and Went, flat on the ground counting belly plant seedlings, and to watch usually lab-bound biochemists digging out the deep roots of desert shrubs.

Because of the revision of the undergraduate ecology courses, my biology teaching, except for the Plants and Human Affairs course, shifted to graduate courses after 1974. In one of these, Experimental Ecology, I alternated yearly between topics in chemical and tropical ecology (although twice I covered the history of concepts in ecology). In many ways it was a fortunate shift in emphasis at this time in my career, as I had a burgeoning number of graduate students and was increasingly involved in national and international activities. Intertwining my major graduate courses with my research resulted in a seamless nourishing of both of them.

My other graduate course was Topics in Advanced Plant Sciences, which had grown out of the weekly Botany Tea meetings. At the Botany Teas, which usually consisted of twenty-five to thirty participants, talks were given by both visitors and our own students and faculty for two terms, while

Dinner with Went around campfire

in the third term I was in charge of the Advanced Topics seminar. Because the students and faculty ranged in background from plant biochemistry, physiology, and development to ecology, we took a multifaceted approach to topics, tackling subjects as diverse as symbiosis and model systems as tools in biology. Often the lively discussions from various, sometimes conflicting, viewpoints led to unexpectedly enlightening experiences. The course provided an intrabotanical perspective that wrapped together research and educational components.

RESEARCH IN AFRICA

1968

I want to do it because I want to do it.
Women must try to do things as men have tried.
When they fail, their failure must be a challenge to others.
—Amelia Earhart

I had spent from 1966 to 1968 helping to establish UCSC, including the founding of Stevenson College, and teaching new courses in the college and the Biology Board of Studies. I had published some of the last results of my research at Harvard and was advanced to tenure as an associate professor in the spring of 1968. I also had managed, in rare spare time during these frenetically occupied two years, to set up my research lab. I had never been in a place where it was necessary to start from scratch—not a single test tube, rubber band, nothing! During this time, my animal ecologist colleague and I had shared a lab, but with our own graduate students due to arrive that fall we each would then expand into full labs.

CHEMICAL AND TROPICAL ECOLOGY

I had been invited to participate in one of the US ecological projects, which were just beginning in 1968 as part of the International Biology Program (IBP). Some ecologists thought that participation in IBP, referred to as "big biology," was the single most important event for the US ecology in thirty years because it lifted the field to greater recognition. The idea was for teams of ecologists to work together on large-scale integrated ecosystem analyses. I had been encouraged by Hal Mooney at Stanford to join a group comparing California desert biomes with those in Argentina. I declined this opportunity, despite the unprecedented funding from the National Science Foundation. I had had enough of adapting my research to other peoples' projects. Now was the time for me to proceed with research of my own conception in the emerging subdisciplines of chemical and tropical ecology, as Barghoorn had encouraged me to do at Harvard. I did, however, participate in an important IBP meeting in Santa Barbara on "Chemical Interactions in Plants and Animals." In many ways, I was glad later that

I hadn't joined a biome project in IBP, which ended in 1974. Although valuable information was accumulated, studying the totality of ecosystems proved to be unworkable. Because the involved scientists could not agree on a central set of hypotheses to test, the myriad of biome projects ultimately lacked the intended integration.

Chemical ecology, which I wanted to pursue in order to understand the ecology and evolution of amber-producing plants, was just becoming recognized as a field of study. Although the roots of chemical ecology go back to the work of Theophrastus in the fourth century BC, it did not develop into a field of inquiry until the 1960s, when an explosion of interest in possible roles that plant chemicals might play paralleled the rebirth of an evolutionary (Neodarwinian) perspective.

G. S. Fraenkel's 1959 paper, "The raison d'etre of Secondary Substances," was the first to articulate clearly the idea that plant secondary chemicals evolved as defense against insect herbivores, and thus insects were important selective agents of plants. Prior to this paper, secondary chemicals—so-called because they do not contribute to a plant's primary metabolic processes—were essentially ignored by ecologists and evolutionary biologists, and simply considered waste products by many chemists. Then in 1964, Paul Ehrlich and Peter Raven published a paper on the coevolution of butterflies and plants mediated by secondary chemicals, which heralded the development of the field. The first college course in chemical ecology was given jointly by entomologists and natural products chemists in 1968 at Cornell University. The first book of collected papers on chemical ecology, edited by E. Sondheimer and J.B. Simeone, appeared in 1970. Cornell ecologists R.H. Whittaker and Paul Feeny displayed the ubiquity of chemical interactions in natural environments in their seminal paper in 1971. The first issues of the journal, *Biochemical Systematics and Ecology* (BSE) followed in 1973 and *Journal of Chemical Ecology* in 1975. By the time J.B. Harborne produced the first introductory text in 1977, the field had become well recognized.

In my tracing the production of terpenoid resins, as amber, through geologic time, I had been intrigued with why certain plants began synthesizing large amounts of this complex of chemicals soon after trees evolved. A few terpenes are physiologically necessary for plants, so the pathways for their synthesis had been developed early in plant evolution. However, the mixture comprising resin had developed in specialized secretory structures that would protect the plant's vital tissues from potentially toxic compounds. Could not this mixture of sequestered terpenes comprising most resins be playing an important defensive role in the survival of some plants? And would not the humid tropics be where long-lived plants would especially need protection from abundant potential enemies thriving there? When I decided to embark on studying the chemical ecology of a model tropical resin-producing tree that produced amber, however, a distinguished colleague retorted that "I was either courageous or crazy to attempt such a project!" I replied that I was probably a bit of both, but that such an undertaking was necessary if I was going to answer the evolutionary and ecological questions I was daring to pose. In 1966, this projected research put me in a pioneering role in chemical ecology investigations—and one initiated from a unique paleobotanical perspective.

Tropical studies were just becoming common among American ecologists—not withstanding the importance of the tropics to the early plant geographers and colonial Europeans. Concepts of vegetation were distorted in American ecology textbooks because they tended to be based on the relative poverty of temperate zone vegetation. Paul Richards' 1966 book, *The Tropical Rainforest,* opened the eyes of many American ecologists. And with its founding in the early 1960s, the Organization of Tropical Studies played a major role (through research and training students) in making the tropics become the standard to which other regions were compared and the place in which ecological theories were generated for American ecologists. Thus, I also was participating at an early stage in the development of ecological studies in the tropics, using the new perspective of the mediation of plant-produced chemicals in interactions with other organisms.

FIELD STUDIES OF AMBER-PRODUCING TREES

Having decided that I wanted to use the legume *Hymenaea* as a model system to study the chemical ecology and evolution of tropical amber-producing trees, I needed to get into the field to obtain an overview I could use to design experiments back at UCSC. Although I had seedlings that had been grown in the Harvard greenhouses from my trips to Mexico and Costa Rica transported to California, I needed to collect more seeds from different species and habitats. Moreover, extending my network of contacts to scientists and government agencies in the tropical countries where *Hymenaea* occurred would be essential for the continued field work that I anticipated both my graduate students and I would be doing. Establishing contacts and site locations for the research also were crucial for obtaining and maintaining grants to fund the research.

Hymenaea species had been described in many parts of South America, but Brazilian Amazonia was the center of its distribution. Having been introduced to personnel at various Brazilian institutions (importantly in Amazonia by Richard Schultes during 1966), I hoped that I could continue to receive support from NSF that had funded the amber studies on which the current research was based. I also needed, however, to collect material in Africa, to determine if *Hymenaea* occurred there and, if so, to establish its taxonomic relationship to other African resin-producing plants. Furthermore, finding it would mean an amphi-Atlantic occurrence of *Hymenaea*, which would imply continental drift, a hot topic at the time, in explaining the distribution of the genus.

Funding for field research in Africa during the summer of 1968 came from an unexpected invitation to join an ongoing project, which also would enable me to collect from populations that I suspected were *Hymenaea*. Desmond Clark, a paleo-anthropologist at UC Berkeley, was attempting to decipher what impact climate and humans had had on the history of decrease in African rain forests. Clark was studying the history of human utilization of Congo forests in the Lunda area of northeastern Angola. Fossil resin had been found in presently unforested areas, and Clark asked me to use chemical analysis as part of determining their botanical source. Knowing that the fossil resin had been produced by a rain forest tree would provide another piece in the puzzle of understanding the disappearance of Congo rain forests in this area of Angola. It also would be a cross disciplinary use of the infrared chemical technique I had used to determine the botanical source of amber in an evolutionary context.

Funds provided by the UC African Studies Center would enable me to visit sites in both eastern and western Africa. I could start in Kenya, where I wanted to collect *Trachylobium*, a genus that had originally been placed in *Hymenaea,* along the coast. I would take a safari interlude, primarily in South Africa, en route to the anthropological project in Angola, and finish in Ghana to collect additional material useful for both the *Hymenaea* and anthropology projects. I had assistance in selecting sites as well as contacts for help in the field in Africa from researchers at UC Berkeley, Harvard, and the Royal Botanic Gardens at Kew. Support for each step of the way opened up for me as I prepared to travel alone in difficult situations, but knowing I would have assistance when it was needed. The only unpleasant aspect at the beginning was the need for more prophylaxis than I had endured for Colombia, Mexico, and Central America. In addition to taking chloroquine for malaria, there were injections for tetanus, typhoid fever, yellow fever, cholera, and others. Preparations seemed endless.

My itinerary began in London, at the Royal Botanic Gardens, where I met with researchers who had worked in Africa. Because Kenya and Ghana had been British colonies, various Kew botanists suggested forest officers and botanists at herbaria there who could help me in the field. Furthermore, I began discussions with J.P.M. Brenan, keeper of the herbarium at Kew, who was one of the world's leading researchers on African leguminous trees and who also would bolster some of my new perspectives regarding *Hymenaea.*

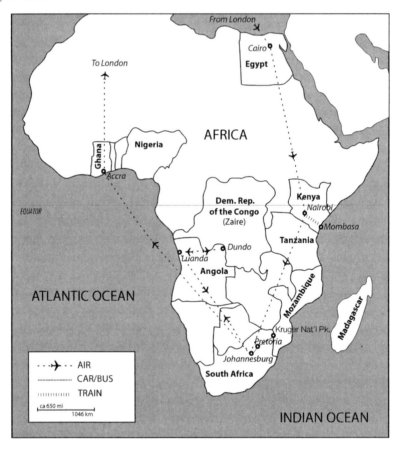

Route of African trip

I next visited the headquarters of the Companhia de Diamantes de Angola in Lisbon because the company's Servicios Culturais was in charge of making arrangements for my field work in Dundo. All of Desmond Clark's paleo-anthropological studies in the Dundo area, in which mine were to be a part, had been done under the auspices of the diamond company. It was also expected that we would publish our research results in their *Publícaçôes Culturais*. I had a preview in Lisbon of later treatment by this company—I was put up at the finest hotel and had a chauffeured black Mercedes at my disposal during my stay.

En route from Portugal to Kenya, I made stops in Madrid, Rome, and Athens—primarily enjoying these famous Mediterranean cities as a tourist. I arrived a week later in Nairobi after an awe-inspiring trip across parts of the Egyptian desert, and its Nile River, with my bird's eye view of the magnificent patterning of the dune formations across what seemed like an endless sea of sand. I remembered again St. Exupery's *Wind, Sand, and Stars*.

HYMENAEA IN EAST AFRICA

I began my research in Kenya with collections to determine whether *Hymenaea* occurred in Africa or whether it was restricted to the New World, as was commonly thought then. Was *Trachylobium* in fact an African species of *Hymenaea,* or was it, as was currently believed, just a close African relative? More intensive study was needed and resolution of the species designation depended upon availability for analysis of as many parts of the tree as possible.

I met with Kenya's conservator of forests and P.J. Greenway, author of *The East African Flora,* in the East African Herbarium at Nairobi, and they suggested localities where I could observe and collect *Trachylobium.* The only species in the genus (*T. verrucosum*) occurred in coastal Kenya, Tanzania, and Mozambique as well as on the offshore islands of Zanzibar and Madagascar. The best collecting sites were both north and south of Mombasa—which necessitated an overnight trip on the British East African Railway from Nairobi to Mombasa.

A ride on this historic train in itself was a thrilling experience. Furthermore, one of the most unforgettable events of my entire trip in Africa was pulling up the shade of the window of my sleeping compartment to see a herd of giraffes gracefully racing the train. It was truly a magnificent sight. Later, while in the field, I saw a giraffe calmly peeking at us over an *Acacia* tree with limpid eyes, incredibly long silken eyelashes, a long purplish tongue, and a prehensile upper lip enabling it to encompass a spiny branch of leaves. If seeing these stately giants racing the train hadn't already hooked me, this close experience would have. I gushed so much about giraffes when I got home that friends and students gave me all kinds of giraffe ornaments.

They are still so prominent in my office that I have had visitors comment, "I didn't know that you had done research on giraffes!"

In Mombasa, the district forest officer made arrangements for me to visit the Kwale and Mida-Gedes forest reserves in my quest for *Trachylobium*. At the Kwale Reserve, which lies south of Mombasa, the forest officers seemed surprised by this lone American woman wanting to collect specimens, including resin, from the tree they called *msandersi*. *T. verrucosum* had been one of the dominant trees in this dry coastal evergreen forest and could obtain a diameter of three to four feet and a height of eighty to ninety feet. Many *Trachylobium* trees had been cut to make *dhows* (Arabian sailing vessels)—I was horrified when my guides happily pointed out piles of *Trachylobium* logs. I had come to see living trees in a forest *reserve!* When I questioned the foresters about timbering in a reserve, they replied the wood was so highly prized that cutting the trees was allowed. When I asked about loss of revenue from resin the trees produced, they replied matter-of-factly that the wood now was more valuable than the resin. However, resin had been removed from the trees for sale, and I later obtained some Kwale *T. verrucosum* resin from an export merchant. Although there were no flowers, we collected branches with leaves and pods. The characteristic pods, which had viable seeds, were invaluable for our later work.

If the foresters were surprised with me, I found it strange to see these Africans dressed in

Kenyan Forest Service officers standing by Trachylobium (Hymenaea)

British Forest Service uniforms and was doubly surprised when they said that it was time for tea. We went to an empty Tudor-style English house, complete with a typical thatched roof such as I had only seen in England, where English foresters had once lived. We sat on the floor in the middle of an empty room with a magnificent silver tea service in the center of our little circle. Their attempts to create elegance seemed incongruous—here were post-colonial black Kenyan forest reserve employees maintaining an English colonial tradition. My thoughts went back to the British couple that had invited David Mason and me to have tea, replete with white tablecloth and silver tea set, along the side of a British Columbian highway when we were en route to Alaska. At least in that case it was the British themselves perpetuating their customs.

Next I went in a van with forest service assistants northward along the Kenyan coast to the Jilore Forest Station in the Mida-Gedes Reserve. Here again, *Trachylobium verrucosum* had been a dominant tree but was now being timbered. Nevertheless, some remained, and a few large trees had long stalactite-shaped resin hanging from the branches, some of which we were able to collect. Throughout my experience in these reserves, I was impressed by the helpfulness of the native Kenyan foresters and their desire to acquire whatever information I could offer them, though this latter seemed strange to me, as I was there to *learn* from *them*. They repeatedly indicated how little training they had compared to the former British foresters, and they hoped it would become possible for them to increase their knowledge. I have wondered over the years if more education did become available for them.

These East African collections were essential in my studies of the evolutionary history of the genus *Hymenaea*. My collections (especially the fruits and seeds from which we grew plants in the UCSC greenhouse), herbarium specimens from the Royal Botanic Gardens at Kew, and plants we grew from a Madagascar population from seed provided by the Madagascar Forest Service, were essential for our taxonomic revision of the genus *Hymenaea*. I, in collaboration with a graduate student, and strong support from several African legume researchers, returned the monotypic genus *Trachylobium* to *Hymenaea*. In our publication we proposed that the reinstated *H. verrucosa* was similar to a group of Amazonian and Cuban species, which may have been derived from a common African stock in the Tertiary period. Later, distinctive petals found in Dominican amber led us to suggest that its ancestors were African *Hymenaea* species rather than American ones.

SAFARI INTERLUDE WITH POLITICAL OVERTONES

After my return to Nairobi, I wanted to see some African savanna animals before returning to my research. First, botanists at the University College Nairobi (part of the University of East Africa) took me to Nairobi National Park on the outskirts of the city. Here I had my first incredible experience of being close to a lion pride, including cubs, as we drove right up to it alongside the road. The lions simply yawned at our presence. Even more amazing to me was the view back to the Nairobi skyline, knowing that no fences enclosed the park to keep the animals contained. This no-fence policy was based on the concept that the animals would not stray from their natural habitat. Now, unfortunately, with the increasing human population in Kenya, the area has to be fenced, except to the south.

I expanded up on this introduction to Africa's savanna animals with a visit in South Africa. This side trip also provided me with an opportunity to observe some important trees in this landscape, while sociologically, it brought me directly into the apartheid controversy.

I flew to Johannesburg and thence to Pretoria, where I was a guest of H.P. (Manie) van der Schijff, whom I had met at Harvard when he had spent a sabbatical leave at the Arnold Arboretum. Manie was professor of botany at the University of Pretoria and a plant ecologist at Kruger National Park. He also was a deacon in the conservative Afrikaner Dutch Reform Church and strongly supported apartheid. It was the Afrikaners, descendants of long-ago Dutch settlers in South Africa, who established apartheid in 1948. While at Harvard, Manie had attended a more moderate Dutch Reform Church in neighboring Framingham, and had extended an invitation to its minister to visit South Africa to see how well the black people were treated under the "separate but equal" concept. Completely by chance, the minister and I arrived in Pretoria at the same time.

Manie and the minister began to argue on our first outing together, a trip in the Transvaal to see how well Bantu people were treated under apartheid. We stopped to cash some traveler's checks at a bank, where there were separate lines for whites and blacks. Manie had told the minister that a basic reason for segregation was that the native blacks were incapable of carrying out many activities of white Africans. Yet here we were standing in line to do similar things, so the minister wanted to know why there were two lines. I completely agreed with him, having struggled through racial issues such as segregated education, housing, and seating on buses as a youth in Oklahoma, including unpleasant arguments with my father, who had deeply ingrained cultural attitudes from his upbringing in the Southern United

States. Furthermore, the Civil Rights Act had only been passed in 1957 and amended in 1964, after Martin Luther King Jr.'s "I have a dream" speech. Then King was assassinated in 1968, the very year of this visit. And, I had lived the last two years in Stevenson College at UCSC among vociferous, proactive students concerned with racial inequalities.

Baobab tree in Transvaal

As we drove north towards Botswana into the Transvaal bush and thorn veldt, I had my first opportunity to see the symbolic plant of dry parts of Africa—the large, hollow, but magnificent baobab tree (*Adensonia digitata*). Many Africans think that these widely distributed trees are the world's oldest living ones, contrary to North Americans touting the greater age of the bristlecone pine. Here I was also eager to see the great expanses of the small mopane trees (*Colophospermum mopane*) a resin-producing legume from which I collected resin globules from the trunks of a few trees. There were extensive fields of peanuts along with *Opuntia* cactus planted to provide water for cattle. We visited houses, schools, and hospitals that had been built by the Afrikaners, ostensibly to provide the Bantu with equal facilities. I am afraid, however, that Manie had not convinced either the minister or me of the validity of the basic tenets of "separate but equal."

On a later trip to Kruger National Park, which is along the northeast border of South Africa with Mozambique, I hoped conversation would focus more on the biota and less on apartheid! However, the angry questioning began again as we were nearing the park boundary in very hot bush veldt country. For the relief of thirsty travelers, a roadside thatched-roof hut contained a self-service Coke machine; however, a large sign announced that it was "For Whites Only" (reminiscent of separate drinking fountains in the United States). The minister cried out, "Now just what does this kind of discrimination have to do with intellectual capacity or education?" Fortunately, I spied an ostrich strutting through the veldt, which distracted everyone's attention, and we moved on without stopping for one of those "Whites Only" Coca-Colas.

We stayed in cabins in the park, and I will never forget hearing the roar of lions at night. Although we were perfectly safe, the sounds had a spine-tingling effect, especially as it seemed there were many of them. The next day we traveled on roads not open for tourists. To my delight, there were many stately browsing giraffes, a curious baboon climbed on the hood of our car to view us, and a leopard was dangling from a branch in a large tree near the road. Grazing zebra and impala were abundant. The imposing size and antipathy between hippopotamuses and crocodiles along the river banks were impressive. I remember hearing the hippos grunting, honking, and emitting a booming, laugh-like sound long before we saw them.

In many ways, however, I was most impressed with the elephants in Kruger Park. Once, while we had stopped in the road to watch some zebra and giraffes, I looked behind us to see five or six well-tusked elephants coming at us at a good rate of speed. When I mentioned this to Manie, he got so excited that he accidentally put the car in reverse. We were hurtling

Manie van der Schijff beside a thorny Acacia tree, Kruger Park

right into the elephants, who started flapping their huge ears, trumpeting and waving their trunks. Manie managed to change gears before making contact, and we sped off in a cloud of red dust. When we were safely away, he explained that he genuinely feared male African elephants, especially rogue young males—capable of crushing a car like a tin can. We later saw some elephants pushing over trees, and Manie said their high numbers were exceeding the carrying capacity of the vegetation in Kruger Park—apparently this is still a major problem.

After living through Manie van der Schijff's stout support of apartheid in 1968, I learned by chance, almost thirty years later, that he had remained an ardent apartheid supporter. While standing in line to see the Lipizzaner horses at the Spanish Riding School in Vienna, Austria, I could not place the English accent of the people behind me. I asked where they were from; when they told me they were from Pretoria, South Africa, I mentioned that I had visited a botanist there who was an ecologist in Kruger Park. Amazingly, they were neighbors of the Van der Schijffs. They reported that Manie had strongly opposed the overturn of apartheid, even after Nelson Mandela's election as state president of South Africa in 1994. "A stubborn man," they said.

I had a completely different experience regarding apartheid at the University of Witwatersrand in Johannesburg where I visited the paleobotanist, Edna Plumstead, whom I had met in England on the International Botanical Congress paleobotany field trip in 1964. She was the only woman professional that I met on this African trip. Edith was adamantly opposed to apartheid and, in fact, was training black students, even though they would not be allowed to obtain a diploma following their studies at Witwatersrand. She had even lost government support for some of her research as a result.

ANGOLAN PALEO-ANTHROPOLOGY PROJECT

Following my sojourn in South Africa, I flew to the city of Luanda, Angola, to begin field study for collaborative research with the UC Berkeley paleo-anthropologists. I again was the guest of the Companhia de Diamantes de Angola. As in Lisbon, I was put up in the best hotel and given a driver with another big black Mercedes that permitted me to visit whatever interested to me. Luanda seemed like a miniature Lisbon; even the patterning of tiles in the sidewalks was the same.

Because I had visited universities in Nairobi, Pretoria, and Johannesburg, I asked to visit the Cidade Universitaria that was shown on a city map.

However, my visit to "university city" kept being put off. Finally, with my constant urging, I was surprised to be taken to a large warehouse, which the driver insisted was the right location. In the office of this so-called university, I met with an official who told me that Angolans were not yet ready for a university. A few individuals were screened annually to be sent to a university in Portugal. Despite undoubted problems during British colonization, at least the British had provided native African people more possibilities for advanced education than either the Portuguese or the South African Boers.

I flew to Dundo in the state of Lunda, the diamond company's field headquarters near the Angola border with what was then Zaire (now Democratic Republic of the Congo). We flew over savanna country with baobab trees standing out prominently amid a burned landscape that seemed to extend almost endlessly. We stopped briefly at one town and I went to the back of the plane to step out, thinking I'd look around the airport. I was startled to be met with soldiers pointing rifles at me, speaking rapidly in Portuguese. I didn't understand their words but clearly I was being told to get back in the plane. This was my first taste of the civil unrest in Angola. It took almost ten years of fighting before Angolans gained their independence in 1975.

When the plane landed near Dundo, I felt I was being deposited in the middle of nowhere. Soon, however, I was met by another one of those chauffeured black Mercedes and whisked off to the diamond mine company town, which again was laid out to resemble Lisbon. It was like being in a dream to land in this isolated island of Portuguese culture in the middle of African savanna and woodland. The town was comprised of mine buildings, an elegant house for the director, wooden homes for others including myself (complete with houseboy and cook), an archaeological and geological museum, a fancy club house, and a park with a botanical garden and bandstand. My luxurious accommodations for field work reinforced the disparity between living conditions of the surrounding native people and the Portuguese owners of the diamond mines.

Dundo is located in northeastern Angola on the edge of the Congo River Basin, which includes the world's second-largest rain forest. Southern tributaries to the Congo River cut deeply into the red Kalahari sands in this part of Angola. Although most of this plateau country is deciduous woodland and savanna, sheltered sites have isolated fragments of mixed evergreen rain forest, which also lines the rivers as gallery forests. This rain forest is what Clark and others thought had been more widespread previously. Clark had assembled a number of specimens of ancient resins that he thought ranged in age from 800 BC into the Pleistocene. He hoped that chemical comparison of resins from extant rain forest trees might enable identification of the fossil ones found today in savanna and dry forest areas, and thus document that rain forest had indeed once been more extensive in the Dundo area in the past.

J. Vicente Martins, keeper of the archaeological and pre-history section of the Museu do Dundo, was my guide in the field. Although he did an acceptable job of helping me collect from trees that might be sources for the fossil resin, I found him to be an arrogant and obnoxious individual, a stereotype of the ugly western colonizer in Africa. I had been upset by Manie van der Schijff in South Africa, but I was even more so with Martins. As we entered local villages, twice he stopped to bring gifts to "wives" who were mothers of children he had fathered. He informed me that he had been doing a real service to the community by introducing "good white genes" into this black population.

We collected abundant resin from the burseraceous *Canarium* in the gallery forests but only obtained limited amounts of resin from the leguminous *Daniellia alsteeniana* and *Guibourtia coleosperma* that occur today in small remnants of mixed evergreen forests. These forests had been so badly burned in successive fires that we did not find much resin left on the trees.

After several days of relatively unsuccessful resin collecting, I had some personal problems with Martins. Following a dinner together one night, he began to read romantic Portuguese poetry to

Angolan gallery forest of type thought previously to have been common

me. He tried to get very close to me while also turning out the side-table lamps. As he turned them out, I turned them back on around the room. He became so wildly upset that I thought I was going to have to call for help.

Then he left, in haste. I was not sure if we could continue doing field work together, but all seemed to have passed over by the next morning, and we continued with no reference to the incident. This is the only time in my field work in numerous foreign countries that I ever had such a problem.

The final straw in my relationship with Martins came when we arrived at my house thirsty from a hot day of collecting. I asked my houseboy to bring some drinks in Portuguese—a language that neither of us knew well. He was such a kind, gentle boy, and strove in every way possible to help and please me. We had developed an effective means of communication using few words and lots of gestures, but I made the mistake this day of trying to communicate only with words. He hesitated—he was both struggling to understand me and fearful of making a mistake in Martins' presence. He had reason to be fearful. When the boy did not respond immediately, Martins stepped forward and slapped him so hard that he knocked him to the ground. When I tried to help the boy, Martins yelled at me to leave him alone, that I must not pamper or sympathize with "them" in any way or they would get out of control. When I persisted in defending the boy, Martins stamped out of the house, claiming that he was going to report me to the authorities in charge of the Companhia de Diamantes in Dundo.

Martins did indeed report my actions to the commandante for reprimand. Fortunately, most of my field work was finished. The commandante gently discussed with me the problem that the mine had with keeping their workers "under control." I was beginning to understand the local people's hatred of their Portuguese colonizers and could see an impending uprising, which is what the diamond mine owners feared. At this time the commandante also invited me to view sorting of the diamonds from the mining operations. Like all people entering the diamond sorting rooms, I had to change clothing and in essence be strip-searched upon leaving. The sight of so many magnificent specimens of diamonds (dazzling even though they were rare uncut specimens) was eye popping and made it abundantly clear what a lucrative business this was. I could now comprehend the serious conflicts in various African countries, including Angola, over controlling ownership of diamond mining operations.

Perhaps by way of lessening the reprimand regarding my defense of the servant, the commandante offered me a choice of several magnificent carvings made by native people. I was hesitant, even embarrassed to select any of them, because they were considered of such ethnographic importance that special governmental permission would be necessary to send them to me. Under considerable coercion, I finally chose a mask, a medicine man, and a woman typical of the area. Later an Angolan expert at UCSC told me that I should ultimately give these special ethnic carvings to a museum in the United States, which I plan to do.

My most prized carving, however, was done by an eleven-year-old native boy, Augustinho, who helped us in the field. On one trip, instead of finding a grove of living trees where we had planned to collect, we found only the charred, skeleton-like remains of a recent intense fire. I was sitting on a rock with my hands on my head looking at the scene in despair. The boy told Martins that I reminded him of his tribe's "thinking lady," and that he wanted to make a carving of her for me. This he did in a few days, using the soft wood of the rubiaceous *Hymenodictyon*. The carving, done with a simple hoe-like knife, is exquisite, displaying considerable artistic talent. Martins only allowed me to pay the boy less than one US dollar! I have often thought about this boy, especially as so many friends have admired the carving. I have wondered whether his family's economic circumstances allowed him to continue to create such beautiful objects.

RESIN COLLECTION IN GHANA
My next challenge was how best to get to Ghana, so I could collect more resin samples to aid in my determining whether or nor the Angolan ancient resin samples were from a rain forest leguminous tree. These collections would also help to increase my background for analysis of the ecology and evolution of leguminous resin-producing trees in general. Political tensions between Angola and Ghana prevented my flying between the two countries; instead, I had to fly all the way from western Africa to Johannesburg, South Africa, which lies in eastern Africa, and from there fly to Accra, Ghana, in far western Africa. Edna Plumstead kindly offered me hospitality in her home during my turnaround in Johannesburg. I was grateful for such friendship, and I always enjoyed hearing more about her exciting study of Gondwana fossil plants. Although there weren't the vexing security problems of today, the hassles of flying in Africa left me exhausted by the time I finally reached Ghana.

The University of Ghana is located at Legon, a short distance north of the capital, Accra, along the more easterly part of Ghana's coast on the Atlantic Ocean. Herbert Baker, who replaced Herbert Mason following his retirement from UC Berkeley, had previously been a faculty member at the university. He put me in contact with authorities there, who arranged for A.A. Enti, the curator of the herbarium and a forest botanist, to be my guide in collecting from resin-producing trees.

Throughout my field work in Ghana, we stayed in simple, but very clean rest houses and I had the most opportunity to visit village markets and take pictures of local products. I was particularly impressed with the use of huge manihot (*Manihot esculenta*) roots as a staple food in western Africa—except for the horrid porridge made from it we had for breakfast, which had the consistency of library paste. I was also fascinated with the operations of a local type of Red Cross. My trip was during the time of the Biafra conflict, a war of secession from southern Nigeria (1967-1970). Ghanians in some areas were giving assistance to the Biafrans through contributing seeds from *Cola bitida* fruits (native in Ghana and Nigeria). The seeds are chewed or pulverized to make a beverage that inhibits fatigue and forestalls hunger. The people couldn't afford to send their own food but could at least help the Biafrans ward off pangs of hunger.

Rain forest occurs primarily in the southwestern part of Ghana, where we visited the Kade Agricultural Station and Ayola Forest Reserve. Here in the rain forest we saw abundant resin produced by the legume *Daniellia ogea.* As with *Trachylobium* (*Hymenaea*) in Kenya, stalactite-like masses of resin hung from branches high (sixty to seventy feet) up in the trees. Local people collected resin for use as incense and glue, and for torches. To the north of Accra in the Ashanti Region, which is mostly mixed forest and savanna, we collected *Daniellia oliveri*, which produced less resin than *D. ogea* in the rain forest. We obtained resin from other legumes, such as *Copaifera salikunda,* in the Bobiri Forest Reserve and *Guibourtia ehe* from gallery rain forest in the Asukese Reserve near Sunayi. All of these leguminous trees in these reserves in Ghana produced more abundant resin than the trees I saw in Angola. The British had established these forest reserves when Ghana was the Gold Coast and timbering of mahogany was destroying the forests. However, Enti was very sad and concerned—just as I had been in Kenya—that numerous economically important trees were being harvested in the reserves that had been established to protect them.

While in the Kumasi area of Ashanti land, Enti stopped at a village compound where I visited his family with him. I met two of his mothers—the older one being his biological mother. Enti had told me that polygamy had worked effectively in his family. The oldest wife chose the younger ones, who then shared in the childbearing, taking care of the family, and doing agricultural work as well. One aspect of compound life that Enti felt had been advantageous for him was that loving arms were always present—if one adult was upset with him another one was there to soothe him. The day of our visit several siblings and "aunties" were also present to

Collecting resin from Daniella *in Ghana rain forest; A.A. Enti to right*

meet the visiting American. They gave me a beautiful Kente cloth with myriad designs stamped with a black dye. It was a very pleasant and warmly welcoming family visit and a special cultural experience for me.

Despite living within the native culture, this family had espoused what Christianity had to offer to some of their children. This was another example of mixing of cultures by accepting some aspects of Christianity—as I had seen with Alaskan Eskimos and Mayan Indians. Enti had been sent to a Christian missionary school that led to his going to the University in Ghana followed by graduate education from the University of London. Several years after my visit Enti left the university and established his own business, Enti Forest Enterprises, which he hoped to ultimately turn over to his son. He wanted his son to study forestry in the United States, and during the late 1970s I got an unexpected telephone call from him from Michigan, excitedly telling me that he was there attending his son's graduation from forestry school. It was marvelous to be able to share the joy of the fulfillment of this father's dream.

Resins collected from both Angola and Ghana as well as Congo resins provided by J. Léonard, the monographer of Congo copal trees, were critical in reaching my final conclusions regarding the plant source of the ancient resins in Angola. Comparison of infrared spectra of the ancient resin with that of modern resins from various species of *Canarium, Copaifera, Colophospermum, Daniellia,* and *Guibourtia* revealed similarities between ancient and current leguminous rain forest species. *Copaifera mildbraedii* or a close relative appeared to be the most likely source of the fossil resin. Although *C. mildbraedii* today occurs about two hundred kilometers north of the site at which the fossil resin was collected, it could well have been a component of the gallery forests that occur along rivers outside of the rain forest proper. The source of this fossil resin supports other evidence for restriction of rain forests in this part of Africa, suggesting that the disappearance of this gallery forest tree probably was the result of a drying and cooling climate, aided by human activities, especially fire, in the last millennium. These results were published in the lavish format of the diamond mine's *Publicações Culturais*.

EVOLUTION OF *HYMENAEA* IN SOUTH AMERICA

1969

It is therefore, an opportune time to examine the floristic relationships between Africa and South America to determine just how strong they are and whether or not continental displacement offers a rational explanation for them.
—Robert Thorne (1973)

I now had my first cohort of four graduate students and a postdoctoral fellow, most of whom would be working with me as part of a team studying the evolution and chemical ecology of *Hymenaea*. Because I wanted to use *Hymenaea* as a tropical model system for studying chemical ecology in the evolutionary context provided by amber, it was essential to understand the systematic framework of the genus, which was poorly known. One of the students was interested in a systematic study and I could collaborate with him on my proposed phylogenetic analysis of *Hymenaea*. My basic need to understand the resin chemistry of the genus would be met by a student who came with an MS in plant biochemistry, and who would be given assistance from Eugene Zavarin, an authority on resin chemistry of conifers at the UC Berkeley Forest Products Laboratory. The third student was interested in studying the ecology of *H. courbaril* in Mexico and Central America, which could be expedited through the Organization for Tropical Studies (OTS). A postdoctoral fellow planned to analyze the development of the anatomical system in which the resin was synthesized, stored, and then secreted in *Hymenaea*, building on our previous microscopic analyses.

Eugene Zavarin, long term chemical collaborator

I also thought that we should initiate studies of Pacific Coast plants in our lab. The fourth student in the first cohort wanted to study allelopathic (inhibitory) effects of terpenes from *Umbellularia,* the California bay tree, on seedlings under the tree—a different kind of chemical interaction than we were pursuing in the tropics. Overall, I was very fortunate with this group of graduate students and the post-doc who provided an excellent start for my research at UCSC, which was characterized throughout the years by a team approach. In terms of training women I also was off to a good start, as half of this first group was female.

STUDIES OF *HYMENAEA* IN BRAZIL

After having potentially re-established the presence of *Hymenaea* in Africa during the summer of 1968, in the fall of 1969 I began a sabbatical leave that would focus on travel across *Hymenaea*'s extensive Brazilian distribution in

Graduate students and faculty planning to attend
XI International Botanical Congress in front of building later named Thimann
Laboratories

South America. I was particularly interested in assessing the African, east coast Brazilian, and Amazonian relationships in the evolution of the genus. Before leaving the country, however, I guided a group of grad students and post-docs (most of whom had been together in the Botany Tea jaunts to Death Valley) along the Pacific Coast to Seattle, Washington, to attend the XI International Botanical Congress over which Thimann presided as president. I used the congress as a launching pad for my ideas, and showed my students just how pioneering our research on *Hymenaea* was. We did a a poster accompanied by a slide and stereo presentation on "Evolution of Resin-Secreting Trees," and I led an informal discussion on "Evolutionary Considerations of Lower Terpenoids in Plants," in which I invited prominent plant biochemists and ecologists to participate.

In 1969, numerous biochemists still held a traditional view that terpenes—of which *Hymenaea* resins are comprised—were primarily metabolic waste products. Except for the few physiologically important terpenes, the multiplicity of others (30,000 presently known!) were considered "indifferent ballast" that probably were of little (secondary) significance to the plant. In my 1969 paper "Amber: A Botanical Inquiry," I had suggested the possible ecological roles of secondary chemicals in the evolution of resin-producing trees. I had agreed with Fraenkel's 1959 proposal that the *raison d'être* of secondary products is to defend plants, but his focus was upon the effects of these chemicals on insect herbivores. With my interest in terpenes defending tropical trees I thought that microbes, especially fungi, should also be considered. This bias persists today; the subdiscipline of chemical ecology has remained dominated by insect ecologists and with relatively few researchers working in the tropics.

Immediately following the congress, I embarked on my several-month *Hymenaea* collecting trip through much of Brazil, but with visits in Venezuela, Trinidad, Uruguay, Argentina, Chile, and Ecuador. The Brazilian part of the jaunt required careful planning to elicit the expertise of numerous researchers at institutions across that huge country (it is larger than the United States in area). I established a network of Brazilian botanists who assisted us as our work progressed over the years. NSF continued to fund our *Hymenaea* studies, including the extensive Latin American fieldwork I was about to embark upon.

My observations of *Hymenaea* began in Venezuela, which was my introduction to *Hymenaea* in northern South America, although there was only a single species, *H. courbaril*, which I had seen throughout Central America and Mexico. At the Instituto Botánico and the Jardín Botánico de la Universidad Centrale in Caracas, I met with Director Tobias Lasser, a connection that became particularly valuable later when we began a comparative study of *Hymenaea* and *Copaifera*.

Route of 1969 South American collecting trip

COLLECTING *HYMENAEA* THROUGHOUT BRAZIL

My first collecting in Brazil was in Amazonia, where I had contacts in Belém and Manaus from my 1966 visits with Richard Schultes, plus those from my new Brazilian colleague at UC Berkeley, Hilgard O'Reilly Sternberg, who was an authority on the geography of the Amazon River. All of my work in

Amazonia would be in the reserves of various research institutions where I could get the necessary assistance in locating *Hymenaea* trees as well as climbing and collecting from them.

My arrival in Belém was a remarkable example of the friendliness and exceptional hospitality I would experience through many years of working in Brazil. It began when I boarded the plane in Trinidad for Belém, and offered to hold a few of the huge stuffed toys from Disneyland that a Brazilian couple sitting next to me was taking home to their children. The flight was delayed due to bad weather, resulting in a midnight arrival in Belém. The couple insisted that I come home with them to spend the night. No protests worked! Following a period of excitement for their children receiving their toys, the mother made room for me in the oldest girl's bedroom. "*No problema*," I was assured. It was all very jolly and welcoming. In the morning, after breakfast, they took me to my destination and encouraged me to drop by for dinner anytime, there was always plenty of food . . . I continued to enjoy their hospitality when I was in Belém, and learned more about Brazilian life and people outside the scientific realm.

Except for that first night, I stayed in rooms in the botanical garden and zoo of the Museu Goeldi while in Belém. The extremely humid heat is always a shock physiologically, at least when I first arrive in Amazonia. My little room at the museum did not have air conditioning; in fact, it did not even have a window. It had a cot, although hammocks (*redes*) are often preferred for sleeping in this environment. On later trips I would always carry a *rede* with me, as the locals do, the way in temperate climes we carry our sleeping bags in the field. I had been warned to keep the door closed to my room at night because harmless animals from the zoo were allowed to roam freely in the garden at that time. The first evening there, after a short time lying in a pool of sweat, I opened the door to let in a little cooler air. I had just started to doze off when I felt something sniffing my feet. From a shaft of light coming in the door, I could see a large bulky animal that was unafraid of my movement. When I turned on the single overhead light bulb, I discovered a somewhat friendly tapir. After briefly viewing each other, I shooed him out and closed the door. But the heat was so overwhelming that I opened it again. And again when I was half asleep, I felt an animal investigating my bare legs. This one had a very mobile snout—it was an anteater. When I leapt out of bed, I landed on a skink, a lizard that commonly occupies the walls of such rooms. It so startled me I let out a cry that sent the anteater scampering and brought the researchers in neighboring rooms running to my assistance. I was embarrassed, but with much laughter my neighbors emphatically insisted that it was necessary to keep the door closed or I would have more inquisitive visitors. They also promised I would soon begin to adapt to the heat and humidity. In a few days, I did.

Because tropical forests are such a storehouse of biological diversity, the collection and naming of tropical plants has always been the first step in studying them. Thus herbaria are critical reference libraries of specimens with their accompanying data, upon which later studies are built. This kind of information is particularly important in Amazonia. While most of the Amazonian specimens of *Hymenaea* I had seen in the US and European herbaria were sterile, the Museu Goeldi collection offered not just abundant specimens, but more with either flowers or fruits. The collection contained numerous specimens of important late nineteenth and early twentieth century Amazonian collectors such as J.E. Huber and W.A. Ducke, who also had developed both the herbarium and the associated botanical garden of the Museu Goeldi. Investigating the specimens collected by these early botanical

explorers was truly a prelude to doing an ecologically-oriented monograph of *Hymenaea*. I spent many hours in the Museu Goeldi herbarium looking at specimens of Amazonian species for data regarding sites of their occurrence along with flowering and fruiting times with which I could begin to build a phenology of *Hymenaea* (annual time of leaf flush and drop as well as flowering and fruiting) to assist us in making our own collections.

I collected specimens from *Hymenaea* growing in the museu gardens with the help of their botanists and their tree climbers, who also accompanied me to the

Collecting Hymenaea oblongifolia *in flooded forest with Museu Goeldi staff*

IPEAN (Instituto Pesquisas e Experimentação Agropecurias

do Norte) reserve where we could collect in the *varzea*, or periodically inundated forest. September is during the low-water period, so we could walk through the *varzea* and collect resin from roots, whereas many trees in my June visit in 1966 had been completely covered by water. Here I saw my first specimen of *H. oblongifolia*, a species that was obviously a close relative of the east African species *H. verrucosa*. I climbed an observation tower built into the rain forest canopy, an early attempt to provide researchers access to observe life in the tree canopy, hoping to catch a glimpse of some insect pollinators on *Hymenaea* flowers (one section of the genus has insect pollinators whereas the other has bat pollinators).

Throughout my fieldwork in Amazonia, we always worked in the early morning hours (5:00 AM or even before) when it was cooler, and we stayed out of the full sun, with all of its intensity, as it was almost directly overhead this close to the equator. The temperature rarely, if ever, reached 90°F, but even when the temperature was 80°F the humidity was still never below 80 percent; it was this combination of high temperature and humidity that took its toll on energy. Before the cloud build-up brought heavy downpours at noon or in the early afternoon, we came in and ate the main meal of the day. Then it was siesta time until late afternoon when it began to cool down. No work was done during this period—not even in an air-conditioned herbarium. I retreated to my room to read about the experiences of the great nineteenth century naturalist, Richard Spruce, in Amazonia. Schultes had strongly encouraged me to read the *Notes of a Botanist on the Amazon and Andes,* which contained Spruce's letters and journal extracts of several years exploring the forests along the tributaries around Santarém and Manaus, where I would be collecting.

When leaving Belém, I had a wonderful early morning flight to Manaus and again marveled at the incredible size of even the Amazon's meandering tributaries. The overview during the flight, which, washed in rosy watercolor hue at dawn, is particularly glorious, and it reinforces the fact that this river contains one-fifth of the water flowing across the face of the earth. The Amazon has ten times the water of the Mississippi, the river with which I had been so impressed as a Midwestern student. The vastness of the rain forest and floating grassy meadows recalled to me the immense areas of boreal forest and tundra I had seen in Alaska in 1956, but the immensity of Amazonia was even more overwhelming, with some tributaries being as large as the "mighty" Yukon River. The tundra patterns, however, were more complex than Amazonian grassy meadows, and more colorful—at least as fall approached. In Amazonia, flying at relatively low altitudes, I could see trees in flower, which, of course, I never witnessed when flying above taiga forests. And, these Amazonian forests host incredible diversity—perhaps a quarter of the worlds' terrestrial species. I would never lose my sense of awe in flying over Amazonia, even after numerous later flights. I feel so privileged to have seen both Amazonian and Alaskan wilderness areas before they were visibly disturbed by human activities.

William Rodrigues, one of the INPA botanists who assisted me in 1966, was a mine of information about *jutahy*—one of the Portuguese common names for Amazonian *Hymenaea*—and he would continue to aid me and my students through all the years we went to INPA. I felt comfortable with him and had, importantly, worked through some of the language problems. It often took a certain "acquaintance interval" with Brazilian researchers to reach the point of understanding each other, especially when you did not speak Portuguese well and their English was fragmentary. Most visiting researchers knew more Spanish than Portuguese and most Brazilians are resigned to visitors using this mixture they call "Portenole." And, as always, we relied on hand gestures and body language—so amazingly helpful when people are eager to communicate but don't know each others' language well.

We spent much time at the Ducke Reserve (in the Rio Negro watershed) where INPA foresters could help me locate *Hymenaea* trees as well as climb them to collect specimens. I was now realizing how widely dispersed *Hymenaea* trees were, with only one to two individuals of a species per hectare (2.47 acres) in the upland forest, and how dependent I was on help in even finding them. I was also questioning just what constitutes a population in this dispersion of individuals in the rain forest. (This issue came up later with some NSF reviewers of a grant proposal, who thought we should sample twenty trees per population. They had never studied trees in an Amazonian rain forest!) I was especially interested in *H. intermedia*, which was restricted to central Amazonia, because it had intermediate floral characters between Amazonian *H. oblongifolia* and the widespread *H. courbaril* that I had known in Mexico and Central America. Could these intermediate characters be a result of hybridization—given the high level of dispersion of the trees? I also wondered just how different these Amazonian populations of *H. courbaril* were compared to the northern ones?

In addition to my botanical research, I was fascinated with the historic city of Manaus and its faded remnants of grandeur from the days of the Amazonian rubber boom. I now had a little more time to explore the city than during my previous visit. I wanted to photograph for use in my Plants and Human Affairs class some of the numerous mansions and the opulent neoclassical Teatro Amazonas, which was built in 1884 during the peak of the wealth of "black gold." The belle epoque interior was a conscious copy of Milan's La Scala and is filled with murals painted by Brazilian artists, chandeliers from Venice, and much more—all transported by boat to the mouth of the Amazon. A platoon system of locking docks was built to accommodate the ocean vessels along the Manaus waterfront to bring the opera singers, a number of whom ultimately died of tropical diseases, from Europe to perform in this opera house during these rubber boom days, which lasted until World War I.

I had planned to stay in a hotel in the center of Manaus, but Hilgard Sternberg had suggested that I contact a friend of his, who was director of the Amazonas State Library, about the best place to stay. She kindly suggested the possibility of my staying in her sister's home. Thus I had another opportunity to witness the daily lives of Brazilians at home and to meet people in Manaus other than scientists. It was a pleasant experience until my farewell dinner! Having a *tartaruga*, the world's largest freshwater turtle, for a feast was traditionally considered a special way to bestow an honor upon a guest. The family had obtained one of

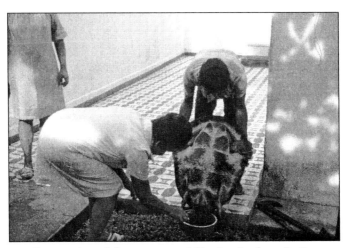

Preparation of the tartaruga, following its decapitation

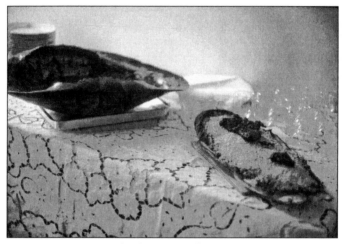

for feast in my honor

these giant Amazonian turtles, which was endangered even in 1969. I was horrified when I saw this magnificent creature on the patio outside the kitchen being readied for its execution. Then my horror reached crisis levels when I was told that part of the celebration was to watch it being decapitated. I managed to escape inside on the verge of tears—this rare animal had been brutally killed in my honor! It was cooked and served in the center of the table in its shell. I could barely choke down a few mouthfuls of this turtle feast that everyone else was exclaiming over. It was a clash of cultures with these kind and hospitable people trying to do something special for me, whereas I was concerned about a lack of sensitivity to conserving this magnificent creature. I also felt hamstrung in expressing my feelings about this special honor.

My next Amazonian stop was Santarém, the headquarters of SUDAM (Superentendenica do Disenvolvimento da Amazônia) where arrangements had been made for me to collect at their FAO (Food and Agricultural Organization) station in the Palhão and Curuá Una Reserves. Some visiting researchers in Manaus were concerned that I was going to an isolated camp with men I did not know, but I was not worried. We traveled in a motorized canoe hewn out of a large native tree, from Santarém along the very large Tapanjos tributary into the much smaller Curuá Una tributary, which runs along the reserves. We maneuvered along quiet waterways amid islands of floating grassy meadows. I had been reading Spruce's account that some of these floating grass islands could reach a thickness of thirty feet. These meadows are often the retreats for large fruit-eating and seed-dispersing fish during low water in the *varzea*, which they inhabit during the flooded period.

As we proceeded to the station, my Portuguese-speaking forester assistants talked about sharp-teethed, flesh-eating piranhas and warned me to keep my fingers out of the water. They also mentioned that anacondas were common along the water's edge in this area and that you could tell when they were hidden among the debris along the edge of the river by a

Anaconda skin pinned to wall of field station cabin

strong characteristic smell. I couldn't understand the details because of my poor Portuguese, but they clearly were testing me to see if they could scare me. Once there, I was given a little screened cabin with simple curtains that could be pulled across the screen for privacy. While I was sleeping, the assistants quietly pinned the skin of a huge anaconda on the wall of the cabin immediately across from mine. When I opened my curtain in the morning I was a bit startled by the incredible size in both girth and length that these snakes could attain. Nevertheless, I was able to maintain my cool at breakfast, and casually mentioned what a beautiful animal it was and how I hoped that I would get to see more than just the skin. I seemed to have passed my test.

Because *Hymenaea* is an emergent tree, towering above the canopy of the *terra firme* forest, collecting specimens from it is always frustrating. Its bare trunk usually extends up at least a hundred feet before the first branches appear. Most of the central Amazonian species are bat-pollinated, so flowers and fruit occur on the end of branches, making it necessary to either climb high in the canopy and out on branches to obtain reproductive specimens or to shoot them down from the ground. The trunk diameter of *Hymenaea* trees in this area was even greater than at sites around Manaus, and this made climbing even more difficult, especially with the climbers using the traditional technique of a belt and spikes on their boots. None of the tree climbers here had heard about new climbing techniques that were just being developed for tall Pacific Northwest trees, and then modified for Costa Rican rain forest. These new techniques enabled easier collecting of specimens as well as facilitating canopy research. As they later developed, it would be possible to access the exciting life in the canopy and be used in tropical forests worldwide. We were unfortunately a little too early to gain the benefits. Although my helpers were good marksmen, they had trouble hitting the tip of the narrow branches containing flowers and/or fruits. Often, even after hitting a flowering branch with a bullet, the specimen fell onto other trees, remaining out of reach. All of my assistants' attempts to collect from *Hymenaea* species in Amazonia made it clear why few herbarium specimens had good reproductive parts! Collecting flowers and fruit, however, was necessary for our monographic revision of the genus. I also needed resin samples for chemical analysis and, characteristically, the resin was also high on the trunks of the trees.

On one day that we had been particularly frustrated in obtaining specimens, either through climbing or shooting, in the Curuá Una and Palhão Reserves, I had retreated some distance to get a full picture of a grand specimen of *Hymenaea courbaril* along a reserve road. While I was taking the photo I noticed that the workers were discussing something together, and soon afterward I heard the sound of a chain saw. I could not believe the devastation caused when the huge tree came crashing down. Again I was horrified! This magnificent *Hymenaea,* in a forest reserve, had been cut down for me. I didn't know which was worse—the demise of *tartaruga* in Manaus or the *Hymenaea* here. And I was reminded of the commercially important trees in Kenyan and Ghanian forest reserves being cut and sold. The foresters didn't seem to understand why I was unhappy.

It wasn't just the *Hymenaea* that was destroyed; the tree brought down other trees with it—some of which were inextricably tied together with vines (lianas). It looked like a bomb had hit the immediate area. I was also seeing, however, the creation of a good-sized gap, a mechanism that enables tree replacement in primary rain forest by opening a space for light to enter. Because it occurred near the road, there also was a good display of the vertical four strata of the forest, and how such structure results in the packing together of so many kinds of plants. Moreover, the downed tree provided a treasure trove of large masses of resin along the tree trunk as well as numerous flowers and pods. I have referred repeatedly to information obtained from specimens from this tree in different publications. The tree itself has achieved a sort of immortality since the picture of it that I had taken when it was still standing has appeared in various of my publications as an outstanding example of an Amazonian emergent rain forest tree.

COLLECTING *HYMENAEA* IN OTHER PARTS OF BRAZIL

The next step was to collect *Hymenaea* species in Atlantic Coast rain forests in the states of Bahia and Pernambuco, a region known to have taxa in common with Amazonian and African rain forests. At the 1966 meeting in Belém I had become acquainted with botanists who, on this trip, significantly enhanced my collecting in these areas. They also became friends and continued to assist me and my students in making collections for over a decade. Moreover, I was able to observe the vegetation and variety of habitats in which *Hymenaea* occurred through the eyes of botanists who knew them well—a priceless experience.

In coastal Bahia, I was the guest of Paulo Alvim, Brazil's preeminent plant physiologist who also had ecological interests and was director of CEPEC (Centro Experimentale de Pesquisas do Cacau) in Itabuna. Alvim was responsible for building the center in the rain forest just south of Salvador, which was being held up as an example of excellent field laboratories for experimental studies of tropical plants. Alvim provided me with assistants and transport to collect *Hymenaea* there as well as in the neighboring forests. I was excited to find a new species of *Hymenaea* (*H. aurea*) and a variant of *H. oblongifolia,* a species that I had first seen in Amazonia.

Hymenaea courbaril, *emergent tree to right of jeep*

CEPEC was also an excellent place to take photos of physiological experiments to determine the best conditions for growing, harvesting, and processing *cacau* (cocoa plant) for my course in Plants and Human Affairs. Alvim was well-known for studying perplexing phenomena such as tree growth periodicity in tropical climates, and I later collaborated with him in organizing a series of seminars on ecophysiology of tropical plants. He also arranged for me to meet with the president of the Federal University of Bahia in Salvador to discuss possible collaboration with members of his biology faculty. While in his office, I admired some tapestries that depicted the diversity of peoples in Salvador, the historic first capital of Brazil. Santos told me that similar tapestries hung in the Brazilian president's palace and offered to introduce me to the artist who had done the paintings that were used as the basis for making the tapestries. I was delighted, of course, for such an unusual cultural opportunity.

I met Genaro de Carvalho at his studio, and he showed me many of his paintings. Then he surprised me by offering a small painting of my choice to have in my college apartment to show students some Brazilian art, which was characteristic of an area in which I was doing some of my research. I was astounded, but picked out a wonderful cubist-type rendition of Bahia—particularly displaying the intense colors of the blue sky and ocean, ochre and deep orange of many houses, and varied greens of the vegetation. The students greatly admired it in my Stevenson College apartment and were amazed at this artist's generosity.

In northeastern Bahia and Pernambuco, the highly acclaimed Brazilian botanist, Dardano Andrade-Lima, who was head of the Botany Department at the Federal University of Pernambuco in Recife, helped me collect in scattered patches of coastal rain forest as well as in the complex savanna and dry forest areas. The open savanna-like vegetation, called *cerrado,* usually has scattered trees and shrubs with a very tortuous growth form and a ground layer of grasses. When the vegetation becomes denser, with taller and less tortuous trees, it is called *cerradão*. In this environment, tree leaves are frequently very leathery or densely pubescent and their bark is thick, often with evidence of fire. We found a number of *Hymenaea* species in these habitats. Again, I felt fortunate in going on a collecting trip with Andrade-Lima as I learned so much from his extensive research in this incredibly diverse dry vegetation. The vast areas of *cerrado* and *cerradão* to which he introduced me cover about a quarter of Brazil and are most conspicuous in the central and southern part of the country. I was reminded that Warming, the early ecologist whose works I had studied as a graduate student, had begun his career in the 1870s with observations of this vegetation. Warming, who wrote the first plant ecology text, was different from the botanists exploring Amazonia, such as Spruce and Bates, who were

In my Stevenson College apartment, with Brazilian artist's painting on wall as a gift for the students

seeking new species to collect and describe. Rather, Warming observed the apparent adaptation of plant species to different habitats and the communities in which they occurred. He used such observations for establishing his concept of ecological plant geography, which differed from previous floristic perspectives. Although I was interested in clarifying the systematics of *Hymenaea*, my ecological perspective necessitated seeing the various species in the communities in which they occurred in different habitats.

The central plateau country near Brasilia was my next stop. In 1969 both the city and the university were still in an early stage of development with a prevailing unfinished look—having been inaugurated in 1960 and 1962, respectively. Embassies of most countries still had not moved from the opulence of Rio de Janeiro to the "barrenness of Brasilia," as it was often put. George Eiten in the Botany Department and herbarium at the Universidad de Brasilia, and E. Heringer at Instituto Brasilero Geographica e Estatistica (IBGE)—both authorities on the central area of *cerrado and cerradão*—accompanied me in the field especially to see the variation of *H. stigonocarpa*, a characteristic *cerrado* tree. We also sought out rain forest species occurring in gallery forests lining the rivers that drain southward from Amazonia amid the dry *cerrado* and *cerradão*. Prominent in the gallery forest is a tall subdeciduous *Hymenaea* that had previously been considered a separate species (*H. stilbocarpa*)—but that my graduate student and I later decided belonged as a member of the complex of several varieties of *H. courbaril*.

HINTS TO EARLY EVOLUTIONARY HISTORY OF *HYMENAEA*

Amazonia had been considered the center of distribution of *Hymenaea*, but I had observed species in the coastal rain forest that established relationships between Africa and Amazonia. *Hymenaea oblongifolia*, the closest relative to the African *H. (Trachylobium) verrucosa*, was a widely distributed Amazonian species. Specimens of *H. oblongifolia* in coastal forests of Bahia and Pernambuco were similar to the Amazonian populations in their flowers and fruits (characters usually used to distinguish legumes). Only distinctly different leaf characteristics had been used to make them different species. Graduate student Eric Lee and I thought we were witnessing another polymorphic complex with differences in leaf characters having evolved in greatly different habitats. We later called this Atlantic coastal variant *H. oblongifolia* var. *latifolia* (meaning *wide leaf*).

The discovery of this African, coastal Brazilian, and Amazonian connection led me to firm up hypotheses regarding the early evolutionary history of *Hymenaea*. I thought that continental drift provided a logical explanation for the distribution of these closely-related species—more than a decade after I had listened to geologists in Berkeley proclaiming that there was no evidence to support such continental movement. By 1969, however, continental drift was becoming a widely accepted concept. In understanding the distribution of *Hymenaea,* my argument centered on when Africa and South America had drifted apart. It was generally accepted—or, at least, would be by the early 1970s—that this continental drifting took place during the mid-Cretaceous. Botanists who were studying plants with amphi-Atlantic distributions thought that most Brazilian plants arrived from Africa via occasional long distance dispersal rather than by vicariance (ancient ranges being split by the drift). Migration during the late Cretaceous or early Tertiary would be easy across relatively narrow seas, especially in the equatorial area.

We found no evidence for the tribe in the largely tropical subfamily in which *Hymenaea* had been placed (Detarieae: Caesalpinioideae) until the Eocene—the time when tropical rain forest reached its maximum development (perhaps more than twice its present distribution according to the paleobotanist J.A. Wolfe). The African legume authority, J.P.M. Brenan, had reported that two-thirds of the genera in the subfamily Caesalpinioideae are not only endemic to Africa but that three-quarters of these are restricted to rain forests. We thus concluded that *H. verrucosa* was probably relictual in coastal East Africa and offshore islands from a former more continuous distribution of evergreen forests from West Africa across to East Africa. Therefore, the highest probability of oceanically dispersed fruit (*Hymenaea* pods are commonly found along seashores and readily germinate afterwards) would have occurred when the continents were relatively close together and when rain forest vegetation was widely distributed.

Ancestors of *H. oblongifolia* could have come from West Africa to Amazonia via the south equatorial current. But, there are two options for the origin of *H. oblongifolia* var. *latifolia*, which is disjunct in the Brazilian Atlantic coastal rain forest from the three Amazonian *oblongifolia* varieties that are restricted to either upland or periodically or permanently flooded habitats. Ancestors could have arrived from Africa via the Brazil current, or these coastal Brazilian populations of *H. oblongifolia* var. *latifolia* could have been more continuous with the Amazonian forest populations at one time. Fossil floras and faunas have demonstrated that moist tropical vegetation occurred as far south as Patagonia, Argentina, until the Oligocene and Miocene, when drying trends caused its northward retreat. We found not only the African-connected variety of *H. oblongifolia* in the coastal rain forests but also a species (*H. rubriflora*) related to another Amazonian species (*H. reticulata*), but as part of a different, later-evolved section of the genus.

With various *Hymenaea* species occurring in the dry vegetation, including several varieties of the widespread *H. courbaril*, it was obvious that the genus had found environmental conditions more favorable in the New World than in Africa. These varieties of *H. courbaril*, along with *H. stigonocarpa* and *H. martiana* and *H. velutina* formed a coherent group of species in the *cerrado* and dry forests of central and eastern Brazil. Species appeared to have radiated from Amazonian-type moist forests into various drier vegetation types over a wide geographic range as climates had become drier through the mid Tertiary. The later evolutionary history became even more complex through alternating wet and dry, and even cooler, conditions during the Pleistocene. (A number of recent pollen studies have confirmed these climatic changes and their impact on the vegetation. Moreover, DNA studies of two southeastern *cerrado* species of *Hymenaea* showed great genetic variation in different phylogeographic populations and have suggested the species habitat differentiation occurred during these Pleistocene or early Holocene climatic changes.)

Having witnessed so many large animals the year before in the savanna and dry forests of Africa, I could not help pondering the striking lack of them in similar vegetation in Brazil. For much of its history, South America had been home to an array of large animals. Although the reasons for their abrupt disappearance are not certain, many scientists, including Jared Diamond, believe the impact of human migration was decisive. In contrast to Africa, where animals evolved alongside early humans and learned to fear them, South America was the last continent to be populated by humans, who by that time had become sophisticated hunters. With no previous association with their new predator, the large animals of South America were prime prey for the humans and most were driven to extinction. Today it is the vegetation that is under attack by humans.

I succeeded in my major goal of obtaining viable seeds from most *Hymenaea* species, so that we could grow plants for experiments at UCSC. Moreover, with my paleo-evolutionary background, viewing *Hymenaea* species in their various habitats throughout their Brazilian distribution was like going back in time. I was reconstructing in my mind an evolutionary scenario of the genus from the migration of an African ancestor to the New World at a time of maximum rain forest conditions—then subsequently evolving through progressively drying trends that resulted in various kinds of more arid vegetation.

OTHER VISITS

The remainder of this trip was primarily visiting friends in other South American countries, essentially as a scientist-tourist. I was always received with warm hospitality and felt blessed with the opportunities to stay in the homes with these families—continuing our friendship established while they were visiting the United States. In Montevideo, Uruguay, I visited an amazingly successful woman professor in a Latin American university, whom I had met at the Cronkite Center. She taught literature and shuddered at my life in the field. Here she insisted that I spend a lazy weekend as Uruguayans do, relishing the Old World charm of Montevideo, and as she predicted, I found the atmosphere delightfully relaxing. My second stop was the University of Argentina at La Plata, to visit the family of a systematist, whom I had met while he was visiting the Harvard Herbarium. Apart from tourist activities with the family, I relished discussions comparing the vegetation of Argentina with parts of Brazil I had covered in my collecting.

In Santiago, Chile, I visited another systematist at the Museo Nacional de Historia Natural. Knowing about my love of alpine plants, he took me on trips into *páramo* areas of the nearby Andes, particularly to see the incredible bromeliad *Puya* with hundreds of flowers on branch extensions that act as perches for pollinating birds. This plant is almost as characteristic of the *páramo* in this part of the Andes as *Espeletia* is in Colombian areas. These visits expanded my cultural experience of the people in other countries, developing a strong cultural thread that would often be woven with my purely scientific thread during my travels doing field work.

HALLMARK YEARS

1973-1978

Anyone who must think intensely and integrate vast amounts of information to solve a problem must feel the thrill of discovery.
—Barbara McClintock

The years between 1973 and 1978 were hallmark years for me. I had moved from field-oriented research to a mixture of both field work and laboratory experiments, including greenhouse and growth chamber. Our lab made a breakthrough in showing that chemical variation of resins could play a defensive role in plants, and could result to some extent from natural selection imposed by insect herbivores. I presented my views regarding the importance of the tropics in the evolution of the diversity of copious resin-producing trees to a world botanical audience, and I explored the potential for collaboration on chemical studies on Yugoslavian *Satureja,* which tied together my ecological and ethnobotanical interests.

The year 1973 saw my promotion to full professor in the spring. Considerable notice was given in the press about my being the first woman on the UCSC campus to be promoted to professor. One of the favorite stories among some of my colleagues about this promotion came from a meeting shortly afterward that included a number of administrators from the UC president's office. Chancellor McHenry proudly presented me to them as a new UCSC professor, and asked me what I thought would most advance my career. (There were still very few women professors in the UC system.) Without hesitation I replied, "A wife, especially one like Jane" (McHenry's wife was well known to be a devoted helpmate). It is the only time either I or my colleagues remember seeing McHenry speechless, and seemingly nonplussed—even for a few moments. Several other men in the group, however, nodded knowingly as well as in amusement.

I also had just been elected as a fellow in the California Academy of Sciences, and happily discovered that Lincoln Constance, the "patriot of Berkeley botany" had nominated me. His having encouraged my career, first while I was in Berkeley, continuing when I was at Harvard, and now again back in California, made the nomination especially meaningful. Also during the 1973-74 academic year, I was elected as a member of the Society of Women Geographers, which was founded in 1925 by a small group of women interested in exploration but who were excluded from the all-male Explorers Club. They established an organization for "traveled women," and it was to this group that such women had retreated in the San Francisco Bay area when excluded from the Biosystematists. Moreover, I had been asked by the vice chancellor for natural sciences to be the first woman chair of the Biology Board of Studies, with my term to begin at the end of my sabbatical leave during the winter and spring of 1974.

Susan Martin and Eric Lee with me at 1973 commencement

Another special event in 1973 was the graduation of two of my first PhD students, Y.T. (Eric) Lee and Susan Martin. Their enthusiasm had given a great boost to the *Hymenaea* project; their research had provided fundamental chemical and systematic information for our subsequent ecological studies of the genus. Eric's completion of his part of the *Hymenaea* monograph gave us clarification of the species names, and I was adding an evolutionary framework in which to place our ecological research. With our thorough analysis of many plant characters, the European legume researchers had heartily agreed with our putting the East African genus *Trachylobium* back into *Hymenaea,* which supported my hypothesis about an African origin of the genus. With Eric's additional collecting and taxonomic analysis of all of our specimens along with those from major herbaria around the world, we could demonstrate a close relationship between African and eastern rain forest Brazilian species as well as the latter species with those in Amazonia. We also now had support for my hypothesis that the dry forest and some desert species probably evolved from rain forest species as climates changed during the Tertiary and later during the fluctuating Pleistocene climate. (DNA analysis today on some southeastern Brazilian *Hymenaea* species is providing additional information regarding the impact of Pleistocene climatic variations in their habitat differentiation.)

To further my goal of understanding the ecological role of resins and their relationship to speciation of *Hymenaea*, we needed to examine the resin chemistry in plants we could grow under controlled conditions in our green house and growth chambers. *Hymenaea* amber was produced from trunk resin that consisted primarily of viscous, nonvolatile diterpenes. In studying young plants we focused on the volatile sesquiterpenes occurring in the small secretory pockets in the leaves. Sue Martin's chemical research, conducted on most of the species grown from seeds Eric and I had collected, had given us the identity of the common fifteen sesquiterpenes in the leaf resin. Sue used gas chromatography, then a technique in its early development days, to separate the resin components, which were laboriously trapped and collected for subsequent analysis by IR spectroscopy and mass spectrometry. Because some compounds in the resin extracts had only small structural differences, special measures were required to separate them for analysis. Sue laughs now to remember hand-packing twenty-foot-long GC columns in the stairwell of our research building, where an assistant slowly poured the packing material in at the top while Sue dashed up and down the stairs, tapping and vibrating the column to pack the filling without air pockets. The necessity for such undertakings today is difficult to imagine!

Sue was able to determine patterns of leaf resin composition, that is, the relative quantity of each resin component. Such repeated, genetically determined compositional patterns are often referred to as *chemotypes*. Sue's research also demonstrated that the chemotypes of intraspecific (populational) variation in *Hymenaea* leaves were more significant than interspecific variation. This result was important in implying that biotic factors could be playing a selective role in compositional variation in the populations, and hence these compositional patterns (chemotypes) were of ecological importance. Additionally, along with Al Cunningham, Sue determined some of the nonvolatile diterpene components in the trunk resin—a prelude to other later work on trunk resins. Al, with MS degrees in both chemistry and biology, had joined the lab in 1970 on sabbatical leave from the Chemistry Department of Monterey Peninsula College, to further assist with chemical studies of *Hymenaea* resins. He would finish his doctorate several years later than Sue because he continued to teach while completing his research.

I distinctly remember the problems in editing my first PhD dissertations. The dissertations were huge tomes, and I empathized with Sue and Eric when they had to retype entire chapters as a result of even small changes as editing progressed. To make matters worse, UCSC's dissertation quality standards required them to use the best-quality typewriters available—the IBM Selectrics® used by the Biology Board's secretaries. Thus, Sue's and Eric's typing often was done in the wee hours of the night! The memory of the many times I had to retype my own dissertation to reach the final copy with no white outs was still with me—plus having to draft by hand all maps and graphs. What a change has been wrought by the wide-spread use of word processing, starting around 1979, followed by the introduction of high-quality printers and the constant improvement in software for illustrations. Each technological advance allowed more careful editing by faculty, making it easier to gear chapters toward publication—and reducing the angst of the student in doing many revisions.

The year 1973 also was an important year in my personal life, because I decided to move out of Stevenson College, after living there as a preceptor for seven years. I had dreaded house hunting, realizing how spoiled I had become by the convenience of living on campus. Serendipity would come to my rescue again. En route to a nearby drugstore for a few items during the late spring I saw a sign advertising a townhouse complex a few blocks from the foot of the campus. One unit was left; it was two stories with a good-sized living room and dining room area that had big windows facing two small patios, where I could putter with some plants. There were three bedrooms upstairs, one of which I could convert into a study. This townhouse seemed to answer my needs very well and I made arrangements to buy it the next morning. The real estate agent emphasized that my being a tenured UC faculty member eased a rapid transaction, because most single woman were still not considered good risks for home loans at this time!

While serving on a university committee with one of the leading landscape designers in Santa Cruz, I found expert assistance in developing patios, and I felt grateful how this comfortable home evolved so naturally. It has served me extremely well during all my travels; its closeness to the campus made it attractive to graduate students or visiting professors who could occupy it and also take care of my successive legions of memorable cats. It provided a venue for social activities with many seminar speakers, Christmas parties, and birthday celebrations for my "lab family," as well as various occasions for my friends and associates. Moreover, it led to several visits from Mother during spring events at the university which she greatly enjoyed. During these times she also became acquainted with both Kenneth Thimann and George Hammond, whom I had told her much about. Although Mother did not have a college degree, as usual, her intelligence and educated viewpoints created admirers of these very erudite academicians.

Mother with Kenneth Thimann at 1975 commencement

*Mother, far right, at lab gathering that included
George Hammond, me and George's mother, at her left.*

SECOND COHORT OF GRADUATE STUDENTS

As Martin and Lee graduated, the team for ongoing *Hymenaea* lab and greenhouse experiments was extended with a second cohort of graduate students. I was constantly being prodded by my skeptical plant physiologist colleague, Kenneth Thimann, and to lesser extent by UCSC plant biochemist, Harry Beevers, to test my hypotheses regarding the evolution of the defensive properties of resin experimentally. They thought that chemical ecology was replete with theories, but with too little hard evidence to support them.

Genetic control of the chemotypes we had been analyzing would be necessary to show their evolutionary significance, i.e., that the chemotypes constituted a fitness characteristic of the plant. Serving as an important genetically-determined character for survival of the plant, they could be selected by herbivores or pathogens. Since we were unable to do genetic experiments on the tropical tree *Hymenaea,* we had to show that abiotic conditions such as light, temperature, and moisture did not influence the compositional patterns (i.e., they were not phenotypically variable) and hence could be inferred to be genetically controlled. We would use our seedlings grown under controlled conditions in growth chambers. At the same time, we could assess whether any of these factors influenced the total amount of terpenoids, which could increase a dose-dependent defensive effect of a particular compound or combination of them.

Although I recognized that the survival of the individual plant (its selection by agents in its environment) was an ecological event, in trying to determine the role that resin characteristics played in the fitness of the plant to survive into future generations, I was considering these characteristics being selected in an evolutionary context of populations. This merger of ecological and evolutionary perspectives was clearly evident in chemical ecology, where the chemicals are understood to provide fitness for the survival of the organism and hence are viewed as having been selected (along with the individual plant that produces them). Focus on the role of various characteristics, and their genetic determination, is now a mainstay of evolutionary ecology—but was an undeveloped part of ecology in 1958 when Mason was trying to convince ecologists that natural selection was an ecological as well as evolutionary concept.

Our experimental studies of potential abiotic effects on *Hymenaea courbaril* leaf resin variation showed that neither temperature nor photoperiod (daily period of illumination) influenced leaf resin composition but longer photoperiods markedly promoted vegetative growth. While Harry Borthwick, preeminent authority on photoperiodism in plants, was a regent's lecturer at UCSC, he assisted us in designing and interpreting the experiments regarding the effects of the photoperiodic extremes on leaf resins of *H. courbaril* across its wide latitudinal distribution from the equator northward to the Tropic of Cancer. Will Stubblebine, first as a senior thesis student and then as a graduate student, participated in the temperature and photoperiod experiments as well as our first greenhouse herbivore study, which showed that total leaf resin of *H. courbaril* significantly affected larval mortality of a generalist noctuid lepidopteran herbivore (*Spodoptera exigua*) commonly used for lab experiments.

I thought by the mid-1970s we had sufficient observational and experimental data to begin to support my hypotheses regarding the defensive properties provided by different kinds of variation in *Hymenaea* resins. We had shown the importance of spatial and temporal variation in

In greenhouse, amid seedlings used in experiments,
holding a large Hymenaea *resin mass and wearing an amber pendant*

making chemicals a potentially effective defense in long-lived plants, such as trees, against a wide array of rapidly evolving enemies during the life cycle of the plant. In *Hymenaea,* volatile sesquiterpenes predominated in the leaf resins and nonvolatile diterpenes in the trunk resins. However, in the young plant, resins did not occur in the roots at all, which we assumed was because the plant was putting its resources into growth of its deep root, rather than in defense. On the other hand, sesquiterpenes predominated in the stem tissue of the seedlings, which was attacked by herbivores and fungi. In both roots and stems, diterpenes began to predominate over sesquiterpenes during secondary development of the woody trunk. Furthermore, changes in the relative as well as absolute concentrations of various sesquiterpene components occurred during the development of the leaf. Thus we were witnessing both significant developmental and ontogenetic (from seedling to adult plant) changes in the resin components. We had evidence that abiotic conditions (initially temperature and photoperiod but soon including moisture stress and light intensity) did not affect quantitative composition, which by implication supported our hypothesis that compositional patterns were under genetic control in individual plants for a particular organ, but could be selected under biotic pressure. There was palpable excitement among the members of the lab group as we had progressed step by step in our understanding of the resins in *Hymenaea*.

Among the plethora of theories being presented by chemical ecologists regarding conditions that led plants to invest metabolic resources in synthesizing chemicals for defense, one, called "Optimal Defense Theory (ODT)," especially spoke to the direction of my research. The principles of ODT were proposed independently by Doyle McKey and David Rhoades in 1979 to explain the ecological and evolutionary forces that generate within plant heterogeneity in the distribution of chemical defenses against herbivory. Our 1978 paper "Implications of Variation in Resin Composition among Organs, Tissues and Populations in the Tropical Legume *Hymenaea*" had strongly suggested that intraplant variation was adaptive and an evolved trait, and thus provided grist for the ODT mill. During the following period in the early 1980s, chemical ecologists often emphasized the importance of host plant variation in "manipulating" herbivore activity—as indicated by such volumes as *Variable Plants and Herbivores in Natural and Managed Systems* edited by R.F. Denno and M.S. McClure. ODT also had been predicated on the idea that these chemical defenses are costly to plants and thus should be preferentially allocated to parts that are of the greatest value—an idea we would increasingly demonstrate as our work progressed.

I expanded on Stubblebine's initial herbivore experiment on *Spodoptera exigua* to show the inhibitory effects of different composition types (chemotypes) of *H. courbaril* leaf resins on different life stages, from larvae to adults, of this generalist herbivore. This was critical in our interpretation of the role of compositional variation versus total amount of resin (which was the usual focus of ecological analysis at the time) in deterring herbivory.

Although genetically controlled patterns in resin composition might be due to random genetic variation, I conjectured that compositional variation in populations at different sites could be selected and maintained by herbivory and hence was a significant character for understanding the "defensive armament" of terpene-producing plants. We now had to find means to get in the field to test this premise.

We published much of our research in the early issues of *Biochemical Systematics and Ecology,* in part to support the fledgling journal in this emerging field. I had attended the symposium in 1972 on "Chemistry in Evolution and Systematics" in Strasbourg, France, where creation of this journal had been proposed as an offshoot of *Phytochemistry.* I became good friends with the editors of both journals, Jeffrey Harborne and Tony Swain, and later served as longtime associate editor of *Biochemical Systematics and Ecology.* Most of the early papers in this journal were chemosystematic. Our studies, which were displaying the importance of understanding terpene patterns of variation from an ecological perspective rather than primarily a systematic one, provided background and some impetus for ecological and evolutionary analyses to be included in this journal.

In another study having evolutionary implications, we examined variation in the size and spatial arrangement of the secretory structures (pockets) containing the resin in *Hymenaea* leaves, tying together our phylogenetic prospectus of the genus with our hypothesis that leaf resin provides defense against different kinds of foliovores. Different sizes and arrangements of the "packaged" resin distinguished species from rain forest to desert ecosystems, which again seemed to imply selection by different feeding patterns of foliovores. This study was designed to entice future studies of different kinds of insect herbivores that attack *Hymenaea* across its wide range of tropical environments. Done in collaboration with Brazilian botanists, it was published in the *American Journal of Botany* for a more general botanical audience than some of our previous papers.

While our experimental work was advancing on *Hymenaea* plants grown in greenhouses from seeds that Lee and I had collected, we began what became long-term studies of monoterpenes in *Satureja douglasii* (yerba buena). This abundant and widely distributed mint grows along the Pacific Coast and often is used for tea, which is how I became interested in its chemical ecology. A colleague who made his tea from plants he collected on campus asked me why his tea tasted "minty" if he collected it in the redwood forest but tasted "like cough drops" if he collected it in the sunny oak-madrone forest bordering the redwoods. I was fascinated as to how these different habitats might affect the composition of the monoterpenes, which in turn determined the aroma and flavor of the tea.

David Lincoln arrived at this time, thinking that he would probably become part of the team working on the tropical *Hymenaea*. However, he had worked at the Todd Mint Company while an undergraduate at Kalamazoo College in Michigan, which fitted him well to study these native mints. He was successful in his dissertation research and he also helped me supervise three senior thesis students' research on *Satureja*. Another collaborative team effort in our lab had been formed. We had a head start on this project because others had used gas chromatography to determine the leaf monoterpenes in yerba buena. Again there was great anticipation as different members of the team provided answers to pieces of the puzzle to our understanding. David had described the chemotypes across the geographical distribution of the species along the Pacific Coast, which gave us the basis for their habitat distribution. The plants were easy to clone and propagate in a short period of time, which facilitated coordinated field, growth chamber, and greenhouse experiments of abiotic and biotic factors that could influence the leaf chemical variation. Abiotic conditions (light intensity, temperature, and moisture) did not affect terpene chemotypes. Therefore, the team moved to study the plant's herbivores. To our amazement we never observed insects on yerba buena. Rather, we found the plant's primary herbivore to be the banana slug (*Ariolimax dolichophallus*), which also turned out to be a good organism for lab and field experiments. Lab experiments showed camphor and biosynthetically related chemotypes were more palatable than the minty menthane group of chemotypes. Differential slug herbivory monitored in the field seemed to explain the difference in the distribution of cough drop-flavored (camphor-type) yerba buena collected from the oak-madrone border forest, where the slugs could not tolerate the high light and dry conditions. In other words, the occurrence there of these chemotypes had been permitted by lack of slug herbivores. The minty menthane chemotypes had survived in the more favorable shady and moist redwood forest habitat for slugs because they found these chemotypes less palatable. Furthermore, the total terpene yields were higher in the dense shade, perhaps indicating selection against herbivory, because terpene yields usually increase with light intensity. The professor who originally asked why his tea tasted differently when collected from different habitats was amazed at our ecological results—and how it involved the banana slug—now the official mascot of our campus.

*Banana slug (left), an important herbivore of yerba buena (right)
in redwood forest floor*

A study of fire ecology in redwood and associated vegetation added a different dimension to our Pacific Coast studies, and became important for the campus as well as the state parks. H.H. Biswell in the UC Berkeley Forestry School had established a program of prescribed burning in Yosemite Park and Giant Sequoia National Monument, which I had visited with some of my students. Biswell suggested that I consider Jason Greenlee, a Forestry School graduate, to do his PhD research on the use of prescribed burning of redwoods, starting with the UCSC campus and then in the surrounding state parks. My college course on redwood ecology came into play, as I had gotten to know various state park personnel. We obtained funding from Big Basin State Park as well as from the campus for Jason's dissertation research, in which he analyzed the vegetation while writing prescriptions for burning in both localities. He also implemented his prescription on campus.

Jason's first prescribed burn on campus caused quite a stir. The chancellor, who had not been fully convinced of using this procedure, came to witness it. Campus fire trucks surrounded Jason's chaparral site and those who came to see the burn gathered around as he started his flame thrower. Alas, he could not get the vegetation to catch fire. He had picked a winter day following rains to make sure that the fire wouldn't get out of control, but had been too conservative in his prescription—perhaps partly because I was so nervous, having been admonished repeatedly by the chancellor not to let Jason burn down the campus. We decided disappointedly that he should try a different prescription on another day. Later Jason successfully burned vegetation on the campus and for a number of years prescribed burning was used as a major means of fire control at UCSC. This work led Greenlee to analyze historic fire regimes in the diverse vegetation of the entire Monterey Bay area. Furthermore, his dissertation on Big Basin resulted in use of prescribed burning in state parks and a period when he was an administrator in the park system for that purpose.

In 1976, all of my graduate students, except one, were men. They and I had a jolting experience that year from a distinguished visitor to the international course in science and technology. I had a dinner for him and the students in the course at my house. He got together with a group of my graduate students and questioned them why they were taking their degrees with a woman sponsor—that this could seriously hamper their professional future! The students managed to change the subject, but they were outraged, and told me about the incident.

Second cohort of students in my lab

LENINGRAD INTERNATIONAL BOTANICAL CONGRESS
In 1975 I attended the XII International Botanical Congress in Leningrad and planned to extend my trip to include a visit to Yugoslavia, primarily to discuss collaborative research on *Satureja*. Although the primary purpose of an international congress is to meet people from other countries, the Soviets thoroughly inhibited this interaction by isolating participants from

each other in different hotels. The Soviets were paranoid about too much mingling of their own people with those from noncommunist countries. This was especially true of the large contingent of American attendees who were put together in the largest Leningrad hotel. Moreover, the meetings were so scattered around town that it was difficult to move from one meeting site to another to attend different sessions.

One of the main reasons I was attending this world assemblage of botanists was to present my ideas regarding the importance of the tropical environment, and recognition of tropical angiosperms, in evolution of resin-producing trees. I had begun to form these ideas at Harvard and my recent experiences in the tropics had only strengthened my belief. Professor Larsson in Denmark had become a stout proponent not only of my hypothesis but also that tropical conditions could help to explain the astounding abundance of Baltic amber. There were skeptics of both of my proposals, particularly among Europeans, with whom I hoped to discuss my ideas. Both Larsson and I were convinced that most European amber researchers had not thought about both physiological and ecological conditions that could influence the abundance of resin production—and how these might be intensified in the tropics. However, under the conditions imposed by the Soviets I gave my paper with limited time for discussion, and I reluctantly gave up trying to contact these people.

Leningrad is an incredibly beautiful city so I turned to taking some tours with American friends in our hotel. The city is located along the banks of the Neva River and its many canals have earned its nickname as the "Venice of the North." Among its 150 museums, the renowned Hermitage with its rich collection of European paintings provided a delightful experience. Of even more significance to me, as an amber researcher, was the Amber Room in Peter the Great's Ekaterinsky palace—although it now only had a few original items. This room was the pinnacle of artistic amber creation in the eighteenth century. Its oak panels, inlaid with 100,000 pieces of amber, had been given to Peter the Great by Frederick William I to celebrate the Russo-Prussian alliance. When the Nazis invaded Leningrad in 1941, the Russians tried to hide the panels of the Amber Room by papering them over. The city heroically survived the nine-hundred-day German siege, but not the Amber Room. When the Nazis discovered the panels, they crated and shipped them away. But where? The survival and whereabouts of the panels remain a mystery—although detective work continues to try to locate this great art treasure. The Russians consider it so much a part of their cultural history that in 1979 they began the almost overwhelming task of replicating the panels from several black-and-white photographs taken before the Nazi invasion. (They overcame many obstacles to reconstruct this incredible paneled room for the celebration of the four hundredth anniversary of Saint Petersburg (its name was also restored) in 2004.)

TRAIN TRIP TO MOSCOW AND KIEV

I wanted to take the train south from Leningrad to Moscow, thence to Kiev, and fly to Yugoslavia—my other main destination for this trip. The train for foreign visitors, however, went from Leningrad to Moscow at night, which would have prevented me from seeing the boreal forest countryside. When I expressed my desire to go to Moscow by day train, Thimann's secretary said that she could get the ticket for me (Thimann had a private secretary provided by the Soviets, because he had been the previous president of IBC).

When I got to the train station ready to board I was told I had the wrong ticket. As a foreign visitor, I was not supposed to be on this train. After much ado, I was finally allowed to board but began to see why they didn't want tourists on it. The seats were uncomfortable wooden benches. I sat down in the front of the car, with people craning to see me with puzzled looks. Thimann's secretary had told me that the train had a dining car. When the conductor came through, also very concerned about my ticket, I found out there was no dining car on this train. As we had stopped at a few stations I noticed kiosks selling food, so at the next stop I started to step off the train to purchase some. Several men in the car, however, shouted "*nyet, nyet*," and dragged me back on the train just as it began to lurch forward. If they hadn't done this, I would have been left behind—and no telling what would have happened. When back on the train, I tried to explain (using body language) that I was hunting for food; people around me started to smile. A little later they began to unwrap food they were carrying with them, and soon afterward some started to offer me chunks of brown bread buttered with something that tasted like lard, small pieces of meat, nondescript cheese, and finally a small apple. I stood in the aisle, smiling and thanking with "*spahseebah, spahseebah*" (thank you) one of the few Russian words I knew how to pronounce. What had been a quiet and seemingly even sullen atmosphere changed to one filled with smiles and laughter. It was an almost magical time and so clearly demonstrated that words are often not necessary for basic communication. After this event, I viewed from the train window this northern country with small lakes and many birch trees along with scraggly conifers—a landscape somewhat reminiscent of the Fairbanks area in Alaska.

And when we made stops I was intrigued with the log and other wooden houses—often with intricate carvings decorating them.

My problems, however, were not over. When I arrived in Moscow I had expected to be met by someone from Intourist, the state agency I had dealt with in Communist countries in 1964, which made all visitors' hotel and transportation arrangements. I got off and stood by the train, but when everyone from the train had departed and no one met me, I began to worry. I had noticed a big burly young army officer several yards away watching me carefully. Finally, he came over to me and asked me in broken but understandable English what I was doing there. I replied that I was waiting for Intourist to take me to my hotel. He told me to stay where I was and that he would call them. He disappeared then returned to his previous location where he continually kept his eyes on me. Eventually, a woman from Intourist arrived, who immediately castigated me for avoiding the tourist train that I should have taken. No explanation was acceptable. However, she did have a reservation for me at a hotel in Moscow immediately across the street from the Kremlin—fortunately not the enormous Rossiya, the world's largest hotel, which looms over the Kremlin.

I spent several days touring Moscow and its environs with the Intourist group and bought some Baltic amber jewelry, which was being featured in many tourist stores. The only difficult situation that occurred in Moscow was my interaction with the *dezhurnaya*, the woman in charge of the room keys, who would check you in and out at the end of corridors in Russian hotels. A rather intimidating and surly woman held this position on the floor of my hotel. I had been warned to take nylon hose, ballpoint pens, and the like to give to such people, but these did not satisfy her. She had taken a liking to my walking shoes and, in fact, said somewhat fiercely that she wanted them! Even though I protested vigorously that these were the only shoes, except for some dressy sandals, that I had brought for an extended trip across Europe, she became so adamant about wanting them that I was beginning to feel desperate. Finally, the inspired idea came to me to ask if I could send her something special she wanted from the United States instead of giving her my shoes now. Yes, she said, she went to the Black Sea for vacation and she had seen a bathing cap with a rubber rose on the top. She would *let* me keep my shoes if I promised to buy and send her such a bathing cap. Fortunately, I left for Kiev before she changed her mind! I wondered in retrospect if she would have been so vehement if I had been accompanied by a man. Maybe not, as I found out much later from Russian friends in the United States that even Russian travelers could be intimidated by the notorious *dezhurnaya*. I did try to keep my promise but was unsuccessful in finding a bathing cap with a rose on top.

I took the train for tourists to Kiev. The next day an Intourist guide arrived to take me on a tour of the city, which emphasized war monuments and buildings emblazoned with huge paintings of Lenin on a red background. I was overwhelmed with facts about Soviet losses in World War II, and was depressed by the majority of paintings in art museums, which were of war scenes—either depicting the war itself or desolate-looking families mourning their losses. I admit that I had not realized the enormous sacrifices of the Soviet people in World War II other than the horrendous ones in the nine-hundred-day siege of Leningrad. I felt depressed in the drabness of Kiev, as I had previously in Warsaw. Even though we suffered privations in the US, and many families lost loved ones, most of us on the home front never realized how many innocent European people suffered so terribly during that war. I was glad to move on to Yugoslavia.

YUGOSLAVIA

My Aeroflot flight to Belgrade was in an old Russian plane that had been converted from war-time use. When I sat down in my aisle seat, the arm fell off. A buxom woman sitting next to me started shouting for the steward to do something, and he managed to get it more or less screwed back into place. When I sat down again, my seatmate smiled broadly and took a pin off her lapel showing the Soyez hookup with Apollo. She handed it to me with great flourish, shouting "peace" in English. People in neighboring seats clapped and smiled. It was a touching moment, especially following my Kiev visit and heavy dose of the effects of World War II on the Soviet people!

The Yugoslavian visit was both a professional excursion and a sentimental journey back in time. George Hammond, in his role as foreign secretary of the US National Academy of Sciences, had been helping Yugoslavian scientists establish cooperative bilateral programs with US universities. Miroslav Gasic in the Institute of Chemistry at the University of Belgrade was interested in collaborating with my lab to study terpene variation in Yugoslavian species of *Satureja*. Nine species, with numerous widely distributed subspecies in Yugoslavia, were frequently used as herbs for flavoring and as medicines, but unknown as a tea, unlike our yerba buena. Chemical analysis of these Yugoslavian species would provide an interesting comparison with our Pacific Coast studies of chemical variation in this genus, as well as data of value for use of the plants in Yugoslavia. For me, it was another case of combining chemical ecology with ethnobotany.

My interaction with the enthusiastic Yugoslavian chemists and botanists was such a pleasure, and I found Tito's Communist rule less a stranglehold on the people than I had witnessed in my travels in Poland, East Germany, and the Soviet Union. I corresponded extensively over several years with some of these scientists regarding preliminary chemical analyses and grant proposals. Unfortunately, as often happens when there is change in the US panel deciding funding for such projects, this Yugoslavian *Satureja* collaboration never came to final fruition. Both sides, nevertheless, had learned much about the chemical variation and herbal values of this widespread member of the mint family. It was regrettable that my lab also could not pursue the chemical ecology in a manner that has been done for thyme (*Thymus*) in France—a result of continuous collaborative studies.

Following my discussions in Belgrade, I flew to the Adriatic Coast and the "magic fortress kingdom" of Dubrovnik, which was of personal sentimental interest in that it had been the summer home of Mirko Feric, my childhood pen pal. Dubrovnik, renowned for its churches, palaces, and medieval libraries that reflect a thousand years of history is today a World Heritage site. (International restoration efforts have repaired most of the damage from shelling by the Yugoslav army during the 1991-92 Balkan siege, although over 30,000 books were burned—another testament to the irrational horror and irreplaceable losses from war.)

I left the Adriatic coast for Zagreb to see the home city of Mirko Feric. I found Zagreb to be a more pleasant city than Belgrade, and while I was having a drink at an outdoor table of a restaurant, as in Paris, a tall, handsome young man asked if he could join me to practice his English. I was startled when he said his name was Mirko, as I had been sitting there wondering if my former pen pal were still alive—and thinking what a joy it would have been to actually have met him.

As a finale for this trip, en route home I visited a former postdoctoral fellow, who had been in Harry Beevers' lab at UCSC. Now at the botanical institute at the University of Munich, he had gone on one of the Death Valley trips, where he was fascinated with the desert "belly plants," which reminded him of some German alpine plants. I happily accepted his invitation for hikes to visit alpine vegetation in the Alps near Shocken. Although over the years opportunities for me to get into alpine areas were sporadic, I took them when I had the chance, and the thread of my love of arctic-alpine plants has persisted ever since my days at Gothic, Colorado, in the mid-1940s.

EXPANDING SERVICE ACTIVITIES

As I was gaining prominence as a UC professor in the mid to late 1970s, my service load continued to increase within the university, and expanded nationally and internationally. On most of these committees or boards, I was the only woman member—in some cases perhaps as a token woman, but in others because I was a qualified woman among the few then available. I thus felt the load of representing "all women" at this time; there was always the specter that if I and other "pioneer" women failed to perform well, it could influence those who followed us, perhaps for a long time. (Even in 1983, Barbara McClintock chafed under the glare of having been awarded the Nobel Prize for her genetic research, stating "It was awful because of the responsibility to women. I couldn't let them down.")

The multiplicity of service roles at times was overwhelming, but since early youth I have always been willing to help when needed. Now, however, it was beginning to seem like a weakness not to "just say no." I had started, at least, to try to tie these commitments more carefully to my research activities. Nonetheless, such a load restricted my personal activities. Among some male colleagues, the pioneering UCSC activities alone were causing burnout, but I continued onward.

In relation to my lab's California botanical research, I served on the Council of the California Botanical Society, as well as on the Editorial Board for UC Publications, first in Geology (1973-1978), then later in Botany. As members of my lab were regularly giving papers at the annual Botanical Society of America meetings, during this time I accepted the chair of its Phytochemical Section.

My growing chemical expertise also led me to be invited in 1977 to be a member of the Ecology Committee of the Scientific Advisory Board of the Environmental Protection Agency (EPA), which had been established in 1970 "to protect human health and safeguard the natural environment." The committee was a major time commitment with voluminous material to assess before meetings that took place, primarily, in Washington, DC. It was an eye-opening but discouraging exercise in discovering how an enormous effort to make scientific conclusions available to decision-makers could be ignored at higher levels of government. The EPA was supposed to assume "leadership in the nation's environmental science, research, education, and assessment," and thus it was even more shocking to our committee to discover the lack of motivation of many current EPA researchers to update their environmental background. When the agency was established, workers from other agencies (such as the USDA) had been transferred to the EPA, and often they were not at the forefront of rapidly moving environmental research. Our committee suggested a sabbatical system be established in which selected researchers could spend a year at a university to be updated on environmental research. The committee was appalled by the lack of interest and even opposition shown by most investigators as we visited their labs to discuss our suggestions.

On another front, I had become increasingly involved with a variety of responsibilities related to the tropics, from membership on the UC Systemwide Tropical Studies Committee to representing UC on the board of directors of Organization of Tropical Studies (consortium of universities). I also served on the research committee of the international Association of Tropical Biology and chaired the US National Academy of Sciences (NAS)/ Brazilian National Research Council (CNPq) subcommittee on the Humid Tropics. Among others, I sat on the NAS panel on "Underexploited Tropical Legumes" and on Projeto Flora Amazônica. Although time-consuming activities, they helped both my research and graduate teaching.

AN ADMINISTRATIVE JOB?
Because of my increasing visibility on the national scene, starting in 1974 I was frequently being asked if I was interested in chairing botany departments (e.g., Iowa State, Maryland, and Oklahoma), in becoming dean of a division or college of botany (e.g., Kansas State and Penn State), and a director of an arboretum (Harvard) and an environmental center (Duke). Despite my qualifications, I think that at least a few of these offers may have arisen from the accelerating pressure during the 1970s for organizations to at least consider women for positions of influence. It seemed that Betty Friedan's political and legal activism for equal access to the workplace and equal treatment were beginning to have some effect. Although I had gravitated toward leadership roles in my youth, opportunities did not become available while I was married. Now, however, after inspecting the possibilities and doing some interviews, I decided to stay on course with my own research at UCSC, which would have been sidetracked by transferring to an administrative position at another institution. I also had helped found UCSC and was committed to helping it progress—I was at that time the chair of the Biology Board of Studies and was still being courted to be the dean of graduate studies. The kind of major administrative work that I did finally accept was to come later with presidencies of four professional societies.

TEACHING BRAZILIAN
BOTANISTS IN AMAZONIA
1974

It is entirely impossible in the Amazon to take stock of the
vastness, which can only be measured in fragments.
—Euclides da Cuha

Big changes had been occurring at INPA (Instituto Nacional de Pesquisas da Amazonia) since my visit in 1969. Paulo Machado, who had become director in 1971, wanted to make INPA the premier research center in central Amazonia. To accomplish his goals he first constructed a campus, carefully located in the forest at the edge of Manaus, so that researchers would be in the forest, even while they were doing library and laboratory work. Importantly, apartments and small houses were available for researchers to live on campus.

Soon after moving into this site, Machado and the Amazonian botanist Ghillean (Iain) Prance, then at the New York Botanical Garden (NYBG), started discussing how to improve the academic quality of INPA staff who lived in Amazonia, as these people were most likely to continue to live and work in the area. At that time most of the qualified Brazilian scientists just came for short periods of field work, then retreated to São Paulo and Rio de Janeiro. Machado and Prance planned a two-year master's program in Amazonian botany for Brazilians who already had a bachelor's degree from one of the three universities in Amazonia—Pará, Amazonas, and Mato Grosso. Prance would direct the program and classes would be taught at INPA by an international team as visiting professors of the Universidade de Pará. Machado's invitation for me to teach in this program was an opportunity to be part of a significant development in the future of Amazonian botanical research through the training of these botanists. This program differed greatly from Organization for Tropical Studies (OTS) courses, which were at that time primarily for graduate students from American universities and taught by faculty from members of the consortium. OTS courses also covered all aspects of biology, not just botany. The two programs provided an interesting comparison in serving different purposes in training tropical researchers.

The opportunity for my teaching in INPA's botany program came in 1974, coincident with a sabbatical leave. I spent several months at Harvard before proceeding to Manaus, making additions to the ecology as well as clarifying my hypotheses concerning evolutionary history in the monographic study of *Hymenaea*. Elso Barghoorn had me appointed as a Harvard Visiting Professor, not just a visiting researcher, because he felt so strongly that women generally did not get their due recognition at Harvard. Such an appointment was a delightful surprise. Eric Lee was still a post doctoral fellow there and hence we could complete the manuscript, which was published the next year as a University of California Publication in Botany.

Machado had become acquainted with our research while Eric, following in my footsteps to collect additional *Hymenaea* material, was at INPA during 1971. He was so impressed with our enthusiasm about work in Amazonia that he invited me to write a short piece on my experience for the first volume of the INPA publication *Acta Amazônica* in 1971. It was great for a woman to be chosen to write such a note for the inaugural issue, and it gave me a chance to express my enthusiasm to have the opportunity to work in Amazonas as well as gratitude for INPA's assistance in my doing so. *Acta Amazônica* was not only established as an outlet for INPA's own researchers but to ensure that foreign researchers made their Amazonian work immediately accessible to Amazonian scientists (preferably in Portuguese), even if they later published their results in other journals. This was a period in which scientists in developing countries such as those of Latin America were strongly proclaiming the need to have scientific publications available in their own language, or at least in their own journals. In 1973, I sent our first research results from Amazonia, "An Evolutionary and Ecological Perspective of the Amazonian Hylaea Species of *Hymenaea* (Leguminosae: Caesalpiniodeae)" to be published in the third issue of this new tropical journal, in order to support INPA's activities as well as support the increasing development of tropical ecology. Publication in general ecological journals may have given our work more exposure outside of the tropics.

For the INPA botany program, I taught a course in Tropical Chemical Ecology. In many ways I had a missionary's zeal to create understanding of a new tropical research perspective—the importance of the abundant production of secondary chemicals by tropical plants and their mediation of ecological interactions with the plants' ever-present and numerous "enemies." After all, so many drugs came from tropical plants; what were these chemicals doing for the plant and even for the organisms with which they were interacting?

The apartments on campus, where investigators and professors could live, were a blessing in many ways. We also had meals at an open-air *canteena* near the apartments. Living on campus greatly facilitated interaction with INPA researchers as well as out-of-class discussion with the students. I had suggested that my course have a seminar format, which was enthusiastically endorsed by Prance because it was a new teaching approach for these Brazilian students. They were used to essentially regurgitating the professor's lectures or material from textbooks. This was so different from what I had become accustomed to at RMBL and UCSC, but herein lay the challenge for both me and my twelve Brazilian students!

My most immediate problem, however, was the language in which the course was to be taught. Machado had emphasized that he wanted me to teach the course in English. The students were studying English as part of this program, specifically because so much of the current scientific literature was in English. Both he and Prance thought that some courses given in English would expedite this language-learning process because most of the courses were being taught in Portuguese by Brazilians. However, even though my course came late in the program, most of the students had not become proficient in English. All of my reading assignments were in English, since there was no chemical ecology literature in Portuguese in 1974. Although most students could read some English, several could barely understand my comments in English, let alone speak themselves or, perish the thought, discuss the ideas they had struggled to read. Thus, I had to compromise on the seminar format and primarily give lectures in a mixture of Portuguese words, Spanish grammar, and a desperate retreat to English with lots of body language to explain some concepts, There were short reports by the students followed by discussion—dominated, of course, by the best English speakers. Interestingly, seven of the twelve students were women, and they, unfortunately, were more hesitant speakers than the men.

Topping these problems was the fact that most chemical ecology research at this time had been done on temperate zone plants with which the students were not familiar. There were some exceptions, notably the research of Dan Janzen on the role of chemical defense against seed predation, and herbivory in determining diversity of trees in tropical forests as well as studies of other researchers on selective chemical attraction of bees to facilitate orchid pollination. The students had some familiarity with the secondary chemicals because they had been given a short course in *fitoquimica* by Otto Gottlieb, Brazil's leading phytochemist.

Overall, however, I became convinced that one of the most important lessons these students learned from my course was neither chemical ecology nor English, but to try to make their own assessments of the research about which they were reading. This had been extremely difficult for them; they first wanted to know what I thought. At the beginning they had little confidence in their own opinions but made amazing progress through the course. They literally seemed freed to present ideas of their own, although some of them were still rather naive. Not to matter, they were beginning to think critically.

Following our lecture/discussions I would rest briefly, have lunch, and start preparing for the next day as the midday storms brought daily heavy rains. After continuing to help students over various hurdles in the afternoon and evening, I would often have to labor late into the night and get up at 4:00 AM to go over the Portuguese part of my lecture. The students also

INPA chemical ecology class in Ducke Reserve

faced an unrelenting schedule, but, somehow, we all survived! They were blessed with characteristic Brazilian senses of humor, and viewing the often agonizing moments humorously sustained us. One day a week we took a break for trips to the Ducke Reserve to rehash ideas in the field. Here I would discuss my current research on *Hymenaea*, emphasizing the parent tree/progeny project and how it displayed problems of doing chemical ecology on tropical trees by people who did not live in Amazonia. We also surveyed the resin-and latex-producing trees in a hectare plot in which the trees had been identified and counted. Several of the students maintained a strong interest in chemical ecology, one doing his thesis on a chemical ecology project and another coming to UCSC to study for his PhD.

Fortuitously, some animals I met while eating in the *canteena* just across from my apartment provided me a little relief from this stress. A feral mother cat with five kittens adopted me after I gave them some extra fish from the *canteena*. I later purchased some dehydrated milk to augment the milk of the very thin mother. The cats quickly made my apartment home and played around me while I was working on class lectures. They even slept huddled on top of me on the small bed. Strangely, I seldom saw the cats scratch very much nor did I suffer from flea bites. It was a mystery to me. Moreover, although feral (at least they had no home), they accepted me without ever expressing fear or any type of aggression. They were just gentle, sweet animals and the good little mother seemed

Three members of class and INPA assistant around Hymenaea intermedia *tree in Ducke Reserve (Roberto Figliuolo, far left, later came to study at UCSC)*

One of feral kittens

so grateful for the extra food and kind attention. I seemed to be benefiting from the colonial American proverb: "You will always be lucky if you know how to make friends with strange cats."

Just before I left Manaus, the mother had weaned the kittens, and she clearly was pregnant again. I was conflicted as to whether in the long run I had done her or her kittens a favor in taking care of them for six weeks, because now what would happen? I talked to some of the permanent INPA staff about adopting them, but taking cats into your home was not a part of the culture of this group of people. I also could not find a vet in Manaus that neutered cats (I hope that has changed since 1974, although I have discovered that even now in some Latin American countries veterinarians are not taught how to spay and neuter domestic pets at veterinary schools). I was able to find a temporary solution with the professor who taught the course after mine agreeing to look after them and to pursue a permanent solution for this little feline family. I never heard what happened.

I had another pleasant and unlikely animal encounter in the *canteena* when, one evening, a three-toed sloth was on one of the benches there. I went over to look at it, sat down, and started to talk to it—as is my wont with all kinds of animals. Moving unbelievably slowly, it crawled into my lap and started to embrace me like a tree trunk, until its arms were around my neck. If you have ever seen the claws on a sloth, you can imagine why I was frozen stiff; however, it did not dig them into my skin. Its rough fur was slightly green from a symbiotic alga that lives in microscopic grooves in the hairs of the animal's fur. These algae give the sloth a greenish sheen that provides protective coloration in the canopy of trees, especially during the rainy season. This particular animal lived in nearby trees but came to the ground occasionally at the *canteena*. Sloths generally like to stay high in the trees; they move so incredibly slow that they can easily be attacked by predators on the ground.

Sloth in INPA canteena

Nonetheless, this animal must have felt safe in these surroundings, and I got to see it up close again another evening. I was the only person anyone had ever seen it crawl up on, although it did grab branches that others held out for it.

Contrary to the relief and pleasure provided by the cats and the sloth, INPA entomologists alerted me to a terrifying insect spectacle—an army ant "visit" on our campus. Acting in concert, columns of hundreds (even thousands) of army ants can fan out in raiding parties up to five hundred feet across at their front lines, consuming roaches, beetles, snakes, and lizards in their path. In this case, it was a minor colony, but still the rapidly moving mass of these large ants was an extraordinary sight.

Fish dominated the meals served at the *canteena*; I had learned from my previous trips to look forward especially to the luscious *tambaqui* and, upon rare occasions, to *pirara̧cu*. However, an initially unpleasant surprise came with my first meal in 1974. While big pieces of fish fillet were being put on the plates of people ahead of me in the food line, when I arrived the server smilingly said "*por a professora*" and placed a fish head on my plate. One of the INPA investigators noticed my dismay and told me that the fish head, which contained the cheeks, was the choice piece, saved for the person of honor that day! Since this fish was a member of the catfish family, it still had whiskers and what seemed to me at the time to be enormous eyes. I was later told that these catfish use their large eyes and whiskers to navigate in the murky Amazonian waters. I got plenty of fillets later, in fact, our meals were dominated by fish, and we sometimes had barbecues following a field trip with fish caught right out of the river.

Fish caught by INPA staff, later barbequed over open fire for class

One of my most exciting trips in the town of Manaus was to the fish market, in which I was accompanied by the INPA ichthyologist. I had never seen such variety (2,500 to 3,000 species of fish have been reported from Amazonia). There was diversity not only in species but also in size—from minnow size to eight-foot *piraraçu*. A salesman holding up a fillet of fish half as big as he was will always stick in my memory. The *piraraçu* is believed to be the largest scaled fish in the world. It can reach nine feet in length and weigh 330 pounds. These fish are large predators, joining the freshwater dolphins and caiman at the river's highest trophic level. Amazonian native people have consumed them as long as they have been known. Fishermen harpoon the *piraraçu* as they come to the surface, which they do every ten to twenty minutes because of the low levels of dissolved oxygen in Amazonian waters.

Manaus fish market; note size of fillet
being held up by seller at far right

Visiting the produce markets was always a pleasure. Manioc, *Manihot esculenta,* here is particularly interesting. Also known as *yuca* or cassava, it is a tuberous root, which is the dietary mainstay of peoples in many tropical areas. It grows well in depleted soils, and with minimum labor yields more starch per acre than any other crop. Manioc is prepared for eating in a variety of ways. When boiled, it has a heavy consistency, like incompletely cooked macaroni. In Brazil the shredded and roasted manioc, known as *farinha*, occurs in various forms. When in coarse grains, it is what we in temperate climes call tapioca. *Farinha* and *farofa* (toasted *farinha* that includes herbs) are popular condiments throughout Brazil. They are sprinkled over soups, stews, and meat dishes, and are commonly kept on the table along with salt and pepper.

The variety of fruit for consumption also was intriguing. Around one hundred and twenty are commonly eaten—65 per cent of which are native—some traditionally cultivated and others only known from the wild. These only appear during certain seasons of the year. When I was in Manaus, at this time there were native species of *Spondias* (*cajarana*), *Anona* (*graveola*), and *Theobroma* (*cupuaçu*) and others amid the usual bananas, mangoes, papayas (*mamão*), pineapples (*abacaxi*), and passion fruit (*maracajá*).

With INPA investigators I took some interesting boat trips, such as a visit to the "meeting of the waters" near Manaus. Here the yellowish, muddy (for some curious reason called "milky" in early reports and now "white") waters of the Solimões River, from the headwaters of the Amazon in Peru, meet the black, clear waters of the Rio Negro near Manaus to officially form the Amazon River. The different-colored waters remain separate for some distance but then gradually begin to mix. It is a dramatic sight; previously I had only seen it from the air. As a result of the convergence of the two rivers, the Amazon is forty miles across at Manaus. Later, I poled a small raft in a canal among the world's biggest water lilies (*Victoria amazonica*). They are so large that a small child can walk on them. Prance and an INPA entomologist had worked out their complex, fascinating pollination by scarab beetles, which are attracted to fragrance emitted as the flowers open at dusk. What a thrill to be among the lilies that until then I had only seen in the tropical conservatory ponds of the New York Botanical Garden and the Royal Botanic Gardens in England.

In addition to my class field trips, I accompanied Ghillean Prance on trips along the newly constructed highway from Manaus to Boa Vista. The road was so new that we generally had it to ourselves, which provided open, easy access for plant collecting and opportunity to view complete soil profiles in the road banks as well. This and other roads of the ambitious Amazonian highway system offered mixed blessings—Prance and others at INPA were becoming very concerned about their environmental impact. Isolation and lack of commercial activity had largely protected Amazonia from 1914 to 1960. Belém had been isolated from the rest of Brazil from 1616 until the

Transamazonian Highway was begun in 1953. When construction of the Transamazonian and other highways began,

Amid Amazonian water lilies

Inspecting new highway near Manuas

agricultural settlements were promoted along them, but farmers along the completed Brasilia-Belém highway were having problems adapting to proper utilization of the land from arid northeastern regions to the humid tropics. In 1974, more environmental impacts were initiated as the Brazilian government promoted large agro-industrial enterprises such as extensive cattle ranching. SUDAM in 1970 had also conferred free port status to kilometers of riverside area, including Manaus. Thus, massive environmental destruction was spreading to the heart of Amazonia.

Realizing the possible impact of these encroaching environmental problems, Prance set up Tropical Ecology, led by Robert Goodland, a highly respected ecologist from NYBG, as one of the early courses in the Amazonian botany program. Prance accompanied the class on the first major field trip to Alamira, Pará, to witness the agricultural projects along the Transamazonian Highway. He not only wanted to see the environmental effects directly but also wanted to think about collecting plants along the natural transects being cut through the forest for the road. However, both Goodland and Prance became convinced on this trip that the highway was an environmental disaster, and felt strongly that the world should be alerted to the wanton destruction that was occurring.

Goodland decided to write a book about the situation and invited Prance to coauthor it. Prance knew Goodland would go all out to expose the problem and therefore declined. He preferred to work from within, training Brazilian Amazonian botany students to think about what they would be able to do regarding conservation as well as work with the Brazilian government on later projects. Goodland instead collaborated with Howard Irwin, director of NYBG, to write a vivid, scathing picture of Amazonia being laid waste. *Amazonian Jungle: Green Hell to Red Desert?* shook the botanical world and its effects soon spread to governments and conservationists worldwide who exerted pressure wherever they could. The Brazilian government was displeased, and informed Goodland that he no longer was welcome in Brazil—the response that Prance had feared in his continuing to work in Brazil

It is difficult today to even recall those times when Brazil had been praised for its ambitious vision in building the Transamazonian Highway system as a means to partially solve unemployment and famine in the northeastern arid parts of their country by settling three million people along the highway. Certainly Goodland and Irwin's book, resulting from an INPA botany class field trip, began the process of alerting the world to what was happening environmentally. I also started to emphasize conservation in discussions in both my Plants and Human Affairs and Tropical Ecology courses, with the idea of aiding my US students to think in terms of relating conservation with utilization of this vast resource of biodiversity. Also, later I served on important US-Brazilian committees concerned with sustainable utilization of resources in Amazonia.

LONG, INTERESTING TRIP HOME

At the end of my course I received payment in Brazilian cruzeiros that I could not take out of the country! Despite having been provided with food and lodging, instructors were paid a fair sum of money in addition. I gave several lavish dinner parties for the students and INPA staff but then decided to use the remainder of the money for a trip across part of the Andes in Peru, Bolivia, and Ecuador en route to Costa Rica for an OTS meeting several weeks after my course ended. Planning a rather complicated trip from Manaus was tricky and I wasn't sure whether my reservations would hold up. In fact, some did not!

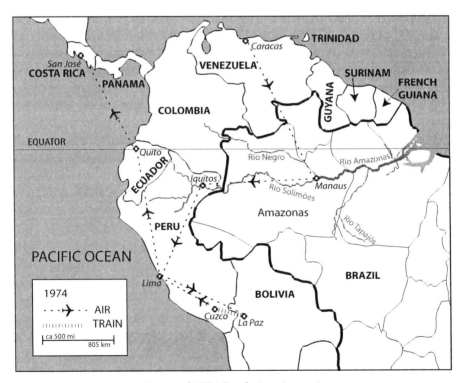

Route of 1974 South American trip

I flew from Manaus to Iquitos, Peru, watching the Amazon narrow into the muddy Solimões River as the plane traveled toward the river's headwaters. It was still during the rainy season, and the *varzea* forests and massive grassy areas were flooded. In Iquitos I was most displeased to see many animals, such as macaws and tropical fish, for sale and being prepared to be sent to buyers in the United States! From Iquitos it was over the Andes to dry and dusty Lima for a brief stop en route to La Paz, Bolivia. I particularly felt the cold in La Paz, having just spent two months in hot Amazonian lowlands. As I walked the steep streets I empathized with the many apathetic looking women selling wares while sitting huddled on the sidewalks, trying to keep warm in their many woolen skirts and black hats. Always their faces and those of the children were rosy from the cold. I soon also began to feel the altitude of the world's highest city (10,800 feet). For the first time in all of my high mountain ventures, I succumbed to the terrible, throbbing headache and nausea of *sirroche*, "mountain sickness."

To top off this misery, the shutter on my Nikon camera got stuck and I was headed the next night for Lake Titicaca and on to Machu Picchu where, of course, I wanted to take photos! I went up and down the incredibly steep streets of La Paz (worse than San Francisco) with a throbbing head, hunting for a camera store where it could be fixed—immediately. No one at any of the stores knew anything about a Japanese camera. Finally, someone suggested I go to the Toyota agency. I first thought I was having a problem understanding their Spanish, but, no, the car shop was what they meant. So off I went to Toyota, where three white uniformed mechanics met me, bowing politely. When I showed them the problem with the camera, they spoke among themselves in Japanese and proceeded to take it completely apart on a counter. I was in despair. Would they ever get it back together, let alone make it work? They were apparently arguing among themselves and I was feeling worse and worse. Then, they were all smiles, holding the camera up for me, indicating that it was fine—which it was! They bowed again and again and would not take any money for their efforts. I suspect that somehow even they were surprised at their success.

That night I took the beginning of another special train trip to which I had been looking forward—to Lake Titicaca on the first leg of a journey to Puno, the capital of Peru's *altoplano*. While waiting for the train I was fortunate to meet a Brazilian physician and his wife, who were very friendly. The train had no heat and so they suggested that the three of us huddle together. They were sympathetic about my having just come from warm Amazonas and being mountain sick as well. Icicles were hanging outside our train window but a full moon was shedding light on a barren-appearing Bolivian part of the *altoplano* at 12,000 or 13,000 feet. Occasionally we could hear the haunting sounds of Andean flutes as we passed a few villages. It was an enchanting experience despite the freezing temperatures. At the first stop we bought native alpaca hats and gloves, which were being sold by colorfully attired people alongside the train. We exited the train at Lake Titicaca, which borders Bolivia and Peru. When we went through the passport check to enter Peru, I signed the forms with a red pen that I had been using to grade final exams in Manaus. This caused a terrible uproar with the officials yelling that red was a sign of communism, and was I a *"communista"*? I was astounded by the question but tried to allay their fears, assuring them that they weren't letting a Communist into Peru by the back door, so to speak. Finally, all calmed down and I was allowed into the country. This was a quite different experience from being in Communist countries where they were afraid of you if you weren't a Communist.

We took a boat across Lake Titicaca to get to Puno. Titicaca is considered the cradle of Inca civilization. At 12,580 feet, it is the highest lake in the Americas and, in fact, is the world's highest navigable lake. The water was intensely blue and the lake replete with many floating islands occupied by fishing families. Fishermen were out in their famous totora reed boats. Totora (*Schoenoplectus californicus*) is a perennial aquatic sedge of fundamental importance to these lake people. Since trees are not available, the totora reeds are used not only for boats, but also dwellings, fences, mats, containers, clothes, food, fodder, and more.

When we got to Puno, I was still suffering from a throbbing headache from *sirroche*. The hotel manager advised me to buy some coca leaves from which he would have a tea made for me. The Brazilian doctor and I went to the market but had difficulty in purchasing only a small amount of coca leaves. The people selling them wanted us to buy kilos! We finally persuaded one woman to sell us several handfuls if I also bought a native woolen pouch in which the locals carry their daily supplies of coca leaves. At the hotel, tea was made that indeed helped.

This part of the Andes is where potatoes (*Solanum tuberosum*) originated. I was fascinated watching local people harvesting potatoes and trampling them to make dehydrated *chuño*. The potatoes were laid out on the ground, and when they warmed up in the sun after having been frozen during the night, people trampled them. They repeated the process until the potatoes were completely dehydrated, making them ready to be stored as reserves against a poor harvest. Markets displayed an amazing variety of potatoes, varying in size and shape (some are smooth, others are lumpy or even curled like plumber's tubes), as well as color (white, yellow, various shades of red, blue, and purple). In fact, 3,000 kinds of Peruvian potatoes are known.

We continued across the planalto via train from Puno to Cuzco, the old imperial Inca capital at 11,000 feet. Along the way we saw people using their colorfully adorned alpacas as beasts of burden—although today these alpine camelids are mainly used for their "wool." I added several capes to my collection of hats and gloves. Cuzco is the gateway to Machu Picchu, and it was the height of the tourist season. I joined the many tourists for the four-hour narrow gauge train trip down from the cold, dry *altoplano* into the humid heat of Aqua Caliente at 5,000 feet. However, Machu Picchu, a sacred location and royal retreat of the ancient Incas, is located on a ridge at 8,000 feet, which one has to ascend 3,000 steps to view the incredible stonework architecture. As with the other visitors, I stood in awe of the engineering achievements, constructed about 1450, of the Inca people here. The geometric patterns established by the multitude of agricultural terraces especially impressed me. (A few years ago Machu Picchu was nominated for recognition as an International Historic Engineering Landmark.)

After my short visit to Machu Picchu and Cuzco, I flew via Lima to Quito, Ecuador, the capital of the northern half of the Inca empire, which occupied all of Ecuador. The flight over the Andes was clear and I was delighted to view the numerous very high (~19,000 feet), snow-laden volcanoes such as Chimborazo and Pichincha. At approximately 10,000 feet, Quito is almost as high as La Paz, but from my tropical lowland experiences, I was interested in it being only about eight-and-a-half miles from the equator, which has an ameliorating effect on the climate. From Quito I flew to Panama and thence to San José, Costa Rica, for my OTS meeting.

ORGANIZATION FOR TROPICAL STUDIES

1971-1987

Botany needs help from the tropics.
Its big plants will engender big thinking.
—E.M.J. Corner

Over the course of the years, the Organization for Tropical Studies (OTS) would be one of the tropical groups with which I would have some of my most sustained activities. I had been introduced to OTS in 1965 while I was at Harvard; that year, OTS sponsored my first field research on *Hymenaea*. OTS had been established in 1963 by a consortium of universities to create a common extension of their graduate schools to carry out programs of field instruction and research in the tropics. From nine charter-member institutions, including Harvard and the University of California, the consortium had increased to twenty-nine by 1971when I became a UC representative to the board of directors. Presently it has a membership of about sixty US, Latin American, South African, and Australian institutions. I played a part in the relatively early stages of the development of what would become a premier organization of its kind.

OTS board meetings were characterized by great camaraderie among its members, especially during the 1970s. This relationship may have been heightened because of the still relatively small size of the consortium and the barn-raising atmosphere, which I had also experienced in the early days at RMBL and at UCSC. Like all academic groups, we had our disagreements and intense discussions but we were all scientists doing research in the tropics and concerned about the best training we could provide for future biologists to understand and conserve this incredible tropical world. Furthermore, OTS board members provided an extraordinary network of faculty with whom to interact about our own research. This was true even in sharing board representation within the UC system. As a result of the friendship developed while sharing these responsibilities with Herbert Baker, the plant ecologist at UC Berkeley, he served as an outside member of committees of my doctoral students who were working on tropical projects.

Board members were imbued with participating in the local culture as much as possible, a practice, of course, with which I was in thorough agreement. We often stayed in small pensions in San José and ate the local dishes, such as the characteristic black bean and rice dish, *gallo pinto*, even for breakfast. We purposely involved Costa Ricans in all appropriate activities of the organization, and struggled with improving our different levels of competence in Spanish. After our board meetings, we had a tradition of purchasing local products such as beautifully crafted leather brief cases, bags, and the like; we also bought freshly roasted coffee beans from local coffee stores and real vanilla from drums in drugstores to carry back home. The latter, which once escaped from the not-well-enough-corked used wine bottle in which I had obtained it, resulted in my suitcase being highly aromatic for some time to come. One of the board members and I even looked into buying a marimba to take home, as we had become so enamored with its music. I had been entertaining such a possibility since I first heard the marimba in the San José plaza in 1953, but alas, it proved too difficult to do.

Part of the very early success of OTS can be attributed to the persuasive leadership of Mildred Mathias of UCLA, who was president of the board of directors from 1968 to 1971. I learned much from Mildred over the years, not only about the role of OTS in tropical studies, but also about how to be a successful woman professor in the University of California system. The efforts of Mildred and various other early proponents of OTS notwithstanding, the development of a particular graduate course, with a unique design, was probably the greatest contribution to OTS's success. In Tropical Biology: An Ecological Approach (often called the Fundamentals Course), the field serves as a classroom, with lectures revolving around an intensive hands-on experience in a series of the easily accessible and diverse tropical ecosystems in Costa Rica. Added to this special design is the diversity of expertise provided by instructors motivated to share their enthusiasm for the world of tropical biology. It is hard to over emphasize the impact this course has had in inspiring and training a core of researchers in tropical biology. My own students found it an invaluable and unforgettable experience. Over the years, courses covering agroforestry and agroecology, as well as marine and coral reef ecology, advanced botany, and numerous others have been offered as well. Some courses were given in Spanish for Latin American students. Since 1963 about 2,000 students from thirty countries have studied tropical field biology under OTS sponsorship. I never taught an OTS course; I always felt a bit wistful that for a variety of reasons it did not work out for me to do so.

I had the privilege of serving as an officer on the decision-making executive committee during the early developmental period of the organization. In 1972, the year after joining the board of directors, I served as its secretary until 1975; then I was vice president for academic affairs until 1978. These years were still during a period when OTS had to overcome many obstacles, with limited finances for development of its organizational structure. The mid-seventies were especially critical times for OTS.

Dan Janzen giving lecture in 1968's "Fundamentals" course

A cash flow problem in 1975, triggered by inadequate accounting procedures, was made worse by NSF refusing to supply further funds until the accounting problems were solved. But these problems couldn't be solved without funds and hence the organization faced de facto bankruptcy in 1976. I clearly remember a special executive committee meeting at which these dire circumstances seemed insurmountable. Dramatic salvation came, however, when Don Stone convinced officials at Duke University, where he was a faculty member in the Botany Department, to serve as the fiscal agent and thus help put OTS back on sound financial footing. Stone was appointed interim director, with the challenge of getting OTS through what he referred to as its "bleakest hours," but we were determined to struggle through the issues. OTS was already playing too significant a role for teaching and research in the tropics not to succeed. And succeed we did!

Before the critical financial times, permanent field stations had been established first in a lowland rain forest at La Selva (1968), then in a lowland dry deciduous forest at Palo Verde (1969), and later at a mid-altitude rain forest and botanical garden at Las Cruces (1983). These, of course, were critical for all aspects of the OTS mission.

EXHILARATING VISITS TO FIELD STATIONS

Loving to fly, I enjoyed the biannual trips to Costa Rica for board meetings, although I was saddened by witnessing the progressive devastating destruction of Central American forests by excessive grazing and timbering. I was grateful for having at least seen the beautiful dense forests on my first trip in 1953. Then there were the four-to five-passenger plane trips to different parts of Costa Rica to inspect current or possible field sites. Adventures were usually in store, adding new strands to the thread of my air travel experiences. On an early trip, a small number of board members flew to the Palo Verde Field Station, near the head of the Golfo Nicoya in northwestern Costa Rica (the only access during the wet season) to inspect completion of lab facilities. The private air strip adjacent to the building had numerous potholes. On our take off for our return trip, the plane accidentally hit one with great force, damaging a wheel. We had to climb out and find assistance from a local rancher. This was in 1971 and, although we were only twenty-five miles from the Pan American Highway, we felt peculiarly remote, ultimately taking a bus back to San José.

Returning from the Wilson Botanic Garden site (which would become Las Cruces Field Station), located in mid-altitude tropical rain forest and cloud forest in the Talamanca Mountains near the Panama border, provided a breathtaking small-plane experience. Several board members were evaluating the rain forest site, but especially the fifty-acre botanical garden emphasizing orchids, tree ferns, bromeliads, and palms among many other plants. The garden was largely of horticultural value, but for OTS it also had relevance for agriculture and forestry as well as various botanical studies. OTS was negotiating to buy the property from the Wilsons, and the team had spent more time viewing it and discussing its appropriateness as an OTS field station than the pilot of the private plane had anticipated. Heavy cloud cover had come in but the pilot decided to proceed through the clouds—as he was afraid they would worsen if we waited any longer. All the passengers were holding their breath as we flew blind through the clouds, in mountainous terrain, with no guidance. We all heaved a happy sigh of relief when the mountains surrounding San José finally came into view.

By far, however, my most exciting flight was in 1974 with Steve Preston, then president of the board, to survey a cabin at Rincon for possible upgrading and use when OTS researchers were doing fieldwork on the Osa Peninsula. I volunteered to go on this jaunt because I could assist in the decision about use of facilities there, but it also gave me the opportunity to again investigate the huge, undescribed species of *Hymenaea*, which produces massive amounts of resin, similar to species in Amazonia.

We had a smooth flight in a small ALPA plane from San José to Golfito, but when we approached for landing, there appeared to be large sticks or tree branches scattered over the little airstrip. Another passenger on the plane, who was collecting fer-de-lance venom on the Osa Peninsula for an agency making an antidote for snakebite, became excited because what had appeared to be branches were the snakes he was hoping to collect. I wasn't too comfortable with the idea that on this visit we would probably be tramping through forests where we could meet up with the notorious fer-de-lance—the most deadly snake in the Americas. I remembered well our fear of encountering them on our Chiapas expedition—and our great relief when a snake that fell out of the low trees onto the neck of one of our group was not the dreaded fer-de-lance. This relatively large pit viper (on average six feet long) often is well camouflaged in the rain forest leaf litter and finds its prey, commonly rodents, by heat sensitivity. A human foot will serve as well. Our plane ran over some of these snakes in landing, but our venom man rushed out to collect others alive.

ALPA plane readying for return to San José after our arrival

Steve and I took a boat across the Golfa Dulce to Rincon, then to the headquarters of Osa Productos Forestales. One vivid memory was seeing children in school uniforms paddling boats across the gulf to school, emphasizing the importance that Costa Rica puts on education. Costa Rica has a greater than 90 percent literacy rate—one of the highest in the Western Hemisphere. I was also thrilled for our boat to move among the *Rhizophora* mangroves, which I had missed in my 1965 Osa trip and had seen only from shore near Acapulco, Mexico, when we were trying to reconstruct the depositional conditions of Chiapas amber.

We stayed in the prospective research cabin, which was primitive indeed; that night I discovered numerous snakes lurking around and even in the outhouse. I had no idea whether they were fer-de-lance, or one of Costa Rica's many other species of snakes, but no way was I going to bare my bottom in that place! So I went back to the cabin to root around for some sort of vessel to use as a chamber pot. The next morning made the whole trip worthwhile for me, however. The huge *Hymenaea* trees had more collectible enormous masses of resin than those I had seen here on my first visit in 1965. Then I could only look longingly, but in frustration, at the stalactites hanging from high branches. This time I was able to collect several stalactites that had fallen to the ground as well as masses of resin that covered large areas of the tree trunks at reachable heights. I have used some of the spectacular pieces I collected on this trip as exhibits, which have impressed many people with the copious amount of resins *Hymenaea* can produce.

The return flight to San José was almost a *"Perils of Pauline"* situation for me, although not quite as gross as the modern movie version *"Snakes on a Plane."* The ALPA plane could hold five people in a squeeze—pilot, passenger next to him in the front, and three in the back. When Steve and I arrived for the flight for which we had made reservations, our snake man was there with a gunnysack of his prized specimens, but along with him were two smiling, partially toothless campesinos with full gunnysacks. That meant there would be four people in back. While the pilot was turning the propeller, the snake researcher quickly put his sack with its squirming contents behind the seat and jumped in with the two campesinos. Steve was sitting in the front seat but I was still standing outside. The three in the back squeezed over, the campesinos still clutching their huge sacks, and the pilot beckoned for me to get in. I was half-sitting on the lap of one of the campesinos, but my fanny was pressed against the door of the plane that wouldn't shut tightly. I was still protesting when the pilot took off down the runway, with the door rattling as we left the ground. Steve reached over the front seat and told me to link arms with him. So I was draped from front to back seat and half over one of the campesinos and his sack, with my fanny against a partially closed door that was rattling like it might open at any moment.

The plane was so heavily laden that it barely cleared the treetops, with sheared branches and leaves flying off. I remembered a similar lift off of the repaired plane in Amazonia. At least in Amazonia we didn't have to fly over mountains, as we did in Costa Rica. On this flight, we would slowly climb over a mountain ridge and then get a downdraft over valleys, with an accompanying violent rattling of the plane's door, which I was firmly convinced was going to fly open, taking me to the outside! Never on any flight, even in storms, or with only one of two engines functioning, have I actually prayed as I was trying to do then. The flight time to San José was almost intolerable; we seemed to be just poking along with our heavy load. When we finally landed, Steve and I could hardly get our arms untwined. When the door was opened I literally fell backward out of the plane, but I didn't mind—I was happy that it was only a short distance to the ground! Throughout this adventure the pilot didn't seem the least concerned. He told Steve he felt that he had to take all of the passengers, even though we were the ones who had arranged the flight, and that we would make it—he said he was often overloaded. This was similar to my experience on buses throughout Latin America—no one was left behind. But a small plane somehow seemed a bit different to me?

Interesting trips on OTS business, as either a board or executive committee member, continued. Among these were numerous canoe trips on the Rio Puerto Viejo to reach the few small buildings of the La Selva Biological Station, which had been acquired from Holdridge of the Tropical Science Center in 1968. Access to the station from the river was only possible from the often muddy landing downstream, near the village of Puerto Viejo de Sarapiqui. NSF provided funding for electric power lines in 1978, but more direct access to the station only came with a cable suspension bridge across the river in 1982. Presently, La Selva is the crown jewel of OTS field stations—recognized by the US National Academy of Sciences as one of the four premier sites for tropical

Access to La Selva via canoe to Puerto Viejo de Sarapiqui

forest research in the world. It can accommodate a hundred visitors, has modern labs, housing and dining facilities, and professional management to aid research, classes, and ecotourism. I could hardly believe my eyes at the developments when I visited in 1992 as part of a meeting of the US National Committee for the International Union of the Biological Sciences (USNC/IUBS) in Costa Rica, which included a workshop on inventorying and monitoring held at La Selva.

OTS ROLE IN ENVIRONMENTAL PROTECTION

OTS personnel, of course, have been consistently aware of the growing devastation of tropical ecosystems, especially in Costa Rica. Although extolled for its incredible biological diversity—packed into an area the size of West Virginia—Costa Rica also has had one of the highest deforestation rates in Latin America. Despite struggling with limited funds, in the mid-1970s the government established a broad system of national parks and biological reserves that protected more than 10 percent of the country's diverse habitats. The election of Oscar Arias as president of Costa Rica also aided conservation efforts; he gave natural resources cabinet-level attention and appointed knowledgeable people to important conservation roles. Arias was on the board of the World Wildlife Fund and knew that OTS could provide valuable assistance in suggesting advisors for a comprehensive analysis of the national park system. I vividly remember a meeting that a group of OTS board members had with this remarkable man, who also was given the Nobel Peace Prize in 1987 for his work in establishing a peace accord among five countries in Central America.

In 1985 OTS was corecipient of the John and Ann Tyler Ecology-Energy Prize for "advancing the understanding and protection of threatened tropical ecosystems." This award demonstrated that OTS's training and research program in tropical studies had made progress long before tropical programs became fashionable. The organization gave a large portion of the prize money to The Nature Conservancy to help purchase the Zona Protectora of Costa Rica's Braulio National Park. This zone extended the park along the southern border of La Selva, thus giving the field station protection from isolation by deforestation.

UCSC MEMBERSHIP IN OTS

Although I had shifted my chemical ecology research to Venezuela and Brazil, my grad students were being trained in OTS courses. I also kept my hand in research by collaborating with the anthropologist/archaeologist Carlos Balser to determine the botanical origin of resin objects from aboriginal burial grounds in Costa Rica. I ascertained by chemical analysis that some of these artifacts had been carved from present-day *Hymenaea* resin and a few specimens even could have been made from Chiapas amber. The results appeared in the first volume of *Vínculos*, a publication of the Department of Anthropology and History of the Museo Nacional de Costa Rica, where the burial objects were on exhibit. Here again I assisted a fledgling tropical journal with an appropriate article, and continued my threads of Costa Rican studies and collaboration with anthropologists as well.

I did have to leave the OTS board of directors in 1987. This was a difficult parting after seventeen years, and having known the organization for twenty-two years! The UC system (except UCLA) had constituted a single OTS member, but the OTS board of directors in 1987 decided that each UC campus had to pay its own way. At the time, UCSC faced severe financial problems and the administration thought the interest in tropical research at UCSC was too limited to justify the annual fee. UCSC did not become an independent member of the consortium for fourteen years—only in 2001 after other tropical researchers had joined the faculty in various departments.

OTS continues to increase its role in tropical research, education and conservation, and is leading the way in sharing information through networks of researchers and educators throughout the tropics. Furthermore, over 40 years of monitoring environmental conditions, along with research, at OTS field stations have put it in a significant position to understand the impact of climate change on tropical biodiversity. I have been pleased to encourage campus growth in expanded UCSC faculty working in the tropics, with additional links to OTS. Furthermore, ever since having fallen in love with Costa Rica on my first visit there in 1953, when I was returning to California from Colombia, I have maintained my commitment to research and conservation efforts to maintain Costa Rica's natural heritage.

INTERTWINED RESEARCH, TRAVEL, AND PERSONAL LOSS

1976-1980

Hymenaea was named for Hymenaeus, the Greek god of marriage.
—Carl von Linne

During the later 1970s I traveled a great deal, mainly for a variety of tropical activities. The extent of my absence from the lab came home to me when I overheard my students telling a visiting researcher that they fought over who would take me to or pick me up from the airport so they would have time alone with me to discuss their work. 1976 was a typical year in which I interdigitated some field research with various tropical meetings. This combined activity provided a bonus for our research—a significant means of helping to supplement NSF funds for my travel to research sites in Venezuela and Brazil during different times of the year. It further helped networking with different groups of investigators who contributed to our research. Researchers not doing tropical work often do not realize how critical these issues are for success of a project—and the necessity for ingenious solutions.

My tropical research had been continually funded by NSF. Reviewers of my proposals, however, were divided as to whether I should increase my understanding of *Hymenaea* or move to another genus. In some ways, I wanted to continue to concentrate on *Hymenaea* because I thought it was an excellent model tropical resin-producing tree—and it seemed that the concept of model systems had not yet permeated chemical ecological/ evolutionary studies. On the other hand, I had been intrigued with the possibility of comparing *Hymenaea* with *Copaifera*, a close resin-producing leguminous relative. Systematic revision of *Copaifera*, however, would be necessary before I could begin comparative chemical ecology studies with *Hymenaea* on a phylogenetic basis. The two genera co-occurred through much of their New World distribution (although in Africa they do not overlap—*Copaifera* occurs in West Africa; *Hymenaea* is in East Africa). The often close occurrence of species of the two genera in various New World habitats posed interesting chemical ecological questions: Were they similar chemically and how did they respond to herbivores and pathogens when in this close association? I decided to ask NSF for funds for this comparison, which would require extensive fieldwork. It would satisfy my reviewers by continuing my study of *Hymenaea* but expanding it to include a new genus. As it has turned out, my interest in and research on *Hymenaea* would continue throughout my career, such that I felt that Linnaeus naming it for the Greek god of marriage appropriately described my relationship with the plant.

INTERTWINED OTS AND NAS ACTIVITIES
WITH *COPAIFERA* FIELD WORK

Exemplary of the kind of complicated travel I was doing from 1976 through 1979, following OTS meetings in Costa Rica I either proceeded directly to Caracas, Venezuela, or first to Manaus and then back to Caracas, to participate in field work for a systematic analysis of the Venezuelan *Copaifera*. Although Brazil is the center of diversity of *Copaifera* in the New World, Panama and Venezuela comprise the northern end of its distribution. I had collected Panamanian species with researchers at STRI and the University of Panama. In Venezuela, Mary Arroyo, a UC Berkeley PhD in systematics and then a professor of botany at Universidad Centrale de Venezuela, had a student who was interested in collaborating on the systematics of the Venezuelan species of *Copaifera* for a master's degree.

A New Zealander, Arroyo had come to the United States for graduate work, married a Latin American, and was energetically using her background in Venezuela. She was an authority on the breeding systems of tropical tree legumes and was fascinated with *Copaifera*. Knowing how few flowering specimens of *Copaifera* were available in herbaria, she understood that numerous field trips would be necessary to catch its irregular, but massive, flowering and the accompanying large numbers of pollinating insects that were of particular interest to her. Two *Copaifera* species, *C. publiflora* and *C. officinalis,* occurred at the university's field station (Estación Biólogica de Llanos, at Laguna de Los Patos) where the caretaker could keep the trees under continual surveillance. Our work in Venezuela brought home to me again the difficulties for Americans studying some tropical trees, because without committed people on the ground year-round significant events can easily be missed.

At the Laguna de Los Patos field station *Hymenaea* and *Copaifera* also were closely associated and I could collect data for comparison of the leaf chemistry and herbivores. On my first trip in the spring of 1976, we found dense carpets of seedlings under the parent trees of both genera, which gave us new data from a dry forest environment for the parent tree-progeny study we had initiated in rain forest. All of these seedlings had leaf chemotypes like those of the parent tree, a quite different situation from the rain forest where several chemotypes were represented under the parent tree.

We also had good luck collecting seeds. A Venezuelan student who was studying the seed herbivores in *Copaifera pubiflora* here, alerted me to ants' removal of the very sticky covering of the seeds. The ants took the seeds into their nests below ground, where they removed the nutritious material for the fungi that they farm in their nests. The ants returned beautifully cleaned seeds above ground, and put them into neat piles. What a wonderfully helpful chore these ants performed for us.

I had been appointed in 1975 to chair an important United States National Academy of Sciences (NAS) advisory committee to meet with a Brazilian National Council on Research (CNPq) committee to discuss bilateral cooperation on research in the humid tropics. Although an honor to be selected to chair this important committee, it was a heavy responsibility. This was a period when Brazil greatly sought collaborative research with the US scientists. One of the NAS subcommittees concerned with rain forest research was a project proposed by Ghillean Prance, called Projeto Flora Amazônica, to produce a computerized database of Amazonian plants. Prance chaired this subcommittee, which then had alternate meetings in Brazil, often in Brasilia, and the United States, usually at NYBG.

Projeto Flora Amazônica meeting in Brasilia; R. S. Cowan (left) with Ghillean Prance on cerrado field trip

In late June 1976, I chaired an NAS/CNPq meeting in Rio de Janeiro, where we decided upon four major areas for future cooperative Amazonian research between scientists in Brazil and the United States. These were: 1) large volume chemicals from forest trees, 2) freshwater biology and fisheries, 3) tropical diseases, and 4) water buffalo. An NAS staff officer accompanied me to

Manaus to discuss plans with the new director of INPA, for a December meeting of selected Brazilian and American scientists to discuss establishing bilateral research on these topics. Such trips to Manaus on NAS business also enabled me to make collections of *Copaifera* at the Ducke Reserve, where workers were watching for flowering, fruiting, and seedling germination. I also could discuss collaborative plans for the *Copaifera* monograph with Marlene Freitas da Silva, a plant systematist at INPA who had taken the chemical ecology course I taught there in 1974.

This planning trip also gave me the opportunity to participate in some fishing trips, as this was a subject to be discussed at the meetings for bilateral research. Developing fish hatcheries was one focal point for discussion, although questions had been raised about the appropriateness of temperate zone practices for Amazonian species such as the huge fruit-eating fish inhabiting the flooded forest *(varzea)*. Unfortunately, the water had reached such a low level in June that there was little chance of catching the huge commercially important *tambaqui*. It was the largest of the Amazonian fruit-eating fish, reaching three feet long and weighing up to sixty pounds. The seeds of the fruit pass unharmed through the fish's digestive system and take root in the mud as the floods subside. Despite the decreasing flood waters in the *varzea*, INPA personnel used nets to catch an amazing variety of small fish, including red-bellied piranha, which were prepared for lunch on our boat.

While on this fishing trip we also intercepted the NSF research vessel, the *Alpha Helix*; its researchers were focusing on understanding electric eels. Although they are freshwater fish, they are commonly called eels because of their elongated bodies, which can reach eight feet and can weigh more than forty pounds. The amount of electricity they could generate was astonishing—these eels can kill or stun prey just by touching them, with the main part of their bodies emitting as much as 600 volts. At this time we also got to see the pink river dolphin jumping and frolicking against a backdrop of a flaming red sunset across an expanse of the river.

Again I stopped in Venezuela to collect *Copaifera* en route to the early December NAS/CNPq meeting in Manaus. November is the dry season and flowering time for the Venezuelan *Copaifera* species. As a bonus, *Tabebuia*, *Jacaranda*, and other members of the Bignoniaceae were putting on a spectacular color display of flowering. We also made large collections of two species of *Copaifera* in a suspected hybrid zone. Documenting putative hybridization was helpful in understanding the amazing morphological variation that characterizes this genus. Hybridization and clonal reproduction, mainly by root grafting, are now considered important in understanding many populations of tropical trees.

Fishing trip with INPA boats in flooded forest

Young caiman caught by fisherman

At the NAS/CNPq meeting in Manaus, I corepresented the United States with the deputy director of the Chemical Biodynamics Laboratory at UC Berkeley for discussion of large volume chemicals from the Amazonian forest. The Brazilian chair was the head of INPA's phytochemical division. The UC Berkeley group proposed studies of a variety of latex-producing trees, as they had been analyzing their hydrocarbons for fuel. I questioned their working with latex for this purpose, which required a complex chemical process to free useful hydrocarbons, whereas resins from *Copaifera* could be used almost directly for hydrocarbons. Later, the simplicity of obtaining hydrocarbons from *Copaifera* convinced the Berkeley lab's director, Melvin Calvin, to concentrate much of their work on *Copaifera*. However, since I had done work at INPA previously, most of the Brazilian collaborative work on *Copaifera* was done with NSF funding at UCSC. On the other hand, Calvin became a strong advocate for *Copaifera*—using his Nobel Laureate status to even suggest to the US Navy to run part of their fleet on *Copaifera* resin obtained from plantations in Puerto Rico.

Following the OTS board meeting in the spring of 1977, I proceeded to Caracas for a major collecting trip of *Copaifera*. It was just before Easter and the Tugues family had invited me to spend it with them at the beach. Tugues, also a professor at the Universidad Centrale de Venezuela, had participated in the Interactions in Science and Technology course that George Hammond and I had taught at UCSC. Although I had previously stayed in the home of Mary Arroyo and her Chilean husband, spending time with the Tugues family provided another opportunity to participate in the life of admittedly upper class Venezuelans.

It was a beautiful clear day at the beach but I did not realize that my bare legs were not covered by the shade of an umbrella. The sun at Caracas tropical latitudes (10 degrees north of the equator) severely burned my legs up to my bathing suit. I was in agony during the first part of our *Copaifera* collecting trip. Much to my embarrassment, numerous pictures that were taken of me on those trips, in shorts with my exposed very red thighs, seemed to get widely dispersed in the botanical world.

We made an east-west transect across central Venezuela from dry savanna (*llanos*), to deciduous and gallery forests, to rain forests. It was the first time we had spent time in the western, more moist portions of *Copaifera* distribution, toward Lake Maracaibo and the Colombian border (not too far from Bucaramanga, Colombia, where I had been in 1953). In comparing the flora and vegetation across this transect, I conjectured that

Copaifera, similar to *Hymenaea,* might have evolved from rain forest into drier forests as the climate changed during the later Tertiary and through Pleistocene oscillations.

Throughout this trip I had been very concerned about my cat Florodoro. I had no way to communicate about her while we were in the field, and my friends in Caracas thought that I was being overanxious. However, my concern was justified. She had slept in my suitcase just before I left, apparently trying to tell me she was not feeling well, but my veterinarian thought she was fine. Nonetheless, soon after I left, Florodoro disappeared. My neighbors taking care of her searched for her to no avail. She finally reappeared, very ill, several days before my return. The vet found that she had feline leukemia, which had not shown up in tests when she was a kitten. She died the morning of the day I returned, before I arrived. It was a very sad time for me.

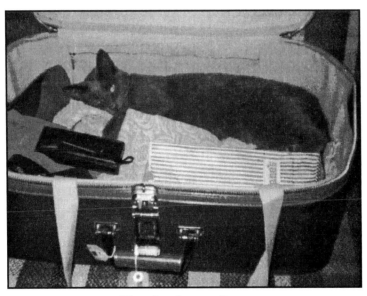

Florodora in my suitcase

This would be my last major collecting trip of *Copaifera* in Venezuela, although I stopped again in Caracas when en route to or from Manaus as the study progressed to lab analysis and writing during 1979 and 1980. The publication of this study of Venezuelan *Copaifera* in *Acta Botanica Venezuelanica* is as yet the most thorough systematic investigation of species in this genus, which is exceptionally difficult to study and understand—and is a testament to close and continued collaborative efforts.

POLYMERIZATION OF RESIN: THE INITIAL STEPS TOWARD BECOMING AMBER

Along with new field work on *Copaifera* we were doing additional chemistry on *Hymenaea* trunk resin in the lab. We had maintained our original interest in the early steps involved in this resin being transformed into amber, but had set this question aside to work on the volatile resin components in the leaves with which we could do experimental studies at UCSC. Now we were ready to investigate the initial chemical transformations of trunk resin.

Polymerization, the linking of chemical units (each unit is called a monomer) into molecular structures consisting of a few to many repeating units, is the main process through which the predominantly nonvolatile diterpene trunk resin in *Hymenaea* becomes hardened enroute to becoming amber. Polymers may range from low to very high molecular weights, and may have simple or complex molecular structures accompanied by changed physical properties. The rapidity and extent of polymerization depends on the chemistry of the monomers involved together with the environmental conditions under which the chain-linking chemical reactions occur. The trunk resin of *Hymenaea*, sticky when it issues from the tree, immediately begins to harden through loss of the small proportion of volatile compounds that enabled it to flow, and through polymerization. Structural characteristics of polymerized resin undergo changes over time in response to various environmental conditions. These progressive changes are considered as "maturation" of the polymerized resin. When exactly in this maturation process the resin can be considered fossilized, as amber, is a persistently controversial question that probably is unanswerable.

Our investigation of the early steps of transformation of *Hymenaea* resin enroute to amber began on the basis of early work by Al Cunningham and Sue Martin, who had elucidated the structures of some diterpenes in hardened (i.e., polymerized) trunk resin of several *Hymenaea* species. However, using standard organic chemical techniques, they had faced major problems in isolating and characterizing the compounds, both because the polymerized resin is poorly soluble under lab conditions, and because the extracted diterpenes continued to polymerize.

George Hammond had long been interested in the processes initiating polymerization. He convinced me to learn more about how *Hymenaea* resins begin polymerization under natural forest conditions—which had previously not been considered by geochemists. With Hammond's assistance in a photochemical analysis, Al demonstrated that the resin starts to polymerize by light-induced chemical reactions (initiation of free radicals), soon after it issues from the tree, through some form of wounding, into the air and light. However, I had found in field experiments in Costa Rica in 1965 that the process can be more complicated. Polymerization was slowed sufficiently during the rainy season that bees could collect resin to use in building their nests. The bees had to be adroit in the timing of their resin collecting—otherwise they would get stuck in the resin and possibly be preserved in amber! If the rain was sufficiently hard, the resin could be washed from the tree and collect in the soil. But we were unable to follow the polymerization process under these circumstances.

With a grant from the American Chemical Society in 1977, I brought a postdoctoral fellow to our lab to continue our investigation of polymerization in *Hymenaea* trunk resins. Hammond had left UCSC and with his influence no longer present, the post-doc preferred to try to further identify the polymeric compounds rather than untangle field conditions that influence polymerization. But she soon had problems similar to Martin and Cunningham in working with the polymerized diterpenes in the lab. On the other hand, she showed, much to our amazement, that a particular group of the sesquiterpenes (cadinenes), amid the small amount of sequiterpenes that enable the predominant diterpenes in the resin to flow, are also involved in polymerization of *Hymenaea* trunk resins. Dutch geochemists later demonstrated in detail that such sesquiterpene polymerization is significant in the formation of some ambers—especially those from Asian dipterocarps.

With the relatively recent availability of pyrolysis gas chromatography-mass spectrometry, geochemists have been able to elucidate all of the diterpene polymeric compounds in hardened *Hymenaea* resin. Importantly, they also have identified these compounds in amber from several Tertiary deposits, and thus added definitive support for these ambers' botanical source as *Hymenaea*.

DEATH OF MOTHER

In the spring of 1978 I had a traumatic personal blow—the death of my mother. She died of a heart attack, and thus fortunately did not have a lingering illness. Losing a mother is difficult for anyone, but especially so for an only child who had been closely bonded to her. Our bond had been so deep that I found it difficult to think of life without her. Her loving support had always been there for me and we had shared so much over 53 years. In the later years, especially following my divorce, our relationship evolved from her being a wise parent to a true friend with whom to confide and share so many interests. My only consolation was that I had her close involvement in my life for so long. Nevertheless, it still was difficult to imagine not writing a weekly letter nor sharing a diary note from the field nor enjoying our many telephone conversations and visits together when this was possible. I only hoped that I had given her a modicum of the joy she had brought into my life.

With no other family member to help, I had to make funeral arrangements and hastily tie up her business affairs in Oklahoma within less than a week, then retreat to finish classes during the spring term at UCSC. I was taken aback when Kenneth Thimann forcefully insisted that my duties at the university must take precedence! I was fortunate, however, again to have the sustaining support of a Christian Science practitioner whom I had known since Sunday School days as a child. Her love saw me through it all. I also felt good in giving the family home to the University of Tulsa to initiate an endowed scholarship in Mother's memory. This was one way that I could memorialize her interests in supporting students to continue their education and furthering the role it would play in enriching their lives.

Recently, reading Hillary Clinton's memoirs, *Living History,* and Tom Brokaw's interview with her for his book, *Boom,* has reinforced my own realization how some mothers, who had been denied advanced education and professional opportunities, lived vicariously through their daughters' achievements. My mother was a product of the first wave of the women's movement—having gotten the right to vote just five years prior to my birth. She was a pillar of enthusiastic support, strongly encouraging me to pursue my interests, and enjoyed so many of my activities, treasuring the letters in which I shared these. Although, along with Hillary's mother, I was a part of Brokaw's "Greatest Generation," my own circumstances, ironically, due in part to my marriage, were such that I did not have to wait to attain my PhD. Since I also did not follow the common pattern of just being a post-war housewife, I fell into the transition period when the opening of professional opportunities was just barely beginning.

Even though my and Hillary's mother were a generation apart, my mother felt the way Hillary's mother did when she said—"I want you to go places I didn't go; I want you to have the chance I didn't have; I want you to see the world." Subconsciously I think that I have felt the same way Hillary has: "There was this sense that we not only had to live our own lives but, to a certain extent, fulfill the hopes of our mothers. I felt that very strongly . . ." Most daughters of Hillary's generation (at least in the western world) probably will not feel this sense of responsibility—even though there always may be the close mother-daughter relationship that provides inspiration and support.

My grieving process was aided by a trip to England in late July, which somehow seemed appropriate, given Mother's persistent English interests. I had developed many English friends over the years, both in Santa Cruz and in England. I had hoped to take Mother on a trip to England some day, especially after the death of my father. He had been essentially an invalid for several years and his death took the heavy burden of his care from my mother, for which I was grateful. Before his death, she had found relief through expressing her creativity and love of flowers by becoming a floral designer for a prominent Tulsa florist. In characteristic fashion, though, she had forsaken taking care of her own health problems to help my father. She was able to make several trips to Santa Cruz with my assistance, but we were never able to take the long and much anticipated trip to England.

I was able to overcome my grief through a diversity of activities. I again enjoyed visiting John Mills, a conservator at the National Galleries in London, who gave me a special guided tour of activities there. He was a chemist who had done extensive research on resins, including *Hymenaea*, because natural resins have been used in various ways in artwork. Getting to know John had been the beginning of a thread of interacting with art conservators and learning about their interest in resins. I also attended the International Legume Conference at the Royal Botanic Gardens, Kew. I lived in Digby Stewart College of the University of London and mixed professionally and socially with legume researchers from around the world. Although I had been a member on an NAS panel on underutilized tropical legumes in Hawaii in 1977, my research had been restricted to two resin-producing genera. The conference broadened my knowledge about this third largest plant family (only behind composites and orchids in number of species), as did research for a paper on terpenoids in the Leguminosae that I contributed to the proceedings. Above all, it was the constant enlivening discussions with fascinating people that helped me partially get over my sadness that Mother was no longer alive.

After the conference I went to Oxford, where I stayed with Jack and Lindsay Harley in their charming, centuries-old stone house with creaky floors. Outside was a typical English orchard and garden filled with a grand display of colorful plants. Jack and I visited the Department of Forestry at the Commonwealth Forestry Institute, whose members had done so much important tropical research. Lindsay accompanied me to Saint Hilda's Women's College, which she had attended. I was fascinated that, although

Saint Hilda's was founded in 1893, it was only in 1910 that Oxford formally *acknowledged* female students and Saint Hilda's became recognized as a "society" for women students. Still, Lindsay emphasized, women in Saint Hilda's waited for another decade before being admitted as undergraduates and eligible for Oxford degrees. My delightful time spent with the congenial Harleys was added balm for my lingering grief.

By the time of my return to Santa Cruz from England, I was ready to move on without Mother's actual presence. I knew that her loving, supporting influence would always be with me.

COMPARING *HYMENAEA*
AND *COPAIFERA* ACROSS BRAZIL

1979

. . . that grand subject, that almost keystone of
laws of creation, Geographical Distribution.
—Charles Darwin

During a sabbatical leave in 1979, I devoted most of February through June to field work in Brazil. I was supposed to have begun my leave in Manaus at an international congress on "Models of Diversification in the Tropics," sponsored by the Association for Tropical Biology. The Brazilian host had problems securing visas for many of the participants, however, and at the last minute the meeting was relocated to Caracas, Venezuela. Overall, this worked out well for me because I spent more time with the Venezuelan botanists discussing our study of *Copaifera* and its relation to *Hymenaea,* which had provided the framework for the expanded Brazilian research. Tropical researchers are always grateful for any extra time with collaborators in other countries, as it is hard to come by. After the meeting I moved to INPA in Manaus to establish headquarters for this research.

ACTIVITIES AT INPA
In addition to planning a collecting trip of *Copaifera* and *Hymenaea* throughout their Brazilian distributions, I supervised the field studies of my first Brazilian graduate student, José Carlos Nascimento. He had been sent to UCSC by Paulo Alvim from the Center for Experimental Research on Cacao (CEPEC) on a Brazilian government fellowship from EMBRAPA to do his PhD dissertation on *Copaifera multijuga*, the Amazonian species most utilized for its resin. His research was stimulated by considerable Brazilian interest in *Copaifera* resins as a possible source of diesel fuel in their petroleum-poor country. This interest had been accelerated as a result of the 1976 NAS/CNPq meeting in Manaus.

Route of 1979 South American collecting trip

José Carlos was focusing on potential effects of different soil types on resin production, which were important in considering cultivation of *Copaifera multijuga* (known locally as *copaiba*) in plantations. *Copaiba* resins had long been collected from native trees for medicinal use but plantations would be necessary for large volumes of resin to be used for fuels. He did not find significant differences in leaf sesquiterpenes in *copaiba* occurring on central Amazonian rain forest soils that were both chemically and physically different. We did not know, however, if the results would be the same for trunk resins.

José Carlos thought that different *Copaifera* species could serve multiple purposes, as an overstory tree on cacao plantations, where the resin also could be tapped for medicinal use. CEPEC and INPA had collaboratively established plots to test this possibility. José Carlos found, however, that cacao plants soon overtopped the very slow-growing *C. multijuga* seedlings. If *Copaifera* were to be used as an overstory tree for cacao, the cacao would have to be planted under existing, mature *Copaifera* trees. Later, research by others at INPA on *Copaifera* plantations showed the slow growth of the seedlings to be one of the most significant limiting factors in use of *C. multijuga* resin for fuel.

I stayed in the apartments on the INPA campus, again a blessing for ease of living arrangements. This way I was able to avoid taking hair-raising taxi rides to a hotel in the center of Manaus. Most Manaus taxis were VW bugs that darted in and out and around other cars at alarming speeds, and I was never sure that I would arrive in one piece. I have often been asked about the dangers of working in Amazonia—if I were afraid of being attacked by animals in the "jungle." My persistent, vehement answer was "No, I have rarely had the privilege of seeing a mammal such as a jaguar, and my real concern throughout Latin America is not getting into a car accident!"

In addition, by staying on the INPA campus, there were more opportunities to network with potential collaborators. One visiting researcher, a chemist, had been brought to *Fitoquimica* at INPA to install a gas chromatography/mass spectrometry (GC/MS) machine to assist in identification of volatile chemical molecules. Using GC/MS analysis, he established for me the strong similarities of the predominant sesquiterpenes in leaf resins of two Venezuelan species of *Copaifera* and *Hymenaea courbaril,* which helped support our ecological comparisons of the two genera.

WORK IN THE RAINY SEASON

I spent the middle of February to the middle of March, which is the height of the rainy season, at INPA. One of my abiding memories of that time was magnificent cumulus clouds that would start building in midmorning, accompanied by an incredible increase in animal noise, especially insects. I had noted the clouds throughout my visits in Amazonia, but this particular year I became entranced. These fluffy clouds formed myriad shapes and I couldn't resist photographing them, especially across expanses of the Amazon. I wanted to capture some of their majesty on film. These lovely clouds were followed by menacing-looking cumulonimbus that brought a noisy period of thunder claps and a dramatic display of lightning along with the midday heavy rain, followed by a sudden quiet. It was as though some tension had been relieved. At the time I was not really thinking about how the evaporation and condensation, so gloriously exhibited by these clouds over Amazonia, are engines of global atmospheric circulation that have effects across South America and even the Northern Hemisphere. Now I would be.

Much of this time I worked at the Ducke Reserve, continuing our comparative study of *Hymenaea* parent tree-progeny leaf resin chemistry. The reserve's long-term weather and phenological records helped us understand the availability of seed crops, and in turn, length of seedling survival under *Hymenaea* trees. Staying overnight at the reserve not just increased the efficiency of my time there, but nights in the rain forest are fascinatingly different from the day. Although the INPA campus had been built in the forest, the rapid growth of Manaus, which now surrounded INPA, had changed the native animal activity and associated sounds. At the reserve, I slept in a hammock either in a dorm room or on the little porch outside. Mosquitoes were not a problem so we did not have to sleep under mosquito nets. Lying awake at night I could hear the "rain forest symphony." It is reminiscent of a dissonant, modern piece of music—monkeys, birds, frogs, and insects making strange croaks, chirps, whistles, and snorts. It made me think about the diversity of animals out there that we simply did not see during the day (in contrast to the numerous animals I saw while working in Costa Rican rain forests). I never saw the bats that pollinated the flowers of *Hymenaea*—but petals and stamens covering the ground under the tree the next day gave evidence of their nighttime activity.

Will Stubblebine at Ducke Reserve dormitory

My former student Will Stubblebine (by then a professor in a Brazilian university) and I were able to maintain plots at the Ducke Reserve over a period of time—although we had some puzzling and unfortunate vandalism of marked seedlings one year. We published two papers serially on these studies in Portuguese in *Acta Amazônica* under the title of "Estudos Comparativos na Composiçao de Resinas da Folha entre Árvore e Progênie de Espécias Selecionadados de *Hymenaea*." In the first one, we compared Amazonian rain forest and Venezuelan dry forest and savanna species, and in the second one we included additional Amazonian species compared with subdeciduous gallery forest species (considered southward extension of rain forest-like vegetation) in southeastern Brazil. We found numerous seedlings and saplings under the parent tree of *Hymenaea* in all cases, and that differences in compositional types (chemotypes) in the leaves between parent tree and their seedling and sapling progeny occurred in rain forest and gallery forests but not in savanna and dry forests. Of special interest in seedling establishment under parent trees in rain forest and related ecosystems was that the chemotype of the leaves of the parent tree (all leaves on an individual tree have the same chemotype) was initially present in leaves of some seedlings—but these seedlings soon disappeared. From growing seedlings in the greenhouse, we also knew that seedlings with different chemotypes could come from seeds in a single pod from a rain forest tree. We thought that this disappearance resulted from lepidopteran larvae that were adapted to the chemotype of the parent tree being able to decimate leaves of seedlings with the same chemotype. With relatively few leaves, these seedlings then perished. We suggested a model in which this terpene variation (production of different chemotypes) could play an important role in defense against lepidopteran herbivores.

Stubblebine and I later summarized all data and presented our model to possibly explain the *Hymenaea* parent tree/progeny chemotype relationships in *Biochemical Systematics and Ecology.* "Variation in leaf resin composition between parent tree and progeny in *Hymenaea:* Implications for herbivory in the humid tropics" became provocative because several previous tropical rain forest studies had shown that seedlings are notably scarce under the parent tree, and some researchers read our paper as a refutation of that. In the early 1970s, Dan Janzen, followed by Joe Connell, had even suggested that herbivore decimation of seedlings under the parent tree could provide a possible explanation for the diversity of tree species in tropical rain forests. Although our research was directed at the specific role of *variability* in *leaf terpenes* (actually different chemotypes) accounting for the success of many seedlings under their parent rain forest trees, some researchers misinterpreted our hypotheses to imply a more general scenario. Although the success of this kind of chemical variation may be an exception to the general rule of seedling success under parent trees, it was an important finding for tropical resin-producing trees. Abundance of seedlings under the parent tree has been reported for the resin-producing New World *Eperua* and the African *Gossweilerdendron,* but with no information regarding the chemical relationships. However, our results have been supported by studies of another volatile-terpene-producing tropical rain forest tree, the lauraceous *Nectandra*, in which numerous seedlings with high compositional variance occurred under or near the parent tree. How general this phenomenon is for other terpene-producing trees is unknown, but I have hoped that our studies would stimulate further analyses on the role of compositional variation of seedlings under parent trees.

Flying insects, such as mosquitoes, were not pestilent in our study areas. However, when I sprayed myself with Off (a brand of insect repellent I had brought from the United States) to avoid whatever insects might be present, my Brazilian helpers would laugh and ask why I didn't use *copaiba* oil. *Copaifera* resin is used both internally and externally, seemingly as a panacea for whatever troubles you! However, neither Off nor *copaiba* oil inhibited the virulent Amazonian chiggers that can create misery for those who respond allergically to them. A chigger is a nasty mite that when newly hatched can bore through human skin, then inject a poison that can cause severe itching for a week or longer. The more a person scratches, the worse the discomfort becomes. I had known chiggers from lawns in Tulsa as a kid, but they did not produce such severe effects as these Amazonian species. After a day in the field I had a mass of red, very itchy welts around my waist and the edges of where my bra had been. I had not experienced this problem in previous Amazonian trips, but this time I was out in the early part of the rainy season when chiggers are abundant. I was told to not wear a bra or even underpants and to wear very loose-fitting trousers and an oversize shirt. These measures helped although I still had some welts persist around my waist and it was weeks before the itching subsided. Although my allergic response to this mite attack was miserably uncomfortable, it did not have any long-term effect on my health. I did not have any serious health problems while working in Amazonia, apart from some unpleasant experiences with diarrhea that fortunately were not serious disorders such as amoebic dysentery.

José Carlos and his wife helped me survive the discomfort of the overwhelming itching of these the chigger attacks by inviting me to their house for dinners, and accompanying me to the Manaus celebration of Carnival. Although the famous samba schools are showcased in Rio, people enthusiastically celebrate this pre-Lenten festival throughout Brazil. It seemed the entire population of Manaus was involved in preparing costumes for the parade of dancers. The children of the Brazilian investigators at INPA learned to samba almost as soon as they could walk.

Little boys also began playing *futbol* (soccer) as soon as they were able to kick a ball, and I later participated in a memorable event that illustrated the role of *futbol* in Brazilian culture. I had been invited to spend several days in the home of Paulo Machado, the former director of INPA, who at that time had moved up professionally to become Brazil's Minister of Health. Brazil was playing Italy for the World Cup championship. The whole Machado family and their servants sat down together (not a usual social mix) and grimly watched as Brazil lost. The entire country went into mourning the next day—certainly no one worked in Brasilia. I knew how much they loved the sport, but it was enlightening for me to see how important world success in soccer was to Brazilians.

POSSIBLE EXPANSION OF AMAZONIAN COLLECTION SITES

In trying to expand my collection sites for *Hymenaea* and *Copaifera*, I came into direct contact with different kinds of Amazonian development problems. Although I was not doing research on the impact of development on Amazonia, I had become seriously concerned about the ecological devastation along the Transamazonian Highway in 1974 when I was teaching at INPA. Therefore I wanted to be careful of the development groups with which I became associated to get into some remote areas.

Botanists at the Museu Goeldi had suggested I talk with personnel at Georgia Pacific Lumber Company about staying at their field facilities and collecting at their timbering sites in the estuary near Isla Marajó. I went to the Georgia Pacific office at Belém where I was tentatively invited to join their forest researcher, who might be able to locate some *Hymenaea* and *Copaifera* trees for me. In discussing their operations, however, I was appalled by their extreme entrepreneurial attitudes toward utilization of the rain forest. Why all the concern about harvesting techniques destroying areas where they worked? they asked. They hoped I wouldn't want to crusade about such practices. After all, there were millions of acres of forest in Amazonia. Knowing I was from California, they probably suspected that I might not approve of their harvesting old-growth redwoods there. As the conversation progressed, I had become visibly uncomfortable, and it became clear to both of us that a trip to their facility was not a good idea for me.

The second possibility for additional collections was at Jari, one of the most famous large-scale projects focusing on capital-intensive investment in Brazilian Amazonia. Touted as a potential model for sustainable development throughout the Amazon Basin, Jari was a group of several enterprises launched in 1967 by the shipping magnate D.K. Ludwig in the state of Pará and territory of Amapá. Located in a huge area approximately three million square acres straddling the Jari River, a northern tributary of the lower Amazon, the project included a number of activities such as the world's largest rice plantation. However, plantation silviculture of exotic trees, native timber extraction, and pulp mill operations were the principal activities. Two FAO foresters at INPA had done some work at Jari. Because native forest was cut to fuel the mill operations, these foresters thought that I probably could collect both *Hymenaea* and *Copaifera* there. When I applied for permission to go, however, I was turned down because I was working under the auspices of INPA. INPA biologists had been highly critical of both Jari's silvicultural practices and agronomic handling of rice cultivation in the *varzea*. The FAO foresters were allowed to visit because they were employed by FAO and just used INPA as their base of operations. They did later make some collections of *Hymenaea* for me. By 1979, however, Jari was in debt and Ludwig (having invested almost a quarter of a billion dollars) in 1982 sold the project to a consortium of twenty-seven Brazilian firms.

COLLECTING THROUGHOUT BRAZIL

In March I began a trip to collect *Copaifera* throughout much of its Brazilian distribution. Marlene Freitas da Silva, an INPA plant systematist who was collaborating with me on the *Copaifera* monograph, accompanied me on part of the trip. I would be collecting leaves for chemical analysis and evidence of herbivore and fungal activity as well as documenting how prevalent co-occurrence of *Hymenaea* and *Copaifera* as nearest neighbors appeared to be. Was the "nearest neighbor phenomenon" more common in certain vegetation types than others?

The two genera occur throughout most of Brazil—which presents challenges similar to collecting throughout the continental United States in a short time. All our work depended, of course, on botanists at numerous institutions assisting us in locating the trees in their area as well as providing means to collect from the tall ones. I turned to some of the same researchers who had helped us with our *Hymenaea* study but added others, especially for the more southerly distribution of *Copaifera* in Brazil. There I wondered if it would also be difficult to find *Copaifera*, let alone *Hymenaea* and *Copaifera* trees together? And I had been warned that we probably would not find *Hymenaea* in many dry forest sites where we had previously collected it. A University of Campinas researcher, who studies rhinochinid weevils that attack *Hymenaea* pods, had tried to follow the collections we made for the *Hymenaea* monograph, and found that trees at numerous sites had been destroyed for their valuable wood, by land clearance, and so on. The situation brought into focus the additional problem of human-induced change in the vegetation in many areas of Brazil.

Marlene and I planned to fly to the southern part of Amazonia in Mato Grosso, detour over to Brasilia, then head for the far coastal rain forests in the states of Paraná and Santa Catarina. I would proceed alone northward up the coast to localities in the states of São Paulo, Bahia, Pernambuco, Ceará, Maranhão, and finally Pará, where at Belém I would turn westward with a stop in Santarém en route to Manaus.

Pressing plants along road with University of Mato Grosso botanists

We started at Cuiabá, Mato Grosso, where Miramy Macedo, another one of my INPA chemical ecology students, now taught at the Federal University of Mato Grosso. It was great to see women students from the INPA botany program obtain good professional positions. Miramy was excited to participate in our activities; she even had a television crew taking pictures for the local news as our group of students got our gear prepared for going on a collecting trip at the edge of the Pantanal. This is the world's largest freshwater wetland and one edge of this great swamp was sufficiently near to Cuiabá that we could approach it from the Transplantaneira highway. I saw islands of rain forest trees amid a sea of grass that reminded me of the "hammocks" in the Everglades (though the Pantanal covers ten times the area of the Everglades). It was on one of these islands close to the highway that I began to photograph the co-occurrence of *Hymenaea* and *Copaifera* in different kinds of Brazilian vegetation. Here they often occurred side by side, frequently with overlapping canopies as nearest neighbors, in different types of vegetation in Mato Grosso, as I had seen them in the dry forests in Venezuela.

In the Ducke Reserve rain forest, José Carlos Nascimento had found *Copaifera multijuga* to co-occur with *Hymenaea intermedia* and *H. parvifolia* in comparing parent-tree progeny relationships, but that they were not in nearest neighbor proximity. He was frustrated in attempting to analyze herbivory on adult *Copaifera* trees as had been the case in our study of *Hymenaea* there. Access to the canopy was very difficult. José Carlos put extension ladders into the lower branches (almost 100 feet up) and then clambered around the canopy as he could. I reluctantly decided that for any sustained and detailed herbivory research we needed to move to an environment where the tree canopy was more accessible. Therefore, I would be assessing such possibilities on this trip.

E. P. Heringer with rare dwarf Copaifera nana

In Brasilia, David Gifford, director of the Laboratory of Ecology at the Federal University of Brasilia, enthusiastically welcomed Marlene and me. Gifford, a Scotsman, was the driving force behind the early establishment of ecological teaching and research at the University of Brasilia. E.P. Heringer, at the nearby Brazilian Institute for Geography (IBGE), gave generously of his time for field trips and discussion of the systematics of *Copaifera*. We learned much from this warm, friendly "oldster," who shared his vast understanding of *cerrado* plants and their leaf-spotting fungi, which we would study later with his continued assistance. He not only introduced us to the common and abundant *C. langsdorfii,* but also took us to a small grassland site in Goiás, the only area where the dwarf *C. nana* is known to occur. He treated it as though he were showing us a buried treasure.

Co-occurring H. courbaril var. stilbocarpa *(prominent round top toward right) and* Copaifera multijuga *(prominent flat top far left) in gallery forest near Brasilia*

With the enthusiasm of both Gifford and Heringer for possibilities of my establishing a long-term study at nearby university and IBGE reserves,

I laid plans with them for one of my graduate students, George Hall, to come the next year (1980) to make a comparative study of herbivory on co-occurring *Hymenaea stigonocarpa* and *Copaifera langsdorfii*. I also was fascinated to see *C. multijuga* and *H. courbaril* var. stilbocarpa in relatively close association in gallery forests running through the *cerrado*. I was hoping future research here would provide better opportunities for comparative studies of chemical defense against lepidopteran herbivores.

From Brasilia, we went into the far southern limits of *Copaifera*—a single species which occurs in the states of Paraná and Santa Catarina. Santa Catarina was beyond reported limits of distribution for *Hymenaea*. The vegetation is essentially warm temperate, and prosperous agriculture was so widespread that finding *Copaifera* in the small remaining patches of native vegetation was a challenge. Led by botanists from the Museu Municipal de Curitibá in Paraná and Herbario Rodrigues Barbaroso in Itajai, Santa Catarina, we finally encountered *C. trapezifolia* in the southern reaches of the Atlantic coastal rain forest *mata pluvial*, which appeared to me similar to a montane cloud forest in Costa Rica. The botanists there had no one available to climb the 75 to 80 foot high trees, so we were only able to collect seedlings. Although we witnessed the kind of habitat in which this species occurs—always important from my ecological perspective—Marlene, as a systematist, was very disappointed in our inability to obtain flowering and fruiting specimens—a disappointment that continued to grow as she studied the genus, unfortunately.

I moved northward to Campinas in São Paulo state to work with Will Stubblebine, now an assistant professor in the Botany Department at the Universidade Estadual de Campinas (UNICAMP). Will was continuing work on the *Hymenaea* parent tree-progeny project in the subdeciduous forest of Mogi Guaçu Reserve and he had some of his students beginning herbivore research on *Copaifera* as well. I also was establishing a relationship with the head of the Chemistry Department to encourage collaborative research on the terpenes in *Copaifera*. I hoped these arrangements would ensure future study of these important genera both ecologically and chemically in Brazil, independent of my work but building upon it.

On one of the trips to Mogi Guaçu, we were pushing our way through some six-feet-high grass (*caña brava*) when, as I turned quickly, a blade of the grass cut my eye. Soon my eye looked like a cherry and I could not see from it. Fortunately, we were not far from the field station, where, a UNICAMP zoologist called his mother who was a physician in Campinas. She told us to return to Campinas at once and that she would contact an ophthalmologist to see me immediately. I didn't know which was the most frightening—my eye injury or the old jeep in which we were hurtling back to Campinas at breakneck speed. We arrived safely, and the ophthalmologist emphasized how lucky I had been. The cut in my cornea would heal without affecting my vision. With several more visits to the ophthalmologist and, a patch protecting the eye for a while, I was soon back in the field, but wary of *caña brava*.

INTERLUDE WITH A WEALTHY BRAZILIAN

Before leaving Manaus, I had had a telex from Jorgé Atolla, a Brazilian graduate of the University of Tulsa in petroleum engineering, who had become a billionaire in the Brazilian oil industry and other businesses. His prominence in Brazil resulted in his having been honored as a "Distinguished TU Alumnus." Through the university he had learned that I also had been so honored (but not for billionaire status!) and that I was currently doing research in Brazil. Thus he wanted to meet me and hear about my Brazilian studies. He invited me to visit his family at their *fazenda* (in this case a country estate) in São Paulo state and offered to send his private plane to Manaus to pick me up and return me. I suggested a better time would be while I was visiting friends in Campinas. Atolla replied he would send his plane to Campinas and that I could bring along the friends with whom I was staying. So my American chemist friends at UNICAMP joined me for this unusual visit.

The Atolla *fazenda* is located in the rich agricultural area of São Paulo, where there are extensive plantations of sugarcane and coffee. After viewing these plantations from the air during our arrival, I mentioned that I would appreciate having the plane on our return trip to Campinas fly over those fields so I could photograph them for use in my Plants and Human Affairs course. About thirty minutes later, Jorgé called to me, as a helicopter landed in front of the extensive veranda surrounding this large house, and he said "Let's go photograph the fields now." I used some of these photos in our textbook and sent Atolla a copy when it was published in 1982.

Atolla fazenda

The number of servants attending us was a bit overwhelming. Breakfast could be served in bed or, happily from my perspective, on a patio with self-service from a table laden with various fruits, breads, and cheeses. But we had three servants in our bedrooms to assist with drawing bath water, whisking off our clothes to the laundry, and so on. I was so uncomfortable with what seemed to be excessive attention that I sometimes avoided going to my bedroom!

Activities while we were there included watching the Atollas' quarter horses perform from the family's private viewing stand. John Connelly, the former governor of Texas who had been in the car with President Kennedy when he was assassinated, had just preceded us in visiting the *fazenda*; he came specifically to discuss quarter horses, as he also bred them. Another day we took a helicopter to have brunch at the estate of a wealthy neighbor. This family had developed a magnificent, professional-quality garden of palms that, unfortunately was being held privately in a somewhat isolated area. Again, food was served elegantly with numerous servants scurrying around. After four days of this opulent life, my friends and I felt relieved to return to our academic lifestyle. The visit had, however, introduced me to another side of Brazilian culture, which had similarities to the expatriate culture I had witnessed in Colombia in the early 1950s. It also dramatically emphasized the gap between the relatively few very rich and many very poor in Brazil.

NORTHWARD IN OUR COLLECTING

Following this interlude, I returned to collecting, moving northward from São Paulo state to coastal Bahia. With the assistance of climbers at CEPEC's Estacão Ecologica and Reserva Ecologia Pau, I finally obtained flowering specimens of *Copaifera trapezifolia*, which occurred here with *C. multijuga*, the common Amazonian species. Again, I was witnessing an interesting Amazonian rain forest connection with some of these Atlantic rain forest *Copaifera* species—similar to the relationship of varieties of *Hymenaea oblongifolia*. We had previously suggested that

Dardano Andrade-Lima introducing me to variation of Copaifera *species in Pernambuco*

such coastal species populations were continuous with Amazonian populations when moist vegetation during the Eocene spanned large areas of Brazil, but then were separated later with drying trends in the Oligocene and Miocene.

Moving even farther northward and inland, my collecting took me into an area of semidesert deciduous trees in the *cerrado* that graded into *cerradão*, and thence into the desert thorn forest (*caatinga*) in the northeastern states of Pernambuco and Ceará. As with our *Hymenaea* studies, Dardano Andrade-Lima of the Federal University of Pernambuco was my guide. He was determined to cover as much of the extensive distribution of *Copaifera* in northeastern Brazil as possible to help me get a grasp of the enormous diversity that this genus displayed here as well as to see if *Copaifera* and *Hymenaea* co-occurred as nearest neighbors consistently. Our observations indicated that close association of species of the two genera was more "hit and miss" here than in the *cerrado* and *cerradão* around Brasilia, but we couldn't be sure why.

Of special interest to me were the hilly areas and their remnant forests, called "*brejos*," which contain a variety of characteristic Amazonian species that are relicts from a moister period when continuous rain forest existed here. Some researchers, such as Ghillean Prance, have suggested that this present-day dry vegetation gives one an idea of what some landscapes were like during the Pleistocene dry periods that even occurred in parts of Amazonia. Towns often have been built around these *brejos* because water is available in the hills (*serras*) that maintain the remnants of the humid forest within the *caatinga*. In one *brejo* with clouds hanging over it, we found 80 to 90-foot specimens of our more southerly rain forest species, *Copaifera trapezifolia*, whereas in the surrounding *caatinga* both *C. martii* and *Hymenaea stigonocarpa* were essentially tall shrubs 12 to 15 feet high.

It was the first time I had been in the *caatinga* when it was green following rains. Several *Copaifera* species were flowering, whereas in the Venezuelan savanna and dry forests, *Copaifera* species flowered during the dry season. I wondered what controlled such differences. Also in comparison to semiarid and arid areas in the southwestern US, there were few herbaceous species evident—perhaps due to the density of tall grasses. I conjectured that *C. langsdorfii*, a widespread variable complex, might be a collection of polymorphic varieties much like Lee and I had interpreted *Hymenaea courbaril* to be in Brazil. Most of the recognized *Copaifera* species here needed considerably more study, and were going to require the concerted effort of local botanists to obtain the necessary flowering and fruiting specimens to clarify species designations as we had done in Venezuela.

Following my dry country trek, I moved northward and back into coastal rain forest near São Luis, Maranhão, where I collected both *Hymenaea* and *Copaifera* from forest remnants on the Ilha de São Luis. It was just a short hop back to Belém and nearby Atlantic Coast white sand beaches (*praias*) where, at Mosquero and Mirapanim, I collected a possible complex of three intergrading *Copaifera* species (*C. martii, coriacea,* and *cearensis*). I wondered if the bewildering variability we witnessed here was due to a hybrid zone of the type we had seen in central Venezuela. We had seen *Hymenaea* species coexisting with *Copaifera* in most Brazilian vegetation types, but *Hymenaea* was conspicuously absent along the Atlantic beaches, though present in nearby rain forests. This seemed strange to me in that *Hymenaea* pods are often picked up on other beaches throughout the Caribbean and Gulf of Mexico, and the seeds are known to germinate readily after having been in salt water. If one or the other of the two genera were to be absent along the beach, I certainly would have picked *Copaifera,* but it was just the opposite here.

From Belém I headed westward back to Santarém to obtain help from the SUDAM foresters for another trip to the FAO Curuá Una station, where I had gone in 1969. Having now read the accounts of the early naturalists, Bates and Spruce, who used Santarém as their headquarters while collecting specimens in the upland forests along the great tributaries of the area, I appreciated more of the historical importance of the town and its immediate environs. On this trip to the Curuá Una station no one attempted to see if I could withstand possible Amazonian dangers, such as anacondas. I apparently had passed those tests on my first visit. Although our goal was to collect several species of *Copaifera* that had been reported to be in this reserve, *C. multijuga,* the common species at the Ducke Reserve, was the only one the foresters were able to locate during my time there. Sometimes it is not a question of being able to find trees with flowers or fruit, but, frustratingly, even to find the trees at all—even with people who know them.

In transit back to Santarém I asked to pause for a closer look at the small kapok trees that commonly characterized the floating grass islands in this area. I wanted to see the floss packed in the pods and it was difficult to do on the very tall trees that I had seen previously. During World War II, as a youth, I had collected milkweed pods for their floss that was used as a substitute for kapok—the supply of which had been cut off by the Japanese. We stopped at an inhabited island where water buffalo were standing on a wooden platform. When we stepped ashore, a smiling woman with a weatherworn face rushed into a thatch-roofed hut and came out with a battered cup containing buffalo milk "*por a señora.*" My two SUDAM workers made excuses to help me with rejecting it. I kept smiling, trying to express appreciation for her kindness with many "*obrigados*" (thank you), but I think she was disappointed. We squished through part of the meadow to collect some of the bright red kapok fruit, which hung on the trees like Christmas ornaments. The woman was the only person present while we were there, and she was still waving as we retreated down the river. One could imagine that she lived quite a lonely existence. She also was the only direct contact I had, brief though it was, with people living along the river.

When I got back to Manaus, I spent time sorting and packing specimens from my entire trip through Brazil. To gain permission to collect in Brazil, agreement is made to leave at least one specimen of each plant collected in a Brazilian herbarium, in my case at INPA. The Brazilians needed a record of their own flora in their institutions, rather than having to depend on the US or European herbaria for collections taken from Brazil and especially Amazonia. Too often this had been the case in the past, and hence the current stringent regulations. Although I was not as successful in collecting *Copaifera* flowers and fruit as I had been in my previous trips collecting those of *Hymenaea*, I was later able to use the large collection of both *Copaifera* and *Hymenaea* leaves to great advantage in studying the variation of chemotypes, the kinds of phenolic compounds in them, and their leaf-spotting fungi.

By the mid-1970s, tropical rain forest conservation was an issue looming ominously on the horizon—with land increasingly coming under the impact of chainsaws, cattle ranches, hydroelectric plants, and more. But how big should protected areas be? Would a single, large reserve contain more species than a series of smaller ones with an area equal to a large one? No one knew. Tom Lovejoy of World Wildlife Fund (WWF-US) proposed an experiment in Amazonia that was both needed and feasible. In 1979, the year I was at INPA, a joint INPA-WWF-US project was approved by the Brazilian CNPq. It was called the Biological Dynamics of Forest Fragments Project (BDFFP). The plan was to establish a series of forest plots ranging in size from 100 to 1,000 hectares in forests north of Manaus that were slated to be cleared for cattle pasture. By arrangement, the ranchers would leave forested plots in the middle of their pastures, which created the world's largest man-made laboratory of island biogeography. Subsets of the flora and fauna would be monitored before and after isolation of these experimental plots. With quantified data the researchers would try to determine how large an area of undisturbed forest would be needed to preserve the full complement of species and their interactions in a given region. The study would involve students, along with researchers, who were experts with certain organisms. This was indeed an exciting and innovative project to aid decisions about conservation of Amazonian upland rain forests and at the same time train future Latin American leaders in conservation. I looked forward to seeing future results.

I started homeward with Surinam the only collecting site left. The best flight at the time was with Air France, from Manaus to Paramaribo via Cayenne, French Guiana. We arrived in Cayenne in early evening and were soon told we would have to spend the night there due to mechanical problems in our plane. However, hotel rooms were not available for all of the passengers. The majority of passengers were businessmen who received priority attention! With only four women aboard, Air France decided to find some other kind of accommodation for us together. They put the four of us (three Europeans and me) in a minibus and took us to a good-sized residence, which had a red light outside the door. Could this be what it appeared to be? Yes, we were taken into the reception area of the brothel and were met by a fancily attired and heavily made-up woman who spoke French in rapid-fire manner with the airline employee. The madam pointed to rooms, which I was eager to see, but a German woman vehemently (even indignantly) stated in English that she certainly was not going to stay in such a place. With the Dutch and English women in agreement with her, I was the only one who thought it would be a safe as well as a totally different and interesting experience. We were then taken to one of the better hotels where they put down mattresses for us on a secluded third-story veranda. Our plane was repaired overnight and we left early in the morning for Surinam.

My contact in Paramaribo was a Dutch woman in a position of some authority in the Surinam Forest Service. The atmosphere in her office was "all business," and indeed her somewhat domineering manner, as well as the way she hovered over me as I looked at herbarium specimens, made me glad that she was unable to accompany me in the field. She had arranged for one of their "tree spotters," Fritz Van Troom, to assist me and had obtained permits to collect in Brownsburg National Park, which is located in rain forest vegetation on the Mazaroni Plateau. Fritz was black but from his name was probably part Dutch. He was a delightful companion and his extensive knowledge of the forest trees, much of it handed down in his family, enabled us to collect several rain forest species of both *Copaifera* and *Hymenaea*. I stayed in one of the rustic cabins in the park, but on the last day of our collecting Fritz invited me to meet his family and have a simple meal (rice and beans and lots of fruit) with them in a predominantly black community near the park. They received me with warmth and were obviously pleased that I accepted their hospitality. For me it was a special pleasure to be afforded such a cultural experience.

RETURN TO A REORGANIZED CAMPUS

Upon my return to Santa Cruz in July, I found Chancellor Robert Sinsheimer had reorganized UCSC by altering the role of the colleges in relation to the boards of studies. It was a strange feeling to have been away in such a different cultural environment and come home to drastic changes in the campus I had known so well.

Sinsheimer had taken over the helm of the fledgling UCSC campus during a period of dire financial stress, initiated during Ronald Reagan's terms as governor. Reagan had made the UC students' disruptive conduct central in his campaign to restore traditional control. In 1967, he became the conservative voice following the liberal years of Pat Brown who had built the UC system into what was acclaimed as the nation's finest public university. For UCSC there was also the jolt of the firing of Clark Kerr, one of the architects of the Santa Cruz idea, as president of the UC system.

UCSC originally had a faculty-to-student ratio of one-to-ten which enabled some of its innovative approaches. However, as the campus had grown, that ratio had steadily grown to the UC norm of one-to-twenty. This created pressures to establish strong disciplinary curricula, which forced the boards of studies to assume educational control. The boards valued scholarship, research, and teaching of particular disciplines, as well as a developing graduate program, generally in accord with systemwide UC standards. The colleges valued their interdisciplinary courses and various services, such as living in the houses as preceptors, giving tutorials, and spending time with undergraduate students outside of their discipline, among others. There also was duplication of committees regarding faculty recruitment. The initial enthusiasm for the educational ideas offered by the colleges had been enough to help faculty carry the extra college burden. But eventually many faculty burned out and felt forced to emphasize scholarly and professional pursuits.

It was faculty promotions, in fact, that brought to a head the conflict between the missions of boards of studies and the colleges. Sinsheimer decided that personnel decisions being split fifty-fifty between the boards and colleges must be changed. He put personnel decisions fully in the hands of the boards of studies. In doing so, he ensured that the faculty would have clear cut academic goals that fit those of the UC system. Having learned about the UC seven-year up or out policy for tenure through the painful experience of my former husband at UC Berkeley, I empathized with the stress felt by untenured faculty (as well as having gone through the same stress myself before being promoted to tenure during my early years at UCSC!).

Yet Sinsheimer wanted to maintain the residential colleges as "intellectual and cultural centers in the liberal arts tradition," so a freshman core course on some broad topic of interest was maintained. However, he abandoned interdisciplinary courses, ignoring the unique opportunities that they offered. In many ways the colleges now looked more like the residential houses at Harvard and Yale than colleges at Oxford and Cambridge.

Sinsheimer was also "re-aggregating" the faculty in colleges more along disciplinary lines. Since most natural scientists had been assigned to Crown College, I reluctantly joined them. I left my founding affiliation with Stevenson College sadly, as it meant losing collegiality among faculty in various disciplines that I had so enjoyed. I have never regained the feeling for "the college" that I originally had.

CHEMICAL DEFENSE OF
HYMENAEA AND *COPAIFERA*

1980-1990

*Our strength often increases in proportion
to the obstacles imposed upon it.*
—Paul DeRapin

Funding from NSF for my research began with the chemosystematic analysis of ambers but soon involved questions regarding evidence for the defensive role that these resins may have played in the evolution of plants producing them. NSF had continued funding as I moved into systematic and chemical ecological studies of *Hymenaea* as a model amber-producing genus. In analyzing the potential defensive role of these tropical resins, I hypothesized that compositional variation of resins (often studied chemosytematically in conifers) could be subject to selection pressures by herbivores and pathogens, which would vary in different environments. This approach had received strong support and praise from the NSF panel's reviewers over the years for "an interdisciplinary but unified approach." I was especially gratified to be given a special NSF "Creativity Award"—a two-year extension to my existing three-year grant—with the "objective of providing an opportunity to attack high-risk adventurous questions." This gave me the chance to try and understand the evolution of co-occurring species of *Hymenaea* and *Copaifera* in terms of chemical mediation of their defenses against herbivores and pathogens in several tropical environments.

RISKY RESEARCH VENTURES IN THE TROPICS
At that time, tropical research in facilities other than those offered by OTS in Costa Rica or STRI in Panama was often considered risky by agencies providing funding for US biologists. As was true for all of our collecting trips, we faced governmental regulations such as visas to enter the country and permits to collect and take specimens out of the country. There were often frustrating delays at times critical for the research. Then there was the necessity of having at least minimal proficiency in the language, either

Spanish or Portuguese in the Neotropics. It also required the assistance of local researchers with knowledge of the biota, and the availability of their institutions' facilities, including protected reserve areas in which to establish projects. Richard Schultes, who introduced me to numerous Brazilian researchers, greatly helped me in overcoming the latter difficulty. They, augmented by my own subsequent contacts, had collaborated with me and my students for more than twenty years. Such collaboration on a long-term project offers particular problems in that the local scientists only have so much time and so many resources they can give to visiting researchers unless the research can intertwine in such a way that all parties benefit from it. Sometimes this balance is difficult to achieve and can jeopardize projects where funding is already only tenuous at best. Because we had previously dealt with most of these issues in Brazil, NSF recognized that we were ready to begin our field herbivore studies.

FIELD HERBIVORE STUDIES
We were not allowed by USDA to bring native herbivores from the tropics into our lab, and thus our early studies of *Hymenaea* defense against foliovores by necessity had depended on a generalist lepidopteran, *Spodoptera exigua*, commonly used in laboratory experiments. Using *S. exigua* we had shown that both the total quantity and compositional variation of leaf sesquiterpenenes were significant deterrents to these generalist herbivores. Now, almost a decade later, special funding for the *Hymenaea-Copaifera* comparison finally provided the opportunity to evaluate defense against both generalist and specialist lepidopterans (those tending to be restricted to a group or even a single species of plant) in the field. Unfortunately, we had to move from the rain forest, where we had evidence of the greatest chemical variation to forests with trees that were easier to access and hence study the herbivores.

Following discussions with David Gifford at the University of Brasilia and E.P. Heringer at IBGE during my 1979 visit in Brasilia, we were well set up to begin our herbivore research at their reserves. Moreover, George Hall had joined my lab group in 1980, planning to do his dissertation on resin defense against insect foliovores on *Hymenaea* and *Copaifera* in Brazil. We knew that the two genera shared very similar leaf sesquiterpenes, and our work in Venezuela and Amazonia had shown that species of each frequently co-occurred. We also had recorded that wherever the species of the two genera were closely associated, as nearest neighbors, the sesquiterpene chemotypes were different. I wanted to find out if this was generally true and, if so, whether such co-occurring species of the two genera shared the same group of foliovores or whether they partitioned them. From our previous field work, supported by information from Latin American entomologists, we knew that lepidopterans comprised the major herbivores—and that microlepidoteran leaf-tying oecophorids were the most obvious ones in Brazil. We obtained the assistance of V.O. Becker, the expert on these leaf-tying lepidopterans in Latin America, who was with Brazil's Agricultural Research group in Brasilia, to identify them on *Hymenaea* and *Copaifera* species in the *cerrado* and *cerradão*.

George began this research intending to compare the herbivory on a species of each genus at the two Brasilia reserves. However, with this preliminary project limited to five months, George finally focused his analysis on herbivory of the dominant leaf-tying *Stenoma ferrocanella* on *Hymenaea stigonocarpa* (which was more abundant here than *Copaifera langsdorfii*), and changes in sesquiterpenes and toughness during leaf development in relation to herbivore activity. The leaves must be sufficiently rigid for these insects to tie them together to build nests where they feed and also gain protection from predators. (When we started to study these leaf tiers I brought some larvae on *Hymenaea* branches into my hotel room, and was fascinated by how they pulled together the leaflets and then sewed them together with a web-like material—and then I could hear them eating the leaflets inside the nest. The leaflet-tying by these microlepidopterans is similar on *Copaifera* leaves.)

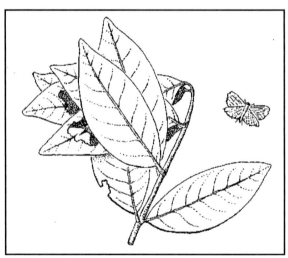

Drawing of Copaifera publifora *leaflets tied together along with proportionally sized moth.*

George found that although the total amount of sequiterpenes was decreasing as the leaf was becoming sufficiently mature to be rigid, high concentrations of particular sesquiterpenes—caryophyllene at one site and muurolene at the other site—were significantly correlated statistically with lower damage by these insects. These high concentrations of a single compound were accompanied by tree-to-tree variation of the suite of other sesquiterpenes comprising the mixture. Despite the limited time of the study, it was the first of its kind in the Brazilian *cerrado*.

During the early part of George's work, David Gifford died of a heart attack, which left the Ecology Laboratory at the university in a state of turmoil. This disrupting event led George to shift his research to coastal redwoods back in California. It also necessitated rethinking my plan for making our headquarters for field experimental studies at the University of Brasilia and IBGE reserves. Without Gifford's leadership, the university began shifting activities away from ecological research, and a stable arrangement in Brazil was essential for my long-term field project. I turned to Will Stubblebine, my former graduate student, now a professor in the Botany Department at the University of Campinas (UNICAMP) in São Paulo state. Will had already started some of his UNICAMP students investigating insect herbivory on *Copaifera*, and one of Will's colleagues was interested in continuing our studies of variation in *Hymenaea*. Thus their botany department was receptive to locating our operations with them. Furthermore, two reserves (referred to as SC for proximity to São Carlos and LA for proximity to Luis Antonio), which were only 50 miles apart and had similar climate and woodland (*cerradão)* vegetation, were available for our research. At the SC reserve, UNICAMP botanists had shown *Hymenaea* and *Copaifera* to be important members of a highly diverse forest community. We also had been offered assistance from biologists at the Federal University of São Carlos when students were working at the SC site. I planned to buy a vehicle to provide transportation for my students and make it available for UNICAMP faculty and their students cooperating with us.

Despite difficulties obtaining visas and collecting permits, as well as finding UCSC students with appropriate field experience (while I was in Australia when all of these changes came about), research got started in 1981. This success came primarily through Herculean efforts of Will Stubblebine. Leaf-tying oecophorid activity begins with the warm rainy season, usually in October and extends until December. The second generation of these insects starts in January and lasts through March. Even with delays due to slow visa processing, students (led by an energetic Charles Convis, who had just graduated from UCSC) were able to start work on the first generation in November. They had to take adult specimens of these insects to Brasilia for Becker to identify; two species were relatively common and two others were rare. One of them, *Stenoma* aff. *assignata,* Becker thought probably had specialized its herbivory on *Copaifera langsdorfii.*

Adult moth of Stenoma aff. assignata

Larva inside tied leaflets, which provide
food and protection from predators

The students also mapped adult trees and quantified seedling production of *Hymenaea stigonocarpa* and *Copaifera langsdorfii* in the two reserves. In contrast to the Brasilia reserves, however, they found *Copaifera* to be more than twice as abundant as *Hymenaea*—despite the LA reserve often being called "*Jatai*," one of the Brazilian common names for *Hymenaea*. The students sent back leaves to UCSC for chemical analysis, where we confirmed that at these sites the species of the two genera had similar sets of leaf sesquiterpenes, but consistently different chemotypes.

Similar to the Brasilia study, the students discovered *Hymenaea* and *Copaifera* did not share similar levels of leaf herbivory. *H. stigonocarpa* sustained much lower levels overall than *C. langsdorfii*; at the SC site, the levels were low for both species (3% vs 10% respectively), but at the LA site *Copaifera* had been heavily attacked (4% vs 50%). In contrast to *H. stigonocarpa* in the Brasila reserves, where oecophorid herbivory predominated, in the São Paulo reserves, non-leaf-tying lepidopterans were more common. This was puzzling because Becker had told us that oecophorids were common on *Hymenaea* throughout its distribution, and especially throughout Brazil. On the other hand, fungal damage was prominent on mature leaves of *Hymenaea* at both Brasilia and São Paulo sites.

The work done in 1981-2 laid the background for the future studies of herbivory at the São Paulo reserves. I decided reluctantly to give up our original intent to compare *Hymenaea* and *Copaifera* at these study sites, because the differences between the two genera made the workload overwhelming. I simply could not get enough researchers in the field at the same time. I had indeed underestimated the complexities of carrying out this research. Moreover, the greater abundance of *Copaifera* at the field sites as well as Brazilian interest in possibly utilizing its resin for fuel, convinced me to focus our research on *C. langsdorfii*.

The next two field seasons were plagued with other frustrations. Heavy El Niño rains especially hampered field work, and a crash in oecophorid populations occurred during 1982-3 and 1983-4—following high populations responsible for the 50% defoliation during 1981-2 at LA. For these years we only found insects at LA sporadically; however, the same low 4% level of oecophorid herbivory occurred at SC. Nevertheless, graduate student Matthew Ross was able to increase the number of developmental sequences of leaves collected from adult trees in which he had monitored the leaf-tying activity. These samples, returned to our lab for chemical analysis, allowed me to allay concerns that chemical data from experiments on seedlings and saplings under greenhouse or growth chamber conditions might not be comparable to those on the adult tree in the field. In the lab at UCSC, we analyzed and compared a variety of parameters in the sequences of leaf development sent back from trees in the field with those of leaf sequences on greenhouse-grown saplings of *Copaifera langsdorfii,* as well as two other species of *Copaifera*. Matthew also expanded our previous work in rearing these oecophorids in the lab at the University of São Carlos, which aided our future field experimental studies. This work greatly interested the Brazilian authority on oecophorid taxonomy, because he only identified the insects from adult specimens, and he knew nothing about their life cycle.

I planned to send Cynthia (Cindy) Macedo to follow Matthew Ross in the field, as she already had experience in surveying herbivory on *Hymenaea courbaril* in Mexico. A Brazilian, Erik Feibert, arrived at that time and I suggested that Cindy and Erik work together on *Copaifera* for their theses at the two São Paulo reserves. At first they were not eager to do collaborative research, but I finally convinced them they could cooperate in the field while doing independent projects. Cindy continued our study of the role of variation in leaf sesquiterpenes in deterring lepidopteran herbivory on *C. langsdorfii*, while Erik did a project on the relation between irradiance and herbivory in determining the high and low sesquiterpene yields in spatial patterns of its seedlings. Soon after Cindy and Erik started field work in Brazil, they both realized that their individual research would have been much more difficult if they had not collaborated. Their two backgrounds were an excellent match; she had more field experience than he, while he knew Portuguese and the Brazilian culture, which were new to her. My initial suggestion that they work together indeed was vindicated as they later married—making the field collaboration doubly "productive"!

In our original questions about the evolution of resin-producing plants, we had focused on terpenes as defensive compounds. Now we began to compare the relative roles of terpenes and phenolic compounds and how they might play different roles at different stages of the leaf's development. This comparison had been encouraged by a senior thesis in which the student had found that the total amount of sesquiterpenes in *Hymenaea* was highest in the early stages and then plateaued as the leaf matured, whereas total phenolics and condensed tannins were highest in the leaf bud and decreased during leaf development. These chemicals together provided a possible "double whammy" effect against *Hymenaea*'s enemies during the early stages of leaf development, when it often was most vulnerable. Therefore, for our *Copaifera* analyses, we determined total phenolics as well as sesquiterpenes, plus several other parameters that influence insect feeding such as nitrogen, water content, and toughness. In all cases, phenolics, nitrogen, and water content decreased whereas toughness increased as the leaf attained maturity. Although the total amount of sesquiterpenes in most species also decreased with leaf development, in two species, including *C. langsdorfii* from the field, it increased until maturity of the leaf. This implied that terpene synthesis was still occurring and could be significant defensively, because leaf-tying oecophorid herbivores feed on mature leaves they have tied. Such differences ran counter to most research, including what we had found in other plants we had monitored, which had indicated that the young leaf was being chemically protected. In these species of *Copaifera*, however, selection for high production of defense chemicals appeared to occur at a different time to meet the plant's greatest need for defense.

Cindy also carried out a field experiment regarding the relationship of *C. langsdorfii* parent trees and progeny seedlings to the oecophorid herbivore *Stenoma* aff. *assignata*. By 1984 this putative specialist oecophorid was essentially the only one found on trees at the São Paulo sites; the other three we had identified had apparently disappeared during the crash of 1982-3. The mean total amount of leaf sesquiterpenes was three times greater in seedlings than in adults and resulted in mortality of almost half of the oecophorid larvae or pupae reared on leaves of seedlings—thus providing experimental evidence of dosage-related effects of sesquiterpenes on the specialist lepidopteran herbivore. Because all leaves from plants at these sites had a single chemotype, Cindy could not analyze the effects of chemotype variation in seedlings the way we had in rain forests—a persistent disappointment in our overall parent tree-progeny studies.

Cindy thought that fitness of the trees at the heavily defoliated site (from oecophorids one year and gelechiids another) might have been affected compared to the site with a "normal" amount of herbivory. The canopy size was unaffected, but canopy vigor and diameter of the trees were much lower at the heavily damaged site—possibly suggesting other infestation years. The use of growth-ring data to evaluate environmental effects on diameter growth, however, is considered unreliable in tropical trees. This is unfortunate, as this kind of evidence regarding tree fitness could assist in drawing evolutionary conclusions.

In sum, for all the trials and travails, what had we learned from our six-year field herbivore study? First, we had confirmed evidence from both the Brasilia *cerrado* site and Saõ Paulo *cerradão* sites that not only were chemotypes of the co-occurring *Hymenaea* and *Copaifera* species different (which we had seen in the Venezuelan *llanos* and Amazonian rain forest), but the two genera could have different kinds and levels of foliovore attack. Although oecophorids occurred on trees of both genera, lepidopterans other than oecophorids predominated on *H. stigonocarpa* in the *cerradão* sites. Furthermore, we had learned that sesquiterpenes reached their maximum earlier in leaf development in *Hymenaea* than *Copaifera*, which meant that *Copaifera* had higher sesquiterpene concentrations during the maximum period of leaf-tying activity of oecophorids. These differences at the São Paulo *cerradão* sites introduced such an overwhelming work load that we were forced to focus on *C. langsdorfii*. In the five years of analysis of the relationship of sesquiterpenes and a specialist oecophorid, *Stenoma* aff. *assignata* on *C. langsdorfii*, at one site we witnessed a comparatively low level of herbivory (although considered a "normal" level for many tropical trees) over the entire study period, which was similar to that at a third São Paulo reserve where herbivory had been monitored by a UNICAMP student. Besides, at our other site, the foliovore activity varied significantly (from outbreak to crash of the specialist insect populations and then gradual increase over the years), thus displaying how activity of one herbivore species on a single tree species can differ between similar nearby sites. One year, fortuitously, we saw a generalist lepidopteran (gelechiid) defoliate immature leaves of more than half of the trees. This event occurred sufficiently early in the rainy season to allow regrowth of leaves, and thus it may have occurred earlier than our arrival in other years or it may be a rare event.

Despite such spatial and temporal variation in herbivory, tree-to-tree leaf variation of sesquiterpenes in *C. langsdorfii*—higher total amounts with usually one compound, often but not always caryophyllene, accompanied by high, more variable amounts, of several deterrent compounds (such as muurolene and cyperene) persistently was a significant factor in defending some trees against these leaf-tying foliovores in the *cerradão*, as it had on *Hymenaea stigonocarpa* in the *cerrado* near Brasilia. Tree-to-tree variation in a mixture of compounds makes adaptation of insects more difficult, and has also been shown to be significant in studies of resin defense in conifer species. I was disappointed that we were unable to continue field herbivore studies to test our hypothesis that the greatest amount of resin variation, which we had recorded in tropical rain forests, could be related to heightened herbivore (or pathogen) activity there. Later development of techniques for access into the canopy of tropical rain forests might make such studies feasible in the future.

Erik Feibert's study emphasized the importance of understanding leaf sesquiterpene variation in *Copaifera langsdorfii* in relation to both irradiance and herbivory. He utilized gardens at the University of São Carlos to establish field experiments in growing seedlings of *C. langsdorfii* under different light intensity. Erik's experiments corroborated my growth chamber studies of selected species of both *Hymenaea* and *Copaifera* seedlings in which I found that high light intensity (in contrast to temperature, moisture, and light duration) significantly increased the total amount of leaf sequiterpenes without changing their relative proportions (chemotype). Thus, although relative amounts of the components were not affected, increased concentration of individual defensive compounds could influence their dose-dependent effects. From these experiments we were in agreement with John Bryant, Phyllis Coley, and their associates in a theory that emphasized the importance of resource availability in influencing the amount of secondary chemical production—particularly, the importance of light intensity for carbon-based compounds such as terpenes. However, the story in our study changed when herbivores were present. Contrary to both the laboratory and field experiments, Erik found that seedlings and saplings growing under natural forest conditions had higher amounts of leaf sesquiterpenes in shade under the parent tree, where herbivory was also high, than in open areas. To explain this difference, we hypothesized that surviving seedlings and saplings growing in the shade of the parent tree had been selected for higher sesquiterpene yields in their leaves, rendering them unpalatable to the foliovores of the adult tree. Cindy's experimental studies with herbivory on seedlings under parent trees supported such an hypothesis. We published Feibert's results in a 1988 special issue of the journal *Phytochemistry* dedicated to Tony Swain (founding and longtime editor of *Biochemical Systematics and Evolution*), who had died in an automobile accident. We were glad to be able to contribute to this memoriam of a friend who had so enthusiastically supported our lab's research.

STUDIES OF LEAF-SPOTTING FUNGI AND
COMPARATIVE STUDIES OF PHENOLICS

The frequent evidence of fungal damage on leaves I had collected throughout the Brazilian distribution of *Hymenaea* and *Copaifera* in 1979 caused me to begin to think seriously about analyzing defense against leaf fungi. I also remembered the general blighting of leaves caused by the leaf pathogenic fungus *Phoma* in a garden of *H. courbaril* seedlings that we had planted in

Costa Rica in our early studies during 1970. We had experimental evidence of leaf resin variation providing defense against generalist and specialist lepidopterans, both in terms of total quantity and compositional variation; could leaf resin variation inhibit some pathogenic fungi, and, if so, how might it differ from defense against foliovores?

Heringer at IBGE actively encouraged my new interest in pursuing fungal research. Graduate student Susanne Arrhenius wanted to move in

Visiting with Tony Swain in Boston

this new direction for her dissertation, and Heringer helped where he could to identify what seemed to be an overwhelming number of fungi growing on our collection of *Hymenaea* and *Copaifera* leaves. With the assistance of the monographer of the fungal genus *Pestalotia (Pestalotiopsis),* Susanne settled on analyzing the distribution of four tropical pathogenic leaf-spotting species. *Pestalotia* is the only genus reported to infect leaves of both *Hymenaea* and *Copaifera* through a range of vegetation types. Susanne also did an experimental study of the inhibitory effects some leaf sesquiterpenes had on *P. subcuticularis,* a widespread species that spanned the distribution of the two genera from Mexico to southern Brazil, and could be cultured. In contrast to caryophyllene being a common deterrent compound of lepidopteran insects we had studied, she discovered it was its oxide that was most inhibitory to *Pestalotia.* Interestingly, other researchers had found that caryophyllene oxide in *H. courbaril* leaves inhibit the fungi cultivated by leaf cutter ants in their nests.

We had observed that leaves on tropical rain forest seedlings of *H. intermedia* and *C. multijuga* had less evidence of fungal damage than their parent trees, and had found the total amount of terpene leaf resins was two-fold higher in seedling leaves than parents. Later, we discovered that total phenolic compounds were also higher in the leaves of seedlings than in the adults, and we hypothesized that these compounds might also play a role in inhibiting fungal growth in the seedlings.

Although we had recorded the presence of phenolic compounds in *Hymenaea* and *Copaifera* leaves, we began to understand some of their important differences in these genera with the arrival of Leo McCloskey in the lab. Leo is an example of the sometimes surprising ways additions are made to one's lab group. He had an MS in biochemistry and, as an owner of a local winery, wanted to increase his knowledge of phenolic compounds, the predominant group of compounds in grape wine. Leo had been doing some research at Ridge Winery and the Stanford chemist Carl Djerassi, who was part owner of Ridge, suggested that analyzing phenolic compounds in plants other than grapes might give Leo more insight into variation in wine chemistry than further analysis of the well-known chemistry of grapes. (Later he was inspired to classify wine styles based on patterns of phenolic compounds, which he applied to predict wine quality.) Ridge Winery was willing not only to support Leo's work but also to provide our lab with specialized analytical equipment (high performance liquid chromatography, which had just come into common use in the 1970s) for a comparative analysis of the phenolic compounds in *Hymenaea* and *Copaifera* leaves.

Evidence of leaf-spotting fungus, Pestalotia, *shown here by*
P. subcuticularis *on* Copaifera multijuga

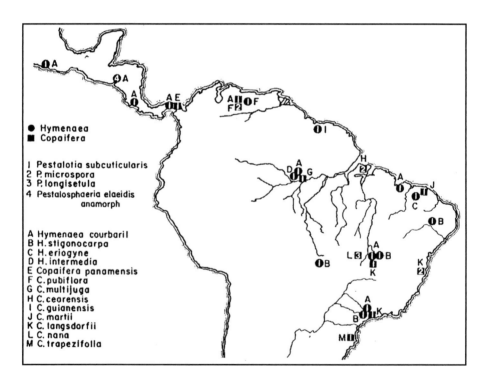

● Hymenaea
■ Copaifera

1 Pestalotia subcuticularis
2 P. microspora
3 P. longisetula
4 Pestalosphaeria elaeidis
   anamorph

A Hymenaea courbaril
B H. stigonocarpa
C H. eriogyne
D H. intermedia
E Copaifera panamensis
F C. pubiflora
G C. multijuga
H C. cearensis
I C. guianensis
J C. martii
K C. langsdorfii
L C. nana
M C. trapezifolia

Location of Pestalotia *species isolated from*
my collections of Hymenaea *and* Copaifera *leaves*

Where we had found leaf sesquiterpenes to be similar between the two genera, Leo found the leaf phenolic compounds to be very different—*Hymenaea* was characterized by condensed tannins (familiarly known for their astringency in black tea and red wine) and *Copaifera* by nontanniferous flavonoids (anthocyanidins known for red-blue color in fruits and flowers). He used a variety of techniques for analysis of these compounds in a wide array of leaf samples that I had collected throughout the New World. For example, he analyzed the levels of condensed tannins in *Hymenaea* species by comparing the proportion of those with low to those with high molecular weight, and found a greater percentage of leaves with a high proportion of high molecular weight condensed tannins in species occurring in rain forests, decreasing progressively to those occurring in very dry forests. Although some researchers had proposed that high levels of condensed tannins reflect selection pressures from the great diversity and abundance of microbial pathogens in tropical rain forests, no one previously had analyzed tannins in species of a genus across tropical forest types.

Leo also found that high levels of cyanidins were responsible for the intense red color of flushing leaves of *Copaifera* species, which so predominated the canopy that they appeared from a distance to be massive flowering. Other researchers had found this red coloration of young leaves may act to inhibit fungi in numerous tropical species. We too began to consider whether the high levels of cyanidins in young *Copaifera* leaves—and the difference in their concentrations in different species—might have evolved under fungal selection pressures in different tropical environments. Preliminary experiments indicated this possibility. It was during such experiments that Susanne and Leo became good friends, ultimately leading to their marriage. I was beginning to feel like a successful, if inadvertent, matchmaker.

Under tropical conditions, it is common for fungi that occur within leaves (fungal endophytes) to colonize the leaves early in their development. Leaf penetration by the fungus may initiate a parasitic or pathogenic relationship, or there may be a dormant phase after fungal entry with disease symptoms not appearing until leaf maturity. The latter situation is referred to as latent infection. Newly expanded field-collected leaves of both *Hymenaea courbaril* and *Copaifera langsdorfii* were infected with *Pestalotia subcuticularis*, indicating that fungal colonization took place soon after leaf emergence. It was mature leaves, however, in my collections that showed evidence of damage. Furthermore, field studies of *H. stigonocarpa* near Brasilia showed progressive increase of fungal damage with leaf maturation.

We thought the fungi might have been chemically inhibited in the early stages of leaf development because their fungal symptoms appeared at the same developmental point at which concentrations of sesquiterpenes and tannins decreased.

We continued our studies of fungi with Gail Fail using light, scanning, and transmission electron microscopy to study the infection process of *Pestalotia subcuticularis*, which Susanne had been analyzing in *Hymenaea courbaril* leaves on saplings growing in our greenhouse. Gail first decided to collect leaf development sequences of *H. courbaril* in the field in Mexico to compare with sequences from *H. stigonocarpa* from Brazil. Finding that the timing of the fungal appearance was similar, she then decided to concentrate on inoculation of developing leaves in the greenhouse for her microscopic studies. With the guidance of Lynn Hoefert, an electron microscope specialist working with the USDA Agricultural Research Service in nearby Salinas, Gail followed the processes of entry, intracellular ramification, latent infection, and lesion formation of this leaf-spotting fungus on *H. courbaril,* as she tracked changes in the amounts of both terpenes and tannins in the leaves. Inoculated unwounded leaves often had symptomless infections for several weeks (typical of leaf endophytes), but

Trio of women, left to right, Gail Fail, Susanne Arrenhius,
and Cindy Macedo, who worked together on related
Hymenaea *and* Copaifera *research*

active infections soon formed in wounded leaves. Tannin vacuoles were dense in the healthy leaves and were degraded with initiation of active infection. Also, destruction of the cell walls of the terpene secretory cells during this time may have released potentially inhibitory terpenes into the intercellular spaces. These observational results supported our hypotheses that both sesquiterpenes and condensed tannins may act to restrict fungal infections in their latent phase in *Hymenaea* leaves.

OUR CONTRIBUTION TO UNDERSTANDING CHEMICAL ECOLOGY IN THE TROPICS

Through our study of two closely-related angiosperm resin-producing trees, we contributed to understanding their chemical defense in several tropical environments—from moist rain forests and gallery forests to arid savanna-like forests and woodlands. We documented that wherever species of the two genera co-occur as nearest neighbors, their leaf sesquiterpene chemotypes differ. We also showed that the greatest variation in chemotypes occurs in Amazonian rain forest, with up to six chemotypes possible from a single parent tree of *Hymenaea intermedia* and *H. parvifolia*, whereas in the dry forests only one chemotype occurs in *H. courbaril* and *H. stigonocarpa* as well as in *Copaifera pubiflora* and *C. langsdorfii*. However, there is considerable tree-to-tree variation within these single chemotypes. Laboratory experiments demonstrated that abiotic conditions did not change the chemotype of an individual tree, but in both laboratory and field experiments we found that greater light intensity increased the total quantity of sesquiterpenes. Knowing there was genetic control of the chemotype, opened the door to the idea that the patterns of variation had been selected by herbivores and/or disease-causing microbes. Initial laboratory experiments at UCSC showed the adverse effects of total leaf sesquiterpenes and different chemotypes in *Hymenaea courbaril* on different life stages of a commonly used generalist noctuid lepidopteran (*Spodoptera exigua*). Field studies in the highly diverse Brazilian woodland (*cerradão*) revealed the impact of sesquiterpene variability on both generalist gelechiid lepidopterans and putative specialist oecophorid microlepidopterans that occur on *Copaifera langsdorfii*. Furthermore, in a field experiment using oecophorid larvae we documented that higher sesquiterpene-yielding seedlings survived under parent trees. In another study, we showed that yields were higher under the shade of the parent tree than in the open, where they would be expected to be higher; we hypothesized this resulted from selection by the oecophorid herbivores.

Our detailed analyses of changes in chemistry during leaf development indicated significant differences that influenced the timing of herbivore attack on *Hymenaea* and *Copaifera*. Although we had always focused our research on terpenes comprising the resin, we began to look into the possible interacting influence of phenolic compounds. Whereas the leaf sesquiterpenes are remarkably similar in the two genera, the phenolics are greatly different—condensed tannins dominating in *Hymenaea* and anthocyanidins in *Copaifera*. We found some evidence that tannins increased the anti-herbivore arsenal of *Hymenaea*, but no suggestion of such effects by the anthocyanidins in *Copaifera*.

We also recovered and identified leaf-spotting fungi from my leaf collections made throughout the distribution of the two genera—as well as from greenhouse specimens grown from seed. We analyzed in detail an endophytic leaf-spotting fungus, *Pestalotia* (*Pestalotiopsis*) *subcuticularis*, which occurs on species of both *Hymenaea and Copaifera* through much of their distributions. In culture experiments, it was the oxide of caryophyllene that inhibited the fungi, which contrasted with caryophyllene often being a primary compound in deterring lepidopterans. Electron microscope studies supported the view that both the terpenes and condensed tannins probably inhibit the development of the endophytic fungus studied.

Although these results only provide initial understanding of these chemical relationships in the leaves of two genera, we hope that they provide significant background to enable other tropical researchers to advance our understanding of their evolutionary implications.

CURRENT MERGING OF CHEMICAL ECOLOGY AND ETHNOBOTANY

Current directions in chemical ecology in the tropics, particularly in the rain forest, appear to be merging with ethnobotany in emphasizing sustainable utilization of forest products. This is evident in Brazilian Amazonia where interest remains high in *Copaifera* resin, now not for diesel fuel, but for the cosmetics industry as well as the resin's age-old uses for medicine. Because of inherent problems of slow growth of saplings in plantations, emphasis is being put on understanding the variability of resin production from the trunk of the adult tree under natural forest conditions, and the best means of obtaining the resin by local people who collect it as an important source of income. Most current research assessing the quantity of resin produced has focused on resource availability of the tree, but the next step is assessment of the impact of pests. Practices that maximize the yield but preserve the tree are becoming a part of a conservation incentive for local collectors.

Interesting recent recommendations have been made by some tropical chemical ecologists to utilize our accumulating understanding of leaf chemical defense. They suggest that knowing when the highest concentration of chemicals occurs within the sequential stages of leaf development could lead to more effective screening for useful chemicals without stripping the trees of their leaves.

THAILAND AND AUSTRALIA ADVENTURE

1980-1981

*A woman is like a teabag. You never know how strong
she is until she is in hot water.*
—Eleanor Roosevelt

From my amber studies, I had been particularly interested in *Agathis*—the most tropical conifer genus, with a distribution from IndoChina to New Zealand. Its resin not only fossilized but also occurred in many deposits worldwide. I was among a group of scientists who had even proposed that *Agathis* or *Agathis*-like resins were a possible source of Baltic amber. My interest in Asian resin-producing trees had been additionally piqued by a graduate student in anthropology and archaeology at Yale University. She was studying the Semalai culture in Malaysia, and had spent several months in my lab, learning IR techniques as a means to identify resins that these people had been using for centuries. Her investigation increased my knowledge of important resins produced by members of several large Asian angiosperm families (Dipterocarpaceae and Burseraceae among others), and continued the thread of my work with anthropologists and archaeologists as well.

BANGKOK SYMPOSIUM

Therefore, I delightedly accepted in 1980 the invitation to participate in a symposium on "Underexploited Economic Plants with Special Reference to Southeast Asia" that NYBG was cosponsoring with the Thai Royal Forest Department, in Bangkok, Thailand. I gave a paper on "Utilization of Resins from Tropical Trees," thereby making the topic sufficiently broad to include my own Neotropical research. I expanded my ethnobotanical knowledge of many interesting Southeast Asian plants, and learned about some of the devastating timbering operations that seemed worse than in Amazonia at the time. I also was pleased with a special opportunity to spend some time there with a long-time friend and an extraordinary Chinese woman botanist—Dr

Shui-ying Hu in Hong Kong in 2007

Shui-ying Hu. I became acquainted with Shui-ying while I was at Harvard in the sixties, and refreshed our friendship in my 1974 sabbatical when she also was helping Eric Lee on his post-doctoral fellowship there. She had an amazing odyssey in arriving at Harvard to obtain her doctorate, working with E.B. Merrill on the flora of China, after Japan invaded China in 1946. She then remained at the Arnold Arboretum making an index to the Chinese flora. During the time that Mao Tse-tung was alive, Chinese botanists were not allowed to see or communicate with any foreign botanist. However, because she was Chinese, Shui-ying managed to get literature to them from the United States and helped them keep up with the field in various ways. After Mao died in 1977, she returned to China and gave several intensive courses for young botanists in various parts of the country. She always was a bundle of energy and indefatigable in her research on the Chinese flora and in helping Chinese botanists. At this symposium we had such fun reliving some of our adventures together at Harvard—such as combing the Cambridge streets lined with gingko tree for fallen fruits and returning to her apartment with them for her to show me they were edible.

I vividly remember getting around Bangkok as a challenging and often bewildering experience even when accompanied by our genial hosts. Walking was difficult in many areas due to incredibly crowded conditions; instead we used either a *sanlor*, a noisy motorized pedicab, or an equally noisy three-or four-wheeled minibus. As ethnobotanists, we investigated with great interest markets filled with abundant produce, often strange to us. One of our host-planned trips was to the floating markets that occur on the major *klongs* (canals) early in the morning. The vendors, mostly women in outsized straw hats, paddled past the canal-front houses with fruits and vegetables and household necessities.

Distinguished ethnobotanist, Charlie Heiser (tall man in back), with Thai Symposium hosts exploring Bangkok

While investigating produce markets and exploring Buddhist temples, I also was witnessing something close to my heart—the reverence for cats among the Thai people. Cats of various ancestry were everywhere, though I saw only a few blue-eyed Siamese and none recognizable as the special Siamese *korat*. The *Cat Book of Poems* produced sometime between 1350 and 1767 presents seventeen good luck cats of Thailand. Although most cats we saw were feral, they were not skittish; often they were very friendly. The cats were fed at certain times in the temples, where they were lounging around in many areas inside. Food and water were abundantly supplied in the markets, with dishes near most of the stands of produce or goods being sold. I was unable to learn if medical help was available for the cats or if there were attempts to neuter them to keep their populations under control. The cats just seemed to be a happy part of the community—knowing they were appreciated. But did they know, as I was told, that they were considered so sacred that killing one was like killing a monk? It was a special memory to carry away from Bangkok.

Cats in Bangkok central market

INVITATION TO AUSTRALIA

I had long wanted to know more about the photosynthetic capacity of the *Hymenaea* and *Copaifera* seedlings with which we were doing our chemical ecology experiments. I had particularly wondered during our parent tree-progeny studies how the seedlings growing in the dark understory would acclimate to the intense light of gaps in the canopy that occur following death and fall of the parent tree. Photosynthetic capacity under different light conditions not only directly affects survival of the seedling but also affects the levels of production of secondary chemicals, which in turn influence herbivory.

An invitation to analyze the question of acclimatization came from the Australian plant physiological ecologist, Barry (C.B.) Osmond. He was the chair of the Department of Environmental Biology in the Research School of Biological Sciences at the Australian National University (ANU) in Canberra, which was a center for ecologically-oriented studies of photosynthesis. Most of their work, logically, was concentrated on desert plants, and Osmond was the senior author of the just-published book *Physiological Processes in Plant Ecology: Toward a Synthesis with Atriplex.* Osmond invited me to come to his department as a visiting fellow to compare tropical tree seedling responses to different light regimes using selected species of *Hymenaea* and *Copaifera* along with

With Barry Osmond at cricket match in Canberra

Australian rain forest species of the important amber-producing *Agathis*. Thus, I would have the additional advantage of learning more about this important tropical conifer. We would be using these resin-producing trees to answer some fundamental questions regarding photosynthetic acclimation in tropical forests. My visit was planned for 1981 because I could also attend the XIII International Botanical Congress meeting in Sydney during the summer.

My Australian adventure began in January where in Canberra I stayed on the ANU campus at University House, a center for university visitors in which I had a large bedroom-study with a little veranda and a bath. There was a hot plate, a toaster, and a few dishes that enabled visitors to fix breakfast. In warm weather, I usually had breakfast on the veranda, where I frequently enjoyed the company of cockatoos that lived in the open courtyard below. These birds could out-compete Santa Cruz scrub jays in boldness and raucousness! A small restaurant at University House was available for other meals; even members of the nearby Parliament often ate there for lunch. As was my wont, I befriended a cat—this one was a young male that hung around University House. He did not come to my upstairs room but liked to accompany me for short walks on the campus with stops for petting. I would often find him waiting for me along paths near University House on mornings when I left for the Research School. In liking to walk with me, he reminded me of Florodora.

To my dismay, the *Hymenaea* and *Copaifera* seeds that I had sent to Australia in the fall of 1980, to grow seedlings for our experiments, had been planted but died because they were not properly cared for during the Christmas vacation. The few that had survived were too small for my experiments, so more seeds had to be planted. Plus, I still had to obtain *Agathis* seedlings from the Queensland Forest Service. I spent considerable effort in encouraging the growth of these plants in the research school's glasshouse—while dodging a large number of spiders that appeared menacing. Although these problems meant quite a delay in beginning the photosynthetic experiments, they gave me time to visit some interesting botanical areas.

BOTANICAL JAUNTS

My first trip out of the Canberra-Sydney area was to the Snowy Mountains in Kosciusko National Park, part of what is called the Australian Alps on the New South Wales-Victoria border. Here the summit of the Australian alpine areas is close to 6,000 feet (elevations similar to alpine areas in New England or summits in the Smoky Mountains). *Eucalyptus pauciflora* was a striking element in the higher mountain forests, with its beautiful white-gray striped bark, and a *Podocarpus* occurred as krummholz, looking so different from the North American krummholz of spruce and pine. Insect herbivory by a chrysomelid beetle that specialized on several species of *Eucalyptus* in these mountains was incredible. I had never seen such decimation of leaves other than from leaf-cutting ants in the Neotropics. High concentrations of volatile leaf terpenes did not provide defense against these voracious beetles, but the possible role of patterns of variation had not been studied.

I was traveling with Joe Connell, prominent ecologist from UC Santa Barbara, and Patrice Morrow who was doing research on these voracious beetles, as well as staff members from the Research School. We stayed in park facilities, where I had a memorable experience with a baby wombat (a small burrowing marsupial endemic to Australia). Wombats are nocturnal and have poor eye sight, hence they are vulnerable to being hit on highways at night. At the park, a mother wombat had been killed by a car and the park ranger's wife had rescued the joey (baby) from the mother's pouch. She carried the joey around with her in a special pocket she had made in an apron, simulating the mother's pouch, and she was feeding the joey special formula on a demanding schedule. The little female, called Harriet, had grown sufficiently large to spend time out of the pouch and followed me everywhere in the ranger's house. So the ranger's wife asked if I would like to care for her while I was visiting the park. I had the delightful experience of taking care of Harriet when we were back from the field in late afternoon and early evening during the short period we were there.

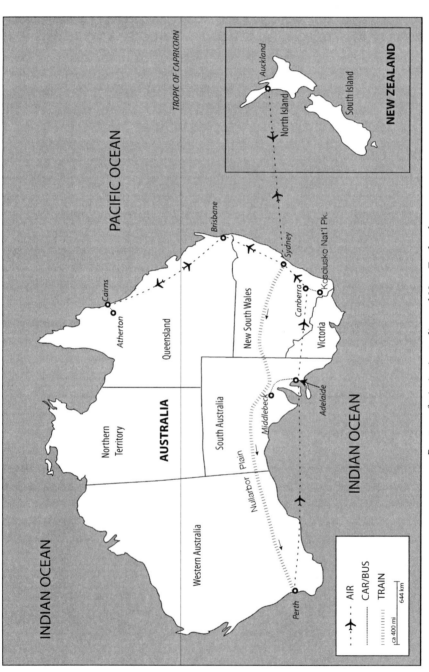

Routes of trip in Australia and New Zealand

With Harriet, the wombat

On a trip to Batesman Bay along the coast of New South Wales, we went into mangrove swamps bordered by eucalypts that had a cycad understory and black cockatoos flying about. Because of my previous study of mangroves in relation to the site of deposition of Mexican amber, I had been asked to serve as an outside member on a dissertation committee of a student studying these Australian mangroves. I had come to find mangrove plant adaptation fascinating as well as the importance of their vegetation to the health of coastal environments, and thus was pleased to have the opportunity to learn more about them in Australia.

While visiting the Tidbinbilla Nature Reserve in the highland region south of Canberra, I collected red balls of resin from the base of burned leaves on the strange-looking grass tree (*Xanthorrhoea australis*). This resin is used industrially in Australia, especially for varnishes or stains. I was thrilled to see many emus, both gray and red kangaroos, and an abundance of birds such as sulfur-crested cockatoos, roselles, and pied currawongs. With my love of cats, I was unhappy to hear about Canberra residents dumping them in the reserve, where they became feral and preyed upon small marsupials. The ANU veterinary school had found that within several generations these cats became tabbies, which provided them excellent camouflage in the bush and increased their predator capacities. The vets feared that these cats would destroy native marsupial populations the way foxes, introduced by the British for hunting, had done.

LIFE IN CANBERRA

These various jaunts outside Canberra were squeezed in between trying to coax my seedlings to grow faster in the glasshouse (I was afraid I would have to leave before they were big enough for experimentation) and carrying on a voluminous correspondence with my students in Brazil and Santa Cruz. I was corresponding with Kenneth Thimann and the John Wiley editors as well regarding proofs for the Plants and Human Affairs textbook. Problems in communication were exacerbated by sequential strikes of workers at Quantas airline and the Australian mail service. The book editors were frantic because for significant periods I could neither receive nor send any mail. For weeks, any correspondence was dependent on the research school's one telex machine—no e-mail then! I had the telex machine jammed with book proofs; since others in the department were also dependent on this means of communication, I became rather unpopular and was soon restricted in my use of the telex. I ultimately had to fly back to Santa Cruz to complete aspects of the book for which Thimann insisted I be responsible as the senior author.

By late March and early April, it was getting cold in Canberra. Although I had spent early to mid year in the Southern Hemisphere of the New World, I had never seen large plantings of temperate zone trees turning brilliant red and yellow in April and May. I had to constantly remind myself of the actual date because it appeared to be October to this Northern Hemisphere inhabitant. The vivid reds and yellows, contrasting with the dull greens and grays of the native eucalypts, not only appeared on the ANU campus but all around Canberra. Canberra, like Brasilia, is a planned city. However, unlike Brasilia, Canberra is renowned for its trees, which link to the suburbs in such a manner that the city seems to have been established in a natural forest. Originally, Canberra was just a windswept plain, but in 1911 a massive tree-planting campaign began. Now Canberra boasts that it has the largest diversity of urban tree species of any major city in the world.

I had become miserably cold in my room. Heat at University House did not come on until mid-April, and even then it provided minimal warmth. I went to bed almost immediately after eating dinner, pulling up the very heavy blankets we were provided. At an elegant dinner in a large Canberra home in April, I had forsaken my long pants, heavy sweatshirts, and sweaters for a dress and pantyhose, assuming naively that the house would be warm. During the meal I was so cold that my teeth almost began to chatter. The woman sitting next to me noticed my anguish and whispered, "Luv, do you have on your woolies?" "No," I said, "What are woolies?" She laughed and replied that she would bring me some at University House. She arrived with woolen underwear that extended partially over the thighs; she also provided me with a warm coat and heavy wool socks.

WESTERN AND SOUTH AUSTRALIA

During Easter vacation at the university I added to my special train trips by taking the Indian Pacific train, which goes from Sydney on the Pacific Ocean to Perth on the Indian Ocean. At the time, it was the world's last remaining transcontinental train (a Canadian transcontinental journey is now again available) and took sixty-four hours to span Australia's 2,715 miles. It was a train trip different from any other I had had—it was more like a cruise, in that passengers had a private berth but ate meals in assigned seating in the dining car. All the other passengers were friendly and jolly Australians on holiday. After the evening meal, they gathered around a piano in the lounge car for a sing-along, which always started with the familiar "Waltzing Matilda."

During the day I was often in the lounge car taking photos from the large windows. As we crossed the barren desert country, the Australian passengers could not understand why I was photographing it. Always thinking about geomorphology in relation to the vegetation, I was fascinated by the landscape. I found the jagged ridges of the Flinders' Range, in South Australia, to be one of the more impressive topographic features we encountered. They appeared before we hit the longest stretch, almost 300 miles, of straight railway track in the world across the vast Nullarbor Plain. The vegetation was different from American deserts but such differences, of course, were meaningless to the Australians. They repeatedly said, "Luv, it's just salt bush" and later added "not even a dingo out there." By happenstance, I did get to see a couple of dingoes near a short stop at Kalgoorlie. We all kept looking for, but were not privileged to see, the wedgetail eagle, the biggest on earth and the symbol of the train.

In Perth I stayed in the home of the Glenn Willsons, which was cozily warm—they had become accustomed to central heating when Glenn had been provost of Stevenson College. He had left UCSC to become vice chancellor of Murdoch University in Perth; I enjoyed this opportunity to see him and his wife again as I had missed the close association we had in Santa Cruz. I also met with the well-known Australian resin researchers B. Dell and J. McComb at the University of Western Australia. McComb took me on several field trips to the university's Carrington Reserve where I saw several species of grass tree (*Xanthorrhoea*) different from those I had seen at south of Canberra. Here they grow under *jarrah* (*Eucalyptus marginata*) and are commonly called "black boy" from the effects of frequent fires. In another area we saw *Xanthorrhoea* as understory of *Banksia. Xanthorrhoea* is fascinating in characterizing such a variety of habitats in the Australian landscape.

J. McComb displaying leaf resins on Eremophila.

In the large collections at King Park Gardens, I saw my first of the over 200 species of *Eremophila*—one of the most significant desert genera in the biogeography of Australia, and a copious resin-producing shrub in Western Australia. Using electron microscopy, Dell and McComb had studied the fine structure of the glandular trichomes (hairs) of *Eremophila,* along with numerous other resin-producing shrubs (such as *Myoporum*), to understand how and why these plants produced such large amounts of leaf resin. They had hypothesized that the thick, shiny resin secretions (typically 5-10 percent of the leaf dry mass but sometimes up to 30 percent) that encase the leaf are especially important in protecting leaf buds against high temperatures, and in decreasing transpiration during times of low availability of water in the extreme desert environments of Western Australia. Dell and McComb had collaborated with chemists who had shown that many of the Australian shrubs also have evolved novel, structurally unique terpenes, which leads to questions regarding the circumstances in which the resin as well as their secretory structures evolved.

I appreciated having the opportunity to see some of these Western Australian copious resin-producing shrubs that had been so intensively studied, and to discuss with one of these researchers their conclusions regarding the importance of desert conditions in determining the function of resin during its evolution. Dell and McComb had concluded that resin produced in external secretory structures protected the plant primarily against harsh abiotic conditions of arid areas and its antiherbivore properties were insignificant. On the other hand, they thought that the function of resin produced in internal secretory structures was to protect against insects but not fungal pathogens. They recognized that resistance to insects and grazing animals provided a functional link between internally and externally secreted resins, but questioned why such resistance would have selective advantage in arid areas. However, studies comparing the chemical ecology of the dominant shrub *Larrea* in deserts of the United States and Argentina had shown antiherbivore activity against a large community of insects that attacked both leaves and stems of the plant. Detailed study of the resistance against these insects did not mean that protection against harsh abiotic desert conditions was not considered important. In fact, integrated studies have been made of antiherbivore, antidesiccant, and ultra-violet screening properties of the shiny resin coating of *Larrea*.

I also disagreed with these researchers regarding their view that internally secreted resins did not protect against both insects and pathogenic fungi that the lush moist tropical environment support. In this discussion, I was reminded of Paul Sears' view of how much an ecologist's interpretation is based on the environment in which he is working—and often of the difficulty in generalizing beyond it. In this respect, I was glad to have an evolutionary perspective from studying fossil resin that led me to think about adaptation to different environments during the long evolution of resins and the secretory structures in which they are produced.

From Perth I flew eastward to Adelaide, South Australia where I gave a seminar at the University of Adelaide and stayed in the home of the artist Rosemary Woffard Garf, who was producing a quarto-sized volume of her prints of Australian animals. When I mentioned to the botanists at the university that I had always wanted to visit an Australian sheep station, they kindly made arrangements for me to stay briefly at their Middlebeck Field Station, which gave me the flavor of the Australian outback. Although it is only 300 feet above the valley, it receives eight inches of rain annually, which is sufficient to support more mesophytic vegetation than the surrounding areas. Salt bush (*Atriplex*), blue bush (*Mariana*), and spinifix grass (*Spinifix*) were common, and unlike their counterparts in Western Australia, the species of *Eremophila* and *Myoporum* here were not noticeably resinous. With about ten sheep per hectare, rabbits (again introduced by the British for hunting) were still a problem, being twenty per hectare despite major eradication attempts. Feral cats were not a problem as they were around the urban areas of Canberra and Sydney. Watching numerous emus, several mobs of western gray kangaroos, a few red kangaroos, and lots of gallas (white and pink cockatoos) made time pass quickly.

From South Australia I proceeded to Queensland to begin field observations of *Agathis*. En route northward I paused at the coastal town of Brisbane, Queensland, where my most memorable experience was holding a koala at a nearby sanctuary. It was cold in Brisbane, with a strong wind from the ocean that penetrated the cracks around the windows of the bedroom where I was sleeping. I was still unprepared for the chilliness in most Australian homes I visited, and I was glad to be heading even farther north, which being in the Southern Hemisphere, meant into the warmer, tropical areas of Australia.

FIELD OBSERVATIONS OF *AGATHIS*

Queensland Forest Service workers had sent me seedlings from three Australian species of *Agathis* for our photosynthesis experiments, but I wanted to observe the trees and their seedlings in their native forest habitat. Foresters met me in Cairns to take me to their headquarters in Atherton. Meg Lowman, who probably was the only person in Australia in the early 1980s with firsthand experience doing research in rain forest tree canopies, had helped prepare me for the kind of field clothing I needed to avoid leeches in the *understory* of tropical Queensland rain forests. I had never encountered leeches before, as they don't occur in New World rain forests. Meg and I had gone to an army surplus store in Sydney and bought boots (canvas mesh so water could escape), baggy pants, and a loose-fitting shirt. We sewed the bottom of the shirt onto the pants and the pants onto the tops of the boots, which made a one-piece suit designed to foil the entrance of leeches. Meg supervised as I practiced scooting into this incredible-looking piece of clothing. Getting out was much easier than getting into it. The Queensland foresters were not only amazed but I think greatly amused by this outfit, having themselves adapted to the ever-present leeches in the forest. The suit helped, but the wily leeches still got inside my boots, as I found when I wrung out wet and bloody socks. However, I never found them attached to my body, for which I was grateful. Unfortunately, I suffered again from chiggers, but they were not as virulent as those in Amazonia, and my special leech outfit may also have kept the chigger numbers lower than otherwise expected. I certainly appreciated Meg's help in preparing me to venture into an Australian rain forest!

Members of the Queensland Forest Service assisted me in observing *Agathis* (which they referred to using the New Zealand name of "kauri") in various state rain forest reserves on the Atherton Tableland. This rain forest was very different from those I had known in the New World and Africa—not only in the occurrence of various conifers but in the lack of complex strata.

We saw the three species of *Agathis* from which the foresters had grown seedlings for our experiments in Canberra. Each of these species was a large tree with a distinctive forest habitat. *A. atropurpurea* (called "blue kauri" because of its unusual dark purple or salmon-red bark) was the dominant tree on ridges in high, more-or-less open forest. However, the many seedlings and saplings, often clustered around the parent tree, tolerated shade. This species not only produced stalactites of resin, but large masses that collected around the base of the trunk and wounded roots. *A. microstachys* (bull kauri) was a huge but more isolated tree occurring in dense, moister luxuriant forest with a palm and tree fern understory. There was no evidence of regeneration, which fit the pattern shown by other rain forest *Agathis* species of not competing well with angiosperms in moist areas. *A. robusta* was dominant, with abundant regeneration of all age sizes, on infertile soils in the dry fringes of the rain forest. This species also occurs commonly following disturbance of primary forest and thus does well when grown in plantations. The field observations of these *Agathis* species would become very useful in interpreting our photosynthesis experiments.

In all the rain forest sites, *Podocarpus* was one of the most common tree associates of *Agathis*. I knew *Podocarpus* was a large conifer genus in the Southern Hemisphere, but I was surprised by the abundance and variety of species I saw in Australia. Although *Podocarpus* is considered a resin-producing conifer, I saw no visible evidence of resin, possibly because of lack of wounding. *Callitris*, the symbolic conifer of Australia—which produces Australian sandarac, a resin used commercially as a varnish—occurred on the dry edge of the rain forest. I was amazed to see small *trees* of *Eremophila* and *Myoporum*, which did not seem to be resinous. In that respect, they were more like the shrubs in the desert areas of South Australia—in contrast to the shrub species in Western Australia that produced such massive amounts of resin on their leaves. These trees also were very different from *Hymenaea* and *Copaifera* in which the greatest resin production occurs in rain forest habitats, not dry forests. *Eremophila* and *Myoporum* are very complex genera with regard to the environments in which they produce resin and would be fascinating to study from ecological and evolutionary perspectives.

In the Danbulla Forest on the shores of Lake Tinaroo, I saw *Eucalyptus grandis*, the magnificent Australian rain forest eucalypt that is being planted in Amazonia. Although I had seen strangler fig trees (*Ficus* sp.) in the Neotropics, their commonness and strong development in the Queensland rain forest were impressive. In fact, strangler figs have been reported to be more important in the physiognomy of the Australian than South American forests. Fig fruits are an important resource for many animals throughout the tropics including birds, which sometimes defecate fig seeds in crotches of various canopy trees. The figs germinate there, sending their roots downward to the forest floor. As the roots are growing downward, they surround the tree's trunk, strangling the host tree until it dies and decays. The fig tree continues to grow, eventually forming a strong woody mesh around the former host tree. In Queensland rain forests, there were numerous kinds of birds, with cockatoos and kookaburras being very common, that might play a role in the development of the strangler fig there.

To add to my field ventures, I had memorable cultural experiences during my stay in the charming old Atherton Hotel, which was a frame building constructed in traditional Australian small-town style. After one of the days in the field, I returned to the hotel very hot and tired (at least it was warm here), eager to quench my thirst. After getting the key to my room, I started toward a pub, attached to the lobby of the hotel, to get a cold drink. The female receptionist flew after me, shouting "No, no, a woman does not enter a pub alone in Queensland. It would be assumed that she was available." Startled by her admonition, I meekly indicated that I only wanted to get a cold drink. She brusquely told me to go to the dining room and she would have someone bring me a soda there.

In the dining room, while awaiting my cold drink, I eavesdropped on the officers of the Atherton Rotary Club, who were meeting at a nearby table. At that time, stores were closed for the weekend after 11:00 AM on Saturday. Some of the town's population, however, wanted the local hardware and grocery stores to remain open Saturday afternoon and even Sunday morning—as some businesses now were being allowed to do in Sydney. Although these Rotarians seemed to agree that having a few stores open would be convenient, they were worried about the employees who would have to work during the weekend. Wouldn't it be like going back to Dickensonian times? "Dickensonian times" sounded a little extreme to me; was this what we were putting weekend employees through in the United States?

The last day set for field work turned out to be a holiday to celebrate the Queen's birthday. The foresters suggested I visit the coral reef on Greene Island just off the coast from Cairns, and here I greatly enjoyed observing fish and other organisms associated with the corals visible from a sunken glass viewing area. The colors were magnificent; it was all too brief but it was necessary to return to Canberra to carry out the photosynthesis experiments on the glasshouse seedlings. I recall being a little nervous about actually *doing* some physiological ecology for the first time.

PHOTOSYNTHESIS EXPERIMENTS

Most of the analytical procedures for the photosynthesis experiments were new to me, and I think my confidence to even join the Australian researchers probably traced back to the time I spent with Larry Bliss and his students in physiological ecology at the University of Illinois. Fortunately, I was given technical assistance for the experiments. We analyzed five rain forest species—two *Hymenaea*, one *Copaifera*, and two *Agathis*—grown under 6 percent shade and full light. The shade-grown seedlings showed lower compensation points (when photosynthesis equals respiration) and lower respiration rates per unit leaf area than those of sun-grown seedlings. Except for one species of *Agathis*, we did not observe photosynthetic acclimation from shade into full sun conditions. My coresearcher Barry Osmond and I could only speculate on the relevance of our data to the question of seedling response to gap formation in rain forests. Researchers doing field studies of *Agathis*, such as the Oxford forester Tim Whitmore, had generalized that canopy dominants or trees emerging over the canopy are shade tolerant and that their seedlings grow slowly until a gap occurs. Whitmore predicted that these shade-tolerant seedlings would grow to maturity in small gaps but the high light in large gaps would probably kill them. All plants in our experiment showed some photoinhibition (and hence lower photosynthetic rates) in transfer from shade to full sunlight. *A. robusta*, which regenerates abundantly in the dry fringe of Queensland rain forests (as well as tolerates even more open situations), however, showed evidence of acclimation; this could make it more competitive in larger gaps. Furthermore, the *Hymenaea* and *Copaifera* species in the study did not support the idea that large increases in light intensity would kill the seedlings. Although all of the seedlings were shade tolerant, they still grew in the full sunlight of Canberra, despite lacking potential for photosynthetic acclimation to high light. Thus Osmond and I hypothesized that survival of tree seedlings following gap formation may depend more on competition from pioneer species—those that occur in open areas following disturbance—with high photosynthetic rates (and hence greater growth rates) than on acclimation of the photosynthetic apparatus of seedlings that have developed in the shade.

I also was left wondering not only whether *Hymenaea* and *Copaifera* seedlings with certain resin compositions might better survive herbivory under some parent trees, but also whether survival of gap formation would depend upon the presence of fast-growing competitors. Furthermore, I didn't know how much an increase in total amount of resin due to high light intensity would increase the seedling's competitiveness—at least with regard to herbivory. This complicated scenario presented a complex of selective agents—biological ones such as competitors and herbivores as well as nonbiological ones such as the role of light intensity in photosynthetic acclimation and influencing resin production that in turn can affect herbivory. Which ones would predominate probably would depend on local conditions.

POST-EXPERIMENT ACTIVITIES

Following my completion of the photosynthetic experiments, Thimann insisted I return to Santa Cruz for a short period to finalize proofs and work on the index for our textbook. One of the last upheavals during proofreading was the Wiley editors' decision to be politically correct regarding gender. We had used a capped "Man" in many cases to refer to all humankind. The editors wanted us to change all such references to "humans." It was a tedious job as we often had to contort sentence structure to fit the correction into the existing typescript. Thimann chafed a good deal about doing it, but it seemed that the times demanded it—especially with me, a woman, being the senior author. During this period, Ghillean Prance also asked if he could use the proofs in an economic botany course he was teaching as part of establishing the new Institute of Economic Botany at NYBG. He thought that our text would be the most up-to-date, and the publisher gave him permission to do so since the book was to be published soon. *Botany: Plant Biology and Its Relation to Human Affairs* was published in 1982 in time for our next class.

I returned to Sydney via a brief stop in the Fiji Islands to catch my breath and prepare my symposium talk for the XIII International Botanical Congress. Soon after my presentation, "Variation in Terpenoid Resins and Implications for Insect Herbivory in the Tropics," I flew to the North Island of New Zealand, where *Agathis australis* (the Kauri "pine") has reigned as the country's national symbol.

I was met in Auckland by a botanist from the University of Auckland, who took me to the Waipoua Forest Reserve near Whangerei to see the giant Kauri pines, which were the source of the copal resin and timber that built the economy of this area of New Zealand in the nineteenth century. At Waipoua we viewed a New Zealand icon, the Tane Mahata, the "Lord of the Forest" in the language of the indigenous Maori people. The tree is estimated to be 2,000 years old and its trunk is more than 15 feet in diameter. The incredible girth of these trees reminded me of the Big Trees (*Sequoiadendron giganteum)* of the Sierra Nevada. *A. australis* was thus a much more imposing tree than the three Australian species of *Agathis* that I had just been studying. My botanist host and I visited a kauri pine museum where I saw some of the enormous pieces of resin that characterize this species. Such pieces are sometimes carved into large works of art; the smaller ones are made into jewelry. We spent the night in Kauri House Lodge in Dargaville, a colonial homestead made from kauri timber; its chandeliers, door knobs, and so on were made from the resin. The owners were true lovers of the kauri tree, such that everything that could be was made from either the wood or resin of *A. australis*. *Agathis* resin is also the source of much amber, not only in New Zealand, but also in various parts of the world where the trees occurred in the past.

My experience in Australia and New Zealand enabled me to expand my thinking from the Neotropical leguminous resin-producing trees to that of a Paleotropical conifer and, importantly, to compare them in a physiological ecology experiment. This research provided another small piece in my ever-increasing understanding of the overall puzzle of resin-producing trees, including their evolutionary record as amber, their impact in forest ecology and their significant human use.

PART IV

CHANGING COURSE

Preparing to pass gavel to incoming ISCE president David Jones;
Jeffrey Harborne, featured speaker to my right

Lab members celebrating the 1983 graduation of Jason Greenlee, Susanne Arrenhius and Al Cunningham. Back row (left to right) Katherine Stopol, David Crankshaw, Leo McCloskey, Lenore Hough, Susanne Arrhenius, Gail Fail, Roberto Figliuolo, Sue Martin, Al Cunningham. Front row (left to right) David Lincoln, George Hall, Jason Greenlee, Mario Lowenstein, Jeff White and me.

EXPANSION OF RESEARCH DIRECTIONS

1980-1995

The hectic beginning to the 1980s continued as I returned from Australia to a large, extremely active lab group. The range of activity was especially reflected during enthusiastic lab meetings full of new ideas that eclipsed the usual problems with failure of lab equipment, lack of funds etc. For the *Hymenaea* and *Copaifera* comparison project, it included reports from the herbivore researchers in the field as well as lab reports from the fungal and related chemical investigators. Discussions also included analysis of possible inhibitory effects of redwood needle monoterpenes on endophytic fungi as well as their effects on nitrifying bacteria in the soil and leaf litter beneath the trees. The agroecology component was involved in projects ranging from allelopathic effects of glucosinolates from different members of the mustard family to management strategies in agroecosystems in Costa Rica. A team approach continued with groups of students working together; in the main it was a harmonious environment based upon sharing information as each young researcher gained experience. Culturally, the group was enhanced by two Mexicans, a Chinese, and a Brazilian. The large group of students resulted in graduations, and associated celebrations from the mid-eighties to the late-nineties.

CONTINUED LAB STUDIES OF *HYMENAEA* AND *COPAIFERA*

In addition to the ongoing lab studies of leaf fungi and variation of both terpenes and phenolic compounds, a visiting scholar from China and a grad student from Brazil were working on different projects and presenting some interesting cultural issues as well.

Jinliang Wang from the Kunming Botanical Institute and Tropical Botanical Garden in Xishuangbanna, Yunnan, China, joined our lab as a visiting scholar from1983 to1985 to learn about chemical ecology. He was fascinatingly different from my Chinese graduate student from Hong Kong. Jinliang's English was poor (his second language had been Russian) and numerous problems arose when he didn't admit he was unsure how to operate some equipment. His answer was always yes, or a nod to that effect, when we asked if he understood our directions. But we were never sure whether he didn't understand our English or he didn't want to admit his technological ignorance. He also arrived with little money, but never complained, so we did not know he needed personal assistance. We only found out by accident that he and another Chinese scholar were sharing a dorm room for one person at Crown College. Jinliang slept in the single bed at night and the other scholar slept in it during the day (he was studying computer technology and it was cheaper to use the computer at night). Dealing with such cultural issues involving pride are bewildering and often seem intractable. Despite new technology baffling him, Jinliang doggedly completed an experimental study of seasonal and diurnal variation in leaf sesquiterpenes of greenhouse-grown saplings of *Hymenaea* and *Copaifera*, which was published in Chinese.

Roberto Figliuolo, who had been a student in my 1974 INPA Chemical Ecology course, joined our lab on a Brazilian fellowship as part of plans developed at the NAS/CNPq meetings in 1976, to study some aspect of the chemistry of *Copaifera* resins for a PhD. Roberto's arrival in Santa Cruz was an unforgettable event and set the tone for his chaotic but always interesting sojourn here. I had told him to let me know his arrival time so he could be met at the San Francisco airport. However, with the usual communication problems from Amazonia, his telex with this information arrived after he did. When he could not find me in the airport, he hopped into a taxi and told the driver to go to Santa Cruz. Although the driver told him it would be expensive, Roberto did not think it would be *that* expensive, as taxis are cheap in Manaus (the only city he knew). He had not thought to bring my home telephone number with him, so I received a frantic call from the taxi driver from a telephone booth, wanting directions to my house—he had gotten the phone number from the telephone book. When they finally arrived, the cab driver wanted over $200—quite a sum at the time.

Roberto was very bright, but scientifically curious to the point of being undisciplined. He started work on *Copaifera* terpenes, but soon got sidetracked in a complicated tangential analysis of an unusual nonprotein amino acid and its prevention of water loss in *Copaifera* leaves. He was fascinated with this compound and became deeply involved in preparing a manuscript, which did get published in *Phytochemistry*. Roberto continued to explore interesting chemical questions tangential to his dissertation, despite my protestations, and was surprised when his five-year fellowship ended, all too soon. INPA insisted that Roberto return to Brazil, but they were displeased with *me* that he was returning with a master's degree rather than the planned PhD. My wounds were somewhat salved by George Hammond, who told me about problems that he at Cal Tech and Carl Djerassi at Stanford also had faced in a program to develop Brazilian organic chemistry. They found that young Brazilian chemists often had difficulty adapting to the intensity and speed with which it was assumed that doctoral research in chemistry would be completed in the US institutions.

PHYSIOLOGICAL ECOLOGY IN THE TROPICS

I participated in a symposium on the "Physiological Ecology of Plants in Wet Tropics" held at the Mexican National University (UNAM) in Mexico City in 1983. My topic, "Roles of Secondary Compounds in Wet Tropical Ecosystems," was different from that usually presented by physiological ecologists. I used the symposium as an opportunity to encourage those working in the tropics to think more about the importance of secondary chemicals in plant survival. The symposium was organized by prominent Latin American physiologists E. Medina and C. Vasques-Yanes as well as Stanford ecologist Hal Mooney. Mooney, like my Illinois colleague Larry Bliss, was another Billings student, and he frequently worked with the Australian physiological ecologists with whom I had recently collaborated at ANU. This event thus represented a complicated, intermittent interweaving of the threads in my work involving physiological ecology.

COLLAPSE OF *COPAIFERA* MONOGRAPH

Although the ecological and chemical comparisons were going well, I traveled to Manaus in 1985 to try to stimulate the progress of Marlene Freitas da Silva, the systematist at INPA, on the monographic revision of *Copaifera*. I had collected *Copaifera* specimens throughout its New World range, with Marlene sometimes accompanying me in Brazil. Collecting flowers in Brazil had not been as successful as in Venezuela, where the phenology had been carefully followed by collaborators. I had obtained specimens, admittedly mostly sterile, from the major herbaria around the world and had funds for Marlene to come to Santa Cruz to study them. In 1985, however, she emphatically declared she was no longer interested in continuing work on the monograph because she thought that there were too few flowers available to adequately sort out the species. I had discovered on our trips in 1979 that she really did not like to do fieldwork herself. Moreover, unlike the Venezuelans, she was not interested in using a network of Brazilian systematists to aid in collecting when flowering was observed. At UCSC, I had invested much time, effort, and money in studying pollen, chromosomes, leaf venation, and distribution of secretory pockets (used by the first monographer, who had been forced to use leaf characters), but Marlene was not interested in using such material without also having reproductive parts simultaneously available.

Because all my other collaborations in Latin America had been so positive, my experience with Marlene was traumatic. I suspected that her refusal to continue was based on cultural issues that she never made explicit to me. I did not find out until much later that she was unhappy I had collaborated with the Venezuelans on that part of the distribution of *Copaifera*. Was the problem that they had done such a good job overcoming the difficult problems of obtaining flowers and fruit that it would be difficult for her to match their achievements? I'll never know the answer, but it took me a little while to get over this failure, especially because of the generous funding provided for the monograph by the NSF Systematics Panel.

While in Manaus on this 1985 trip, my spirits were uplifted with a visit to the Biological Dynamics of Forest Fragments Project, which had begun while I was at INPA in 1979. Although the primary purpose was to assess the effect of reduction of rain forest area on biodiversity, the researchers had found that individual species responded to fragmentation idiosyncratically and in unexpected ways. This demanded more and more assistance from experts studying different groups of plants and animals. I witnessed exciting progress in 1985, which continued apace. A summary of twenty-year progress was published in a special volume in 2001, where the organizers re-emphasized that "the study of habitat fragmentation has been gathered into a sizable discipline." More than sixty graduate student theses and over 300 scientific articles had appeared by that time. Their results were directed to two audiences—field biologists interested in new information on tropical taxa, and wildlife managers and conservation planners needing more data to help deal with loss of species with deforestation and how best to sustainably develop the mosaic of forest remnants. It was exciting to directly witness progress of some of this significant field experiment.

Although I would have liked to continue Brazilian studies of *Hymenaea* and *Copaifera*, the systematics panel at NSF had let me know that due to numerous difficulties—especially governmental ones relating to visas and work permits—they would not continue to fund research in Brazil for the foreseeable future. How different from the mid-seventies, when I was chairing a committee for bilateral projects in the humid tropics of Brazil and serving on the NSF-funded Projeto Flora Amazônica. But with this turn of events I began to shift my research emphasis to various Pacific Coast species on which we already had considerable background information from previous studies. I was also reflecting on how many approaches we had learned in our tropical research had already been useful in advancing research at home, and additional studies could provide even more interesting comparisons between tropical and temperate zone plants.

RESEARCH SHIFT

Throughout the late 1970s and into the 1980s, chemical ecologists were beginning to theorize about the conditions that led plants to invest metabolic resources in synthesizing chemicals for defense. Among the plethora of theories, "Optimal Defense Theory (ODT)" especially fit the trajectory of my research. The principles of ODT were proposed independently by Doyle McKey and David Rhoades in 1979. ODT focuses on explaining the ecological and evolutionary conditions that lead to within-plant heterogeneity in the distribution of plant defensive chemicals. We had, in fact, documented in 1978 that terpene variations within Hymenaea plants strongly suggested that intraplant variation was adaptive and an evolved trait. ODT also was predicated on the idea that these defenses are costly to plants and thus should be preferentially allocated to parts that are of the greatest value—later fully expanded by A.R. Zangerl and F.A. Bazzaz.

Other chemical ecologists, such as Phyllis Coley and associates, took a physiological approach, which emphasized resource availability in determining a plant's chemical defense (both the kind of chemical and its amount). Terpenes, which are carbon-based, depend on availability of appropriate abiotic resources for synthesis, and we had demonstrated in both laboratory and field experiments that some, such as light intensity, may increase the total amount produced in leaves. On the other hand, we also had shown that higher total quantity in seedlings under the shade of parent tree, contrasted with those in open sunlight, suggested selection by herbivores. We, however, were emphasizing another aspect of chemical defense—compositional variation—which we thought to be particularly noteworthy in terpene defenses. We had shown experimentally that repetitive patterns of compositional variation (chemotypes) in leaves of *Hymenaea, Copaifera, Satureja*, and *Sequoia* are not influenced by abiotic environmental conditions and thus are apparently under genetic control. We hypothesized that some patterns (chemotypes) could have been selected by biotic components, such as herbivores and fungal pathogens, in various populations. Our hypotheses focused on terpenes, the largest and most diverse group of secondary chemicals (and the starting point of our evolutionary consideration that amber provides); however, our ideas regarding compositional variation could apply to other groups of chemicals that comprised mixtures of numerous components that produce compositional patterns. In a 1996 symposium on "Phytochemical Diversity and Redundancy in Ecological Interactions," Rex Cates reviewed the extensive research on conifer-insect-pathogen interactions and strongly endorsed our hypotheses regarding the significant defensive role of mixtures and compositional variation of terpenoid resins.

In studying the role of terpenes in Pacific Coast plants—resins in *Sequoia* (coastal redwood), and essential oils in *Umbellularia* (California bay tree) and the herb *Satureja douglasii* (yerba buena)—we already had been and would continue to follow numerous approaches similar to those we had used for *Hymenaea* and *Copaifera*. (As a reminder, resins contain both volatile mono-and sesquiterpenes, called essential oils when they are the sole components, and nonvolatile diterpenes.). A significant difference, however, was that coastal redwood and California bay tree are monotypic (have only one species), and we therefore were not analyzing the phylogeny of species within the genus. Although *Satureja* is a large genus, throughout all of our studies, we had restricted our work to one species with a widespread Pacific Coast distribution. Furthermore, instead of sesquiterpenes, we analyzed variation in monoterpene patterns through the geographic range of these plants and determined experimentally that all chemotypes were under genetic control. With no evidence of insect herbivory on either yerba buena or redwood leaves, we had considered the impact of slug herbivory on the distribution of chemotypes in yerba buena and the effects of several terpenes on the fungal endophytic activity in redwood needles. We additionally would expand our studies to look at the effects of California bay tree monoterpenes on deer herbivory, and inhibition of nitrification (oxidation of ammonium to nitrites and then to nitrates through activity of special bacteria) in the leaf litter and soil under redwood, Douglas fir, and later, bay trees.

One of the hallmarks of our studies of trees both in the tropics and along the Pacific Coast was the analysis of changes in concentration of components in the terpene mixture throughout a leaf's "lifetime," and the importance of these changes in understanding the temporal actions of the trees' enemies. Furthermore, we pioneered careful assessment of the variations in the terpenes in trees through changes in leaves from the seedling, to the sapling, and finally adult plant. I have characterized our overall contribution as a phytocentric approach to chemical ecology. We were thinking not just about the plant's (especially long-lived trees) response to rapidly evolving insect herbivores, but how the variation of its terpenes help it face diverse enemies (e.g., fungal pathogens and vertebrates), and how such variation occurs within plants, within populations, and in different species of a genus occurring in different habitats.

REDWOOD TERPENE EFFECTS ON FUNGAL ENDOPHYTES

General interest in leaf fungal endophytes was especially high during the 1980s. We had been investigating endophytic activity of leaf-spotting fungi in *Hymenaea* and *Copaifera*, and then discovered that endophytic fungi are thought to be ubiquitous in conifers. Prominent researchers on endophytes, such as George Carroll, have assumed that most leaf endophytes in conifers are inactive after colonizing the leaf, and that their active growth and reproduction occurs when the leaf senesces or is damaged. Carroll convinced me and Francisco Espinosa-Garcia, who had just arrived from Mexico with a special interest in endophytes, that coastal redwoods were an excellent endophytic system to study and that our campus was an ideal location for detailed analysis. Furthermore, we thought that the chemical ecology of redwood leaf endophytes offered an interesting comparison with our *Hymenaea* study. However, monoterpenes, which produce the characteristic odor in conifer forests, rather than sequiterpenes, predominate in redwood leaves.

Francisco Espinosa-Garcia

Another new graduate student, Jeanette Rollinger, joined Francisco in studying fungal leaf endophytes in coastal redwood. They used the background work on redwood leaf monoterpene variation done by George

Hall, who had analyzed changes spatially within the tree, temporally during ontogeny from seedling to mature tree as well as geographically. By comparing leaves from wild native trees to those from similar locations in planted populations of a twenty-year provenance (place of origin) study established by UC Berkeley foresters, George demonstrated the genetic control of monoterpene compositional patterns through redwood's geographic range. His work also showed that a single tree in these planted populations was capable of producing progeny with different monoterpene compositions—similar to what we had found in rain forest species of *Hymenaea*.

We hypothesized that the leaf monoterpene variation in redwoods has a role in keeping the fungal symbionts inactive, as had been indicated for sesquiterpenes in *Hymenaea* leaves. Thus we were moving away from the commonly held view that conifer endophytes are inactive until the needle senesces or is damaged. Our first and major job was to identify the numerous fungal endophytes in the tree's needles. Fortunately, George Carroll assisted in this process, drawing on his own previous study of redwood endophytes. Jeanette did a geographic analysis of this community of endophytes, focusing on the most prominent fungus in redwood needles. Francisco found much tree-to-tree monoterpene variation in campus populations, as George Hall had also documented, and experimentally tested the effect of various redwood monoterpene patterns as well as individual terpene components on different fungal endophytes (ranging from harmless mutualists to virulent pathogens). A diversity of fungal responses suggested that redwood monoterpenes may have differential intraspecific significance in regulating pathogenic and nonpathogenic activity in its foliage. Francisco found that effects of the monoterpenes were dose-dependent, and some terpenes were apparently acting synergistically in relation to the degree of specialization of the fungal endophyte.

AGROECOLOGY

Steve Gliessman became a faculty member of the Environmental Studies Board of Studies and founding director of the UCSC Agroecology Program in 1980. He came from Colégio Superior de Agricultura Tropical (CSAT) in Tabasco, Mexico, where he had discovered that an ecosystem approach could provide long-term solutions to some problems facing tropical agriculture. At that time the Environmental Studies Board of Studies did not have its own graduate program, so its graduate students had to be cosponsored in Boards of Studies that did. My previous membership in the Environmental Studies Board, my Stevenson College course in Agriculture and Ecology, and my tropical work in Mexico and Costa Rica made me the natural cosponsor for Steve's students. Furthermore, Steve had done his PhD research on the inhibitory effects of chemicals from bracken fern (*Pteridium aquilinum*) in Costa Rica. Thus the research of Gliessman's students would pick up several threads, including chemical ecology, that were already interwoven with my interests.

Steve Gliessman thanking me for cosponsoring agroecology students; one student, Francisco Rosado-May next to him and Deborah Letourneau, another agroecology faculty member to the right

The first five agroecology MS students interacted with our lab group and took my courses, but were not a part of my lab's mainstream research. Their thesis topics ranged from analysis of home garden agroecosystems in Mexico to the effects of weed borders on aphids and their natural enemies in brussels sprout crops. One topic, however, followed later, more detailed PhD dissertations that involved the effects of chemicals from plants in intercropped systems, that is, the mechanisms of yield increase in broccoli intercropped with wild mustard. I felt privileged to be in on the ground floor of the development of UCSC as one of the leaders in another emerging subfield of ecology. Interest in applying ecology to agriculture had gradually gained momentum with the growing influence of ecosystem approaches. By the beginning of the 1980s, agroecology had developed a conceptual framework for study of agroecosystems, and was being influenced by traditional farming systems in developing countries as examples of ecologically-based agroecosystem management. These UCSC agroecology students gave me an opportunity to participate in ecosystem research—different from my focus at the populational level of organization as well as agricultural rather than natural systems. Their research provided me with a continual stimulation of new concepts and approaches to analysis. Additionally, it furnished interesting, developing information for my teaching of Plants and Human Affairs.

By the mid-1980s four PhD students cosponsored with Steve Gliessman were pursuing agroecology projects for their dissertations. Several were studying the allelopathic effects of chemicals from some plants, particularly in the genus *Brassica* in the mustard family, on weeds or intercrops in agroecosystems. In these studies, I added the analysis of glucosinolates (mustard oils), the predominant group of compounds in *Brassica,* to our mainline analyses of terpenes and phenolics. Another Mexican student, Francisco Rosado-May, studied the chemical ecological role of wild mustard (*B. kaber*) in the management of soil-pathogen fungi and nematodes, and Jim Paulus studied the contribution of *B. kaber* as a cover crop where apple trees were being converted to organic production. Robert Kluson worked on the responses of a three-part mutualistic symbiosis of *Phaseolus* (bean), *Rhizobium* (nitrifying bacteria*)*, and *Glomus* (mycorrhizal fungus) to allelopathic effects from cabbage (*B.oleracea*) in an intercropped system. Because soil fertility is a major problem in sustainable crop production in the tropics, Martha Rosemeyer, on the other hand, compared the symbiotic role of mycorrhizal fungi and nitrifying bacteria in two slash/mulch bean agroecosystems in Costa Rica. The last doctoral agroecology student I cosponsored, Philip Fujiyoshi, arrived later in 1990. His dissertation concerned both the chemical and shading effects of squash (*Cucurbita* spp.) on weeds in a corn and squash agroecosystem. The growing success of the agroecology program—the first of its kind in the world—was greatly assisted by the research of these excellent graduate students, and by Gliessman's later writing of a textbook that brought agroecology and sustainable agriculture to the forefront.

BIG EVENT ENDING THE EIGHTIES

Apart from the complex research activities, the 1980s ended with a "jolt." In the fall of 1989, the big Loma Prieta earthquake hit the San Francisco and Monterey Bay Area. We had just moved into the new Sinsheimer Labs and had not gotten bungee cords to protect materials on shelves from falling in my lab; thus we sustained loss amounting to thousands of dollars in broken specialized glassware. Fortunately, FEMA provided replacement funds for these. Also, the monoterpenes that we used in chemical studies poured out of some broken containers, giving our lab a pleasant fragrance that filled our wing in the fourth floor of the building. As with books in the university library, those in my office came tumbling down into heaps. But, overall, we were so fortunate in the small damage, considering that the earthquake essentially destroyed much of downtown Santa Cruz.

TERPENES EFFECTS ON NITROGEN CYCLE
FROM REDWOOD FOREST TREES

I had also become intrigued during the early nineties by the possibility that monoterpenes could be affecting the nitrogen cycle through their effects on

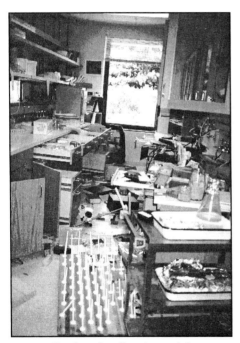

Earthquake effects in our lab

nitrifying bacteria in the leaf litter and soil in forests dominated by resin-producing trees. Here the trees can provide extensive terpene-rich fallen leaf litter than can accumulate on and in the soil. A chemical ecologist working in western conifer forests had shown that monoterpenes could inhibit nitrifying bacteria in ponderosa pine forests, and I wondered if we could demonstrate similar effects for monoterpene-producing trees in the redwood forest. If so, these terpenes could significantly affect ecosystem-level properties, despite only occurring in concentration in parts per million in forest soil. It would also help explain the extremely low nitrification rates observed in redwood forests. A faculty colleague in microbial ecology, Bess Ward (now at Princeton), expanded one of my MS student's research on the inhibition of nitrifying soil bacteria (*Nitrosomonas europea*) by redwood monoterpenes, using analysis in whole cell cultures to experimentally document inhibition by certain of the most common of these monoterpenes.

A little later, a visiting Korean faculty member, Jong Hee Kim, also demonstrated the inhibitory effect of monoterpenes on nitrification from

Douglas fir (*Pseudotsuga menziesii*), a common associate of redwoods. In initial correspondence with Jong Hee about her spending a sabbatical leave in my lab, I fell into the trap of assuming that I was corresponding with a male. She finally corrected my cultural blunder and I weakly apologized that I had no idea that Jong Hee was a Korean female name! Her background was also interesting in that she had obtained her doctoral degree from Ewha Woman's University, founded in 1886 as a mission school for Korean girls, and was fortunate that as a woman she was able to become a member of the biology faculty at Kyung nam University in Masan, Korea.

Our research of the effects of terpenes on nitrification from component trees in the redwood forest was continued by Swarup Wood's analysis of the influence of *Umbellularia californica* monoterpenes in the leaf litter and soil beneath trees. Brian Lawrence, an essential oils chemist, had earlier analyzed the chemistry of the leaves of this tree for us. Swarup concluded, in laboratory-amended soils, that inhibition was dose-dependent and that oxygenated monoterpenes were more inhibitory than certain monoterpene hydrocarbons. However, concerned about understanding the complexity of allelopathic inhibition under natural conditions, he also showed that humic acids and other organic matter in soils, may buffer nitrifying bacteria against the inhibitory effects of these monoterpenes. Unfortunately, I was unable to continue these studies to see if the complex soil conditions in the field could have negated some of our laboratory experiments on redwood and Douglas fir.

At graduation of Swarup Wood

EFFECTS OF *UMBELLULARIA* TERPENES ON DEER HERBIVORY

In our only chemical study of herbivory by a vertebrate, Ray Goralka focused on the effects of the variation of monoterpenes in *Umbellularia* leaves on seasonal browse quality for black-tail deer. Study of these deer was particularly interesting on our campus because their relatively large population and their obvious differential browsing of reachable leaves. Ray discovered that a significant increase in total amount of monoterpenes and a compositional shift to high concentration of a toxic component (accompanying low total nitrogen, increased dryness, and toughness) during leaf development made the mature leaves less palatable to black-tail deer herbivory—indicating that the plant is not protecting the young leaves chemically, as in the majority of other plants we had studied (two species of *Copaifera* had been the only exceptions). Controlled artificial feeding trials of these deer supported our conclusions regarding the effect of higher monoterpene yield in the mature leaves on palatability, which also have the highest concentration of the toxic compound umbellulone. (Some humans also have a severe reaction to umbellulone and should not use *Umbellularia (California bay tree)* leaves as a spice; true bay tree, *Laurus nobilis*, leaves do not have this toxic compound). Thus, although the California bay tree was not chemically protecting the young tissue against early browsing, it was protecting the mature leaves against the relatively long season of deer browsing. These results point out the fallacy of generalizing about patterns of terpene variation without understanding the impact of different kinds of biotic selection pressures.

Ray also found insignificant monoterpene variation in mature leaves across the geographic range of the species, as well as in the changes of total quantity during ontogenetic stages from seedling to sapling to adult tree that might influence black-tail deer herbivory. This lack of geographic and ontogenetic changes was quite different from

With Ray Goralka at commencement

those in leaf monoterpenes in redwood and leaf sesquiterpenes of *Hymenaea* and *Copaifera*. Ray's results did allow us to predict, however, that chemical defense against black-tail deer would be similar throughout the distribution of *Umbellularia*— a fact of some interest to wildlife managers.

During the shift to study the Pacific Coast plants in the nineties, Wendy Peer joined the lab, adding another perspective by providing background to analyze the effects of phytochrome in several different ways. First, we had always wondered if the quality of light, as indicated by phytochrome effects, would have a different influence on terpene production than light intensity. She found that phytochrome affected leaf monoterpene variation in *Satureja* in a chemotype-dependent way, indicating that this variation apparently results from adaptation to light environments where the chemotypes usually occur. She also analyzed the shade avoidance response of redwood seedlings growing in the redwood forest. Although growing in a shaded environment, they responded as sun-adapted plants.

Wendy Peer with renowned phytochrome physiologist, Winn Briggs, and me celebrating after her dissertation defense seminar

Completion of Wendy's doctorate brought to a close my having my own lab. Although I would continue to sponsor or cosponsor three other PhD students, their research was done in a lab available because of the professor's leave for administrative work. Use of someone else's lab created a different atmosphere and was more difficult for me to adapt to than it seemed to be for the students. But adapt we did.

MADAME PRESIDENT

1983-1988

Activities that centered around professional societies and, ultimately, my serving as president of three of them, dominated several years following 1983.

A significant societal commitment arose in 1983 as a result of my having been invited to give a lecture at a Gordon Research Conference on "Chemical Mediation of Insect-Plant Interaction." Gordon Research Conferences are international forums for discussing cutting-edge research in the biological, chemical, and physical sciences. A conference leader selects a small group of scientists who come together for a full week to exchange ideas in an informal atmosphere. The leader also selects the lecturers, who speak during morning and evening sessions—with the afternoons free for informal discussions and activities, which increases interactions among the attendees. Participants are housed together in a site away from cities and tourist distractions. My lecture focused on the incredible variation, which the complex mixture of terpenoid resins provide, as a *modus operandi* for plant defense. I emphasized tropical environments, where I proposed that plants faced the greatest onslaught from insects and pathogens.

I was surprised to be elected by the scientists attending this meeting to a committee to found an international society for chemical ecology. Gerald Rosenthal later hosted the four elected members, in addition to the co-editors of the *Journal of Chemical Ecology,* for this task at the University of Kentucky. Rosenthal was one of the early proponents of chemical ecology and a co-editor with Daniel Janzen of the seminal 1979 volume *Herbivores: Their Interaction with Secondary Plant Metabolites.* Our committee proposed that this organization, formally named the International Society for Chemical Ecology (ISCE), "be organized for scientific purposes, more specifically to promote the understanding of interactions among organisms and their environment that are mediated by naturally occurring chemicals. Research areas include chemistry, biochemistry, and function of natural products, their importance at all levels of ecological organization, their evolutionary origin, and their practical application." We wrote a constitution and bylaws for the founding membership to vote on and considered future activities of the society, which would be discussed at the first annual meeting at the University of Texas the next year (1984). Because of the worldwide interest in chemical ecology and the potential for the organization to be truly international, the committee wanted to ensure that the society was not seen to be run by an overwhelming number of Americans. We were successful, in that by 1993, five out of ten, that is, half of the presidents were from outside the United States. Similarly, by 2007 half of the twenty-four presidents represented countries other than the United States (primarily from Europe and Canada), but the members of the advisory council were from countries spanning Europe, Latin America, Asia, and the Mideast. Currently, the society has members from thirty-five countries; and it has become the global organization that its founders hoped it would.

ISCE presidents attending 10th anniversary meeting in 1993. Left to right: Lincoln Brower, me, David Jones (UK), Wittko Franche (Germany), David Zigler, Jacques Pasteels (Belgium), Kenji Mori (Japan), and William Fenecal—Gunnar Bergstrom (Sweden) not present

I was elected by the executive committee as the vice president of ISCE in 1984, and gave a lecture on my favorite subject of "Patterns of Variation in Plant Defensive Compounds" at the inaugural ISCE meeting as well. I also participated that year in a symposium on "Micromolecules in Evolution" at the University of São Paulo, where I further developed my interaction with Otto Gottlieb, Brazil's premier phytochemist. By this time I was beginning to assemble sufficient data from various components (chemical, systematic, and ecological) of our studies of leguminous, resin-producing tropical trees to synthesize an evolutionary overview—a novel approach for Brazilian chemists, in particular.

PRESIDENT OF THE ASSOCIATION FOR TROPICAL BIOLOGY

The following year (1985) I was elected president of the Association for Tropical Biology (ATB), the first woman to be so honored in this group. As it was more-or-less a figurehead position, I had few responsibilities—most were assumed by an executive group at the Smithsonian. ATB had split off from OTS in the early planning stages in 1963, with ATB to serve the role of promoting tropical research primarily through international symposia and publication of the journal *Biotropica* (which was established in 1969, having grown out of the *Bulletin of the Association of Tropical Biology*). More recently, in 2002, ATB expanded its objectives to include understanding of human impact on the tropical environment and accordingly changed its name to the Association for Tropical Biology and Conservation.

SURPRISING DUAL PRESIDENCIES

When I returned from my 1985 sabbatical leave in Brazil, I discovered that I had been elected to move from vice president to president of ISCE *and* had been elected president of the Ecological Society of America! At this time the executive committee and council were still electing incoming officers rather than having the general election by the membership. Neither the letter nor telex asking me to become president of ISCE had reached me in Manaus, given the unreliable mail and telex service in Amazonia at that time. Although the executive committee of ISCE had not received an answer from me, its members proceeded with my selection. Knowing that I had been on the ground floor in founding the society and was serving as vice president, they thought I would consider moving to the helm an honor. (At that time, women did not generally move to the presidency of professional societies, even though in some cases they had served as vice president.)

I *had* been asked if I would accept the nomination for presidency of ESA before I left for Brazil. I answered affirmatively to the nomination thinking that I probably would not be elected, despite having been elected as vice president four years earlier, in 1981. In the case of both ISCE and ESA I still had the mindset that professional societies tended to see a "woman's place" as vice president but not president. The only other woman president during the 71-year history of ESA had been E. Lucy Braun, and that was in 1950!

After discussing with the chair of the Biology Board of Studies the challenges of coping with both presidencies simultaneously, he suggested that sufficient secretarial help was available to provide me with a half-time secretary. This was my deliverance. I could not have handled both presidencies without this assistance because each entailed several years of very active service. Despite some anxiety regarding my extra-heavy work load, directing my energies toward the varied administrative responsibilities of national and international import was helpful in surmounting my disappointment over the failure to complete the systematic part of my *Copaifera* research.

PRESIDENT OF INTERNATIONAL SOCIETY
OF CHEMICAL ECOLOGY

I accepted the gavel as president of ISCE at the third annual meeting in 1986, which was hosted by David Wood, the bark beetle pheromone expert at UC Berkeley. The well-attended sessions, which included numerous members from foreign countries, the papers were well received with enthusiastic responses to those on topics such as the frontiers and future of chemical ecology, defensive strategies against tannins (one of the chemicals that received focus in early studies), and others.

One amusing incident sticks in my mind regarding the potential clash of cultures in arranging meetings for an international organization. We were housed in UC Berkeley dorms in which males and females occupied the same floor and used the same bathrooms. The first morning of the meeting I went to the communal bathroom in my robe, ready to take a shower. I met a distinguished-looking white-haired gentleman who turned out to be a chemistry professor from Germany. He politely informed me that I was in the wrong bathroom (there were urinals in this one). When, in turn, I informed him that the bathrooms in the dorm were unisex, he flushed and fled, muttering in German. He angrily reported to the organizers of the meeting that in no way could he remain in the dorms under these conditions and promptly moved to a hotel—so much for embracing UC student liberation.

After a busy year as president, especially assisting with planning the annual meeting, the ISCE past president continues to serve on the executive committee, becomes chair of the nominating committee for future officers, and remains a member of the advisory council for another three years. All of this activity for officers with experience in the society was deemed necessary during its formative stages.

The year following the Berkeley meeting, I assisted David Jones in planning the fourth annual meeting at the University of Hull in northeastern England. I would pass the gavel to David, who was not only the host of the meeting but the incoming president. David was a chemical ecologist/geneticist well known for his studies of polymorphisms in cyanogenic glycosides, especially in species of *Lotus* and *Trifolium*, against snails, slugs,

With Jeffrey Harborne

and voles. A number of papers at the Hull meeting were directed toward the application of chemical ecology and the mechanisms of defense compounds, which led to much spirited discussion. The featured evening speaker was Jeffrey Harborne, who, as longtime editor of the journal *Phytochemistry* and author of the first chemical ecology text, was generally so instrumental in developing plant chemical ecology.

Harborne impressed me by giving credit in this lecture to a generally unrecognized British woman, Miriam Rothschild, for developing a conceptual basis for some aspects of chemical ecology. I had just been reflecting about how few women were prominent in the field as yet, and remembering with humor my situation at the 1972 international symposium on "Chemistry in Evolution and Systematics" in Strasbourg, France. The organizers had paired single people in hotel rooms, purposely putting chemists with biologists and Europeans with Americans to facilitate interactions in the development of an emerging field that combined chemistry with systematics, ecology, and evolution. They had not considered gender, as they assumed all of the participants were male, accentuated by the fact that "Jean" is the male spelling of my name in France ("Jeanne" being female). Accordingly, I had a surprise when I arrived in my room at the hotel. My roommate was taking a shower, but the clothes on the bed obviously belonged to a man. I retreated to the hotel reception desk and found out that my roommate was German male chemist. The small hotel was fully occupied, so I had to be sent to another one where I was the only person from our symposium. This sparsity of women in the field was evident for some time, although now there are numerous outstanding women researchers. It was ten years after my presidency that ISCE had another woman president. She was from Switzerland and was followed in 2004 and 2005 by two more—one from the US and the other from Norway.

It was my job as past president at the Hull meeting to chair the nominating committee for the next officers. Thus far, officers had been elected by the executive committee and council rather than by the membership. The founders of ISCE thought that it was important for the society to be led by persons known to be devoted to its development (in other words, to be willing to do considerable work) during its early years. Now that ISCE had passed its fourth annual meeting, I suggested that perhaps it was time for a general election. I was totally unprepared for the reaction of the European members of the executive committee and council, who thought that, since we were still a small society, it was unseemly to pit one person against another in such an election. They did not consider it "unseemly," however, to continue to let a small group elect their successors nor to suggest that Americans always supported "competition." I yielded to the views of the Europeans and, with their dominant opinions, it was several years before general elections were held.

PRESIDENT OF THE ECOLOGICAL SOCIETY OF AMERICA
In contrast with ISCE, the Ecological Society of America (ESA) was and is a large, well-established society. It had been one of the first ecological societies, founded in 1915, following impetus from the founding of the British Ecological Society in 1913. The large size of the society demanded a president-elect period, a time of learning how the officers operated as well as being apprised of numerous and often major issues that the society currently faced. The president shouldered all aspects of running the organization because assistance was not available as yet from an executive office. Mid-year meetings were essential at the business office, then located

at Arizona State University. The past president's duties were not as great as in ISCE, but he/she gave the banquet address, which is considered a major event of the annual meeting.

In the busy 1987 year as president of the ESA, I chaired the annual meeting at Ohio State University. The society had so many critical issues that the need for an executive office, with its assistance for officers and year-round functions, was starkly evident. Nonetheless, the old guard, especially at the business office, resisted the idea, thinking that the society could not afford paid assistance. ESA had always been run by volunteers or elected, unpaid officers. The executive office situation was complicated by general consensus among officers and active members that ESA must have an effective public affairs outreach with an office in Washington, DC to make ESA and its experts available for legislative matters concerning environmental issues.

The society, research-oriented since its founding, had for many years stayed out of the political arena, declaring itself to be strictly a scientific society. This did not mean there had not been concern about preserving natural areas. In 1917 Victor Shelford had chaired the Committee for Preservation of Natural Conditions, which in 1926 published a catalog of relatively undisturbed areas in North America and parts of Latin America (*The Naturalist's Guide to the Americas*). During the 1940s, however, influential members became concerned that environmental activism with government officials might compromise the society's image of scientific objectivity. After disputatious debate, a constitutional provision was passed preventing the society from taking a direct role in lobbying. The Nature Conservancy Committee (a descendant of the 1917 committee) was spun off from the society in 1951 and incorporated as the nonprofit Nature Conservancy that is now a large non-governmental organization.

Segregation of strictly scientific concerns from matters of public policy, however, is not easy. Although both public affairs and applied ecology committees were established in the 1950s, it essentially was in the aftermath of one woman's courageous book, Rachel Carson's *A Silent Spring* (1962), that ecologists began to write openly about their social responsibility, and that ESA began to connect with the public. Paul Sears in 1964 wrote his famous statement that ecology by nature was a "subversive subject," providing information for a "continuing critique of man's operations within the ecosystem." Others in the discipline began to clamor about the ivory-tower tendencies of ecologists, who were only beginning to become aware of the need to apply their knowledge to solving societal problems as well as inform the public about their research and explain its relevance. In the early 1970s, ESA began to produce position papers on important issues; some members pressed for the formation of a National Institute of Ecology about the time that the Environmental Protection Agency was being formed.

A fledgling ESA Washington office was established 1983, which later was expanded into ESA headquarters, with an executive director, where finances were managed and annual meeting assistance was provided. The public affairs office was included within this one main office.

During my period as president we were continually dealing with media problems concerning the definition of ecology—just what was it? I felt like I was back with Mason and the UC Berkeley ecologists—although I did not dust off the tools of language analysis in these discussions. The executive committee wrestled with at least three different relevant meanings: 1) the relation of any organism to its environment—its ecology, 2) the professional science of ecology, and 3) the political philosophy and associated movement incorporating a variety of environmental concerns. We were particularly grappling with the results of Earth Day, which had led some members of the media as well as the public to equate ecologists with recyclers and had revealed nothing about the basic scientific research done by ecologists. It was in this context that the executive committee decided to establish some sort of roster of ecological experts who could provide information to the media as well as to environmental managers. The Ecological Information Network (EIN) now comprises a database of experts who have volunteered to answer questions or provide input on various ecological issues. Five years later, another woman president, Jane Lubchenco, established the Science Program (originally the Sustainable Biosphere Initiative), which promotes the integration of ecological science with management and decision-making in government and private sectors.

One of my lasting impacts as ESA president probably was emphasizing global perspectives. As President of ISCE I worked with various members from foreign countries, but, of course, this was not true in ESA. In the tapestry of my professional life, this is a strong thread that I have long been weaving. At ESA, I encouraged the development of foreign chapters, starting with Mexico and Canada. Chapters enhance communication among ecologists regionally as well as within the parent society. The Mexicans at that time were concerned that they would lose their identity if they became a chapter in a large American society. During my presidency, Mexican universities were still sending many of their bright young scientists to obtain advanced degrees in the United States or Europe. It was only later, after they began providing their own graduate education and developing a cadre of "home-grown" ecologists, that they gained confidence they could hold their own within ESA. In 2003, a Mexican Chapter was finally formed. An official Canadian Chapter was formed in 1992. With these two chapters, ESA now spans North America in its official operations. An International Affairs Section supports relationships between ESA and the worldwide community of ecologists and promotes effective communication among all ecologists about international issues.

Making ESA publications available to ecologists in developing countries was another of my international interests. Allen Press, publisher of the society's journals, was having a problem housing all of the past volumes of *Ecology* and *Ecological Monographs,* and I suggested that they be made available to libraries in developing countries. This turned out to be a more complicated issue than it seemed on the surface. For example, how could we be sure that the volumes would be properly cared for and actually made available to the ecological community, and who would pay for shipping? ESA did send some sets of past volumes of *Ecology* and *Ecological Monographs* to developing countries and sought funds to help pay for having them shipped. Today these volumes seem less necessary for libraries, at least in some countries that can afford to obtain the journals online. However, there are others that can't afford the high fees and these greatly benefit from receiving the hard-copy journals.

Finally, to further support communication across borders, I advocated giving free ESA memberships to worthy ecologists from developing countries who could not afford them. After my presidency, I continued to serve as chair of the Committee on Ecologists in Developing Countries from 1990 to 1993 and as a member of the International Relations Committee from 1993 to 1995. Funding is still being requested from members to support grants for libraries and memberships for needy individuals in developing countries.

During the mid to late 1980s some members of the publications committee questioned whether ESA should continue publication of *Ecological Monographs* because more researchers were writing smaller articles rather than syntheses of the components of a large project. This situation came about in part because granting agencies were expecting a show of more immediate results. Having served as chair of the publications committee from 1982 to 1985, I felt strongly about making such a precipitous decision while I was president. While it was true that *Ecology*, the first society journal (established in 1917), was overwhelmed with smaller articles,

I also knew that *Monographs* had been established in 1931 in response to a similar situation. I was convinced that the time would soon return when publishing longer synthetic studies, which deal with complicated questions involving multiple components, would be deemed invaluable. I was right. *Monographs* is not just flourishing again, but in 2004 it had the highest rating for impact of any journal publishing primary research articles in the ecological sciences.

During 1987 and 1988 the executive committee also discussed launching a new journal, *Ecological Applications*, to make space available for increasing applied research, and it began publication four years later in 1991. *Frontiers in Ecology and the Environment*, with international and interdisciplinary emphasis, later joined the ESA family of journals.

Lab family present at UC Davis for my ESA presidential address

I gave my past president's address at the 1988 annual meeting at UC Davis, and the number of my "lab family" members who came to be there was imposing. The previous year, in preparation for giving the commencement address for UCSC women in science, I had given considerable thought to recognition of women scientists. I also had become concerned that I had been the first woman president of two professional societies—the Association for Tropical Biology and the International Society of Chemical Ecology—and was only the second female president (and the first in 36 years) of ESA. I knew numerous women who had significantly contributed to ecology but had not received adequate recognition for their work, nor had they held important positions in the society. Therefore, I decided to give my address on "The Path and Progress of Women Ecologists." I had been warned that such an address might produce a backlash from prominent men in the society, which had occurred when women had addressed such issues in other societies. However, I focused my address as a *tribute to the accomplishments* of women ecologists, not how they had been treated, and I received a standing ovation and numerous personal commendations from men as well as women. Later the editors of *Annual Reviews of Ecology and Systematics* asked me to write a more in-depth paper on early women ecologists' accomplishments, which I did, again in tribute to recognized and unrecognized excellent research.

ESA certificate of appreciation

The certificate I was given for serving as president of ESA had been printed years before and "expressed appreciation for *his* service"—on the assumption, of course, that every ESA president would be a man. (I don't know what E. Lucy Braun's certificate said.) Margaret Bryan Davis, the incoming president—amazingly, another woman—was furious and insisted that new certificates be made immediately. One has to wonder whether the previous lack of elected women leaders in ESA was intentional or simply benign neglect, with a certain amount of pressure being needed to prompt the society to recognize women. I propose the latter, but have no evidence to support it other than the fact that there have been eight women presidents since my time and numerous women have been elected to other important society positions. One historian of women scientists thinks that to a far greater extent than is realized the fate of top women in a scientific field says as much about the attitudes and behavior of the most prominent men in that specialty! Aside from increased recognition in ESA, it is interesting that in 1988, women comprised eighteen percent of the society and in 2005 only seventeen percent!

Past ESA presidents who attended 1990 annual meeting (note three women by this time): Back row (left to right) Jane Lubchenco, Lawrence Bliss, Ron Pulliam, Eugene Odum, Bob Paine, Richard Root, Eugene Likens, Simon Levin, Paul Risser, Frank Golley, Dwight Billings, Dennis Knight; Front row (left to right) Forrest Stearns, Francis Evans, Jean Langenheim, Harold Mooney, Rexford Daubenmire,Stanley Aurbach and Margaret Davis

POST-PRESIDENTIAL HONORS

Although I was thoroughly occupied with being at the helm of both ISCE and ESA, this prominence led to my being selected for several lectureships.

The first came from the Radcliffe Institute for Independent Studies (by then called the Bunting Institute and later incorporated into the Radcliffe Institute for Advanced Studies), which invited me to be the 1986 Annual Bunting Science Lecturer. I greatly appreciated this honor, which provided me an opportunity to express my gratitude for the role the institute had played in launching my career twenty years earlier, and was touched by the warmth and pride that members of the institute expressed toward one of their first scholars. I was especially delighted that Polly Bunting, the founder of the institute, attended the lecture and congratulated me for my achievements. She appreciated that I displayed in my lecture how research initiated partially under the institute's auspices had progressed to become part of the emerging subfield of chemical ecology and its expansion into the tropics.

Although many of my botanical friends in the biology labs, herbarium, and botanical museum at Harvard had passed away, Fakhri Bazzaz, whom I had known at Illinois as a student of Larry Bliss, was now the physiological ecologist at Harvard. While going to lunch at the Harvard Faculty Club with Fakhri, I discovered women no longer had to enter their own dining room through the side door. I could enter the front door and eat in the main room! Recently, there have been even more far-reaching signs of progress for women at Harvard—in 2007 the university selected a woman president, who was promoted to that position from being dean of the Radcliffe Institute for Advanced Study.

I was struck by comments Drew Gilpin Faust made in a *New York Times* interview just after the announcement of her appointment as Harvard's president. She said, "One of the things that characterizes my generation (born in 1947 and graduated from college in 1968)—that characterizes me, anyway, and others of my generation—is that I've always been surprised by how my life turned out. I've always done more than I ever thought I would. Becoming a professor—I would never have imagined that . . . Getting a PhD—I'm not sure I would have even imagined that. I've lived my life a step at a time. Things just sort of happened." I would use very similar words to characterize my professional trajectory such as obtaining my PhD, being a scholar of the Radcliffe Institute, becoming a UC professor—although, significantly, I was a generation before that of Faust. "Things just sort of happened," such as this wonderful return visit to Harvard for the Bunting Science lecture.

During 1986 I also was elected by the UCSC Academic Senate to give the Faculty Research Lecture. This is considered the highest campus honor that can be bestowed by faculty peers. It was a surprise and pleasure for me to follow my distinguished biology colleagues Kenneth Thimann and Harry Beevers in this role. I was the first woman so elected on the UCSC campus, but happily others followed as their numbers increased among the faculty. I was invited to give other lectures as well, such as the Sandia Foundation Lecture at the University of New Mexico in Albuquerque in 1987, and in 1989 the UCSC Graduate Student Commencement Address.

In the late eighties I served on the Council of Scientific Society Presidents—a fascinating experience to hear the views of leaders across the sciences, especially regarding how to increase funding for research. I also began my long tenure on the National Research Council/International Union of Biological Sciences Committee on Biodiversity. In the latter I could be involved in global discussions of biodiversity, and potential ways to ameliorate it—even though it was not the specific focus my own research.

EVOLVING SOCIAL
AND FAMILY LIFE

1966-2007

Raising cats is like having children but without the tuition.
—Ron Reagan

My social life was very university-oriented. This had begun while I lived in Stevenson College, where I socialized a good deal with other faculty preceptors. I also developed close association with the families of the biology faculty as their numbers increased over the years. And similarly I had many social activities with my graduate students as they increased in numbers. Moreover, with the amount of traveling I was doing both in the field and to meetings of various kinds, I appreciated the availability of concert and theater offerings on campus when I got home.

SOCIAL CIRCLE OF ENGLISH FRIENDS
Although I had known the Thimanns while I was at Harvard, I had not interacted with them socially there as much as with other friends. After my arrival at UCSC, however, I became great friends with Anne Thimann, who was constantly making sure that I diversified some of my activities apart from work. She also was at my side as I furnished my townhouse—from shopping in San Francisco furniture stores to helping me make curtains for upstairs rooms and having hand-crafted rugs made by local weavers (she was a master weaver herself).

Anne Thimann

Anne Thimann reminded me of my mother in some ways. She too had not attended college; she told me that only the boys in her English family

423

were sent to the university. Nonetheless, she was a highly educated woman, particularly in literature and the arts, and could hold her own in conversations with the many erudite visitors to her home. Kenneth was a renaissance man, similar in some ways to W. S. Cooper. He was a fine musician and during his youth had had difficulty deciding whether to pursue a career as a concert pianist or as a chemist. In choosing the latter, he felt he could still continue his love of music, whereas the reverse would have been more difficult. He organized the Crown College Chamber Players and brought in top musicians with the aid of the former music director of the Boston Symphony Orchestra, who had retired in Carmel. Thimann, like Cooper, was a perfectionist in writing. He emphasized that numerous drafts often were necessary to achieve the desired clarity—and stressed the importance of not giving up on revising drafts even if your busy schedule made it necessary to work on them piecemeal. When I dropped by their home for informal visits, I often found him working in this piecemeal way. This idea became influential in helping me with writing as my life became evermore busy.

In his constant international travel and many relationships with researchers around the world, Thimann felt he should attempt to communicate in the language of his peers. As president of the XI International Botanical Congress, he gave his introductory remarks in five languages. Anne told me that when they were visiting another country, they always practiced basic phrases of the language of that country during breakfast as well as any other times that they could find. This rubbed off on me and, although I did not have anyone with whom to practice at breakfast, my shelves of Berlitz phrase books and travel dictionaries attest to my attempts to learn about the languages of the countries in which I traveled.

The Thimanns became among my closest personal friends and I was blessed in so many ways with our relationship. It came to an end when Kenneth, following Anne's death, left for the East Coast to be near his children in the mid-1980s.

I also gravitated to two other English couples, both from County Durham in northern England. I became well acquainted with Glenn and Jean Willson when he was provost of Stevenson College, and our friendship continued after he left UCSC in the early 1980s to go first to Murdoch University in Australia and ultimately to the University of London. I knew Harry and Jean Beevers when Harry was the plant biochemist in the Biology Board of Studies. While the Willsons were at UCSC, I was involved in numerous social interactions with all three couples. I was often the only single woman at our dinner parties, which didn't seem to matter to them. I just seemed to fit in with these English people. The Beevers were the last to leave Santa Cruz, during the late nineties. I have greatly missed these three couples who had provided such close friendship and social pleasures.

Close circle of English friends at UCSC; left to right,
Harry Beevers, F. M. Glenn Willson, Jean Beevers,
Kenneth Thiman and Jean Willson

Many of my European trips started and ended in London, where I also developed long-term friends—Jack and Lindsay Harley at nearby Oxford, and Swain and Brennan, among others, at the Royal Botanical Gardens at Kew. My friendship with Tony Swain and his chemical ecologist wife, Ghillian, became even closer when they moved to Boston University. When Ghillean Prance became director of the Royal Botanical Gardens, I also socialized with him and his wife Anne. I had gotten to know them when I taught in the INPA Botany Program as well as later when I interacted with him at the New York Botanical Gardens. I wondered if my affinity for English friends went back to my own English heritage, which was bolstered by the influence of my Anglophile mother.

SURROGATE LAB FAMILY

I had begun to develop familial-type relationships with my graduate students early on. And then there were undergraduates doing senior theses, who had often been integrated into the teams of graduate students. As times went by, my "family" also included some graduate students with whom I had become good friends while serving on their doctoral committees. I suppose that the nurturing instincts I felt toward my graduate students were a type of replacement for not having children of my own. I knew, too, I could depend upon them in emergencies. Such relationships were intensified after the death of my mother in the spring of 1978—the group's attempt to console me led to what became a cherished event for all of us.

Previous to 1978, I had gone to Tulsa every Christmas vacation to be with Mother. As the Christmas season was approaching that year, I had mentioned in an offhand way in the lab that I was going to miss decorating a tree and sharing festivities with her. To my great surprise and delight, the group arrived one evening in mid-December with a tree, handmade ornaments, and fixings for a dinner. How lovely, thoughtful, and representative of the lab group's developing role of a surrogate family. It really emphasized how much certain members of my lab group were becoming long-term close friends and indeed serving in lieu of children.

Every year since then, until very recently, I have had Christmas festivities that began with a trip to a local tree farm to select and cut a tree. We then got together over pizza, salad, beer, and brownies to decorate my townhouse and the tree. I had a hobby of collecting Christmas ornaments from my travels, so it was truly an international tree. Then we met for the big celebration in which I provided the turkey and fixings and each student brought a dish that was traditional in his or her family. I usually brought back some little gift for each lab member from my many trips and these became the basis of a Santa Claus feature in these parties. Each year a different person donned the Santa Claus hat to hand out the packages under the tree. When Mexican students joined the lab, we added a piñata to the festivities, which resulted in some especially humorous sessions of adults battering the piñata strung from a tree outside my townhouse. After my students began to have children, they often replaced the adults in banging the piñata. We also ended the party with a special Christmas dessert and singing carols. Our singing was enhanced by accompaniment of guitar and flute when students with those skills arrived. A real sense of joy and merriment characterized these celebrations for which I was so grateful.

I always celebrated each student's birthday, an idea I had brought with me from the Botany Department at the University of Minnesota. My students reciprocated with a surprise party for my sixtieth birthday, followed by a gala one for my seventy-fifth (which was also the turn of the twentieth century) at a local conference center. Seventy-five people accepted the invitation, including university-related friends. Students came from Mexico, South Carolina, Colorado, and Oregon as well as different parts of California. Various former students

Traditional Lab Christmas party;
clockwise from top left: cutting tree,
student Santa, Flora watching from
stairs, dinner, carols, and pinata.

organized the event, particularly Gail Fail and Al Cunningham, who live nearby. My first graduate student, Susan Martin, was mistress of ceremonies, and Tom Hofstra, whom we all thought would be my last graduate student, gave a slide show and talk about the major events in my life. He also made posters of photos displaying my various activities, and adorned the walls of the center with them. Numerous guests added their personal comments following Tom's talk, and it all was videotaped. These comments were in addition to the letters that many students sent, detailing memories of their relationships with me. These letters, which were collected in a volume, were testament to how most of my students have continued as a part of my life beyond their graduation. Indeed, the whole event provided lovely, unforgettable reminders that these students, along with my mostly university-associated friends, have formed a loving surrogate family.

With Susan Martin and Tom Hofstra at my
75th birthday celebration

Thus Christmas celebrations and remembering everyone's birthday—as well as going to national meetings together, making annual special field trips, and having associated dinners—brought a special familial sense into my life. As the years passed, in some cases I also got to know some of my students' parents and even became incorporated into their families in spirit. I particularly remember several events. Susanne Arrhenius' father, a professor at UC San Diego, has the same birthday as I do, which has led to our often celebrating together at their family home in La Jolla, California. If not together for that day, we always have been in contact for mutual expression of best wishes.

Lab picnic on trip to Pt. Lobos; Back row (left to right) Stephen Jacques, Al Cunningham. Francisco Rosado-May, Martha Rosemeyer, Gail Fail, Jeanette Rollinger; Front row (left to right) Jason Greenlee, Francisco Espinosa, me, Cindy Macedo and Erik Feibert.

I also had an extraordinary visit with the parents of one of my Brazilian students (Erik Feibert) in a part of Portugal rarely seen by Americans. Following the meeting of the Society for Economic Botany in 1998 in London, I met with Erik's parents at a lovely *fazenda* in the northern hill country of Portugal. It had been owned by the Portuguese family of Erik's mother for generations. Located in a small remote village, the family now seldom visited it and his mother was thinking of selling it. In this process, she discovered that she held title to the entire village. Although previous members of the family had given rights for land, via a handshake, to various people in the village, these rights had never been written down and legalized.

No one had questioned the legality of their property ownership. The Feiberts thus found that they owned what was essentially a medieval fiefdom and were in the process of deciding what to do.

The remoteness of the area, which was strange to my thinking of Europe, was brought home to me personally in several ways. First, my luggage had not arrived in Porto from London, and as we wended our way on the long drive along the Douro River into the hills of the Trans-Os-Montes, I was afraid that British Airways would never find the *fazenda*. With constant urgent calls from Erik's father, however, late on the third day a truck from a little bakery in the nearest small commercial center finally arrived with my luggage. I was especially grateful as I had been wearing some of the cook's warm clothes as I was too big to fit in those of Erik's petite mother. The degree of isolation of this center was further made clear when I tried to cash a travelers check at the bank. There was a problem not only about signing for this check, but also about misinterpretation of the expiration date of my passport. Our attempted negotiations were closed when the bank manager came and declared that he could not understand either my English or Erik's father's "Spanish." When his father angrily claimed that he was speaking Portuguese, the bankers looked at him in disgust—and we left with Erik's father stormily declaring that "Portugal was more backward than Brazil!"

In much of the area, lovely vineyards were located on terraces supported by steep walls that gave them the appearance of giant staircases. When we returned to Porto, the major city of northern Portugal, which was built on its trade of port wine, we visited the Instituto Vinho do Porto. Erik's father was a member of this institute which enabled us to taste the best years of the various kinds of port. From Porto I took the train through coastal farmland with groves of olive and cork oak trees to Lisbon to meet with another of my other Brazilian graduate students, José Carlos Nascimento and his family. José Carlos was continuing research in Cordoba, Spain and it was an easy drive to Lisbon. We shared much laughter in usual adventures—often surrounding José Carlo's unorthodox driving in Lisbon, its nearby coasts and the Sintra Mountains. We were constantly lost because he kept taking what appeared on the city map to be shortcuts to our destinations. We crept down steep passageways with people sitting in front of their common-wall stone houses looking in amazement as we squeezed past. Finally, in one place an elderly man stopped us to inform us that we weren't on a street but on an alley separating the houses! In another location, José Carlos tried to turn around illegally. He paid no attention to my warning that a police car was following us, until the officer came up parallel to us with his siren blaring. When José Carlos started speaking in agitated Brazilian Portuguese, the cop stopped him with "Please speak English," which, of course, only exasperated José Carlos further. As with Erik Feibert's father, José Carlos' Brazilian Portuguese apparently was not understandable in Portugal—true either in the country or big city. Confusion with language led the policeman to give up and simply give us a warning with directions to the famed restaurant we were attempting to find.

With José Carlos and Maria Conçeicão Nascimento
in Lisbon, Portugal

The Nascimentos were representative of enjoying visits with former students in places such as South Carolina, Colorado, Mexico, among others, but in their case, celebrating *festas* in Manaus, visiting churches in Salvador, interesting sites in Brasilia and much more in Brazil. When initiating research in Cordoba in 1995, the Nascimentos also had traveled across Europe to Prague to join me in visiting this lovely ancient city. It all indeed was surrogate family activity.

BIOLOGY BOARD FAMILY

A marvelous bonding of the members of the closely knit Biology Board of Studies also grew incrementally over the years. Although we had differences of opinions on various issues, we were always able to reach a consensus—and gave each other much support. I felt fortunate to have initiated my full career with such wonderful colleagues and appreciated the friendship of many of their wives. We also were blessed with marvelous staff, from secretaries to greenhouse keepers. And I found out how they could rise to meet personal emergencies—such as mine.

In 1991, I developed *tic douloureux*, an excruciating nerve pain in my face. An MRI showed this was due to a tumor on the acoustic nerve—and I was facing brain surgery. I was referred to a surgeon at UCSF who told me that my career was probably over. A biology colleague, a PhD-MD, accompanied for this visit and we together decided not to accept this verdict. Then a series of serendipitous events led to a positive outcome. Following a meeting in Washington, DC, I visited George Hammond, who was now located at the University of Virginia. At a dinner party at his home, we discovered that a neurosurgeon in their medical school was trying to develop radiation to avoid acoustic neuroma surgery. George contacted him, but after reviewing my MRI, he concluded that surgery would be necessary. However, he suggested that I go to the House Ear Clinic in Los Angeles, where one of their neurosurgeon associates, W. E. Hitselberger, had helped to pioneer a successful approach to this difficult surgery.

My colleague accompanied me to visit this neurosurgeon, and we both were convinced the House Ear Clinic was the place to have the surgery done. I would be in the hospital or under evaluation for ten days, so biology faculty members, faculty wives, graduate students, and staff members decided they would fly to Los Angeles in a relay every other day so that I would not be there alone. Two people drove down with me to help me check in and so my car would be available for the relay team. They all stayed at the famous old Sheraton Town House Hotel near St. Francis Hospital, where arrangements had been made by the clinic for family and friends of their patients to stay; it is also where patients recuperated immediately after leaving the hospital. Its small size, friendly atmosphere, and faded elegance were highly appropriate for recuperation, and enjoyable as well for all my caregivers. A grad student in my lab and a friend flew down to drive my car home. Moreover, a partner of one of my first grad students came from Colorado and stayed at home with me until I was able to take care of myself. Happily I made rapid recovery from the surgery, and I was filled with gratitude; in fact, I was overwhelmed by such loving care shown by so many colleagues as well as present and former students during the entire event.

CAT COMPANIONS

In addition to my lab family and close-knit group of friends, my pets were important companions—as they had been when I was growing up. Instead of dogs, I had cats, as they were more adaptable to my housing and continual travel. First had been the handsome and affectionate Snuggles, who became the mascot of my Stevenson house as well as of the college, but who disappeared mysteriously. I brought the fearful Tiger, who arrived after Snuggles, to my townhouse when I moved from the college. However, he kept thinking that his real home was my apartment on campus and periodically made his way several miles back there. Then he disappeared entirely, when a visiting professor was living in my townhouse while I was on sabbatical leave in Amazonia. I was so sad about his mysterious disappearance that one of my graduate students left an adorable kitten in a basket on my patio for me. As expected, I was immediately smitten! She was so charming that Mother suggested I call her Florodora, referring to the girls in the most successful musical during the early twentieth century. She became my constant companion and took walks of several blocks with me. I lost Florodora, when she was only two-years-old, while I was on a several-week trip to Venezuela.

Shortly afterwards, when a neighbor found out about Florodora's death, she asked if I would like to have a replacement. A friend's cat had just produced a charming mixed litter of Royal Burmese and "gentleman alley-cat" (as she put it) kittens and was looking for homes for them. When I went to choose one, two little females crawled on my lap. The owners said that these kittens were always a pair and they wanted them to go to a home together. Because the kittens had selected me and were Florodora's replacement, they came home as Flora and Dora for more than a twenty-year stay.

Flora and Dora on my desk

During Mother's Santa Cruz visits, both cats developed a strong bond with her—but especially Flora. I called Mother regularly every Sunday and

Flora seemed to know that she could hear her voice then. She frequently spent Sunday mornings on the desk from where I called and would wait for the receiver to be put where she could hear Mother's voice. Flora, in fact, liked to "answer" the phone when I was not at home. When the telephone rang, if she was near one of the phones that she could knock off the receiver, she would do so and meow into it. When some friends who knew her found out about this antic, they would call to see if she'd answer. As a result, I was sometimes told to hang up and let Flora answer the phone!

From kittenhood on, Flora was clearly the dominant cat; Dora's whole life was ordered by Flora—except for one strange incident. As part of Merrill College's international program, a group of United Nations ambassadors were invited to visit UCSC and, as a way of introducing them to American family life, to stay in faculty homes. I was asked to provide hospitality for one of the ambassadors, who was from the African country of Guinea. She was a large black woman who arrived in an elegant and colorful long dress with an equally colorful turban wrapped around her head. Little Dora stood looking at her briefly, and then ran straight up her dress and leapt to the top of the turban. The ambassador started shrieking and I quickly retrieved Dora and grabbed Flora before she tried a similar stunt. The ambassador disdainfully declared that cats only lived in the barns in her country. She wanted to take a bath before we went to a dinner in honor of our United Nations guests; she found the bubble bath near the tub and used it liberally. When I used bubble bath, Flora and Dora often sat on the edge of the bathtub—loving to bat the foam. I had checked that the bathroom door was tightly closed (there is no lock) when the ambassador entered, but working together Flora and Dora had managed to get the door open and rushed to jump on the side of the tub. More shrieking from my guest and I rushed again to gather up the "kids."

The next day, the ambassador was not feeling well and stayed at home in the morning while I was teaching. When I returned, she was in bed with a kitten on each side of her. She gushed about what lovely, comfy little companions they were! After she left, she wrote a letter of thanks for staying in my home, but especially for introducing her to those "adorable kittens." I received Christmas cards for several years from her, always sending her fondness for those little ones. I'm sure that she returned to Guinea talking about staying in an American home with two little kittens!

For almost ten years Flora and Dora comprised my cat family. They always wanted to be where I was and part of what I was doing—sometimes too much so on my desk when I was trying to prepare lectures. Then I began to run a neighborhood orphanage for cats that were left behind—much as Mother had cared for the homeless animals during the Depression and afterward. As author Ernest Hemingway famously observed (once having kept 57 cats)—"One cat leads to another." The first one was a little black female who arrived hungry at my back door; I finally discovered that she had belonged to some students who had moved and left her behind. She settled into a friendly relationship with Flora and Dora, and followed me everywhere. "Blackie," as she was now called, was a delight and soon had grabbed the hearts of my students and other visitors to the house. Her vet, however, found lymphatic cancer in one of her check-ups, and predicted that she wouldn't live more than six months. Although relatively soon, she seemed normal, a couple of years later I noticed a large lump on her shoulder, which was diagnosed as another kind of cancer—a sarcoma that probably had resulted from her feline leukemia vaccination. I consulted with the vet oncologist in our area, who advised surgery for Blackie despite her two cancerous conditions, pointing out that her bright little eyes seemed to say that she wanted the chance to live. Removing the cancerous growth meant amputation of her front leg, but she was soon moving around on three legs as if it were normal—and being her sweet loving self.

Soon after Blackie's recovery, a beautiful purebred Himalayan began appearing at my back door, howling in hunger. I discovered that her name was Tasha and that she had been left behind when one of the townhouses was sold. The new owners did not want her; the neighbors convinced me, though I was somewhat reluctant, to add Tasha to my cat family. This did not turn out to be as easy an addition as Blackie had been. Tasha wanted to be "top cat" and asserted herself in a dominating manner, which did not go over very well with the current residents. Ultimately Tasha was not allowed upstairs where Flora, Dora, and Blackie happily co-existed. They came downstairs to eat in the kitchen and to go out to the front and back patios. Being sociable, Flora and Blackie always rushed downstairs to greet visitors when they came, and Tasha fortunately retreated outside.

Being completely healthy throughout almost twenty years, Flora and Dora had been poster girls for their vet. Then disaster struck. Flora suddenly became ill while I was away on a trip, and was diagnosed with advanced lung cancer—having shown no evidence of illness until this terminal condition. When she had to be confined to an oxygen chamber, and had desperately and unsuccessfully tried to crawl on my shoulder where she loved to be, I reluctantly conceded to the vet's recommendation to euthanize her.

This was my first and traumatic experience with euthanizing a longtime, very special animal companion. But Flora's demise may have been even worse for Dora, who all her life had been a constant companion and subordinate to her sister. It was pathetic to watch Dora search the house and patios again and again for Flora. She was so depressed and obviously bewildered that she would not eat. Although Dora got along well with Blackie, she was no replacement for Flora. Strikingly, however, after several weeks Dora apparently decided that her sister was not going to return and her behavior changed dramatically. Now she was the dominant cat and she soon started acting like Flora, coming downstairs to greet visitors.

This went on for a year and then Dora started to show signs of kidney failure. She didn't like her low-protein diet; in fact, she wouldn't eat the food if I didn't soak it in the water from canned tuna. It was my time now to become desperate from eating every tuna recipe I could get my hands on—in order to supply Dora's food with the tuna flavoring. Finally I found a solution through the proprietors of a small restaurant that served tuna salad on bagels, who were willing to save the water from the very large cans of tuna they used. I soon had lots of tuna juice that I froze as ice cubes, melting them as needed. After a while, however, Dora needed injections of fluids, and she became progressively more depressed.

Pumpkin (AKA Orange Cat)

By this time a male orange tabby had appeared on the scene. After being abandoned as a kitten, he had been mistreated, and became terrified of most people. My mailman, another cat lover, told me of the tabby's plight and hoped I would take him in. This I did as he trusted me and seemed so grateful for kindness. And it was Pumpkin (more usually referred to as Orange Cat) who comforted Dora. When she was lying on the bed dispiritedly, he would wash her face and ears and lie close to her—the only cat other than her sister that

Dora would allow such closeness. Finally, she fought her fluid injections and seemed to lose interest in living. So my vet came to the house and put her to sleep while she was basking in the sun in her favorite place on my bed. It was a difficult process for me to endure but at least it was different from Flora's situation, because Dora appeared to signal me that she was ready to go.

Now my cat family consisted of the beloved little three-legged Blackie, the arrogant Tasha, and the sweet Orange Cat. One by one, over the next six years, they succumbed to various problems. Blackie was first to go, finally being overcome by the lymphatic cancer. It took me longer to get over Blackie's passing than even Flora's, as she was such a special animal who had overcome so much so gallantly. I decided to establish an endowment at the Santa Cruz SPCA in her memory. Called Blackie's Senior Friends, it provides funds for matching senior citizens who cannot afford to have companion animals with senior animals that might languish or even be euthanized in a shelter (since most families adopting pets from shelters prefer puppies and kittens)—a win-win situation for both people and animals.

**BLACKIE'S
SENIOR
FRIENDS**

*Santa Cruz SPCA brochure
for Blackie's Senior Friends*

Several years later both Tasha and Orange Cat succumbed to illness, and I now faced euthanasia more calmly than at first. Tasha went first; Orange Cat's death was in some ways reminiscent of Blackie's, because he was such a sweet animal. He had spent the day among the shrubs near the back door where most of the cats in the neighborhood came to visit him. At night, he wanted to be on the bed with me. He had a lingering end with various medical problems until it became clear it was time to ask the vet to come to help say good-bye.

After Orange Cat's passing, even though the house seemed sadly lonely, I had decided to wait awhile before getting another cat. But I had offhandedly mentioned at the university that it was the first time in thirty years there had not been at least one cat in my house. When the word got to our SPCA, I had an immediate call from the president of the board of directors informing me they had a perfect cat for me. My pleas that I planned to wait were to no avail. She was bringing this special animal to my house the next morning! I had expected an older cat of the type that I wanted to protect in the Blackie's Friends program, but a handsome, long-haired tuxedo *kitten* stepped out of the carrier. He immediately jumped into my lap and started purring—sealing arrangements for his new home, of course. He opened and inspected every cabinet, ate house plants (specializing on orchid flowers), used the litter box as a sandbox to play in, and more! The house definitely no longer had an empty feeling. Mr. Tux as he was named, continues to charm all visitors.

Mr. Tux, current ruler of the house

Although my cat family has constituted a wonderful part of my home life, I never realized how closely my graduate students identified with them. Over the years they had taken care of the cats while I was traveling, and at my seventy-fifth birthday celebration, a special poster displayed pictures of most of them. I overheard a group of students in front of this poster identifying the time intervals they had spent in the lab with specific cats they had taken care of.

Despite having lost family with my divorce and having no children of my own, my life as a single woman with no siblings has been filled with interesting and devoted friends here and in other countries, and I have enjoyed a sense of community and family in various living arrangements.

Instead of surrogate family members in a Girl Scout troop, as I had when a child, I've had my graduate student Lab Family, and instead of dogs I've had cat companions. The strong and colorful threads that were spun when I was an only child have been woven through my whole life's tapestry, and consequently I have experienced the true meaning of family as something beyond blood bonds.

SOJOURNS IN HONG KONG AND CHINA

1980; 1988

During the 1980s, several symposia provided me the opportunity to visit former students and Chinese scholars, and thus to participate in Chinese culture in both Hong Kong and the People's Republic of China. I went to Hong Kong twice to see Yin Tse (Eric) Lee, one of my first graduate students, and his family. For the first visit, in 1980, I was on my way to the NYBG symposium in Bangkok, Thailand. As part of this visit I also took a short train trip to Guangzhou, China, which had just been opened for tourist travel. In 1988, I paused in Hong Kong again, this time en route to a symposium in Kunming, China, which included visits with two former UC visiting scholars—Cao Riqiang in Nanjing and Jinliang Wang in Xishuangbanna.

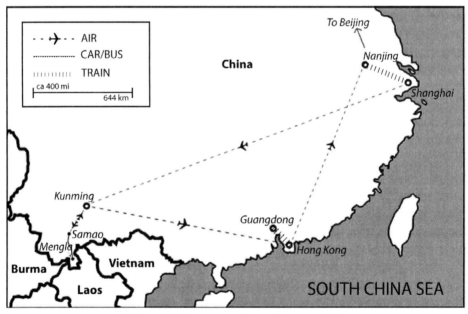

1980 and 1988 visits to Hong Kong and China

FIRST TRIP TO HONG KONG

Once again, I had the good fortune to be invited to stay in a local person's home and see how his family lived—in this case how an upper middle-class Chinese family lived in bustling and vibrant Hong Kong. Eric Lee's apartment was in the Happy Valley area near the racetrack, where he was in charge of the beautiful gardens surrounding the British Royal Hong Kong Jockey Club and the turf on which the horses raced. Although this was an interesting and well-paid job, it was not what Eric had hoped for.

Eric Lee with colleagues at Chinese University, Hong Kong

Following his two-year postdoctoral fellowship at Harvard, Eric had been offered, by letter, a position to teach plant systematics at Chinese University, one of Hong Kong's best universities and the school from which he had received his bachelor's degree. When he arrived at the university, he was told that a new administration had eradicated his position, with a mandate that the department should move in different research directions. The letter offering him the position was not valid because he had not yet signed a contract. It was an unbelievably difficult situation and Eric struggled to accept it for some time. He ultimately had come to grips with it psychologically and maintained contacts with faculty at the university, but he had a continued nagging sense of disappointment in not being able to pursue the academic career for which he had prepared himself so well. At least he was still working with plants at the Jockey Club and actively doing research on turf grasses, in fact, becoming an expert on them in Asia. He also was living a good life in Hong Kong among his and his wife's extended family.

I was soon to be greeted and feted by all of Eric's family. The Chinese give older people, especially teachers, great respect. While Eric was a grad student, his family had sent me many gifts, including beautifully colored silk brocade dresses, gorgeous silk jackets, intricate ivory carvings, and much more. On this visit to Hong Kong, the whole family went overboard with their hospitality. Some Chinese care about food with a passion only rivaled by the French, and Hong Kong is considered a gourmet's wonderland. In addition to fascinating sightseeing jaunts, each night we had a many-course banquet in the style of a different region of China—not just Canton but Chou Chow, Peking, Shanghai, and Szechwan. Of course, we sat around a large round table, and members of the family would continue to add food to my rice bowl until I simply could eat no more. I knew good manners dictated that I should continue to eat as long as food was put in my bowl, but there were limits to my capacity to consume it all—especially after several nights of these banquets.

FIRST VISIT TO CHINA

China opened its doors to visitors in 1980, with Hong Kong the principal gateway to the favorite destination of Guangzhou (Canton)—only 113 miles away by rail. Eric and his family encouraged me to take the China Travel Service tour to Guangzhou. They would have liked to go with me, but Eric's father was fearful about any of them entering Communist China because they had had such a traumatic departure when the Communists took over in 1949. Eric's father had been a civil servant in the former government and made a harrowing escape after sending the family to Hong Kong ahead of his departure.

I boarded the "soft seat train," part of the Chinese national railroads especially for foreign tourists, from Kowloon to Guangzhou. The seats were comfortable and I remember fancy lace curtains at the windows. We traveled in an air-conditioned bus around Guangzhou; it is located on the Pearl River, which was congested with ferry boats, junks, sampans, freighters, and naval ships. Although Guangzhou is the third largest city in China, outside of trucks and a few buses, the streets were jammed with bicycles at that time.

Cars had not arrived as yet. Everywhere the labor-intensive economy was evident and many billboards or paintings on walls showed happy-looking workers. Even tall buildings were being constructed, amazingly to me, using bamboo scaffolding (although later I was told that some timber bamboos, on a per-weight basis, have higher tensile strength than iron or steel). Roads were being built using hand tools such as picks and shovels. (As I watched the Olympics on TV displaying the modern structures and extraordinary economic boom in Beijing, it was difficult to think of these experiences I had in China were only twenty years ago.)

Wherever our bus stopped, a crowd collected around it and people stared wonderingly at us. We were indeed strangers to these people who had been completely enclosed in their own world. I had previously found in my travels what a marvelous effect a smile can have in such situations. I smiled broadly and soon most of the people in the assembled throng were happily reciprocating. The Pearl River irrigates surrounding farmland, and we visited a communal farm. After a Chinese-style country lunch, we toured model flats and met families of leading farmers. We were taken to a school with a large picture of Mao looking over smiling children who sang to us, and a hospital of which community members were especially proud. I was particularly fascinated with the hospital's pharmacy, where herbs were being dispensed from innumerable boxes. The pharmacists were piling different herbs on a piece of paper and wrapping them up, ready to be made into a tea, tincture, or whatever was prescribed. They told us about their extensive use of acupuncture, and proudly pointed out its use even in major surgery.

Upon my return to Hong Kong, Eric and his family asked many questions, eager to know what it is was like in China but still fearing to go themselves to see.

SECOND HONG KONG VISIT

In 1988, my stay in Hong Kong was briefer than in 1980, but included a visit with Eric to Chinese University for a discussion with faculty whom he was informally assisting with studies of the secondary chemicals in herbs used for medicine. My visit coincided with the Chinese Mid-Autumn or Moon Festival in September (the Chinese use a lunar calendar to determine the day on which it will fall each year). We ate moon cakes (patties of ground sesame and lotus seeds or dates, which can be enriched with duck egg) and watched the full moon rise as children with paper lanterns congregated in the park across from Eric's apartment. We also visited a huge open-air market where Eric bought a seal of my name in Chinese and my birthday animal symbol—the water buffalo. At the time, I thought it rather unromantic to have the water buffalo as my animal symbol but later, on my trip to Yunnan, I saw that people so revered and respected these hard-working animals that they often lived in their houses with them. Looking back over my life, maybe a hard-working animal who has received respect and affection reflects my existence very well!

Eric's son, Frank; note full moon and typical lantern children carry during Autumn Harvest Festival.

This was still a time of dramatic contrast in lifestyle and economy between Hong Kong and the People's Republic of China. Eric's family was very concerned about a transfer of sovereignty of Hong Kong from the United Kingdom to China (which did occur in 1997). Eric's two children had been born in the United States, so they had US citizenship, which was a comfort for an anticipated move from Hong Kong.

SECOND VISIT TO CHINA

My most lengthy and informative trip to China resulted from an invitation to give a plenary address at an international symposium on plant resources, to honor the fiftieth anniversary of the Kunming Institute of Botany in Yunnan Province. I also lectured at Nanjing University, at the request of Professor of Biology Cao Riqiang. I had known Cao when she was a visiting scholar at UC Berkeley. She had written a book in Chinese on plant secondary compounds and was responsible for Jinliang Wang becoming a visiting scholar in my lab. Jinliang was now back in China,

Professor Cao Riqiang at Nanjing University

working at the Tropical Botanical Garden in Xishuangbanna Prefecture under the auspices of the Kunming Institute of Botany.

In Nanjing I stayed in the guest house on the campus of Nanjing University and ate in an adjacent campus restaurant. The guest house was a faded example of what it probably had been in pre-communist years but was still comfortable and very convenient. I gave two lectures—one presenting recent advances in chemical ecology and the other centering on how general biology is taught at UCSC—and held discussions on advances in ecology as well. All of this was done via translation, and a fifty-minute lecture took about two hours before questions began (some of the faculty and students asked their questions in English). I had given a translated lecture in 1964 in Costa Rica, but I was much tenser during this Chinese session—perhaps because I understood most of the Spanish but absolutely none of the Chinese. I gave one lecture in the morning, followed by a many-course banquet lunch, then another lecture in the afternoon. I was exhausted by the end of the day. However, I was not done yet, as I was awakened past midnight by loud knocking on my door. Three students, who were studying English in the hopes of making money translating correspondence for businesses, presented me with a long list of questions about "American English." They were being taught "English English" and faced the same problem as the young men who had asked to practice their English with me in Paris and in Zagreb (except they asked in the late afternoon!). I pointed out how late it was and said I was very tired. Nevertheless, they insisted on coming in and there I was, bleary-eyed in my pajamas. I finally convinced them to have breakfast with me the next morning, and I helped them once again before I left Nanjing. They were very eager, indeed.

My stay in Nanjing occurred during Chinese National Holidays, and I was able to witness the local celebrations. Cao had arranged for a car from the university and several students accompanied me to practice their English while informing me about some of the many attractions of this first capital of China. In 1988 the few cars, such as ours, had to wend through streets clogged with bicycles—the numbers of which did not seem much different from those I had seen in Guanzhou in 1980. There was even a bicycle parking problem; in many places there were rows and rows of them and I wondered how people distinguished theirs from all of the other bikes of similar make. (Again, how different today with traffic gridlock of automobiles.) We joined the throngs of holiday visitors at Sun Yat Sen's Memorial and on the bridge overlooking the Xangtse (Changjiang) River, one of the three largest rivers in the world. Although the river is small here, it was great to have a glimpse of it. We also visited the marvelous Nanjing Botanical Garden (the oldest in China), the old capital's walls, and the memorial to the Nanjing Massacre, when the Japanese killed thousands of Chinese citizens. One learns early, and somewhat wearily, that reaching most Chinese attractions requires climbing stairs with many steps.

Parking area for ubiquitous bicycles in Nanjing

To get to Kunming by air, we had to take the train to Shanghai. I wanted to accompany Cao, which meant taking the Chinese "hard seat" train—the type that I was *not* supposed to take in the Soviet Union. This train was much more interesting culturally, if not as comfortable, as the "soft seat" tourist train I had taken to Guangzhou in 1980. On the trip to Shanghai people gaped at me as Cao and I squeezed into bench-style seats with all the other passengers. The train made numerous stops, so it took us three-and-a-half hours to reach Shanghai.

When the train arrived in the Shanghai station, all I could see from the window was a sea of black-haired heads. The terminal was so packed as we left the train that I literally was swept away. I had never before been so jammed among so many people, truly as in the proverbial tin of sardines. Cao finally got hold of my hand and we fought our way out to the street to get transportation to the airport. We had missed the bus, so Cao hailed a "taxi" even stranger than the pedicabs in Thailand. There were no seats in the back and we had to sit cross-legged on the floor for a very bumpy, somewhat harrowing ride through thousands of cyclists and many more trucks and cars than in Nanjing—these motorized vehicles were a sign of the economic boom that would later characterize Shanghai.

Although the new international terminal at the airport was much nicer than the older domestic one, it was a far cry from the sleek airport shown on TV in 2008—also with a 220 mph magnetic levitation train to get to town in a blink! The gate area to our domestic flight to Kunming had no seats. Since we had more than an hour before our flight, we sat on the floor, fortunately getting a space where we could lean up against the wall. It was late afternoon when our flight left; in the air we were served tea and a snack. After the stewardesses took our trays, I went to the back of the plane to use the restroom and found them taking uneaten food off the trays and putting it into plastic bags. When I looked somewhat aghast, one of the stewardesses said, in broken English, "Food is never wasted in China."

The host of the symposium, the Kunming Institute of Botany (part of Academia Sinica—Chinese Academy of Sciences), is located on a thousand hectares in a tree-lined suburb of Kunming. The institute does basic scientific research on utilization and protection of Yunnan Province plants. Over 15,000 species of vascular plants occur in Yunnan; because this is nearly half of China's total, the province is known as "kingdom of plants." To study this plant wealth, the institute has departments for taxonomy, phytochemistry, plant physiology, and ethnobotany. Resource projects at that time were focused on forestry, medicinal and aromatic plants, and fruit trees.

Getting acquainted with a wide-ranging group of European, Chinese, and Japanese botanists and chemists whom I had not met previously was one of the most interesting aspects of the symposium. It was difficult to understand the English of numerous speakers, but walks in the botanical gardens around the institute provided opportunities for casual conversation where some language problems could be ameliorated.

We also visited areas near Kunming. I sat with Cao on the bus and it was here for the first time that she told me about her experiences during the Cultural Revolution. As we passed vast rice fields, she described how in the late 1960s she had contracted schistosomiasis standing in water for long hours while planting rice. When she recovered from the debilitating effects of this fluke parasite, she was put in a factory where she had to spray-paint machinery; she then came down with lung problems. By the time she had regained her health, in the mid-1970s, the Cultural Revolution was over.

During the era of reconstruction afterwards, she returned to teaching at the university and was sent to the United States as a visiting scholar to catch up—the authorities had realized how far they had fallen behind in education and research. Especially during such conversations, and over the course of our longtime friendship, I found myself seeing Cao and Shui-ying Hu (the researcher I had known at the Arnold Arboretum) as two women who had transcended tremendous difficulties in pursuit not only of their own research but also of educating their compatriots.

The most exciting part of the meeting for me was the trip to Xishuangbanna Prefecture, situated in southernmost Yunnan Province on the border with Laos and Myanmar (Burma). Over 4,000 of Yunnan's 15,000 species of vascular plants have been recognized there; it supports about 12 percent of all of China's species on less than 1 percent of the area. About a thousand of these species are economically important, with about half of these used in Chinese medicine. More than one hundred tree species are fast-growing and high quality timbers—a number of them are used in plantations in other tropical areas, such as *Gmelina arborea* in Amazonia.

With Jinliang Wang and wife

Our main goal was visiting the Tropical Botanical Garden in Mengla, which is part of the Kunming Institute and Academia Sinica's Yunnan Institute of Tropical Plants. The garden is located on a gourd-shaped peninsula surrounded by a tributary to the Mekong River. Our traveling group included German and Japanese biochemists as well as French, English, and American botanists, all of whom were eager to visit Xishuangbanna and the botanical garden. We had a Chinese translator from Academia Sinica and a Chinese American from the University of Hawaii who also helped with translation whenever this was needed. I had a special advantage at the garden, because Jinliang Wang, who had been in my lab for two years as a visiting scholar, had spent the Cultural Revolution helping build it. He was a fountain of information and eager to make sure that I saw everything in which I had interest. I also had the opportunity here to meet his wife and two children, who he was not allowed to bring with him to the US.

To reach Mengla, we flew through mountainous terrain to Simao, in a vintage Russian plane that still had the bucket seats it had been furnished with as a war plane. I was sitting in the second row; a Frenchman was in front of me. Although basically a sunny day, we were flying through thick clouds amid high mountains and so low you felt you could touch the side of the mountains as we exited the clouds. The door to the cockpit was open and the Frenchman leaned forward so he could see some of the instruments. He turned back to me with alarm, shouting, "The *altimitaire*. It's not working!" This was something I would have rather not heard; I was uncomfortable already but now this flight was beginning to fit into the category of "another hair-raising plane trip." It only seemed all the more so when we *rapidly* descended through clouds with only radio contact guiding the pilot to make a very bumpy and bouncy, but fortunately safe, landing on a small airstrip in Simao. Here a minibus was waiting to take us to Mengla, where we would be staying in the guest facilities of the botanical gardens.

It was a lengthy trip to Mengla on roads filled with people and their water buffaloes. Crowds of people and animals on mountain roads were familiar to me from my experience in Colombia, Mexico, and Costa Rica. Likewise, the Chinese crazy fast driving was similar! We careened around curves on the wrong side of the road and met, in addition to people and water buffalo, open trucks often loaded with soldiers ominously carrying rifles. The wife of a German biochemist from Heidelberg would shout *"nein, nein"* as we hurtled along, swerving to miss people or their animals. To release tension, others started shouting *nein* with her, and it soon became a humorous chorus when any one or all of us questioned the wisdom of our driver, who remained inscrutable or at least didn't seem to mind our outcries. Our exhortations didn't do much good, but somehow we felt relieved by our shouting.

We were doubled up in rooms at the garden, and my roommate was a Japanese chemist from Yokohama National University. Though unaccustomed to the rustic conditions we encountered at the garden, she was interested in seeing some of the plants that she and others were analyzing chemically for use in herbal medicine. Since this was her first venture in the tropics, she had never slept under a mosquito net. When she untied the net suspended from the ceiling over her bed, it fell down around her; in alarm she thrashed around and got herself hopelessly entangled in it. With the help of other women on the trip I managed to get her calmed sufficiently to extricate her. She then refused to use the netting; instead she kept me awake all night swatting insects.

We had only cold showers (all that was needed in the tropical heat) but this fastidious chemist unhappily thought she wouldn't get clean without warm water. I was much more concerned about the communal wooden chopsticks that were just put into a jar of cold water following a meal. In Hong Kong the Lee family had given me some beautiful ivory chopsticks to use in such situations, but the Chinese botanist from the University of Hawaii told me that to do so would be considered impolite.

Among the 3,000 species in the botanical garden, focus was on the preservation and utilization of economically important tropical plants. A research laboratory and library was associated with the extensive garden, which had been cut out of the native forest and adjoins the Menglan Nature Reserve. It was here that Jinliang made sure that I got my first look at *Dipterocarpus* and *Shorea*—members of the very large resin-producing family Dipterocarpaceae. Genera of this family produce so much resin that its amber is used to produce petroleum products in Southeast Asia. We walked among the bamboo collection of over eighty species from Xishuangbanna; especially impressive were the giant *Cephalostachyum* and *Dendrocalamus*. I had not previously considered the amazing diversity and myriad uses (over a thousand documented) of the bamboos. Agroforestry here included tea (*Camellia sinensis*) plantations with an overstory of rubber trees (*Hevea brasiliensis*). Xishuangbanna is the homeland of the tree that produces famous Pu'en tea, considered to be one of China's finest, and I listened with interest to accounts of the history of tea drinking.

Xishuangbanna is an area with numerous ethnic minority groups, such as the Dais, Bulangs, Lahus, and Jinues amid the usual Hans. The Dais predominated in the areas we visited, and their Buddhist temples with characteristic narrow spires made me think I was in Thailand rather than China. We had dinner in Dai farming village; most of our meals were botanical explorations as we tried to identify what we were eating. Even with experts in our group, such as Jules Vidal—who had worked on the floras of Thailand, Laos, and Vietnam—often we could not definitely identify the plants. We sometimes got into humorous arguments such as whether the part of the plant we were eating was a stem or a petiole (leaf stalk)—only a group of botanists could be so interested. I was unpleasantly amazed at how oily the food was; it often seemed to be floating in rape seed oil. The Chinese with us suggested dipping the food in beer, but then the whole meal began to taste like beer. I began to eat a great deal of rice—separately. It was available for every meal from a big bamboo container set apart from the table. Bread was the food I missed most; I didn't have a single piece of bread while I was in China (the Chinese don't have ovens in which to bake bread). Missing bread was similar to my missing green salads in the New World tropics, but in that case it was because of the fear of intestinal bugs, not lack of availability.

Me on far left among our international group
crossing river to visit Dai village

We returned to Simao to spend the night before boarding our plane back to Kunming—and discovered that the hotel only changed the towels and bedding every week, no matter how many people used the rooms. The Lee family had warned me of this possibility and had given me a beautiful pillow case to use if this happened, but I had left it in my luggage in Kunming. My Japanese roommate was horrified. I must admit that I didn't use my towel, preferring to use some of my own clothes to dry parts of my body that I couldn't just let air dry. It was bad enough the first night, but when we had to stay over again, my roommate began more-or-less to whimper continuously. The second night, as she kept muttering "I shall never come back to China again," I kept answering, "but we have to get out of China first," sometimes leaving her almost in tears. Couldn't help it!

More alarming to me than the stay itself were the circumstances that led to our spending an extra night. We had gone to the airport to board our plane to Kunming, but waited and waited. Finally we were told that the plane had "disappeared." Although this was the word used by our translator, most of us thought (and hoped) that the plane had not really disappeared. We found out that, in a way, it had. The mountain weather had become severe during the trip to Kunming, and the pilot had found a place to land but could not immediately contact anyone because the radio was not working. We had to spend the extra night in Simao and wait for the next day's flight. The following morning, however, much to our horror, a large group of people was waiting at the airport for that day's plane. Things got ugly when our Academia Sinica translator tried to convince these people that we had priority because our flight had not arrived the day before. Some declared there was no way they were going to be bumped for a bunch of foreigners! They even threatened to lie down under the wheels of the plane. What a dilemma for our Academia Sinica representative. Several members of our group were important participants in the banquet that night in Kunming celebrating the fiftieth anniversary of the institute. Furthermore, several of us had flights leaving China the following morning. After *much* negotiation among our translator, the airline officials, and a representative of the local people with tickets, a compromise was reached: half our group and half of theirs would fly that day. We then sat down and figured out who in our group most needed to get to Kunming. I was one of those selected because of my early flight to Hong Kong the next morning. As it turned out, the Kunming Institute director was so upset when he got word of the situation that he convinced the airline to send another plane, which made the round trip the same day. The other half of our group arrived in Kunming not too much later than the first half.

I was a bit weary at the banquet; the trauma of our trip back from Simao had finally taken its toll. I was seated next to one of the Yunnan Province Communist officials, who looked sternly officious in his Mao suit. He knew a few words of English but we spoke little. He primarily sat very stiffly, occasionally looking at me out of the corner of his eye, especially as I was chasing chicken wings around my plate (as well as on the adjacent tablecloth), trying unsuccessfully to get meat off them with my chopsticks. I had discovered that wings are considered special by the Chinese, and they were among the first courses served (and deftly eaten by experienced chopstick users) at several banquets I attended. There were lots of toasts at the Kunming banquet, but in-between the Communist party official would look straight ahead and ignore me. Of course, there *was* a major language barrier. However, he did know the words to "Happy Birthday to *You*," which we sang in celebration of the institute's fiftieth anniversary.

The next morning I flew to Hong Kong on China Airlines—an international flight with accoutrements much better than the domestic flight from Shanghai to Kunming. All went well until our approach to the Hong Kong (Kaitak) airport. At that time, landing there was a bit dramatic—best not to watch from your window as you skimmed over the rooftops of Kowloon onto a single runway projecting into the harbor on reclaimed land. Our pilot attempted to land and then pulled up at almost a ninety-degree angle because the plane was going to overshoot the landing strip. We circled and tried three times before we made a very bumpy landing—confirming again my feeling that the Chinese were still just "getting the hang" of handling mechanisms of transport.

I was met by the Lee family and spent the evening with them; they were full of questions again about my adventures in China. I left the next day on Hong Kong's Cathay Pacific through-flight to Vancouver, feeling much safer in a United Kingdom pilot's hands, but, nonetheless, having thoroughly enjoyed my Chinese sojourn.

EMERITUS BUT NOT RETIRED

1990-1996

The early 1990s were a build up to change in my faculty status—to professor emeritus in 1994. Before that event, I still had my active group of graduate students completing their doctoral research, and I couldn't seem to let go of active participation in professional societies that I had led for a few years. I continued my push for Ecological Society of America's global activities by serving as the chair of their committee on ecologists in developing countries, and I participated in a symposium on the history of ecology at the ESA annual meeting in Snowbird, Utah. Former presidents of ESA had been encouraged to attend, which made for quite an historic event. After three years on the International Society of Chemical Ecology Council following my presidency, I continued as a member of the committee on future meetings, and also began my long tenure as an associate editor of *Biochemical Systematics and Ecology*. I was elected in 1990 as vice president and then in 1992 as the second woman to be president of the Society for Economic Botany, extending my reach into a leadership position in the world of ethnobotany.

Preparing to become associate editor of Biochemical Systematics and Ecology

I was invited to be the Distinguished Nieuwland Lecturer at Notre Dame University in 1991, and was requested to give three lectures. I chose: "The Path of Women Ecologists: Progress from the Nineteenth Century to Present," "From Amber to Chemical Ecology in the Tropics," and "Amazonian Rain Forests: Past, Present, and Future." Although my audiences expressed interest in all of the topics, the lecture on women provoked some of the most intense discussions—centering on the problems of attracting and hiring women faculty at this traditional, Catholic university as well as the issues of accommodating highly trained spouses. Although at that time and place the matter of accommodation usually was for the spouse of a male faculty member seeking employment, university officials admitted to the possibility of the reverse situation when hiring women faculty.

Also during my time on the Notre Dame campus, I spent time in enthusiastic discussions with Robert McIntosh, who had written extensively on the conceptual history of ecology and had previously spent a week at UCSC assisting me with my graduate course on that topic. He had been hoping that we might collaborate on publishing the timelines that the UCSC grad students had put together for the development of concepts in different subfields of ecology. We all had shared a sense of excitement in our increase in understanding that such projects produced.

With Robert McIntosh at Notre Dame University

During the summer of 1993, I was still fully occupied with the activities of both SEB and ISCE. I took over the presidency of SEB from Michael Balik at the annual meeting at the Fairchild Tropical Gardens in Miami,

Florida, in June and organized a symposium for the ISCE meeting in Tampa, Florida, which took place in August. Focusing the symposium on the largest group of secondary chemicals (terpenes) and what they do for the plants that produce them was such a different but successful approach for an ISCE symposium that it was published as a separate volume of the *Journal of Chemical Ecology* in 1994. My introductory paper, "Higher Plant Terpenoids: A Phytocentric Overview of Their Ecological Roles," created sufficient interest to become a ten-year citation classic and the third most-cited paper in the journal. The meeting also celebrated the ten-year history of ISCE, which eight of the former presidents attended.

EMERITUS STATUS

In the 1993-1994 academic year UC offered an incentive retirement package designed to move the highest-paid faculty onto the university's pension funds, thus freeing more of the system's regular funds for other faculty. Although I had not been thinking about retirement, I was 68 and the incentive offer was financially too good to pass up. I did not know how retirement would affect my life style, but it seemed to offer the possibility of continuing pursuits that I thought important without having to carry out activities I found less rewarding. So I accepted this official retirement package, taking the title of professor emeritus, but I did not accept retired inactivity. Ten graduate students had graduated between 1990 and 1993 but I still had four students with dissertation research in progress. Thus without question I was allowed to maintain my lab and office. In addition to my presidency of the UCSC chapter of Sigma Xi—the national scientific research society—I also continued to serve on various UCSC Academic

Assuming presidency of the Society for Economic Botany from Michael Balik

Senate committees. These included education abroad, which maintained my persistent thread of interest in furthering global education, and as the chair of the faculty research lecture committee, which had the task of selecting the annual lecturer. I considered it a privilege to continue to participate in university activities on a campus that I had helped develop since essentially its inception.

During this early emeritus period, my alma mater had not forgotten me. Having honored me in 1979 with its Distinguished Alumni Award, in 1994 the University of Tulsa invited me to become a member of the Board of Visitors of the College of Arts and Sciences, and the following year to give the keynote address at the Phi Beta Kappa inauguration of new members. My address, "Global Vision: A Challenge for the 21st Century," was a plea for finding ways to tie the world's peoples together, a topic that had long been very much on my mind. I was pushing the importance of the World Wide Web in helping with global communication—and indicating the rapidity of its development, which then only spanned 81 countries. It is hard to imagine that this was only a little over twenty five years ago!

Two years later I continued this theme of a global vision for the future as one of the keynote speakers at a triennial meeting of the Society of Women Geographers in Washington, DC. In many ways what I presented was already a perspective of a confirmed group of believers—as women who had exciting adventures in many parts of the world. They were in solid agreement with how our global perspectives were changing with rapidly developing technology. Nonetheless, it was a theme I was expressing in whatever arena it seemed appropriate.

Hernando Garcia-Barriga just after receiving the Richard E. Schultes Award

SEB MEETING IN MEXICO

In late June of 1994, as president of the Society for Economic Botany, in Mexico City I presided over the first annual meeting of SEB to be held in a foreign country. Several prominent members were apprehensive about having an international meeting, fearing it might not be successful. But the event was a great success, due in large part to the expert planning of the local SEB committee. The primary hosts were Jardin Botanico and Facultad de Química of UNAM, with collaboration of other Mexican institutions. All scientific sessions were held in the magnificent colonial-period Antigua Palacio de Míneria. The meeting was characterized by joint participation of US, Mexican, and Central American ethnobotanists, thus achieving the desired kind of interaction for an international meeting. Many participants enjoyed the field trips to a large regional market and to sites where the *chinampa* agricultural system was introduced, as well as to agricultural teaching and research centers. During this meeting I visited my former student Francisco Espinosa-Garcia, now a professor and researcher in the Instituto de Ecología of UNAM, and his students. I also spent time with a longtime friend and colleague in ISCE, Ana Luisa Anaya, who is a researcher in the Instituto de Ecología Functional, professor of postgraduate programs in Ciencias Biológicos in UNAM, and later author of the book *Ecología Química.*

Periodically, the president of SEB has the privilege of making an award in honor of a specific occasion. Because the first international meeting was being held in Mexico, I appointed a committee to advise me as to whom I should honor. I assumed that a Mexican would be chosen, but the committee decided that the awardee should be considered in terms of Mesoamerica. Since the late Efraim Hernandez- Xolocotzi had been honored as Distinguished Economic Botanist by SEB, the committee unanimously suggested that this President's Award should honor the other Mesoamerican giant—Jorge Léon-Argüedes from Costa Rica. I was happy with this selection as I had admired his work during my OTS days in Costa Rica. Moreover, I was delighted to hear that the Colombian Hernando Garcia-Barriga had been selected to receive the Richard Evans Schultes Award, given by the Healing Forest Conservancy. Hernando had helped introduce me to Latin American plants in my 1953 trip to Colombia and now, 41 years later, as president of SEB, I had the opportunity to present an award to him!

As a result of the resounding success of the first international meeting of SEB, the society decided to expand its international activity. The society's first international chapter, in the United Kingdom, was flourishing and was already planning to host the 1998 annual meeting in London. Furthermore, Ghillean Prance was president of SEB that year as well as Director of the Royal Botanic Gardens. The meeting was held jointly with the International Society of Ethnopharmacology at Imperial College of London University, and the topic "Plants for Food and Medicine" was selected to bridge the two societies. This meeting sealed the idea of international meetings for SEB, which would range from Denmark to Thailand (as of now), and which increased its worldwide membership. (Furthermore, in a 2006 survey, the vision most consistently expressed by members was for SEB to become "truly global," with greater numbers of members and more meetings outside of

With Kaplans at Royal Botanic Gardens at SEB
meeting in London; she was SEB secretary and
he was editor of Economic Botany *when I was president*

North America to encourage collaborative partnerships. I greatly appreciated this turn in perception of SEB becoming internationally oriented.)

VARIOUS PLENARY ADDRESSES
From 1994 to 1996, I gave plenary lectures at meetings of geochemists, isoprenoid chemists, and chemical ecologists. The diversity of perspectives among those groups was intriguing. During the summer of 1994, following the SEB Mexico meeting, I gave the opening address in a symposium on "Amber, Resinite, and Fossil Resins" in Washington, DC, at meetings of the American Chemical Society's Division of Geochemistry. This symposium was cosponsored by Ken Anderson, a geochemist doing groundbreaking

work on the botanical origin of amber using pyrolysis gas chromatography/ mass spectrometry, a technological advance that enabled identification of the structures of amber's major polymers. Anderson was interested in learning more about the biology of resin-producing plants, which distinguished him from most geochemists. He asked me to open the symposium with an address on the biology of amber-producing trees, hoping I could encourage other geochemists to increase their understanding about the plants whose fossil products they were analyzing. To give some focus to such a broad topic, I used case studies of *Hymenaea* and *Agathis*, the latter being the most prominent source of coniferous amber. It was great fun to get back to thinking in depth about amber—as my focus during recent years had been toward chemical ecology of the living trees. Papers from the symposium were published in a book as part of the *American Chemical Society Symposium Series*, which has become widely used by amber researchers with a variety of perspectives.

After the symposium, Anderson and I collaborated on a paper with an archaeologist, Ishimada Shimada, in suggesting that *Hymenaea* was the source of amber found in tombs in northern Peru. Later I published work with Israeli geochemists in which we used *Hymenaea* resin as a model system for study of stable isotypes in resins. Continuing this thread of collaborating with archaeologists and geochemists on fossil resin research, and utilizing samples and information I had derived from modern *Hymenaea* resin over many years has added a rewarding freshness to my thinking and expansion of my horizons.

The following year (1995) I shifted to giving a plenary address to a different group of chemists at the European Isoprenoid Congress in Prague, Czech Republic. This invitation was an outgrowth of my phytochemical approach to terpenoids in organizing an ISCE symposium in Florida in 1993. I almost had to abort this trip, as in the late spring I was diagnosed with early-stage uterine cancer. I was told that if I had immediate surgery, I could still make the European trip. Although I recovered rapidly following the surgery, the trip did take a physical toll.

En route to Prague, I stopped to consult with Professor Marianne Popp at the Plant Physiological Institute at the University of Vienna about our joint project on *Hymenaea*. I became acquainted with her during 1981 in Australia, and had visited her previously at the University of Münster, Germany, where we had started collaborating on a paper about leaf cyclitols (chemicals that regulate water retention in plant tissue) in *Hymenaea* from a phylogenetic perspective. She had been amazingly successful in the overwhelmingly male Austrian university world—even later becoming a dean at University of Vienna. Besides discussing our project and getting to know Marianne's research group, since I was still recuperating from surgery, I was encouraged to enjoy some of the many Viennese pleasures such as coffeehouses, a Mozart concert at the State Opera House, and the Lipizzaner stallions. On a short round trip cruise from Vienna to Budapest, Hungary, I dolefully found the "beautiful blue Danube" less than so, with much evidence of pollution along this part of the river at least.

In Prague, my address was the first given by a plant chemical ecologist to the European Isoprenoid Congress, which is constituted primarily of natural product chemists. Although these chemists analyze isoprenoids derived from plants,

Dinner in lab with research group of Marianne Popp (in center)

they had given little thought to the ecological roles the chemicals play for the survival of the plant. The organizer of the conference, Jurj Harmantha, thought that my previously presented and now published overview of the ecological role of higher plant terpenoids would be a good way to introduce these chemists to a plant-oriented perspective. Following my presentation, many of them did tell me that my talk had opened their eyes. Although their focus had been on use of these chemicals for the benefit of humans, it seems strange to me that they could extract chemicals from plants without having thought seriously about their possible value for the plant. Some of their perspective may also still derive from a traditional view of many biochemists, that isoprenoids (terpenoids)—other than the few known to be physiologically essential—were simply plant waste products. I never cease to be amazed by how persistent this view of plant secondary chemicals is, especially among chemists.

The conference was held in a convention center built by the Soviets. A large cafeteria for meals was available (with lots of characteristic Czech sausages, dumplings, and cabbage) but the small rooms where we slept were truly spartan. I had picked up a cold, including a very sore throat in Vienna. It got worse in Prague and a doctor there prescribed the usual rest and liquids—which meant continued isolation in my bare room. I thus missed some of the tours of Prague and its surroundings organized for the conference attendees. However, near the end of the conference my former Brazilian grad student, José Carlos Nascimento, who was in Cordoba, Spain on sabbatical leave from EMBRAPA, and his wife came to visit me. Together we enjoyed much of this beautiful city with its 600 years of striking architecture—historic castles, bridges, and so much more.

A plenary address at an international conference on *Ecología Química* in the fall of 1996 took me back to Mexico, but this time to Oaxtepec. Ana Luisa Anaya was the primary conference organizer, but my former student, Francisco Espinosa, assisted her. The conference coincided with the November 1 Mexican celebration of *Dia de Los Muertos* (Day of the Dead), which is a mixture of Old World Roman Catholic and Mexican indigenous rites. It is a cultural event marked throughout Mexico, and many people make offerings of food such as fruit and bread to departed relatives around a little altar in their homes, as I witnessed in the home of Ana Luisa Anaya, with whom I stayed in Mexico City before the conference. The Day of the Dead, however, is most assiduously observed in heavily indigenous regions, such as the beautiful colonial town of Pátzcuaro, in Michoacán. Because Francisco Espinosa now lived in Morelia, Michoacán, he took me to see the celebrations at Tzintzuntzan, the ancient capital of the Parépecha Kingdom near Pátzcauro, where some people spend the night in cemeteries with memorials of *cempasuchitl* (marigold) flowers along with other offerings. My friends and colleagues provided me with another Mexican cultural opportunity—and such an antecedent to the conference.

With Ana Luisa Anaya in Mexico City

My lecture, "Contributions of Long-Term Studies to Theory of Chemical Defense: Perspectives from Resin-Producing Trees from Temperate and Tropical Zones," which was translated into Spanish for publication, opened the conference. It was a partial synthesis of my pioneer studies of the tropical angiosperm tree genera *Hymenaea* and *Copaifera* in comparison with other studies of the widespread and economically important temperate-zone conifer *Pinus ponderosa*. I discussed a question I had long been pondering—why does the greatest *diversity* of tree taxa producing copious amounts of resin occur in the moist tropics? I had hypothesized that conditions favoring active photosynthesis throughout the year provide abundant carbon for growth and that, furthermore, there was low utilization of carbon in the slow-growing trees in mature forests on the low-nutrient soils typical of resin-producing trees, thus making carbon available for terpene defense compounds. David Lincoln, a former grad student, had shown experimentally that carbon availability alone does not account for increased terpene synthesis—that copious production is influenced by defensive pressures. Of course, the selective pressure exerted by the relentless attack of a diversity of insects, mammals, and pathogenic fungi is exceptionally high in the moist tropics, which supported my hypotheses regarding the evolution of the defensive role of tree resins that have been preserved as amber. My corollary to this hypothesis was that compositional variation evolved under these biotic selection pressures because of the variety of dependent organisms (which demanded that compositional variation was genetically controlled and related to the fitness of the tree). These implications were what we had laboriously been working to demonstrate for *Hymenaea* and *Copaifera*.

I compared the corollary of terpene compositional variation evolving under biotic selection in our topical legumes with the long-term studies of biotic selection in the temperate zone ponderosa pine. The chemical ecology of insect attack on numerous conifers had been studied in some detail (later Cates, in a summary of many of these studies, recognized my ideas regarding the importance of compositional variation in defense). However, population ecologist, Yan Linhart, with grad students and associates at the University of Colorado, had approached studies of ponderosa pine from both ecological and evolutionary perspectives. They had been able to do research on selection of monoterpene variation by different organisms representing a broad spectrum of behavior (bark beetles, Abert's squirrels, dwarf mistletoe, and more in Colorado). In addition to their insightful results, these studies pointed out the great value of working on a tree in which various aspects (including secondary chemistry) have been analyzed, and facilities to do such work have long been available and funded.

I also designed my presentation to initiate discussion of model systems and their value in chemical ecology compared with those used in genetics and molecular studies, such as *E. coli*, *C. elegans*, and *Arabidopsis*. An increasing question in ecology is whether focusing research on a single organism or group of organisms can be justified when whole ecosystems that are not yet understood are being modified and even destroyed. I wanted to justify some model systems in plant chemical ecology, where *depth* of information is needed to answer fundamental questions. A major problem in chemical ecology is the complexity of the interactions—requiring in-depth information not only about the interacting organisms but also about the chemicals and their variations, which mediate the interactions. Each new system requires considerable natural history background study before experiments can be designed to address the most interesting questions. Don't we at least need to know a few systems in depth, I queried? I had compared ponderosa pine with *Hymenaea* and *Copaifera* to show how valuable years of basic and applied study in established reserves were for an economically important pine compared to a more frustrating situation for chemical ecological analysis of these tropical genera. But what is the best way to choose these model systems and, importantly, get them financed for study? Do they necessarily have to be of economic value, as was true with ponderosa pine? My questions went unanswered; I felt, with disappointment, that they were not even adequately discussed. Yet I knew they were important to all the researchers present—just that they couldn't seem to address the issues at this point in time for essentially this still emerging field.

Nonetheless, this symposium served in many ways as a Mexican Gordon Research Conference—that is, the coming together of a small group of leaders in chemical ecology for fruitful interaction covering a wide range of topics in a place away from distractions. Moreover, it resulted in a book in Spanish, *Relaciones Químicos entre Organismos: Aspectos Básicos y Perspectivas de su Aplicación*. The organizers hoped to stimulate interest in chemical ecology amongst Spanish-speaking researchers who might not read specialized chemical ecology journals in English.

Considering the range of my interesting activities, continuing research in my lab with several graduate students completing their degrees, along with travel, culminating with the series of plenary addresses, I decided that emeritus status was a blessing—with loss of some burdensome duties but with ever continuing opportunities to still be useful.

RETURN TO THE
NORTHERN ENVIRONS

1994-1997; 1971-1989

Despite my research being focused in the tropics since the mid-1960s, threads representing the northern boreal forests and their bordering arctic and alpine tundra—which were spun during my graduate student days in Minnesota and Colorado, a trip to Alaska, and later days in New England—have remained strong and visible in the tapestry of my life. The history of this vegetation is closely interwoven with glacial activity, and my interest in that topic also has varied threads, woven from different experiences during numerous journeys over the years. I mention only a few, most of which also were associated with memorable train trips.

BOREAL FOREST IN CANADA

During the summer of 1994, I accepted with alacrity an invitation from a relative, who lives in Toronto, to visit Ontario's Algonquin Provincial Park. The park is located in typical Canadian boreal forest replete with glacial lakes dotted with lovely islands—a scene I remembered with great pleasure from my transect through such forests en route along the Alaska Highway in 1956. Having just had its one-hundredth anniversary, the park was advertised as a "reasonable facsimile of the wilderness that once covered Ontario."

I immediately noted numerous sugar maples (Ac*er saccharum*) amid the balsam fir (*Abies balsamea*) and other conifers, and was told the maples' abundance is dramatically displayed in the fall. Algonquin Park is where Ontarians come to view spectacular fall colors, highlighted by the brilliantly red maples. We stayed on one of the park's many islands in an artist's picturesque cabin with no electricity or piped-in water and accessible only by canoe. At night we could hear the wild call of the loons—in this case, real ones. Sharing the solitude and beauty of this lovely island for a few days was a special experience. We did not see any of the park's noted bear population, only moose wandering along the edge of lakes.

Canoeing amid islands of conifers in Algonquin Park

(In 2008, Ontario's premier scored another extraordinary environmental victory when he announced that 55 million acres, half of the province's boreal forest, will be off limits to development and industrial use The scale of this decision is staggering; it commits Ontario to setting aside lands more than twice the size of Pennsylvania as parks or wildlife refuges as part of a plan to help thwart climate change. Canada's boreal forest is the world's largest and mostly intact forest ecosystem. The decision not only helps ensure that carbon currently stored there stays put, but also protects the habitat of abundant wildlife. Moreover, the protection of large unfragmented blocks of habitat may help the survival of species that are forced to move north to adapt to warming conditions.)

From Algonquin Park, we drove around the edge of Georgian Bay to Kilarney Provincial Park, known for its quartzite hills. The landscape is so charming that it has lured artists to the area since the 1920s, including the Canadian Group of Seven. These artists are known for their paintings of landscapes, based on love of land they thought to be typically Canadian. Initially they focused on the land of northern Ontario; later they expanded their vision to include areas around Lake Superior. The beauty of the Kilarney area so impressed these artists that they were instrumental in having a forest preserve created, which ultimately became Kilarney Provincial Park in 1964.

When I returned to Canada five years later, I was again thinking about the paintings of the Group of Seven. This 1999 trip was expressly to see the spectacular fall coloration, especially of those maples in Algonquin Park, and also in Algoma. In Sault Saint Marie, Ontario, which is located between Lake Superior and Lake Huron, we boarded the Algoma Central Railroad for another special train ride, this time to see fall color in the famous Agawa Canyon. The train snaked its way along for 114 miles, passing numerous lakes and rivers with continuous views of red maple, yellow poplar, and bronze oaks. For several years the Group of Seven had spent a month in the Algoma area in autumn—painting the spectacular landscapes with the blazing reds of the maples and ghostly effects of early snow. They lived in an old converted boxcar; the freight train would pick them up periodically and deposit them at different sites along the tracks. Having now seen several of the areas that they painted in both summer and fall, I could understand their passion for Canadian landscapes. On these various trips, I continued to weave new strands into my long thread of interest in art—strands often related to natural landscapes in different parts of the world.

SOUTHEAST COASTAL ALASKA AND GLACIER BAY

I decided in 1997 that I should not put off any longer seeing Glacier Bay, a place I had heard so much about as W.S. Cooper's student. An Alaskan chemical ecologist colleague had told me Cruise West offered small-vessel excursions different from large cruise ships, which provided an easy way to get to Glacier Bay in a short time, see other glacial sights, and take in Gold Rush history as well. That sounded right from my perspective, so I booked a cruise on the eighty-passenger *Spirit of Alaska* for Alaska's Inside Passage.

We passengers met the vessel in Ketchikan—it looked like a fishing boat docked beside the huge cruise ships. While waiting for our ship's passengers to assemble, I took a hydroplane flight over Misty Fjords National Monument and viewed vast areas of magnificent mixed conifer forest clothing spectacular, glacially created U-shaped valleys and bordering the many fjords and lakes.

The next day, the *Spirit of Alaska* negotiated narrow inlets around the northern tip of Prince of Wales Island. The ship had a front ramp from which passengers could disembark to explore the forest, and I used the opportunity to sort out the conifer species I had seen from the air the day before. Late that afternoon, back on board the ship, passengers were summoned for a safety drill, which we were told would simulate a disaster. As we were struggling into our life jackets, there was a terrible bumping and scraping below the ship and then the bow tipped upward. The alarm signals began clanging, and we all were told to congregate in the dining room, which helped balance the tipping ship. "What a dramatic simulation," we thought!

Disembarking Spirit of Alaska to explore forests

We had gone aground on a shoal in the northwest corner of Prince of Wales Island. Two Coast Guard cutters arrived, and a Coast Guard officer was deposited dramatically on board from a helicopter. He officiously entered the dining room to inform us that we now were safely in the hands of the Coast Guard. The Coast Guard planned to have the cutters pull the ship off the shoal, but decided first to see if high tide would float us free, because the captain thought that the exceptionally low tides that year were responsible for the grounding. Meanwhile passengers were not allowed to leave the dining room. We were offered free drinks to help pass the time—especially since the Coast Guard wanted us to stay in our uncomfortable life jackets until the ship was freed. Divers under the ship were unable to determine if the hull had been seriously damaged. We ate a picnic-style dinner, and the free alcohol produced a jovial group; the incident resulted in a special camaraderie among the passengers that might not have developed otherwise. The captain was right; when the tide came in, the ship floated free, but the Coast Guard insisted on having one of their cutters escort us out of narrow waters to the frontier town of Wrangell. Here the next day, it was confirmed that the ship had not been seriously damaged, so we were able to proceed with the remainder of the trip.

Wrangell was a jumping off point in the late 1800s for three gold rushes—each of which used the Stikine River for four hundred miles of transport through the coast ranges that separate southeast Alaska from British Columbia. I took a jet boat across the large Stikine Delta to the Shakes Glacier along the river. For the first time I saw chunks of a glacier front calving into the river—leading to the formation of small icebergs.

Because of its shallow draft, the *Spirit of Alaska* could make its way through winding, narrow passages, where we could closely view the forest edge on both sides of the ship, into Sitka, on Baranof Island. Founded in 1804, Sitka is the oldest nonnative settlement in southeast Alaska, and a treasure trove of Tlingit, Russian, and American history as well as the site of the Alaska Raptor Rehabilitation Center. Leaving Sitka, we entered Tracy Arm, a forested fjord with spectacular waterfalls cascading down its steep walls. The fjord was headed by two active tidewater glaciers, the actual builders of this topography. Good-sized icebergs that had calved from the glaciers choked the fjord, which made for exciting passage as we wended our way through them. Some were populated by seals who had hauled out on the ice to sun themselves.

We sailed in fairly open waters into Lynn Canal to Skagway, the major jumping-off point for various routes over mountain passes to the Klondike gold fields. During the "Days of '98," steamships arrived daily with prospectors who were part of the largest gold rush the world has ever known. Some prospectors chose to go over the very steep Chilkoot Pass and had to make many trips to carry the tons of supplies themselves to the summit. Others elected to use pack horses along the less-steep route over White Pass, but inexperienced packers overburdened their horses and thousands of animals died in a place that came to be called Dead Horse Gulch. In 1898 two men decided to do the impossible and build a narrow-gauge railroad.

The building of the White Pass and Yukon Railroad is among only twenty engineering feats in the world to be declared an International Historic Civil Engineering Landmark. The road was blasted through the coastal mountains in twenty-six months. Besides, the climb to White Pass is one of the steepest railroad grades in North America. From tidewater at Skagway, it climbs 2,865 feet in the first twenty miles—with grades up to 3.9 percent and cliff-hanging turns of 16 degrees. Furthermore, construction was done through winters with temperatures of minus 65 degrees Fahrenheit and drifts of snow up to thirty-five feet! I was delighted to be a passenger on this railroad on a pleasant summer day.

White Pass and Yukon Railroad, taken from
window of train as we approached White Pass

No matter how the Klondikers got over the passes, they still had six hundred miles to go, often in crudely made boats, across lakes and up the Klondike River to get to the gold fields. My ride on this railroad not only added to my long thread of interesting train trips, but also resonated with earlier travel because I had seen, on my 1956 trip along the Alaska Highway, the area to which the Klondikers were headed. At that time, I had not realized the inconceivable difficulties prospectors faced in getting to the region around Dawson City. As I sat on the train, I appreciated not only the engineering accomplishment but also the courage of those who constructed the railroad and the hard times they had suffered—not to mention the travails of the Klondikers themselves. The thought of riches that gold might bring was an amazing motivator that tested endurance. How many actually survived and achieved great wealth? All of this went through my mind while riding this train.

The *Spirit of Alaska* finally arrived at Glacier Bay, my primary destination on this trip. Though I had glimpsed tundra succession in front of the Muldrow Glacier at the foot of Mount McKinley in 1956, I felt I had grown up professionally, so to speak (almost half a century earlier!), hearing Cooper and Lawrence talk about forest succession at the front of the tidal glaciers of Glacier Bay.

Cooper's research on glacial succession began when he examined vegetation on the deglaciated terrain near Mount Robson, British Columbia, which stimulated him to explore sites in Alaska where glacial retreat and development of vegetation from bare ground to forest would be proceeding rapidly enough to follow the whole process in a single lifetime. He found that possibility at Glacier Bay and in 1916 made his first scientific expedition there to study the earliest, pioneer stages of mosses and *Dryas drummondii,* which formed extensive, dominant mats shortly after the moraine had been exposed. *Dryas* has nitrogen-fixing root nodules and Cooper found that it is joined, about thirty-five years later, by another nitrogen-fixing plant alder (*Alnus*) that occurs amid patches of several species of willow. Sitka spruce (*Picea sitchensis)* saplings begin to come through a thicket of alder at around eighty years; between 115 and 200 years, a spruce forest forms and later two hemlock species (*Tsuga heterophylla* and *T. mertensiana*) come in with an understory of *Vaccinium* shrubs. Cooper also realized the importance of working out the history of past glaciations in order to establish the rates of development of the different successional stages.

During my visit, I was astounded by the rapid rate of glacial recession shown on maps at park headquarters. A little over two hundred years ago (1794), the explorer George Vancouver found Glacier Bay filled with ice more than 4,000 feet thick and twenty miles wide—and it extended more than a hundred miles inland to the Saint Elias Mountain Range. But in 1879 John Muir found the ice had already retreated forty-eight miles up the bay. By 1916, when Cooper arrived, the Grand Pacific Glacier was sixty-five miles from Glacier Bay's mouth. This rapidity of glacial retreat was still considered unique in 1997. Its documentation has been considered important in understanding climate change, and the relative rapidity of change in primary plant succession makes it an exciting area for continued ecological study. With the degree of global warming recognized today, however, the rapidity of glacial retreat at Glacier Bay is no longer quite so unusual.

The Glacier Bay successional sequence also has provided a rare opportunity to study, with some degree of precision, the rate of development of soil properties. Robert Crocker, a prominent Australian soils scientist, came to the University of Minnesota to discuss soil development at Glacier Bay with Cooper. I first met Crocker at Minnesota when he joined a Glacier Bay expedition in 1952; later we interacted again when he came to UC Berkeley. During 1955 he collaborated with Jack Major at UC Davis to produce an elegant study of the soils in the Glacier Bay succession. Among the various relationships between development of vegetation and genesis of soils at Glacier Bay, Crocker and Major found the rate of accumulation of nitrogen to be the most important. Although the *Dryas* mat accumulates considerable quantities of nitrogen, it does so less effectively than the alder thicket as it forms a closed canopy. Subsequently, nitrogen is lost from the forest floor with the loss of alder and the emergence of spruce forest.

As a result of his research at Glacier Bay from 1921 to 1936, Cooper recognized that the area should be preserved. In 1922 the Ecological Society of America selected Cooper to chair a committee to explore the possibility of making Glacier Bay either a national monument or a park based on its scenic and scientific merits. Although Congress was skeptical, Cooper's ESA campaign was so vigorous that President Calvin Coolidge declared Glacier Bay a National Monument in 1925, under the American Antiquities Act—but with an area much smaller than that which had been recommended. In 1980, President Jimmy Carter made it a National Park with an enlarged area. In 1986, Glacier Bay became a Biosphere Reserve, and in 1992 a World Heritage Site.

In 1980, the US Board on Geographic Names, in recognition of Cooper's research and efforts to preserve the area, gave the name *Mount Cooper* to the mountain located on the side of Johns Hopkins Inlet in Glacier Bay. As the *Spirit of Alaska* went into John Hopkins Inlet I viewed Mount Cooper, taking me back in memory to the Minnesota classroom where Cooper had shown us so many glorious color slides of Glacier Bay.

FJORDS OF NORWAY

The trip in 1989 to the ISCE meeting at the Institutionem fur Kemist Ekologi in the western Swedish town of Göteborg provided me an additional opportunity to explore spectacular evidence of past glaciation in some of Norway's fjords. En route to this meeting I stopped in Germany to visit Marianne Popp, who was a professor at the University of Münster at that time. With my usual enthusiasm for train travel, I planned to take the train from Münster to Göteborg to see the countryside in a way not possible when flying. I would have to change trains in Hamburg; most of the trip from Hamburg to Copenhagen would be at night, but afterward I would see western coastal landscape of Sweden. Friends in Münster questioned the wisdom of this plan because of recent reports of robbery on night trains, but I decided to do it anyway.

Well-tended farms and occasional castles characterized the lovely German countryside between Münster and Hamburg. In the Hamburg *bahnhof* (railroad station), I turned my luggage over to a service for securing luggage. Later as I was standing in line to retrieve my luggage for the night train, a thief grabbed my purse. I was devastated; now what would I do, with neither identification nor money? The *bahnhof* police were sympathetic, suggesting that the American Consulate could help, but it was Sunday and it would not be open until the following morning.

While I was giving my deposition, a couple of young Americans, waiting to report having lost a watch on the train from Berlin, overheard me saying I was a professor at UCSC. They interrupted, saying they were UC San Diego students; they offered to use their credit card to pay for a night in a hotel and accompanied me to one nearby. The next day, the consulate relatively quickly took care of a new temporary passport and American Express had all of my travel arrangements under control by mid-afternoon—I lacked for nothing except 300 Swedish krona and about 50 American dollars! I then caught the evening train I had missed the night before. What good fortune (in an unfortunate situation) that a couple of UC students would go out of their way to help a UC professor—even from another campus! It helped take away the bitter taste from the only unhappy train trip I had ever taken.

Immediately following the ISCE meeting I spent several days with the daughter of Al Cunningham, one of my early graduate students. Carole had met her Swedish husband while they were both students in chemistry at UC Berkeley. They lived in Floda, a Göteborg suburb, and it was fun to stay in the home of a Swedish and American couple. She was finishing her chemistry degree at the University of Göteborg—and would go on later to get a medical degree while raising two children. Although her husband was not too helpful with household chores, she benefited from the generally liberal Swedish attitude toward support of educating and promoting professional women.

The train from Göteborg to Oslo took me through the Swedish coastal boreal forests of spruce and fir with numerous birch. From Oslo we bused to Stryn, crossing rich farming lands through Lillehammer (the former Winter Olympics site), and traversing mountain areas where tundra plants were still in flower. From the bus window I could see mats of moss campion, tufts of cotton grass, abundant gentians, and soldanelles along snowy patches. How I wanted to stop to look at them. I knew I would be seeing boreal forest along the walls of the fjords, but this trip showed me that the mountain environment with its tundra was more important in Norway than in Sweden and Finland. This was my first realization that almost 70 percent of Norway is mountainous—with most of it above treeline.

In Stryn we picked up a small former fishing boat, *Nordbrisa*, and proceeded along the Nord Fjord to Maloy. The weather was cloudy and cold, but without rain; in some ways, the low-hanging clouds made the steep-walled, narrow fjords—with their thundering waterfalls and surrounding snow-topped mountains—appear even more dramatic than in bright sun. From the westernmost town of Floro, we sailed in sheltered waters through narrow sounds, between islands and skerries, skirting mouths of several fjords past small picturesque villages to the northern shore of the huge Sogue Fjord, the "King of Fjords". From this trip it was easy to grasp that, except for Iceland, Norway is the least populated country in the world.

We ended our cruise in a small branching fjord at Flam. From here I had another spectacular train trip on the famous Flam Railway, which climbed out of a beautiful, very steep, narrow valley, taking many hairpin curves and going through twenty tunnels to reach Myrdal at 3,000 feet. The railroad grade is so steep that the train has five sets of brakes, but the mountain views here are considered some of the most spectacular in Norway. From Myrdal en route back to Oslo, we had magnificent vistas across the Hardangen Mountain Plateau down into the smaller areas of forests and farmlands of eastern Norway.

Shortly after my return home from this trip, I received my large leather travel purse in the mail from the police at the Hamburg *bahnhof*. It had been found in the bushes outside the station and contained my wallet with credit cards, traveler's checks, passport—everything except the money. The police had written a little note saying they were sending it to me with their apologies that this untoward event had occurred in Hamburg.

TAIGA AND TUNDRA OF FINLAND

I saw European boreal forest as it reached arctic tundra for the first time a number of years before. Although it goes back to 1971, numerous aspects of it are especially memorable. I had been visiting G. Larsson, the preeminent Baltic amber researcher in Copenhagen, Denmark and took a hydrofoil from Copenhagen to Malmo, Sweden to visit another amber researcher. From there I took a train that went northeastward to Stockholm. I was impressed with how similar the gently rolling, glacial landscape was to that of southern Minnesota, which I had gotten to know as a graduate student. I now could imagine how Swedish farm immigrants might have felt very much at home in that part of Minnesota.

I stayed briefly in stately Stockholm; my main goal was to visit nearby Uppsala to photograph the home of the legendary botanist Linnaeus, who had established the binomial system of nomenclature. The shutter on my Nikon camera was not functioning properly, so I needed to get it fixed before taking the train to Uppsala. I went from one camera shop to another, but no one knew how to repair this Japanese camera! In despair, at the last store, I groaned that I was a professor of botany at the University of California who wanted to take pictures of Linnaeus' home and gardens to use in a class. The clerk said, "Oh, wait a minute, let me talk to the manager." A dignified gentleman arrived and said, "Of course, we must get a botany professor to Uppsala with her camera in good condition." I appreciated such respect for a botany professor.

The manager thought that the Nikon repair center on the outskirts of Stockholm could take care of the problem. When I told him I was taking the train to Uppsala the next day and would be leaving the same evening on the overnight ship to Turku, Finland, the manager flew into immediate action, calling the Nikon center to make an early-morning appointment. The next day he took me there by car, and emphasized to the service personnel the urgency of my taking the noon train to Uppsala. We just made the departure of the train, with my camera now working properly. The camera store manager sent me off with a hearty farewell, saying he was so happy for American students to learn more about the famous Swedish botanist. (Today it would be easy to obtain the kind of photos I sought from the Internet, but I also think about the interesting experiences I would have missed in Sweden if I had obtained them in this manner.)

Because it was mid-September, the color of the maple, aspen, and birch leaves was glorious on the train ride to Uppsala; they also lighted up the famous gardens—now in a dormant state—at the home of Linnaeus. The train returned me to Stockholm just in time to board the ferry to Turku. Swedes often take this ferry for an all-night party, with a magnificent smorgasbord of meats, cheeses, fish, seafood, breads with different spreads, and dessert delicacies continually being replenished—until another elegant spread is laid out for breakfast before landing in Finland.

I was met in Turku, Finland's oldest city, by Reino Alava, whom I had known at UC Berkeley and who was head of the Botany Department at University of Turku. I was "horrified" to discover that the botanists had planned a great smorgasbord for me, having just consumed two enormous ones on the ferry. I managed to put off eating for a few hours by asking to tour the famous market and its turn-of-the-century market hall. Amid all of the wonderful berries (16 of 57 native berries are commonly eaten) was a featured vegetable—iceberg lettuce from the Salinas Valley! It was flown in from California daily and apparently was eagerly snapped up, even at high prices. This seemed strange indeed in 1971, but would not today, with produce commonly being transported over the world in our global economy. After making my way through the smorgasbord prepared especially for me by the Turku botanists, we toured their new botany building. Here Reino proudly pointed out the banks and banks of lights, which he proclaimed had greatly increased the activity of the students in the winter when the almost 24-hour darkness depressed many people.

In the late afternoon, I flew to central Finland to visit the family of a Finnish artist who was a good friend in Cambridge. Her sister, Ellen Uranniemi, taught English in an elementary school in the farming community of Multia. The small plane ride from Turku was one of the bumpiest I have ever had, which reflected the size of the plane and the plethora of small lakes—with many encircling larch trees turning bright yellow, amid the dark green conifer forest—over which we were flying. More than two-thirds of Finland is still forested, with settlements and agricultural areas only forming small patches in the forest landscape. The constant change of moving over land or water seemed to control the ups and downs of the plane and I was glad for our arrival.

I was whisked off to the family's farm in Multia, where they were preparing yet another incredible spread. But first, especially since it was Saturday night, I had to have a sauna. I was taken to the sauna hut along the edge of one of those small lakes. It was early evening and quite cool. Although the Uranniemis said that they had cooled the sauna down especially for me, in a few minutes I was as red as a cooked shrimp, and I soon asked please to leave. But I was then told to jump in the lake. I tried to demur but was gently shoved in; the water was icy and I let out a blood-curdling scream. Ellen quickly fished me out of the water, and, after getting warmed up and into dry clothes, I just had to "survive" my hospitable hosts urging me to try this or that Finnish specialty at their smorgasbord.

The next morning we went to church in a charming, sharply spired wooden building characteristic of many Scandinavian Lutheran churches. I couldn't understand a word of the Finnish service, but it included much singing, which I joined by humming. After the service, coffee and *pulla* (sweet cardamom-flecked bread) and various sugar-coated rolls were available for the parishioners. As I was observing it all from a world of my own, my "family" was talking to another one and they began laughing and pointing to me. Loons had not been seen for a while on the lake that adjoined their farms, but neighbors across the lake thought they had heard one last night. They were mystified, though, that they had only heard one loud call! Could that have been . . . ?

On Monday I visited Ellen's class and was amazed as the small children all immediately stood when I entered and recited in unison, "Good morning, Professor Langenheim." We later went for a walk in a nearby spruce-fir-birch forest and these kids knew the Latin names of the plants. When I said, "Oh, cranberries," I was castigated—they were *Vaccinium vitis-idaea* (the common name there in English actually would have been lingonberry). This was followed by a little lecture for me from one of the youngsters about the importance of using the Latin (scientific) names because then people all over the world would understand what plant you were talking about! I wished I could have made a recording of that little speech to share with those of my UCSC students who abhorred learning the Latin names of plants! The boreal forest is very much a part of Finnish life (more than 20 percent of families own forest land) and the forest flora is small and hence easy to learn, but nevertheless . . .

I flew to Rovaniemi on the Arctic Circle because I wanted to at least get a glimpse of European arctic tundra. I was the only passenger on the plane by the time we arrived in Rovaniemi, as mid-September was too late in the season for most tourists to venture that far north. As the door of the plane was opened for us to disembark, an astonishing display of the aurora borealis burst before us. The entire sky was lit up with dazzling streaks of green, yellow, scarlet, and blue-purplish red colors that danced and quivered—along with bright white light that appeared to touch the ground. We all were awestruck. The explanation for the aurora involves subatomic particles that stream from the sun to earth's magnetic poles in the upper atmosphere and generate light. The green-yellow and red are produced by atmospheric oxygen; the blue and purplish-red by nitrogen. I had seen the northern lights before, in northern Minnesota, Alaska, and over-the-pole flights—but never anything as overwhelming as this display.

A few miles north of Rovaniemi I saw the border of the boreal forest and beginning of arctic tundra. The sparse scotch pine (*Pinus sylvestris*) forest was ablaze with color—the leaves of various shrubs turning red and those of small aspen turning golden. Another lasting impression was the amount of lichen covering the tundra; as far as the eye could see, the ground was white with what I assumed to be *Cladina (*formerly known as *Cladonia),* and I saw reindeer being herded by Laplanders. Although I had seen massive amounts of *Cladina* covering the forest floor in the boreal forest edge in Alaska being eaten by caribou, I now could understand why this lichen is commonly called "reindeer moss".

FULL CIRCLE

1997-2007

But thousands die, without this and that,
Die, and endow a college or a cat.
—Alexander Pope

I had assumed that the graduate students who had arrived in the early 1990s, before I became an emeritus faculty member, would be the last ones that I would sponsor. But I was delightfully surprised to be asked to sponsor two doctoral students after the last of my pre-emeritus students graduated. Neither of them did research involving secondary chemicals, but their dissertations have given me the opportunity 'and challenged me' to keep abreast of some of today's fast-moving research utilizing molecular techniques.

In 1997 I accepted Tom Hofstra, who furthered my interest in tree disease by doing a molecular study of the distribution, genetic diversity and compositional variation of the bacterial communities, called wetwood, within and among native California *Populus* species. When Tom graduated in 2003, Susanne Altermann immediately came on board. Her dissertation research has taken me back to the mountain experiences where I became fascinated with lichens, as well as my interests in plant geography (although lichens comprise a symbiosis between a fungus and an alga, they commonly are classified with plants). Using molecular techniques, Susanne has studied geographic patterns in the mountain wolf lichen (*Letharia lupina*) symbiosis over its western North American distribution. Thus more than a dozen years since I officially retired, I still have the privilege of supervising PhD students and serving on others' qualifying examinations.

REFLECTIONS ON MY ROLE IN GRADUATE EDUCATION

Now, as I approach the end of sponsoring (but not mentoring) graduate students, I have been reflecting on my role in graduate education at UCSC. I was involved in helping establish the graduate program, first as a member of planning committees for graduate studies at UCSC, then as an advisor to four graduate students starting the first year of the program. I continued to gain graduate students over the years and have either sponsored or cosponsored forty-one students (as well as having served on a dozen students' dissertation committees—including those from Yale University, University of Texas at Austin, and Australian National University.) As I progressively was able to spend more time on graduate courses, I integrated class topics with research centered on my group of graduate students and those with similar interests from other labs. In later years, because of my interest in graduate education, I was asked several times if I would consider being dean of the Graduate Division. I consistently refused, preferring to concentrate at that time on the students as well as on being an officer in national and international scientific societies that supported their research. Nonetheless, the Graduate Division asked me to give the commencement address in 1989. In "A Global Vision: A Mandate for the Future," I exhorted graduate students across the campus to accept the responsibility of international outreach as highly educated people.

Among my forty-one graduate students, twenty-seven (66 percent) were men and fourteen (34 percent) were women. Nearly two-thirds of both women and men received doctorates. The remaining one-third received masters, and they were pretty evenly divided among men and women. Thus within my group I saw signs of progress for women since the time of my graduate student days, when women commonly were only allowed a masters degree.

As a woman PhD student in the mid-1940s, who obtained the degree in the early 1950s and who has been working professionally since the beginning of the women's movement in the mid-1960s, I have followed with interest how my women PhD students have fared since they received their degrees. The first two women students arrived in 1968, and the other seven women have been more or less evenly spaced over the years since then, with a few more in the 1990s and later. Four are unmarried. One of these obtained a faculty position in a four-year liberal arts college (Evergreen), one in a California community college, and two in either federal (USDA Agricultural Research Service) or state (California Regional Water Control Board) agencies. Five are married and two have children. One is a faculty member in a four-year liberal arts college (Coker); her husband is a faculty member at nearby University of South Carolina. Another is a full-time faculty member and department chair in a California community college; her husband has a job in a nearby town. One has a research appointment at the research university (Purdue) where her husband is a faculty member, another has done research in a private research company that she and her PhD husband own. All of these married women have been constrained in their own work opportunities by the location of their husbands' positions. The fifth student is just finishing her degree; she will not restrict her choice of jobs, because her husband is retired.

Apart from my students, I have seen breakthroughs in barriers for married women ecologists at UCSC during my time here. There are now three married couples with full-time faculty appointments in either the Environmental Studies (ES) or Ecology and Evolutionary Biology (EEB) Departments. One of these couples came with a split appointment in the Biology Department; recently both were raised to full-time status in EEB. Another woman has a full-time appointment in EEB and her husband has one in ES, whereas in the third case both husband and wife have appointments in ES. All three couples have children. Having children after their appointment at UCSC has been made more manageable with maternity and family leave policies established in 1975.

Among my male students, four of the seventeen PhDs became faculty in research universities. Two of them are in Mexico; one first became the rector of the state University of Quintana Roo and currently is rector of the new Intercultural Maya University of Quintana Roo, which focuses on training indigenous Maya people in areas such as agroecology. The other has had numerous research students, including some in chemical ecology, at UNAM's Institute of Ecology, both in Mexico City and in Morelia, Michoacan. The third is an American who was an assistant professor of ecology in the Botany Department of UNICAMP in Brazil but resigned because of low salary to enter the US industry as a senior computer analyst. The fourth became a member of the Biology Department at the University of South Carolina, where he has been active in chemical ecology research and has had numerous graduate students, resulting in his being awarded one of the university's distinguished professorships.

Another student became a faculty member in California State University of Monterey Bay, and three became full-time faculty in California community colleges, all assuming administrative positions in addition to their teaching courses in either biology, forestry or chemistry. Two of the students were constrained to taking their community college positions because of personal commitments to partners who did not want to leave Central California, often a problem for those who fall in love with this part of the world! Another four students became researchers. Two are at UC and one is at the University of Texas at Austin, whereas the fourth established his own company for wine research. Three became environmental or agroecology consultants, including one who provided guidance regarding wildfires for the US Forest Service and California State Parks. One of these later used this background to head a forestry program in a community college. A Brazilian became a high-level administrator in EMBRAPA—Brazil's equivalent of USDA, and a Chinese student did research and supervised turf and plantings for the Hong Kong Jockey Club.

If these jobs of my students obtaining doctorates seem diverse, it is even more so with those taking masters degrees; I will not try to present them here. Overall, I now look in amazement of having trained such a broad diversity of professionals.

In addition, doing a rigorous senior thesis, an aspect of undergraduate education on which UCSC has put some emphasis, has propelled many students into professional careers. I supervised senior theses of numerous undergraduate students, some of whom went on to receive doctorates at other institutions and garner good positions in a variety of academic and research institutions. One, for example, took his PhD at Michigan State University and now is back in California as a professor at Humboldt State University. Another took his PhD at Johns Hopkins and currently is a researcher at the US Geological Survey. Two have obtained prestigious positions in other countries after having received their doctorate degrees. One woman completed her PhD at UC Davis, married a Spanish researcher, and is now a researcher in the Institute of Sustainable Agriculture in Cordoba, Spain. Particularly noteworthy is Jonathan Gershenzon who completed a PhD at the University of Texas; after a research position at the center for terpene biochemistry at Washington State University, he was selected to be the director of the Max Planck Institute for Chemical Ecology in Jena, Germany, which is currently considered "the number one address in the field."

With Jonathan Gershenzon on recent visit to UCSC

Thinking about the success of these students, apart from the many others with whom I had contact over the years, makes me feel like a "proud parent"—even being a small part of their lives has greatly enriched my own life.

GALÁPAGOS VISIT

In another realm of contemplation, I have always thought that field biologists, in particular, should make a pilgrimage to the Galápagos Islands that so influenced Darwin's concept of natural selection. I felt I would be filling a gap in my biological experiences by actually seeing this classic group of tropical desert islands with its unusual biota, and a visit there also would enable me to put more recent research there into better perspective. I had resisted going on a commercial tour until in 1999 a colleague from the American Museum of Natural History (AMNH) suggested one of their cruises on *Polaris*, a refurbished research vessel. The expedition leader had done her PhD dissertation on the islands' giant marine iguanas, and she would be accompanied by outstanding guest lecturers from AMNH as well. So I decided the time was right to make this journey of reflection.

Ecuador's Galápagos National Park Service has established forty-eight visitor sites, and we visited many of them, on the various volcanic islands, each for a different purpose. Often in the calm of early morning, before breakfast and our morning trip, I went on deck and reread relevant parts of *Voyage of the Beagle*. Moreover, I also traveled back in thought to the late 1950s, when Mason and I were agonizing over why ecologists had not incorporated natural selection into their thought, and to a later time when some ecologists and historians of science were referring to Darwin as an "inadvertent sire of ecology."

Contrasts dominate the Galápagos scene—islands are from very small to large, and their elevations range from barely above sea level to highlands up to several thousand feet. Everywhere there is evidence of seismic activity that formed the archipelago, with volcanic cones present on each island of appreciable size and lava flows and ash deposits of ages from ancient to very recent. Accompanying such variety in local habitats, the vegetation ranges from none on recent lava flows to scattered giant *Opuntia* cactus stands in arid lowlands to lush moist tropical uplands with surprisingly diverse vegetation. These environmental differences are accompanied, of course, by variation in the animals adapted to these local habitats. However, it was not only the isolation of these islands and these varying conditions that illuminate the concept of natural selection today.

Major environmental events can also play a significant role in selection of plants and animals. My visit coincided with a period of El Niño years. At Punta Suarez, on the island of Española, one of the richest wildlife locations in the Galápagos, we witnessed the results of the warm waters killing or severely diminishing the growth of the algae that are the main source of food for the marine iguanas, the world's only truly marine lizard. This had resulted in many of them being very thin, even emaciated. It was a sad sight to behold, but emphasized the impact a few years of major climate change can have. On the other hand, Galápagos scientists were surprised that the small (only fourteen-inch-long) endemic penguins did not seem to be impacted by the warm waters of El Niño. They had feared devastating effects on these penguins. These are the only penguins to live north of the equator in the cold upwelling waters of the western Galápagos Islands, such as Fernandina where we saw them, and breed entirely within the tropics. They are probably descended from the Humboldt penguins that occur in the cold waters off Peru, carried north by the Humboldt current from Antarctica.

On several beaches, the marine iguanas and sea lions glanced languidly at us, and Darwin's finches and mockingbirds not only closely approached us but also perched on us sometimes. Not fearing humans, a mockingbird perched on my hat and a yelping sea lion tagged after me as I walked along one beach (which would not happen with sea lions along a California beach). Seeing animals so friendly made me ponder the terrible influence humans have had on most wild animals—such that they have to fear us to survive—unless living in a few protected areas!

We also visited the lush highlands of Santa Cruz Island, which were a pleasant contrast to rocky Fernandina with its recent volcanic activity. Puerto Ayara, the main town on Santa Cruz Island, is home to 8,000 people and is the economic hub of the archipelago. It is also the location of the Charles Darwin Research Station (CDRS), where scientists gather data for the conservation of the Galápagos' unique biota. CDRS runs the giant tortoise breeding program, one of the most successful and significant programs of ecological restoration on the Galápagos Islands. In these highlands, I was impressed by the forest of *Scalesia*, a tree in the sunflower family, which displays adaptive radiation on the islands comparable with Darwin's finches. Most discussions of evolution in the Galápagos Islands emphasize the finches and bypass *Scalesia*. Unfortunately, from my perspective, plants often take the back seat to animals! Many botanists also may not realize that Darwin's collection of Galápagos plants formed the basis for the first flora of the archipelago.

Darwin finches have been intensely studied by generations of researchers, including Peter and Rosemary Grant and their associates from Princeton University. On the very small island of Daphne Major, they have spent over thirty years recording resident birds' births, deaths, and eating habits as well as weather and food-supply information—the detailed kind of long-term data that has enabled them to build on Darwin's observations of natural selection. They have recently been able to demonstrate rapid character displacement (change in beak size) due to interplay between population numbers of two species of finches (one large-beaked and the other small-beaked) and a major environmental event (a drought that set the stage for fierce food competition). Their work is an amazing demonstration of evolution in action, and an example of the incredible value of long-term research, which in this case culminated with a fortuitous combination of populational and environmental events.

Although the initial impetus for Darwin's insight into the role of natural selection is generally thought to have been the radiation of the Galápagos finches, apparently his thinking was also triggered by an endemic genus of mockingbirds. Until recently, however, the mockingbirds, like *Scalesia,* have been the victims of benign neglect. Darwin thought that the mockingbirds had descended from a single colonization event brought about by wayfarers from Chile or Argentina. Now with the availability of molecular techniques, studies have confirmed that the mockingbirds arose in a single location, but the closest relatives are in North and Central America, not South America.

The trip also emphasized what an uphill struggle it is to conserve this rare and special area for posterity. Economic forces, both local and foreign, are ever-present. Fishermen are a constant threat; in fact, while we were there, a tourist ship reported a Japanese ship fishing illegally in Galápagos waters. And despite some Ecuadorean park controls, there are daunting challenges to protecting the fragile ecosystems from ecotourists, partially because of the sheer numbers that come to visit the famed islands.

A BOOK ON PLANT RESINS

In early 1999 I signed a contract with Timber Press to write a reference book on plant resins. I had been inspired by my spring trip to the Galápagos Islands, followed by the XVI International Botanical Congress during the summer in St Louis, Missouri. There, I had cosponsored with my Mexican former graduate student, Francisco Espinosa, a symposium on one of my favorite themes, "Multiple Ecological and Evolutionary Roles of Secondary Metabolites in Plants: Significance of Chemical Variation." Our speakers from Austria, Sweden, Finland, Mexico, and the United States produced the kind of lively discussion that set me up well for settling down with my book writing. Timber Press wanted an update of Howe's 1949 *Vegetable Gums and Resins*, the only reference on the subject available at that time. I suggested the book be restricted to resins, as I knew they alone would provide information for a large volume, due in part to rapid advances in chemical technology that enabled better understanding of the biosynthesis and ecological relationships of resins.

The overviews I had written, such as those for the ISCE and ACS symposia, helped me to launch the book by providing synthesized thought from a large and disparate literature. I did not want the book to be encyclopedic in the sense of a mere packaging of factual information, and neither did Timber Press. They hoped I would produce a readable reference for the scientist as well as for the broad audience of people who might have some interest in resins. My goal was to enable the reader to understand the biosynthesis of these plant products—how and in what kind of anatomical structures they are stored and secreted as well as how these structures aid plants in defense and help humans extract the resin for their use. I wanted to provide an evolutionary perspective developed from the fossil record—when were resins first produced and what evidence do we have, through the ages, of their possible effectiveness in defense? I would analyze ecological studies of defense in both well-known conifers and little-known tropical angiosperms. Furthermore, I would tackle the ethnobotany of both fossil and modern resins, tracing their use from the Stone Age to the present. Although I had the breadth of background to accomplish these goals, it was an ambitious project to carry out in the two to three years set by Timber Press! In many ways, it controlled the activities of my life until the book was well into production.

I had numerous black-and-white as well as color photographs to illustrate topics covered in the book. Timber Press, however, put limitations on the number of photographs, and suggested that I augment them with line drawings. I did not have time to do these myself, but an amazing event came to my rescue. A bright undergraduate student, Jesse Markman, who was teaching a seminar on plants, lost his supervisor to death. He asked me to become his advisor, but with time pressure from Timber Press to complete the book, I hesitated. On the other hand, I felt obligated under the circumstances, and so agreed to assist him. As the seminar progressed, Jesse told me he had taken a course in scientific illustration and would like to introduce the students in his seminar to making drawings of the plants they were observing. When I saw some of his drawings, it occurred to me that he might like to do some illustrations for the book. We were soon working "hand in glove" and ultimately Jesse produced over fifty line drawings for the book, which have received considerable acclaim. This all developed out of an act of compassion regarding the passing of a colleague, but it enabled the development of a latent artistic talent and greatly enriched the quality and quantity of illustrations in my book. I always stand in awe of the results of such serendipitous events.

Plant Resins: Chemistry, Evolution, Ecology and Ethnobotany was published in May 2003, just in time to stimulate an invitation to give the John Dwyer Distinguished Lecture at the Missouri Botanical Garden. Adding to good reviews of the book in diverse journals, it also received the Klinger Book Award from the Society of Economic Botany in 2004. Since the book's publication, I have received a continual stream of e-mail messages from resin researchers around the world. Our small electronic world has made me aware of the many people with interests in various aspects of resins—and is representative of the global networking that I spoke about in my "Global Visions" lectures long ago.

AN ADMINISTRATIVE CHANGE FOR BIOLOGISTS

In 1997, the Biology Board of Studies was given a more traditional designation of Biology Department. This shift in nomenclature was campus-wide with the prime justification being that people outside of the UCSC campus did not know what *Board of Studies* meant. Was it essentially the same as a department or did it have a different connotation? Because the changes in 1979 introduced with Chancellor Sinsheimer's "reaggregation" fundamentally put the focus on disciplinary education, the change in the name from Board of Studies to Department was devoid of internal administrative changes

In 2000, the biology department split into two departments, which did have administrative consequences. The discipline of biology had become so complex that molecularists at one end of the spectrum, for example, found it difficult to identify with ecologists and evolutionists at the other end of the spectrum. In fact, some biologists working at the molecular level identified more with chemists and physicists than other biologists. A lack of background and consequent understanding across the subdisciplines also complicated the participation of faculty in such matters as recruitment and promotions. Likewise, undergraduate majors covering all of biology had become unrealistic. The two new departments followed the national trend of dividing into Molecular, Cell, and Developmental Biology (MCD) and Ecology and Evolutionary Biology (EEB). In retrospect I am glad that I had the opportunity to know and work alongside biologists at both ends of the spectrum when this was still feasible.

LATE HONORS

In the last several years I have been pleased to receive additional recognition of my long-term professional contributions. My friends had begun comparing me to the Energizer Bunny—I just keep going and going.

Each year a volume of *Madroño*, the journal of the California Botanical Society, is dedicated to an individual selected by the council of the society. In 2005, I was chosen as the person to whom the 2004 volume should be dedicated. This honor came fifty years after I had published my first research paper in *Madroño*.

Receiving BSA Award from Peter Raven (left)

With Hal Mooney at BSA reception (below)

In 2006, the Botanical Society of America (BSA), in its centenary meeting, gave me one of its Centennial Awards for contributions to the advancement of the plant sciences. This meeting was held on the arboretum-like campus of California State University at Chico in the foothills of the Sierra Nevada. The large yard of the former president of the university provided a pleasant atmosphere for the special awards ceremony and following reception. The opportunity to interact with this incredible assembly of recipients, some of whom I had known from grad school days at Minnesota in the late 1940s (Shirley Tucker), while at UC Berkeley during the 1950s (Peter Raven and Don Stone), at Illinois (David Dilcher) in the 1960s or through the years since (Hal Mooney at Stanford), and numerous others, was a great joy and emotional experience. One of the awardees from the earlier years commented that we were the survivors among those who had made major contributions to the advancement of American botanical science during the twentieth century, and this special occasion provided what might be the last privilege of seeing such a group of distinguished colleagues together again.

Another surprise in 2006 was the announcement that I was going to receive the Fellow's Medal, the highest research award given by California Academy of Science. In my remarks after receiving the medal, I recalled with appreciation the late Lincoln Constance, who had been so prominent in academy activities and long a supporter of professional women. It was he who made sure that I had a research appointment in the Botany Department at UC Berkeley in the 1950s, and he who nominated me for fellowship in the academy after my obtaining professorship at UCSC in the early 1970s. I felt that he would have been happy to see me receiving the Fellow's Medal which was presented to honor "Decades of excellence in contributions to the advancement of science."

Receiving the California Academy of Sciences
Fellow's medal from Ward Watt

The award, was presented by the President of the Academy, Ward Watt, at a gala dinner held at the Presidio in the former officer's club overlooking San Francisco Bay. It was announced during dinner that all of the wine was provided by a former undergraduate student of mine who is now the co-owner of a small, elite Napa Valley winery. He sent the wine, explaining that he had developed a passion for plant biology in my Plants and Human Affairs course. "Thanks in part to the excellent teaching of Jean Langenheim," he wrote, "my days are filled with Applied Plant Secondary Chemistry." This expression of gratitude for my teaching, which he connected to an award for research, was a quintessential representation of UCSC.

Speaking about what it was like at TU in 1946

Amid these scientific honors came a quite different kind of recognition. One of the themes for 2006 Homecoming at the University of Tulsa was "student government through the years," and a committee going over the history of TU student government discovered that I was the first woman president. They invited me to come to be honored and speak about what student government was like during the 1945-1946 academic year. It was a journey back in time, bringing me from my student days sixty-years-ago to the very different world of today. My description of student government at that time, especially the lack of university funding for our activities, left the current members of student government wondering how we could have been so successful in ambitious projects such as hosting the leadership conference of southwestern colleges and universities. Even when I emphasized the context of my generation having endured the Great Depression and World War II—and thus being used to finding ingenious ways to accomplish our goals despite lack of money—these students, who have grown up in a time of affluence, were still puzzled! Although I have worked in an educational setting these sixty years, it was a fascinating generational experience talking with these students about what it was like for the "We make do" generation. (An interesting aside is that there have only been five other women presidents in TU student government since 1946.)

Being able to attend the luncheon for induction of 2006 Distinguished TU Alumni was an added special event. It was the first time I had participated since my own induction twenty-seven years earlier (1979), and I was pleased to be among five women of the seventeen Distinguished Alumni present at this luncheon.

GIVING BACK

During 2004, the state was in financial turmoil and cuts to the University of California budget led to a dramatic forty percent increase in fees for graduate students and cuts in teaching assistantships as well. Although most graduate students, with assistance from their advisor, could cobble together various small sources of funding for research, endowed graduate fellowships were needed. The thriftiness I had learned as a child during the Depression had enabled me to include funding one for plant ecology and plant evolution in my estate trust. Now it began to seem as though I ought to activate it sooner. I had been thinking about how important AAUW fellowships had been to me in times of need when little other support was available—especially for women at that time. As the Nobel Laureate, Barbara McClintock had expressed her appreciation of AAUW for their fellowships, "For the young person, fellowships are of the greatest importance. The freedom they allow for concentrated study and research cannot be duplicated by any other method." Thus I set the wheels in motion, and in 2005 I endowed a Graduate Fellowship in Plant Ecology and Evolution. Although it is not restricted to women, as this seems of less concern now, I am happy to give back a little of the kind of assistance that made a difference in my education as well as to continue to assist the graduate education with which I have been so involved at UCSC, and to advance the study of plants with which I had been so fascinated during my professional career.

With first of my fellowship recipients, Krikor Andonian

Endowment of a Chair in Plant Ecology and Evolution in the Department of Ecology and Evolutionary Biology was also in my trust to be established upon my death. However, again the timing seemed right to bring this about during my lifetime, and I endowed a chair in 2006. By doing so, I was adding to the movement in the department to bolster the plant program; this endowment is the beginning of continued—and I hope increasing—support for a number of plant-related activities of the chair holder.

With first recipient of my Chair in Plant Ecology, Ingrid Parker

Plant sciences can often be neglected, although they were particularly strong during an earlier period at UCSC. I not only wanted to help increase the current strength in studies of plant ecology and evolution of the unique Central California flora but to include a global perspective—with some emphasis on the tropics. I considered evolution to include the interaction of plants with animals and microbes but hoped to keep appropriate focus on the plants in these interactions. I also wanted to acknowledge not only the importance of native plants (and the effects of invasive plants on their evolution), but the central role they play in the life of humans and the need for the development of sustainable agriculture and forestry. Moreover, plants are giving us clear evidence of the effects of global warming—another expanding area to investigate.

Presently I am enjoying the reward of watching the fellowship's effects on the progress of the students receiving them, seeing the influence of the chair on faculty activity and their ripple effects both on local studies about plants and on those in the tropics.

FINAL REFLECTIONS

When reviewing the first draft of these memoirs, I was struck with my frequent use of certain words—*enjoy, delighted in, fascinated with, appreciated, grateful for.* These words were chosen in haste, simply as a means to get my ideas down on paper. To avoid redundancy, I have had to eliminate them from many places in the text. In doing so, however, I also realized their significance. Their overuse summarizes my feelings about my life. I have always been enthusiastic about whatever I was doing. Not that there weren't down times. But a sense of joy and expression of gratitude for the good entering my life was instilled in me by my mother; she also exposed me to a spiritual philosophy that strengthened these attitudes.

My life's trajectory has taken me through the dark days of the Great Depression, the Dust Bowl in Oklahoma, and World War II. A period of societal affluence followed, which, however, included the Cold War with the Soviets, social upheaval regarding civil rights, an unpopular war in Vietnam, and young peoples' revolt against authority. I saw the enormous changes in women's opportunities and status in society—from the right to vote and obtain a quality graduate education having come only a few years before my birth to now seeing women becoming US Secretaries of State and presidents of Ivy League universities. I was a participant in the "in between period" of struggles for women professionally—with marriage providing an opportunity to obtain a doctorate, but nepotism restrictions and societal views constraining its use. I've witnessed and been a part of great changes from classical plant community studies in ecology to the use of biochemical and molecular techniques to solve both ecological and evolutionary questions. I have seen major conceptual advances, from accepting natural selection as an ecological as well as an evolutionary concept, to validating the occurrence of plate tectonics and continental drift, to recognizing new pathways to terpene biosynthesis. The explosive rapidity of technological changes cannot be overstated—from increasing sophistication of chemical and molecular technologies to those of computers, satellites, the World Wide Web, and Internet communication. I have seen electronic communication bringing to fruition the global vision I had earlier heralded. They have so impacted lives that students today cannot imagine living in a world without them!

Many threads have been woven into the complex design of my life's tapestry. Threads representing love of learning (from science to philosophy and literature) and interest in the natural world (from arctic-alpine to equatorial tropics) are strong throughout the tapestry. An associated thread of interest in art, especially of landscapes and plants, was spun early with drawing and painting, but developed into photography during my ecological research. Another persistent thread visible even in my childhood is the love of travel, first on trains, later by airplanes, and then continuing with transport all over the globe. The travel thread has many branches, but prominent ones are related to research and involvement in the cultures of people in different parts of the world. These branching threads were woven in and out with various intensities depending upon travel experiences as diverse as plant collecting in the early days along the Alaska Highway and visiting an Eskimo family; collecting amber by mule train amid local Indians in Chiapas, Mexico; doing field work during a military coup in Colombia; visiting the compound of a polygamous family of a field assistant in Ghana, and being a guest in a billionaire's *fazenda* in Brazil. Another solid thread initiated during childhood was my love of animals and their importance as companions in my daily life. This thread was less visible during my marriage but became strong again during my full professional life—especially in later years. Similarly, the thread of leadership roles began during my youth, was diminished during marriage, but became substantial again as my professional career advanced. The tight interweaving of various threads representing research (exploring knowledge) and teaching (communicating knowledge) has been present ever since my graduate student years.

Although I never had a woman professional role model, I was pointed in the direction I took in my graduate studies by an extraordinary woman. Women in the Radcliffe Institute also provided inspirational guidance at a critical time of my career. Moreover, I was inspired in meeting women scientists in other countries who have overcome obstacles to contribute their talents. I also have felt privileged to have been stimulated intellectually by, and to work with and become long-term friends with numerous male leaders in my fields of interest. They gave critical professional and personal support even during times when institutional regulations prevented them from promoting my professional achievements. Obstacles to sharing knowledge and friendship never existed.

Recognition for my efforts across most of the areas in which I have done research since the late 1940s primarily began with opening of opportunities for women during the late 1960s and 1970s. I never restricted my research contributions to a particular field but have worked within and across several disciplines. I have been most lauded for the big-picture, synthesis publications in which I have welded together paleobotany, plant ecology and ethnobotany, including chemical approaches, often with a tropical perspective. Cross-disciplinary research was not common when I embarked on it—now it is being heralded as necessary to address many critical questions facing us today

My life of learning and discovery, and my surrogate family relationships have been so rich that I have seldom felt lonely. I have pondered why, when early on in my solo career I felt overwhelmed with responsibilities, I did not rebel. I think, partly, I was driven by a sense that I didn't want to let down the women who might follow me. I didn't consider myself a martyr to this cause, but I can't deny I was endowed in childhood with a strong sense of duty, including taking seriously the Girl Scout pledge? "To do my duty . . ."

Passion, persistence, and patience are the three characteristics that have carried me through. Passion for my work was the driving force for the persistence to succeed, and patience was needed when developments seemed painfully slow. However, it is not the accomplishments, per se, that I feel the most happy about, but rather having been able to share the excitement and joys (along with overcoming trials) of these intellectual adventures with my students and associates—at home and around the world. I also hope that I have encouraged others along my odyssey to embark on the rich rewards of a life of learning and discovery, in whatever form it may take.

REFERENCES

PART I BEGINNINGS

THE EARLY YEARS

Debo, A. 1943. *Tulsa—From Creek Town to Oil Capitol*. Norman: University of Oklahoma Press.

Earhart, A. 1932. The Fun of It. New York: Harcourt Brace Jovanovich.

_____. (arranged by G.P. Putnam) 1988. *Last Flight*. New York: Orion Books.

LAYING THE FOUNDATION

Clements, F.E. and V.E. Shelford. 1939. *Bio-Ecology*. New York: John Wiley.

Cooper, W. S. 1923. The recent ecological history of Glacier Bay, Alaska. III. Permanent quadrats at Glacier Bay; an initial report upon a long-period study. *Ecology* 4: 355-65.

Cowles, H.C. 1901. The physiographic ecology of Chicago and vicinity: A study of the origin, development and classification of plant societies. *Botanical Gazette* 31: 73-108, 145-82.

Sears, P. 1935. Deserts on the March. Norman: University of Oklahoma Press.

Weaver, J. and F. E. Clements. 1938 (2nd ed.). *Plant Ecology*. New York: McGraw Hill.

Letters to Richard Zahner

PART II DUAL CAREERS

GRADUATE-STUDENT YEARS

Chu, Kwei-ling and W.S. Cooper. 1950. An ecological reconnaissance in the native home of *Metasequoia glyptostroboides*. *Ecology* 31: 260-78.

Clements, F.E. 1916. Plant Succession: An Analysis of the Development of Vegetation. Carnegie Institute of Washington Public. 247: 512 pp.

Coleman, W. 1986. Evolution into ecology? The strategy of Warming's ecological plant geography. *Journal of the History of Biology* 19: 181-96.

Cook, R.E. 1977. Raymond Lindeman and the trophic-dynamic concept of ecology. *Science* 198: 22-6.

Cooper, W. S. 1913. The climax forest of Isle Royale, Lake Superior and its development. *Bot. Gaz.* 55: 1-44, 113-40, 189-235.

_____. 1926. The fundamentals of vegetational change. *Ecology* 7: 391-413.

_____. 1928. Seventeen years of successional change upon Isle Royale, Lake Superior. *Ecology* 7: 1-5.

_____. 1931. A third expedition to Glacier Bay, Alaska. *Ecology* 12: 61-96.

_____. 1935. The Late Wisconsin and Postglacial history of the Upper Mississippi River. *Minnesota Geological Survey Bulletin*, No 26.

_____. 1936. The strand and dune flora of the Pacific Coast of North America: a geographic study. In *Essays in Geobotany in Honor of William Albert Setchell*, pp. 141-87, ed. T.H. Goodspeed. Berkeley: University of California Press.

_____. 1958. *Coastal Sand Dunes of Washington and Oregon.* Geological Society of America Memoir 72. Baltimore: Waverly Press.

Cowles, H.C. 1901. The physiographic ecology of Chicago and vicinity: a study of the origin, development and classification of plant societies. *Bot. Gaz.* 31: 73-108, 145-82.

Daubenmire, R.F. 1943. Vegetational zonation in the Rocky Mountains. *Bot. Rev.* 9: 325-93.

_____. 1947. *Plants and Environment: A Textbook of Autecology.* New York: John Wiley.

De Candolle, A.L. 1855. *Geographie Botanique Raisone.* Paris: V. Masson.

Drude, O. 1890. *Handbuch der Pflanzengeographie.* Stuttgart: Verlag von J. Engelhorn.

Egler, F.E. 1951. A commentary on American plant ecology, based on textbooks of 1947-1949. *Ecology* 32: 673-95.

Egler, F.E. 1977. *The Nature of Vegetation: Its Management and Mismanagement.* Connecticut: Norfolk.

Humphrey, R. 1962. *Range Ecology.* New York: Ronald.

Humboldt, A. and A. Bonpland. 1807. *Essai sur Geographie des Plantes.* Paris

_____. 1850. *Views of Nature: or Contemplations on the Sublime Phenomena of Creation; with scientific illustrations.* 3rd edn, London: Henry G. Bohn.

Kittredge, J. 1948. *Forest Influences.* New York: McGraw Hill.

Langenheim, J.H. 1949. *Physiography and Plant Ecology of a Subalpine Earthflow,* Gunnison County, Colorado. MS Thesis, University of Minnesota.

Langenheim, R.L. Jr. 1952. Pennsylvanian and Permian stratigraphy of the Crested Butte Quadrangle, Gunnison County, Colorado. *Bulletin of American Association of Petroleum Geologists* 36: 543-576.

Lawrence, D.B. 1978. Obituary William Skinner Cooper (1884-1978).

Lemon, P.C. 1962. *Field and Laboratory Guide for Ecology.* Minnesota: Burgess.

Lindeman, R. 1942. The trophic-dynamic aspect of ecology. *Ecology* 23: 399-418.

Nicholson, M. 1996. Humboldtian plant geography after Humbodlt: the link to ecology. *British Journal for History of Science* 29: 289-310

Oosting, H.J. 1948. *The Study of Plant Communities. An Introduction to Plant Ecology.* 2nd edn 1956, San Fransisco: Freeman.

Schimper. A. F.W. 1903. *Plant Geography on a Physiological Basis.* Translated by W.R. Fisher, revd. and edited by P. Groom and I. B. Balfour. Clarendon: Oxford University Press.

Warming, E. 1895. *Plantesamfund, Grundtraek af den Okologiska Plantsgeografi.* Denmark: Pilipsen.

_____. 1909. *Oecology of Plants; An Introduction to the Study of Plant Communities.* Transl. by P. Groom and I.B. Balfour. Oxford University Press.

WESTWARD TO CALIFORNIA

Barbour, M.G. 1995. Ecological fragmentation in the fifties. In *Uncommon Ground: toward Reinventing Nature*, pp. 233-55, ed. William Cronon. New York: Norton.

Cain, S. 1948. *Foundations of Plant Geography*. Harper and Bros.

California Women in Botany Regional Oral History, Bancroft Library, University of California, Berkeley.

Chaney, R.W. and H.L. Mason. 1933. A Pleistocene flora from the asphalt deposits at Carpinteria, California. Carnegie Institution of Washington Public. 415: 45-79.

Clausen, J., D. D. Keck, and W. M. Hiesey. 1940. Experimental studies on the nature of species. I. The effect of varied environments on western North American plants. Carnegie Institution of Washington Public. 520.

Cooper, W. S. 1917. Redwood, rainfall and fog. Plant world 20: 179-184.

_____. 1922.The broad-sclerophyll vegetation of California: an ecological study of the chaparral and its related communities. Carnegie Institution of Washington Public, 319.

Letters to and from W.S. Cooper

Daubenmire, R.F. 1938. Merriam's life zones of North America. *Quarterly Review of Biology* 13: 327-52.

Gleason, H.A. 1926. The individualistic concept of the plant association. *Torrey Bot. Club. Bull.* 53: 7-26.

_____. 1939. The individualistic concept of the plant association. Amer. *Midland Naturalist* 21: 92-110.

_____. 1953. Dr. H. A. Gleason, Distinguished Ecologist. *Bull. Ecol. Soc. Amer.* 34: 40-2.

Jenny, H. 1941. *Factors of Soil Formation*. New York: McGraw Hill.

Kruckeberg, A.R. 1954. The ecology of serpentine soils. III. Plant species in relation to serpentine soils. *Ecology* 35: 267-74.

_____. 2005. Introduction to California Soils and Plants. Berkeley: University of California Press.

Langenheim, J.H. 1953. Plant Ecological Reconnaissance of the Crested Butte Area, Gunnison, Colorado. PhD Dissertation, University of Minnesota.

Lidicker, W.Z., Jr. 2000. An assay on the history of the Biosystematists of the San Francisco Bay Area. In *Cultures and Institutions of Natural History and Philosophy of Science*, pp. 315-27, eds. M. T. Ghiselin and A.E. Leviton. California Academy of Science Memoir 25.

Major, J. 1951. A functional, factorial approach to plant ecology. *Ecology* 32: 392-412.

Mason, H.L. 1946 I. The edaphic factor in narrow endemism. I. The nature of environmental influences. *Madroño* 7: 209-25.

_____. 1946 II. The geographic occurrence of plants of highly restricted patterns of distribution. *Madroño* 8: 241-57.

Rossiter.M.W. 1984.*Women Scientists in America. Struggles and Strategies to 1940.* Johns Hopkins University Press.

Smocovitis, V.B. 1994. Organizing evolution: founding of the Society for the Study of Evolution. *J His. Bio.* 29: 241-309.

_____. 1997. G. Ledyard Stebbins, Jr. and the evolutionary synthesis (1924-1950). *Amer. J. Bot.* 84: 1625-37.

Stebbins, G. L. 1950. *Variation and Evolution in Plants.* New York: Columbia University Press.

_____. 1999. A brief summary of my ideas on evolution. *Amer. J. Bot* 86:179-89.

Whittaker, R. H. 1957. Recent evolution of ecological concepts in relation to the eastern forests of North America. *Amer. J. Bot.* 44: 197-206.

Wahlin, M.D.L. 2009. *Sigma Delta Epsilon-Graduate Women in Science, Inc. 87 Years of History (1921-2008).* San Diego, CA, Bordeaux Printers.

COLOMBIAN EXPEDITION

Fluharty V. 1957. Dance of the Millions: Military Rule and the social revolution in Colombia 1930-56.

Langenheim, R.L. Jr. 1959. Preliminary report on the stratigraphy of the Girón Formation in Santander and Boyaca. Boletin de Geología, No 3, Universidad Industrial de Santander, Bucaramanga: 35-50.

Langenheim, J.H. 1959. Preliminary notes on plant fossils from Late Paleozoic and Early Mesozoic rocks in the Cordillera Oriental of Colombia. *Boletin de Geología*, No 3, Universidad Industrial de Santander, Bucaramanga: 51-3.

Letters to Jeanette Harmon

Luteyn, J.L. 1999. *Páramos: A Checklist of Plant Diversity, Geographical Distribution, and Botanical Literature*. New York: New York Botanical Garden Press.

TEACHING DURING BERKELEY YEARS

Brower, D.R. (ed.) 1953. *Going Light with Backpack or Burro*. San Francisco: The Sierra Club.

Hagen, J.B. 1986. Ecologists and taxonomists: Divergent traditions in twentieth-century plant geography. *J. Hist. Bio.* 19: 197-214.

Letters to Jeanette Harmon

Langenheim, J.H. 1955. Flora of the Crested Butte Quadrangle, Colorado. *Madroño* 13: 64-78.

——————————. 1956. Plant succession on a subalpine earthflow in Colorado. *Ecology* 37: 301-17

ALASKAN TREK

Billings, W.D. and H.A. Mooney. 1959. An apparent frost-hummock-sorted polygon cycle in alpine tundra of Wyoming. *Ecology* 40:16-20.

Letters to Jeanette Harmon

Vierick, L. A. 1966. Plant succession and soil development on gravel outwash of the Muldrow Glacier, Alaska. *Ecol. Monog.* 36: 181-99.

EXPANDING HORIZONS WITH COLLABORATIVE RESEARCH

Axelrod, D.I. 1967. Geologic history of the California insular flora. In *Proceedings of the Symposium on the Biology of the California Islands*, pp. 267-, ed., R.N. Philbrick. Santa Barbara Botanical Garden, Inc.

Binder, P. M. 2008. Frustration in complexity. *Science* 320:322-3.

Cain, S. 1944. *Foundation of Plant Geography*. New York: Harper and Bros.

Chabot, B.F. and Billings, W.D. 1972. Origins and ecology of the Sierran alpine flora and vegetation, *Ecol. Monog.* 42: 143-61.

Chaney, R. 1938. Paleoecological interpretations of Cenozoic plants in western North America. *Bot. Rev.* 9: 371-96.

Cowles. H. C. 1908. An ecological aspect of the conception of species. *Amer. Nat.* 42: 265-71.

Darwin C.1859. *On the Origin of Species*. London: John Murray.

Einstein, A. 1940. Considerations concerning the fundamentals of theoretical physics. *Science* 91: 487-92.

Egler, F. E. 1951. A commentary on American plant ecology, based on textbooks of 1947-1949. *Ecology* 32: 673-95.

Erman, D. C. 1975. Peat depth of Sierra Nevada fens, and profile changes from 1952 to 1972 in Mason fen. *Great Basin Naturalist* 26: 101-7.

_____. 1976. Peat depth of Sierra Nevada fens, and profile changes from 1958 to 1972 in Mason Fen. *Great Basin Naturalist* 36:101-7.

Grant,P. R. and B.R. Grant. 2008. How and Why Species Multiply. Princeton University Press.New Jersey, Princeton.

Gurevitch, J., S.M. Scheiner, and G.A. Fox. 2002. *The Ecology of Plants*. Massachussets: Sinauer Associates, Inc Publishers.Hagen, J.B. 1992. An Entangled Bank. *The Origins of Ecosystem Ecology*. New Jersey: Rutgers University PressHarper, J. L. 1967. A Darwinian approach to plant ecology. *J. Ecol.* 55: 247-70.

Hayakawa, S. I. 1949. *Language in Thought and Action*. New York: Harcourt Brace.

Hodges,K. 2008. Defining the problem: terminology and progress in ecology. *Front. Ecol. Environ.* 6:35-42.

Holmes. M. A. and S. O'Connell 2003. *Where are the women geoscience professors?* Report on the NSF/AWG Foundation Workshop, Washington, D.C.

Hospers, J. 1953. *An Introduction to Philosophical Analysis*. New York: Prentice-Hall.

Jones, C, G.J.H. Lawton, and M. Shachak. 1997. Ecosystem engineering by organisms: why semantics matters. *Trends Ecol. Evol.* 12: 275.

Langenheim, J. H. and J. W. Durham. 1962. Quaternary closed-cone pine flora from travertine near Little Sur, California. *Madroño* 17: 33-51.

Lewontin, R. 1970. The units of selection. *Ann. Rev. Ecol Syst.* 1:1-18

Mason, H. L. 1936. The principles of geographic distributions as applied to floral analysis. *Madroño* 3: 181-90.

_____. 1947. Evolution of certain floristic associations in western North America. *Ecol. Monogr.* 17: 201-10.

_____. and J. H. Langenheim 1957. Language analysis and the concept of environment. *Ecology* 38: 325-339.

_____. 1961. Natural selection as an ecological concept. *Ecology* 42: 148-165.

McIntosh, R. P. 1985. *The Background of Ecology. Concept and Theory.* New York: Cambridge University Press.

_____. 1999. The succession of successions. *Bull. Ecol Soc Amer.* 80: 256-65.

Orians, G. H. 1962. Natural selection and ecological theory. *Amer. Nat.* 96: 257-63.

Rae, S. 1970. Studies in the ecology of Mason bog, Sagehen Creek, California. MS Thesis, University of California, Davis.

Reichenbach, H. 1951. *The Rise of Scientific Philosophy.* Berkeley: University of California Press.

Shanahan, T. 2004. *The Evolution of Darwinism. Selection, Adaptation and Progress in Evolutionary Biology.* Cambridge University Press.

Watkins, N.W. and M.P. Freeman.2008. Naural complexity. *Science* 320:323-24.

Wegener, A. 1920. *The Origin of Continents and Oceans.* London.

BACK TO THE MIDWEST

Bliss, L.C. 1956. A comparison of plant development in microenvironments of arctic and alpine environments. *Ecol. Monog.* 26: 303-37.

Braun, E. Lucy. 1950. *Deciduous Forests of Eastern North America*. Philadelphia: Blakiston.

_____. 1956. The development of association and climax concepts: their use in interpretation of the deciduous forest. *Amer. Jour. Bot.* 43: 906-11. And in *Fifty Years of Botany: Golden Jubilee volume of Bbotanical Society of America*, ed. W.C. Sterns, 329-39. New York: McGraw Hill.

Curtis, J.T. 1956. The modification of mid-latitude grasslands and forests by Man. In *Man's Role in Changing the Face of the Earth*, pp. 721-36, ed. W. L. Thomas, Jr. University of Chicago Press.

_____. 1959. *The Vegetation of Wisconsin: an ordination of plant communities*. Univ. of Wisconsin Press, Madison. 657 pp.

_____. and R.P. McIntosh. 1951. An upland forest continuum in the prairie-forest border region of Wisconsin. *Ecology* 32: 476-96.

Delcourt, H.R. and P.A. Delcourt. 2000. Eastern deciduous forests. In *North American Terrestrial Vegetation*, 2nd ed., pp. 357-95, eds. M.G. Barbour and W.D. Billings. Cambridge University. Press

Dyer, J, M. 2006. Revisiting the deciduous forests of eastern North America. *Bioscience* 56: 341-52

Fosberg, F. R. 1951. Review of the Eastern Deciduous Forests of North America. *Scientific Monthly*, July: 66-7.

Keever, C. 1950. Causes of succession on old fields of the piedmont, North Carolina. *Ecol. Monogr.* 20: 229-50.

_____. 1985. *Moving On*. Brady Printing Co., Statesville, NC.

Kuhn, T. 1962. *The Structure of Scientific Revolutions*. Chicago: University of Chicago Press.

Langenheim, J.H. 1961. Late Paleozoic and Early Mesozoic plant fossils from the Cordillera Orientale and correlation of the "Giron Formation." *Bol. Geol. VIII, Servicio Nacional de Colombia*: 99-118.

McIntosh, R. P. 1967. The continuum concept of vegetation. *Bot. Rev.* 33: 130-87.

_____. 1993. The continuum continued: John T. Curtis' influence on ecology. In *John T. Curtis. Fifty Years of Wisconsin Plant Ecology*. pp. 95-127, eds. J.S. Fralish, R.P. McIntosh and O.R. Loucks. Wisconsin Academy of Sciences, Arts and Letters.

Quarterman, E. 1950. Major plant communities of the cedar glades. *Ecology* 31: 234-54.

Stuckey, R. L. 1973. E. Lucy Braun (1889-1971) outstanding botanist and conservationist: a biographical sketch with bibliography. *Michigan Botanist* 12: 83-106.

Williams, J, W., B. N. Shuman, T. Webb, P. J. Bartlein, and P. L. Ledue. 2004. Late Quaternary vegetation dynamics in North America: Scaling from taxa to biomes. *Ecol. Monog.*74: 309-34.

http:// biology.usgs.gov/npsveg/classification/sect3.html
http:// www.esa.org/vegweb/

New Directions:*Amber and Divorce*

Carey,S., J. Harte, and R.delMoral. 2006. Effect of community assemby and primary succession on the specie-area relationship in disturbed ecosystems. *Ecography* 29:866-872.

Curtin, C. G. 1994. The Gothic earthflow revisited: a chronosequence examination of colonization of a subalpine earthflow. *Vegetatio* 111: 137-47.

Langenheim, J. H. 1956. Plant succession on a subalpine earthflow in Colorado. *Ecology* 37: 301-17.

_____.1962. Vegetation and environmental patterns in the Crested Butte Area, Gunnison County, Colorado. *Ecol. Monog.* 32: 249-85.

Miranda, F. 1952. *La Vegetación de Chiapas.* Dept. de Prensa y Turismo. Mexico: Tuxtla Gutiérrez.

Peet, R.K. 2000. Forests and meadows of the Rocky Mountains. In *North American Terrestrial Vegetatión*, 2nd ed., pp. 76-121, eds. M.G. Barbour and W.D. Billings. Cambridge University Press.

Radcliffe Institute for Independent Studies Brochure

Sears, P.B. 1956. Some notes on the ecology of ecologists. *Sci. Monthly* 83: 22-37.

Whittaker, R. H. 1956. Vegetation of the Great Smoky Mountains. *Ecol. Monogr.* 26: 1-80.

_____. 1960. Vegetation of the Siskiyou Mountains, Oregon and California. *Ecol. Monogr.* 30: 279-338.

_____. 1962. Classification of Natural Communities. *Bot. Review* 28: 1-239.

PART III SOLO CAREER

BEGINNING A NEW CAREER

Bliss, L.C. 1963. Alpine communities of the Presidential Range, New Hampshire. *Ecology* 44: 678-97.

Cittadino, E. 1980. Ecology and professionalization of botany in America 1890-1905. *Studies in the History of Biology* 4:171-98

Langenheim, J. H. 1964. Lichen and Mosses. In *Mountain Flowers of New England*, pp. 1-9. Appalachian Mountain Club.

_____. 1965. *Baltic amber as compared with Mexican amber.* Yearbook of the American Philosophical Society: 332-33.

_____. 1966. Botanical source of amber from Chiapas, Mexico. *Ciencia* 24: 201-11.

_____. and C. W. Beck. 1965. Infrared spectra as a means of determining botanical source of amber. *Science* 149: 52-5.

_____., B. Hackner, and A. Bartlett. 1967. Mangrove pollen at the depositional site of Oligo-Miocene amber from Chiapas, Mexico. *Harvard Bot. Mus. Leaflets* 21: 289-324.

_____. and C. W. Beck. 1968. Catalogue of infrared spectra of amber. Pt. I, North and South America. *Harvard Bot. Mus. Leaflets* 22: 65-120.

_____. and A. Bartlett. 1971. Interpretation of pollen in amber from a study of pollen in present-day coniferous resins. *Bull. Torrey Bot. Club* 98(3): 127-30.

Kingsland, S. 2005. *The Evolution of American Ecology, 1890-2000.* Baltimore, MD John Hopkins University Press.

Miranda, F. 1963. Two plants from Chiapas amber. *Jour. Paleo.* 37: 611-14.

Wilson, E. O. 1994. *Naturalist/E.O. Wilson.* Washington DC: Island Press.

COLLECTING AMBER FROM EUROPEAN MUSEUMS

Bachofen-Echt. 1949. *Der Berstein und seine Einschlüsse.* Wien.

Conwentz, H. W. 1890. *Monographie der baltschen Bernsteinbaume*. Danzig Commissions-Verlag W. Engelmann, Leipzig.

Czeczott, H. 1961. The flora of the Baltic amber and its age. Prace Museum Zeimi 4: 119-45.

Goeppert, H. R. and A. Menge. 1883. *Die Flora des Bernsteins und Ihre Beziehungen zur Flora der Tertiärformation und der Gegenwart*, Band 1. Danzig.

Grabowska, J. 1983. *Polish Amber*. Warsaw: Interpress Publishers.

Langenheim, J. H. 1964. Present status of botanical studies of amber. *Harvard Bot. Mus. Leaflets* 20: 225-87.

—————————. 1969. Amber: a botanical inquiry. *Science* 163:1157-69.

Larrson, S. G. 1978. *Baltic Amber—A Paleontological Study*. Denmark: Scandinavian Science Press.

Schubert, K. 1961. *Neue Untersuchungese über Bau und Leben der Bersteinkiefern [Pinus succinifera (Conw.) emend]. Beihefte zum Geologischen Jahrbuch 45.*

Takhtajan, A. 1969. *Flowering Plants: Origin and Dispersal.* Washington DC: Smithsonian Institution Press.

FAR-REACHING HARVARD ACTIVITIES

Bernholdt-Thomsen, V. 2005. Matriarchal principles for today's economics and societies: what we can learn from Juchitan. Second Congress on Matriarchal Studies. University of Texas at San Marcos.

Brokaw, T. 2007. *Boom. Voices of the Sixties*. New York: Random House.

Cavalcante, P. B. 1976. *Frutas Comestíveis da Amazônia*, 2nd ed. Brazil: Falangola.

Clinton, H. R. 2003. *Living History*. New York: Simon and Schuster.

Davis, W. 1996. *One River. Explorations and Discoveries in the Amazon Rain Forest*. NBew York: Touchstone.

Friedan, B. 1963. *The Feminine Mystique*. W. W. Norton & Co.

Gomez-Pompa, A., C. Vasquez-Yanes, and S. Guerera. 1972. The tropical rain forest: a non-renewable resource. *Science* 177: 762-5.

Goodman, E. 2006. *Remembering Betty Friedan*. Boston Globe, Feb 6.

Janzen, D. H. 1977. The impact of tropical studies on ecology. In *Changing Scenes in the Natural Sciences*, 1776-1976, pp. 159-97, ed. C. E. Goulden. Sp. Public 12, Philadelphia Academy of Sciences, Philadelphia, PA

_____. 1983. *Costa Rican Natural History*. University of Chicago Press.

Kaliner, M. 2004. *Views of 1950s graduates have changed dramatically*. Radcliffe Quarterly.

Langenheim, J. H. 1967. Preliminary investigations of *Hymenaea courbaril* as a resin producer. *J. Arn. Arb.* 48:205-27

O'Brien, T.P. and M.E. McCully, 1969. *Plant Structure and Development. A Pictorial and Physiological Approach*. New York, McMillan Co.

Paiva, E.A. S. and Machado,S. R. 2007.Structural and ultrastructural aspects of ontogenesis and differentiation of resin secretory cavities in *Hymenaea stigonocarpa* (Fabaceae-Caesalpinioideae) leaves. *Nordic Journal of Botany* 24:423-31.

Shapiro. A. R. 2004. *A Radcliffe girl at Harvard or Why members of class 1958 staged a revolution in 1993*. Gender in Harvard and Radcliffe History. Yards and Gates.

_____. 2005. Birth of a feminist. Remembering Radcliffe in the 1950s. *Harvard Magazine* March-April issue:15-7.

Schultes, R. E. and G. Von Reis. 1995. *Ethnobotany. Evolution of a Discipline*. Portland, OR: Timber Press.

University of California, Santa Cruz. 1965. General Catalogue.

RETURN TO CALIFORNIA-*UCSC* RESIDENTIAL COLLEGES

Norena, C. 2004. *The Rise and Demise of the UC Santa Cruz Colleges*. Institute of Government Studies, University of California, Berkeley. Berkeley Public Policy Press.

Thimann, K, V. 1989. *Early UCSC History and Founding of Crown College*. UCSC Oral History Report interviewed and edited by Randall Jarrell. UCSC Special Collections.

Willson, F. M. Glenn. 1989. *Early UCSC History and Founding of Stevenson College*. UCSC Oral History Report interviewed and edited by Randall Jarrell. UCSC Special Collections.

BOARDS OF STUDIES AND GRADUATE PROGRAM

Langenheim, J. H. and K.V. Thimann. 1976. Introducing students to plants through their relationship with Man. *Plant Science Bull.* 22: 14.

McIntosh, R. P. 1985. *The Background of Ecology. Concept and Theory*. New York: Cambridge University Press.

Odum, E. P. 1953. *Fundamentals of Ecology*, 2nd ed.Philadelphia: Saunders.

Schmitz,O.J., J.H. Grabowski, B. A. Peckarksky, E. L. Preisser, G.C. Trussell and J.R. Vonesh. 2008. From individuals to ecosystem function: toward an integration of evolutionary and ecosystem ecology. *Ecology* 89:2436-45.

Tansley, A. G. 1935. The use and abuse of vegetation concepts and terms. *Ecology* 16:284-307.

RESEARCH IN AFRICA

Clark, J.D. 1968. Further palaeo-anthropological studies in northern Lunda. *Publicações Culturais, Companhia de Diamantes de Angola* No. 78.

Ehrlich, P. R. and R. H. Raven. 1964. Butterflies and plants: a study in co-evolution. *Evolution* 18: 586-608.

Feeny, P. P 1992. The evolution of chemical ecology: contributions from study of herbivorous insects. In: *Herbivores: Their Interactions with Secondary Plant Metabolites*, Vol. II, *Ecological and Evolutionary Processes*, pp. 1-44, eds. G. H. Rosenthal and M. R. Berenbaum. New York: Academic Press.

Fraenkel, G. S. 1959. The raison d'être of secondary substances. *Science* 129: 1466-70.

Harborne, J. B. 1977. *Introduction to Ecological Biochemistry*. New York: Academic Press.

Hueber, F. M. and J. H. Langenheim. 1986. Dominican amber tree had African ancestors. *Geotimes* 31: 8-10.

Janzen, D. H. 1977. The impact of tropical studies on ecology. In *Changing Scenes in the Natural Sciences* 1776-1976, ed., C. Goulden. Special Publication 12, Philadelphia Academy of Sciences, Philadelphia, PA.

Langenheim, J. H. 1972. Botanical origin of fossilized resin and its relation to forest history in northeastern Angola. *Publicações Culturais*, Companhia de Diamantes de Angola No. 85: 15-36.

_____. 1973. Leguminous resin-producing trees in south America and Africa. In *Tropical Forest Ecosystems in Africa and South America: a Comparative Review*, pp. 879-104, eds. B.J. Meggars, E. S. Ayensu, and W. D. Duckworths. Washington DC: Smithsonian Press.

_____. and Y. T. Lee. 1974. Reinstatement of the genus *Hymenaea* (Leguminosae: Caesalpinioideae) in Africa. *Brittonia* 26: 3-21.

Léonard, J. 1950. Étude Botanique des Copaliers en Congo Belge. *Publications de l'Institut National pour d'Étude Agronomique du Congo Belge, Série Scientifique* 45: 1-158.

McIntosh, R. P. 1985. The Background of Ecology: Concept and Theory. Cambridge University Press.

Richards, P. W. 1963. What the tropics can contribute to ecology. *Jour Ecol* 51: 231-41.

_____. 1966. *The Tropical Rainforest*. Cambridge University Press.

Sondheimer, E. and J.B. Simeone (eds.). 1970. *Chemical Ecology*. London: Academic Press.

Whittaker, R. H. and P. P. Feeny. 1971. Allelochemics: chemical interactions between species. *Science* 171: 757-70.

EVOLUTION OF HYMENAEA *IN SOUTH AMERICA*

Alvim, P. 1964. Tree growth periodicity in tropical climates. In *The Formation of Wood in Forest Trees*, pp. 479-98, ed., M. H. Zimmerman. New York: Academic Press.

Brenan, J.P.M. 1965. The geographic relationships of the genera of the Leguminosae in tropical Africa. *Webbia* 19: 545-78.

Coleman,W. 1986. Evolution into ecology. The strategy of Warming's ecological plant geography. *Jour. Hist. Bio.* 19: 181-96.

Diamond, J. 1999. *Guns, Germs and Steel: The Fates of Human Societies*. New York: W. W. Norton and Co.

Eiten, G. 1972. The Cerrado Vegetation of Brazil. *Bot. Rev.* 38: 586-608.

Langenheim, J. H. 1969. Amber: a botanical inquiry. *Science* 163: 1157-69.

——————————. 1973. Leguminous resin-producing trees in Africa and South America. In *Tropical Forest Ecosystems in Africa and South America: a Comparative Review*, eds., B. J. Meggars, E. S. Ayensu, and W. D. Duckworths. Washington DC: Smithsonian Press.

Ramos, A.C.S., J. Lemos-Filho, R.A. Ribeiro,F.R. Santos and M. B. Lovato. 2007. Phylogeography of the tree *Hymenaea stigonocarpa* (Fabaceae:Caesalpinioideae) and influence of quaternary climate changes in the Brazilian cerrado. *Ann. Bot.*100:1219-28.

——————————and M.B.Lovato. 2008.Phylogeographical structure of the neotropical tree *Hymenaea courbaril* (Leguminosae:Caesalpinioideae) and its relation with the variant *H.stigonocarpa* from cerrado. *Journal of Heredity* In press.

Spruce, R. edited and condensed by Wallace, A. R. 1908. 2 vols., London: McMillan.

Sternberg, H. O. 1975. *Amazon River of Brazil*. New York: Springer-Verlag.

Thorne, R. F. 1973. Floristic relationships between tropical Africa and tropical America. In *Tropical Forest Ecosystems in Africa and South America: a Comparative Review*, eds. B. J. Meggars, E. S. Ayensu, and W. D. Duckworths. Washington DC: Smithsonian Press.

Wolfe, J. A. 1971. Tertiary climate fluctuations and methods of analysis of Tertiary floras. Paleogr. *Paleoclimatol. Paleoecol.* 9: 27-57.

Zavarin, E. 1970. Qualitative and quantitative co-occurrences of terpenoids as a tool for elucidation of their biosyntheses. *Phytochemistry* 9: 1049-63.

HALLMARK YEARS

Cunningham, A., S. S. Martin, and J. H. Langenheim. 1973. Resin acids from two Amazonian species of *Hymenaea* (Leguminosae: Caesalpinioideae). *Phytochemistry* 12: 633-5.

Gershenzon, J., D. E. Lincoln, and J. H. Langenheim. 1978. The effect of moisture stress on monoterpenoid yield and composition in *Satureja douglasii*. *Biochem. Syst. Ecol.* 6: 33-44.

Greenlee, J. M. 1983. *Vegetation, Fire History, and Fire Potential of Big Basin State Park, California*. PhD dissertation, University of California, Santa Cruz.

——————————. and J. H. Langenheim. 1990. Historic fire regimes and their relation to vegetation patterns in the Monterey Bay of California. *Amer. Midland Naturalist* 124: 239-55.

Langenheim J. H., Y. T. Lee, and S. S. Martin. 1973. An evolutionary and ecological perspective of the Amazonian hylaea species of *Hymenaea* (Leguminosae: Caesalpinioideae). *Acta Amazonica* 3(1): 5-38.

_____, C. E. Foster, D. E. Lincoln, and W. H. Stubblebine. 1978. Implications of variation in resin composition among organs, tissues, and populations in the tropical legume *Hymenaea*. *Biochem. Syst. Ecol.* 6: 299-313.

_____, W. H. Stubblebine, and C. E. Foster. 1979. Effects of moisture stress on leaf resin composition and yield in *Hymenaea courbaril*. *Biochem. Syst. Ecol.* 7: 21-8.

_____., C. E. Foster, and R. M. McGinley. 1980. Inhibitory effects of different quantitative compositions of *Hymenaea* leaf resins on a generalist herbivore *Spodoptera exigua*. *Biochem. Syst. Ecol.* 8: 385-96.

_____, D. E. Lincoln, W. H. Stubblebine, and A. C. Gabrielli. 1982. Evolutionary implications of leaf resin pock patterns in the tropic tree legume *Hymenaea* (Caesalpinioideae: Leguminosae). *Amer. Jour. Bot.* 69: 595-607.

Lincoln, D. E. and J. H. Langenheim. 1976. Geographic patterns of monoterpenoid composition in *Satureja douglasii*. *Biochem. Syst. Ecol.* 4: 237-240.

_____. and _____. 1978. Effect of light and temperature on monoterpenoid yield and composition in *Satureja douglasii*. *Biochem. Syst. Ecol.* 9: 153-60.

_____. and _____. 1979. Variation of *Satureja douglasii* monoterpenoids in relation to light intensity and herbivory. *Biochem. Syst. Ecol.* 7: 289-98.

_____. and _____. 1981. A genetic approach to monoterpenoid compositional variation in *Satureja douglasii*. *Biochem. Syst. Ecol.* 9: 153-60.

McGrayne, S. B. 1993. Barbara McClintock In *Nobel Prize Women in Science: Their Lives, Struggles andMomentousDiscoveries*, pp157-80, ed S. B. McGrayne. Washington DC: Joseph Henry Press, National Academy of Sciences.

Martin, S. S., E. Zavarin, and J. H. Langenheim. 1973. Compositional variation of leaf pocket sesquiterpenes in *Trachylobium verrucosum*. *Biochem. Syst. Ecol.* 1: 35-7.

_____, _____, and _____. 1974. Quantitative variation in leaf pocket resin composition in *Hymenaea courbaril*. *Biochem. Syst. Ecol.* 3: 75-87.

_____, _____, and _____. 1976. Quantitative variation of leaf resin composition in *Hymenaea. Biochem. Syst. Ecol.* 4: 181-91.

_____, _____, and _____. 1976. Biosynthesis of sesquiterpenes in leaf pocket resins in *Hymenaea* inferred from their quantitative co-occurrence. *Phytochemistry* 15: 113-19.

Prance, G. T. 1985. The increased importance of ethnobotany and underexploited plants in a changing Amazon. In *Change in the Amazon Basin.* Vol. 1, pp. 129-36, ed. J. Hemming. Manchester: Manchester University Press.

Rice, R. L., D. E. Lincoln, and J. H. Langenheim. 1978. Palatability of monoterpenoid compositional types of *Satureja douglasii* to a generalist herbivore *Ariolimax dolichophallus. Biochem. Syst. Ecol.* 6: 45-53.

Stone, D. E. 1988. The Organization for Tropical Studies: a success story in graduate training and research. In *Tropical Rainforests. Diversity and Conservation*, pp. 143-88, eds. F. Almeda and C. M. Pringle. California Academy of Science Memoir #12.

Stubblebine, W. H., D. E. Lincoln, and J. H. Langenheim. 1975. Vegetative growth and leaf resin composition in *Hymenaea courbaril* under photoperiodic extremes. *Biochem. Syst. Ecol.* 3: 219-28.

_____. and J. H. Langenheim. 1977. Effects of *Hymenaea courbaril* leaf resin on the generalist herbivore *Spodoptera exigua* (beet army worm). *J. Chem. Ecol.* 3:633-47.

TEACHING BRAZILIAN BOTANISTS IN AMAZONIA

Bates, H. W. 1962. *The Naturalist on the River Amazons.* Berkeley: University of California Press (abridged reprint).

Cavalcante, P. B. 1976. *Frutas Comestíveis da Amazonia.* Edição Comemorativa XII Congresso da Sociedade Brasileiro de Medicina Tropical. Belém, Pará.

Goodland, R. J. A. and Irwin, H. S. 1975. *Amazon Jungle: Green Hell to Red Desert?* Amsterdam: Elsevier.

Goulding, M. 1980. *The Fishes and the Forest.* Berkeley: University of California Press.

Langenheim, J.H. 1971. My experience in Amazonia. *Acta Amazônica* 1: 91.

_____, Y. T. Lee, and S. S. Martin. 1973. An evolutionary and ecological perspective of the Amazonian hylaea species of *Hymenaea* (Leguminosae: Caesalpinioideae). *Acta Amazônica* 3(1): 5-38.

Langmead, Clive. 2001. *A Passion for Plants: the Life and Vision of Ghillean Prance, Director of the Royal Botanic Gardens*, Royal Botanic Gardens, Kew, UK.

Lee, Y. T. and J. H. Langenheim. 1975. *Systematics of the Genus Hymenaea* (Leguminosae: Caesalpinioideae, Detarieae). University of California Publications in Botany 69: 190 pp.

Prance, G.T. 1985. The increased importance of ethnobotany and underexploited plants in a changing Amazon. In *Change in the Amazon Basin*, Vol. 1, pp. 129-36, ed. J. Hemming. Manchester, UK: Manchester University Press.

ORGANIZATION FOR TROPICAL STUDIES

Clark, D. B. 1988. The search for solutions: Research and education at the La Selva Station and their relation to ecodevelopment. In *Tropical Rainforests. Diversity and Conservation*, pp. 209-22, eds. F. Almeda and C. M. Pringle. California Academy of Sciences and Pacific Division, American Association for the Advancement of Science, San Francisco, California.

Gamez, P. and A. Ugalde. 1988. Costa Rica's national park system and the preservation of biological diversity. In *Tropical Rainforests. Diversity and Conservation*, pp. 131-42, eds. F. Almeda and C. M. Pringle. California Academy of Sciences and Pacific Division of American Association for Advancement of Sciences, San Francisco, California.

Langenheim, J. H. and C. S. Balser. 1975. Botanical origin of resin objects from aboriginal Costa Rica. *Vinculos* 1(3): 72-82.

Stone, D. E. 1988. The Organization for Tropical Studies (OTS). A success story in graduate training and research. In *Tropical Rainforests. Diversity and Conservation*, pp. 143-84, eds. F. Almeda and C. M. Pringle. California Academy of Sciences and Pacific Division, American Association for the Advancement of Science. San Francisco, California.

INTERTWINED RESEARCH, TRAVEL, AND PERSONAL LOSS

Arroyo, M. T. K. 1981. Breeding systems and pollination biology in the Leguminosae. In *Advances in Legume Systematics*, Part II, pp. 135-70, eds. R. M. Polhill and P. H. Raven. Royal Botanic Gardens, Kew, UK.

Calvin, M. 1983. New sources of fuel and materials. *Science* 219:24-26.

Cunningham, A., P. R. West, G. S. Hammond, and J. H. Langenheim. 1977. The existence and photochemical initiation of free radicals in *Hymenaea* trunk resins. *Phytochemistry* 16: 142-3.

_____, I. D. Gay, A. C. Oehlschlager, and J. H. Langenheim. 1983. 13C NMR and IR analyses of structure, aging and botanical origin of Dominican and Mexican ambers. *Phytochemistry* 22: 965-8.

Langenheim, J. H. 1981. Terpenoids in the Leguminosae. In *Advances in Legume Systematics*, Part II, pp. 627-55, eds. R. M. Polhill and P. H. Raven. Royal Botanic Gardens, Kew, UK.

Polhill, R. M. and P. H. Raven, eds. 1981. *Advances in Legume Systematics*. Royal Botanic Gardens, Kew, UK.

Van Aarssen, B. G. K., J. W. Leeuw, M. Collinson, J. J. Baon, and K. Goth. 1994. Occurrence of polycadenine in fossil and recent resins. *Geochimica et Cosmochimica Acta* 58: 223-9.

Xena de Enrech, N., M. T. K. Arroyo, and J. H. Langenheim. 1983. Systemática del genero *Copaifera* L. (Leguminosae: Caesalpinioideae, Detarieae) en Venezuela. *Acta Botanica Venezuelica* 14: 239-290.

COMPARING HYMENAEA AND COPAIFERA ACROSS BRAZIL

Alencar, J. C. 1982. Estudos silviculturais de uma população natural de *Copaifera multijuga* Hayne—Leguminaceae, na Amazônica central 2-produção de óleo-resina. *Acta Amazônica* 12: 75-89

Arrhenius, S. P., C. E. Foster, C. G. Edmonds, and J. H. Langenheim. 1983. Sesquiterpenes in leaf pocket resins of *Copaifera* species. *Phytochemistry* 22: 471-2.

Andrade-Lima D. de 1982. Present-day refuges in Northeastern Brazil. In *Biological Diversification in the Tropics*, pp. 245-54, ed. G. T. Prance. New York: Columbia University Press

Bates, H. W. 1863. The Naturalist on the River Amazon London: John Murray.

Bierregaard, R. O., Jr., C. Gason, T. E. Lovejoy, and R. C. G. Mesquito, eds. 2001. *Lessons from Amazonia. The Ecology and Conservation of a Fragmented Forest*. Connecticut: Yale University Press.

Connell, J.H. 1970. On the role of natural enemies in preventing competitive exclusion in some marine animals and rain forest trees. Proc. Adv. Study Inst. Dynamic Numbers Popl. (Oosterbeck): 298-312.

Fearnside, P. M. 1982. Deforestation in the Amazon Basin. How fast is it occurring? *Interciencia* 7: 82-8.

_____. 1986. *Human Carrying Capacity of the Brazilian Rainforest*. New York: Columbia University Press.

Hemming, J. ed. 1985. *Change in the Amazon Basin*, vol. 1. Manchester: Manchester University Press.

Janzen, D. H. 1970. Herbivores and the number of species in tropical forests. *Amer. Nat.* 104: 501-28.

Langenheim, J. H., W. H. Stubblebine, C. E. Foster, and J. C. Nascimento. 1977. Estudos comparativos da variabilidade na composição da resina da folha entre árvore parental e progenie de especies selectionadas de *Hymenaea*. I, Comparação de populacoes Amazônicas e Venzuelanas. *Acta Amazônica* 7: 335-54.

_____, and W. H. Stubblebine. 1983. Variation in leaf resin composition between parent tree and progeny in *Hymenaea*: Implications for herbivory in the humid tropics. *Biochem. Syst. Ecol.* 11: 97-106.

Loman, M. D. 2000. *Life in the Treetops. Adventures of a Woman in Field Biology*. Yale Nota Bene. Connecticut: Yale University Press.

Nadkarni, N. M. 1988. Tropical rainforest ecology from a canopy perspective. In *Tropical Rainforests: Diversity and Conservation*, eds. F. Almeda and C. M. Pringle. California Academy of Science Memoir #12: 189-208.

Nascimento, J. C. 1986. Leaf sesquiterpenes and phenolics in *Copaifera multijuga* (Leguminosae) on contrasting soil types in a Central Amazonian rainforest. *Biochem. Syst. Ecol.* 14: 615-24.

Sanchez-Hidalgo, M. E., M. Martinez-Ramos, and F. J. Espinosa-Garcia. 1999. Chemical differentiation between leaves of seedlings and spatially close adult trees from the tropical rainforest species *Nectandra ambigeus* (Lauraceae): an alternate test of the Janzen-Connell model. *Functional Ecology* 13: 725-32.

Spruce, R. 1908 (ed. A.R. Wallace) *Notes of A Botanist on the Amazon and Andes*. 2 vols., London: Macmillan and Co.

Stubblebine, W. H. and J. H. Langenheim. 1980. Estudos comparativos da variabilidade na composição da resina da folha entre árvore parental e progênie de espécies selectionadas de *Hymenaea*. II. Comparacão de populacoes adicionais Amazônicas e do sul do Brasil. *Acta Amazônica* 10(2): 293-307.

CHEMICAL DEFENSE OF HYMENAEA AND COPAIFERA

Adams, S. A. 1988. Interview. Chinese Botany and the Odyssey of Dr. Shui-ying Hu. Arnoldia, spring 1988: 30-31.

Arrhenius,S. P. and J. H. Langenheim. 1983. Inhibitory effects of *Hymenaea* and *Copaifera* leaf resins on the leaf fungus *Pestalotia subcuticularis*. *Biochem. Syst. Ecol.* 11: 316-66.

_____. and J. H. Langenheim. 1986. The association of *Pestalotia* on the leguminous tree genera *Hymenaea* and *Copaifera* in the Neotropics. *Mycologia* 78: 673-6.

Bryant, J. R.,F.S. Chapin III, D. R. Klein. 1983. Carbon/nutrient balance of boreal plants in relation to vertebrate herbivory. *Oikos* 40:357-68.

Cates, R. G. 1996. The role of mixtures and variation in the production of terpenoids in conifer-insect-pathogen interactions. In *Phytochemical Diversity and Redundancy in Ecological Interactions*, pp. 199-216, eds. J. T. Romeo, J. A. Saunders, and P. Barbosa. New York: Plenum Press.

Coley, P. D. and T. M. Aide. 1989. Red coloration of tropical young leaves: a possible fungal defense? *J. Trop. Ecol.* 5: 293-300.

Crankshaw, D. R. and J. H. Langenheim. 1981. Variation in terpenes and phenolics through leaf development in *Hymenaea* and its possible significance to herbivory. *Biochem. Syst. Ecol.* 9: 115-24.

Fail, G. 1990. Ultrastructural studies of leaf/fungal interactions and secondary chemical production in *Hymenaea courbaril*, a tropical leguminous tree. PhD dissertation, University of California, Santa Cruz.

_____. and J. H. Langenheim. 1990. The infection process of *Pestalotia subcuticularis* on leaves of *Hymenaea courbaril*. *Phytopathology* 80: 1259-65.

Feibert, E. B. and J. H. Langenheim. 1988. Leaf resin variation in *Copaifera langsdorfii*: relation to irradiation and herbivory in a Brazilian woodland. *Phytochemistry* 27: 2525-32.

Gartlan, J. S., D. B. McKay, P. G. Waterman, C. N. Mbi, and T. T. Struhsaker. 1980. A comparative study of the phytochemistry of two African rainforests. *Biochem Syst Ecol.* 8: 41.

Heringer, E. P. 1971. Flora micológia des especies de *cerrado* di Paropeba e arredores, M. G. *Cerrado* 3: 9-14.

Hubbell, S., D. E. Weimar, and A. Adejare. 1983. An antifungal terpenoid defends a Neotropical tree (*Hymenaea*) against attack by a fungal-growing ant (*Atta*). *Oecologia* 60:321-27.

Kursar,T.A.,T.L. Capson, P.D. Coley, D.G. Corley, M.B. Gupta, L.A. Harrison, E. Ortega and D.Windsor. 1999. Ecologically guided bioprospecting in Panama. *Pharmaceutical Biology* 37 (Supplement):1-14.

Langenheim, J. H., S. Arrhenius, and J. C. Nascimento. 1981. Relationship of light intensity of leaf resin composition and yield in the leguminous genera *Hymenaea* and *Copaifera*. *Biochem. Syst. Ecol.* 9: 27-37.

_____ and G. D. Hall. 1983. Sesquiterpene deterrence of a leaf-tying lepidopteran *Stenoma ferrocannella* on *Hymenaea stigonocarpa* in Central Brazil. *Biochem. Syst. Ecol.* 11: 29-36.

_____., C. L. Convis, C. A. Macedo, and W. H. Stubblebine. 1986. *Hymenaea* and *Copaifera* leaf sesquiterpenes in relation to lepidopteran herbivory in Southeastern Brazil. *Biochem. Syst. Ecol.* 14: 41-49.

_____., C. A. Macedo, M. K. Ross, and W. H. Stubblebine. 1986. Leaf development in the tropical leguminous tree *Copaifera* in relation to microlepidopteran herbivory. *Biochem. Syst. Ecol.* 14: 51-59.

Macedo, C. A. and J. H. Langenheim. 1989. Intra-and interplant leaf sesquiterpene variability in *Copaifera langsdorfii*: relation to microlepidopteran herbivory. *Biochem. Syst. Ecol.* 17: 551-7.

_____. and _____. 1989. A further investigation of leaf sesquiterpene variation in relation to herbivory in two Brazilian populations of *Copaifera langsdorfii*. *Biochem. Syst. Ecol.* 17: 217-24.

_____. and _____. 1989. Microlepidopteran herbivory in relation to leaf sesquiterpenes in *Copaifera langsdorfii* adult trees and their seedling progeny in a Brazilian woodland. *Biochem. Syst. Ecol.* 16: 217-24.

McCloskey, L. P. 1984. Leaf phenolic compounds in the tropical tree genera *Hymenaea* and *Copaifera*. PhD Dissertation, University of California, Santa Cruz.

Medeiro,R. S. and G.Veira.2008. Sustainability and production of copaiba (*Copaifera multijuga* Hayne) oleoresin in Manaus AM, Brazil. Forest Ecology and Management. In Press.

Ross, M. K. 1986. Oecophorid herbivory on *Copaifera langsdorfii* in relation to sesquiterpene variation in Southeastern Brazil. MS Thesis, University of California. Santa Cruz.

Zucker, W. V. 1983. Tannins: does structure determine function? An ecological perspective. *Amer. Nat.* 121: 335-65.

THAILAND AND AUSTRALIA ADVENTURE

Connell, J. H. 1978. Diversity in tropical rainforests and coral reefs. *Science* 199: 1302-10.

Dell, B. and A. J. McComb. 1978. Plant resins: their formation, secretion and possible functions. *Advances in Botanical Research* 16: 277-316.

Gianno, R. 1990. *Semelai Culture and Resin Technology*. New Haven: Conn. Acad. Arts and Sci.

Kingsolver, J. G. and D.W. Pfennig. 2007. Patterns and power of phenotypic selection in nature. *Bioscience* 57: 561-72.

Langenheim, J. H. and K. V. Thimann. 1982. *Botany: Plant Biology in Its Relation to Human Affairs*. New York: John Wiley.

——————————., C. B. Osmond, A. Brooks, and P. J. Ferrar. 1984. Photosynthetic responses to light in seedlings of selected Amazonian and Australian rainforest tree species. *Oecologia* 63: 215-24.

Lowman, M. D. 2000. *Life in the Treetops. Adventures of a Woman in Field Biology*. Yale Nota Bene. Connecticut: Yale University Press.

McNeil, J. 1991. Northlands buried treasure. *New Zealand Geographic* 10: 17-45.

Morrow, P. A. and L. R. Fox. 1980. Effects of variation in *Eucalyptus* essential oil yield on insect growth and grazing damage. *Oecologia* 45: 209-19.

Rhoades, D. G. 1977. Integrated antiherbivore, ant desiccant and ultraviolet screening properties of creosote bush resin. *Biochem. Syst. Ecol.* 5: 281-90.

Whitmore, T. C. 1984. A monograph of *Agathis. Plant Syst. Evol.* 135: 41-69.

PART IV CHANGING COURSE

EXPANSION OF RESEARCH DIRECTIONS

Bierregaard, R. O., Jr., C. Gason, T. E. Lovejoy, and R. C. G. Mesquito, eds. 2001. *Lessons from Amazonia. The Ecology and Conservation of a Fragmented Forest.* Connecticut: Yale University Press.

Carroll, G. C. 1986. The biology of endophytism in plants with particular reference to woody plants. In *Microbiology of the Phyllosphere*, pp. 205-22, eds. N. Fokkema and J. Van den Huevel. London: Cambridge University Press.

_____. 1988. Fungal endophytes in stems and leaves: from latent pathogen to mutualistic symbiont. *Ecology* 69: 2-9.

Cates, R. G. 1996. The role of mixtures and variation in the production of terpenoids in conifer-insect-pathogen interactions. In *Phytochemical Diversity and Redundancy in Ecological Interactions*, pp. 199-216, eds. J. T. Romeo, J. A. Saunders, and P. Barbosa. New York: Plenum Press.

Coley, P. D., J. P. Bryant, and F. S. Chapin III. 1985. Resource availability and plant antiherbivore defense. *Science* 230: 895-9.

_____. and T. M. Aide. 1991. Comparison of herbivore and plant defenses in temperate and broad-leaved forests. In *Plant-Animal Interactions: Evolutionary Ecology in Tropical and Temperate Regions*, pp. 25-49, eds. P. W. Price, G. W. Fernandes, and W. W. Ransom. New York: John Smiley & Sons.

Espinosa-Garcia, F. J. and J. H. Langenheim. 1990. The leaf fungal community of a coastal redwood population: diversity and spatial patterns. *New Phytologist* 116: 89-97.

_____. and _____. 1991. Effect of some leaf essential oil phenotypes of coastal redwood on growth of its predominantly endophytic fungus, *Pleuroplacanema* sp. *J. Chem. Ecol.* 17: 1837-57.

_____. and _____. 1991. Effect of some leaf essential oil phenotypes of coastal redwood on growth of several of its fungi with endophytic stages. *Biochem. Syst. Ecol.* 19: 629-41.

_____. and _____. 1991. Effects of sabinene and terpinene from coastal redwood leaves acting singly or mixtures on the growth of some of their fungus endophytes. *Biochem. Syst. Ecol.* 19: 643-50.

522   REFERENCES

——————, P. Saldivar-Garua, and J. H. Langenheim. 1993. Dose-dependent effects *in vitro* of essential oils on growth of two endophytic fungi in coastal redwood leaves. *Biochem. Syst. Ecol.* 21: 185-94.

——————,J. Rollinger, and J. H. Langenheim. 1996. Coastal redwood leaf endophytes: Their occurrence, interactions and response to host volatile terpenoids. In *Endophytic Fungi in Grasses and Woody plants*, pp. 101-20, eds. S. C. Redlin and L. C. Carris. Minnesota: American Phytopath. Soc.

Feeny, P. 1976. Plant apparency and chemical defense. In *Biochemical Interaction Between Plants and Insects*, pp. 1-40, eds. J. W. Wallace and R. L. Mansell. New York: Plenum Press.

Figliuolo, R., S. Naylor, and J. H. Langenheim. 1987. Unusual nonprotein imino acid and its relationship to phenolic and nitrogenous compounds. *Phytochemistry* 26: 3255-9.

Fujiyoshi, P. T., S. R. Gliessman, and J. H. Langenheim. 2001. The inhibitory potential of compounds released by squash (*Cucurbita* spp.) in an ecological significant manner. *Allelopathy* 9:1-18.

——————, —————— and —————— 2007. Factors in the suppression of weeds by squash intercropped in corn. *Weed biology and Management* 7:105-14.

Goralka, R. J. and J. H. Langenheim. 1995. Analysis of foliar monoterpenoid content in the California Bay Tree, *Umbellularia californica*, among populations across the distribution of the species. *Biochem. Syst. Ecol.* 23: 439-48.

—————— and——————. 1996. Comparison of foliar monoterpenoids among ontogenetic stages of the California Bay Tree, *Umbellularia californica*, in relation to deer herbivory. *Biochem. Syst. Ecol.* 24: 13-23.

——————, M. A. Schumaker, and J. H. Langenheim. 1996. Chemical analysis of California Bay Tree, *Umbellularia californica*, foliage during leaf stage development in relation to seasonal browse quality. *Biochem. Syst. Ecol.* 24: 93-103.

Gliessman, S. R. 1998. *Agroecology. Ecological Processes in Sustainable Agriculture*. Michigan: Sleeping Bear Press.

Hall, G. D. and J. H. Langenheim. 1986. Within-tree spatial variation in the leaf monoterpenes of *Sequoia sempervirens*. *Biochem. Syst. Ecol.* 14: 625-32.

——————. and J. H. Langenheim. 1986. Temporal changes in the leaf monoterpenes of *Sequoia sempervirens*. *Biochem. Syst. Ecol.* 14: 61-69.

_____. and J. H. Langenheim. 1987. Geographic variation in leaf monoterpenes of *Sequoia sempervirens. Biochem. Syst. Ecol.* 15: 31-45.

Kim, J. J. and J. H. Langenheim. 1994. The effects of *Pseudotsuga menziesii* monoterpenoids on nitrification. *Korean J. Ecol.* 17: 251-60.

Langenheim, J. H. 1994. Higher plant terpenoids: phytocentric overview of their ecological roles. *Journal of Chemical Ecology* 20: 1223-80.

McKey. 1979. The distribution of secondary compounds within plants. In *Herbivores. Their Interactions with Secondary Plant Metabolites*, pp. 53-133, eds. G.A Rosenthal and D. H. Janzen. New York: Academic Press.

Peer, W. A. and J. H. Langenheim. 1998. Influence of phytochrome on leaf monoterpene variation in *Satureja douglasii. Biochem. Syst. Ecol.* 26: 25-34.

_____, W. R. Briggs, and J. H. Langenheim. 1999. Shade avoidance responses in two common coastal redwood forest species, *Sequoia sempervirens* (Taxodiaceae) and *Satureja douglasii* (Lamiaceae), occurring in various light environments. *Amer. Jour. of Botany* 86: 640-5.

Rhoades, D. G. and R. G. Cates.1976. Toward a general theory of plant antiherbivore chemistry. In *Biochemical Interactions Between Plants and Insects*, pp. 168-213, eds. J. W. Wallace and R. L. Mansell. New York: Plenum Press.

Rhoades, D. G. 1979.Evolution of plant defense against herbivores In *Herbivores: Their Interactions with Secondary Plant Metabolites*, pp4-48, eds., G. A. Rosenthal and D. H. Janzen. New York: Academic Press.

Rollinger, J. and J. H. Langenheim. 1993. Geographic variation in the fungal endophyte community composition in leaves of *Sequoia sempervirens. Mycologia* 85: 149-56.

Unsicker. J. E. 1974. Synecology of the California Bay Tree, *Umbellularia* (H. & A.) Nutt. in the Santa Cruz Mountains. PhD Dissertation, University of California, Santa Cruz.

Wang, J. and J. H. Langenheim. 1990. Seasonal and diurnal variation in leaf sesquiterpenes of greenhouse-grown saplings of *Hymenaea* and *Copaifera. Acta Botanica Yunnanica* 12: 851-9 (in Chinese).

Ward, B. B., K. J. Courtney, and J. H. Langenheim. 1997. Inhibition of *Nitrosomas europea* by monoterpenes from coastal redwood (*Sequoia sempervirens*) in whole cell cultures. *J. Chem. Ecol.* 23: 2583-98.

White, C. S. 1994. Monoterpenes: their effects on nutrient cycling. *J. Chem. Ecol.* 1381-406.

Wood, S. E., J. F. Gaskin, and J. H. Langenheim. 1995. Loss of monoterpenes from *Umbellularia californica* leaf litter. *Biochem. Syst. Ecol.* 23: 581-91.

MADAME PRESIDENT

Carpenter, C. 1970.The political use of ecological information. *Bioscience* 20: 1285.

Carson, R. 1964. *Silent Spring*. Massachussets: Houghton Mifflin Inc.

Harrison, P. 2007.The path of a president. *Radcliffe Quarterly* 1111: 9-11.

Jones, D. 1972. Cyanogenic glycosides and their function. In *Phytochemical Ecology*, pp. 103-24, ed. J. B. Harborne. London: Academic Press.

Langenheim, J. H. 1988. The path and progress of American women ecologists. Address of Past President. *Bull. Ecol. Soc. Amer.* 69: 184-97.

——————. 1996. The early history and progress of women ecologists: emphasis on research contributions. *Ann. Rev. Ecol. Syst.* 27: 1-53.

McGrayne, S.B. 1993. Barbara McClintock. In *Nobel Prize Women in Science: their Lives, Struggles and Momentous Discoveries*, pp157-80,ed S B. McGrayne, Washington DC: Joseph Henry Press, National Academy of Sciences.

Rimer, S. 2007. *A rebellious daughter to lead Harvard*. New York Times, Feb 12, 2007.

Rosenthal, G. and D. Jansen. 1979. *Herbivores: Their Interaction with Secondary Plant Metabolites*. New York: Academic Press.

Sears, P. B. 1964. Ecology—a subversive subject. *Bioscience* 14: 11-13.

Shelford, V., ed. 1925. *Naturalist's Guide to the Americas*. Baltimore: Williams and Wilkins.

EVOLVING SOCIAL AND FAMILY LIFE

Sinsheimer, R. L. 1994. *The Strands of a Life. The Science of DNA and the Art of Education*. Berkeley: University of California Press.

EMERITUS BUT NOT RETIRED

ANDERSON, K. B. AND B. A. LEPAIGE. 1995. Analysis Of Fossil Resins From Axel Heiberg Island, Canadian arctic. In *Amber, Resinite and Fossil Resins*, pp. 170-92. American Chemical Society Symposium series, No 167.

Cates, R. G. 1996. The role of mixtures and variation in the production of terpenoids in conifer-insect-pathogen interactions. In *Phytochemical Diversity and Redundancy in Ecological Interactions*, pp. 199-216, eds. J. T. Romeo, J. A. Saunders, and P. Barbosa. New York: Plenum Press.

Langenheim, J. H. 1995. Higher plant terpenoids: a phytocentric overview of their ecological roles. *Journal of Chemical Ecology* 20: 1223-80.

_____. 1995. Biology of amber-producing trees: focus on case studies of *Hymenaea* and *Agathis*. In *Amber, Resinite and Fossil Resins*, pp. 1-30, eds. K. B. Anderson and C. J. Krelling. American Chemical Society Symposium Series, No. 617.

_____. 2001. Contribuiciones de los estudios de largo plaza de la Theoría de la Defensa Quiímica: perspectivos con árboles resinosas da zonas templadas y tropicales. In *Relaciones Quimicas entre Organismos: Aspectos Básicos y Perspectivas de sus Aplicación*, pp. 251-304, eds. A. L. Anaya, F. Espinosa-Garcia, and R. Cruz-Ortega. Instituto de Ecologia, UNAM and Plaza y Valdes, S.A. de C. V.

Linhart, Y. B. 1988. Ecological and evolutionary studies of ponderosa pine in the Rocky Mountains. In *Ponderosa Pine: the Species and its Management*, pp. 77-89, eds. D. M. Baumgartner and J. E. Lotan. Washington State University Cooperative Extension, Pullman.

Nissenbaum, A., D. Yakir, and J. H. Langenheim. 2005. Bulk carbon, oxygen and hydrogen stable isotope composition of recent resins from amber-producing *Hymenaea*. *Naturwissenschaften* 92: 26-29.

Shimada, I., K. B. Anderson, H. Haas, and J. H. Langenheim. 1997. Amber from 1000-year-old prehistoric tombs in northern Peru. *Materials Issues in Art and Archeology* 1: 3-18.

RETURN TO THE NORTHERN ENVIRONS

Cooper, W. S. 1924. Report of the Ecological Society of America Committee on Glacier Bay, Alaska. *Ecology* 5: 208-9.

_____. 1937. The problem of Glacier Bay, Alaska: A study of glacial variations. *Geogr. Rev.* 27: 37-62.

_____. 1939. A fourth expedition to Glacier Bay, Alaska. *Ecology* 20: 130-55.

Crocker, R. L. and J. Major. 1955. Soil development in relation to vegetation and surface age at Glacier Bay, Alaska. *Journal of Ecology* 43: 427-48.

Harris, L. 1964. *The story of the Group of Seven*. Canada: Rous and Mann Press.

FULL CIRCLE

Altermann, S. 2009. Geographic structure in a symbiotic mutualism. Ph D Dissertation, University of California, Santa Cruz.

Arbogast, B. S., S. V. Drovtski, and R. L. Curry. 2006. The origin and diversification of Gálapagos mockingbirds. *Evolution* 60: 370-82.

Grant, P. and R. Grant. 2006. Evolution of character displacement in Darwin's finches. *Science* 313: 224-26.

Hofstra, T. 2003. Distribution, genetic diversity and compositional variation of wetwood procaryotic communities within and among native California *Populus* species. PhD Dissertation, University of California, Santa Cruz.

Langenheim, J. H. 2003. *Plant Resins: Chemistry, Evolution, Ecology and Ethnobotany*. Portland, Oregon: Timber Press.

Porter, D. M. 1979. Endemism and evolution in Gálapagos Islands vascular plants. In *Plants and Islands*, ed. D. Bramwell. New York: Academic Press.

PHOTO AND ART CREDITS

Most of the photographs are my own—either taken directly or taken by others, often using my camera—or as part of family records. A few, however, should be credited to others, including institutions, and for which I express my thanks for their generosity.

Photo on cover—Jim MacKenzie, UC Santa Cruz; Residential college chapter—Picture of college course published in prototype copy of *Science Notes*—photographer unknown; OTS chapter—Puerto Viejo photo by Dan Janzen, Rafael Rodriguez and Louis Fournier photo by Mildred Mathias and Dan Janzen lecturing by Carl Retenmeyer (photos provided by Don Stone); Chapter on evolution of *Hymenaea*—Photo of students and faculty going to Botanical Congress in Seattle—Unknown UC Santa Cruz photographer; Thailand and Australia Chapter—photo of Shui-ying Hu by Y.T. Lee; Chapter on expansion of research—photo of Swarup Wood and me at his commencement by Bess Ward; Chapter on evolving social and family life—Santa Cruz SPCA brochure of Blackie's Friends; Full Circle Chapter—Receiving Botanical Society of America Centennial Award, photo from BSA; Talking with Hal Mooney photo by Susanne Altermann, Displaying California Academy of Science Fellows Medal photo by Dong Lin, California Academy of Sciences; Speaking at University of Tulsa homecoming, photo from U. of Tulsa Alumni Office; With first Langenheim fellowship recipient., photo by Jim MacKenzie, UC Santa Cruz; Me with Jonathan Gershenzon and with first Langenheim Chair in Plant Ecology, Ingrid Parker, photo by Tim Stephens, University Relations, UC Santa Cruz.

Frontispiece depicts me with *Hymenaea* and shows its major distribution in South America. It was drawn and presented to me by Karen Kaplan when she was a UCSC undergraduate student.

INDEX

A

AAUW (American Association of University Women), 64, 491
graduate student fellowship, 62, 160
postdoctoral fellowship, 160
undergraduate scholarships, 30, 62
Academia Sinica, 447, 449, 452
Acta Amazônica, 299, 339
Agathis, 378–79, 386–87, 389, 391, 460
amber, 356
Australian photosynthesis study, 386, 389
australis, New Zealand icon, 390–91
Alcan (Alaskan-Canadian Highway), 106
Algonquin Provincial Park, Canada, 466
alpine plants
arctic affinity, 141
calcareous rocks, 191
Colombia, 88, 278
Colorado Rockies, 88
Crested Butte, 56–57, 165
German, 295
Mexican (see Mexico: Popocateptl)
Mount Eielson, 112
Presidential Range, 178–79
trek in Switzerland, 195
alpine tundra, 113, 466
Altermann, Susanne, 12–13, 479, 527
Alvim, Paulo, 271, 335
Amazonian fish, 269
Amazon River, 262, 306
amber, 160, 181, 199–203, 210, 241–43, 247, 259, 261, 281, 291, 293, 318, 321, 356, 391, 475
Baltic, 152, 182–83, 185, 190, 192–93, 291, 374
botanical origin, 182, 190, 192, 321, 460, 516
Chiapas expedition, 152–56, 158
collection in museums, 182, 184–85, 187, 189–90, 192–95
determining fraud, 173

formation, 330–31
jewelry factory, 187
Mexican, 171, 202, 381
pollen content, 171–72, 174–77
Amber Room, 291
AMC (Appalachian Mountain Club), 179–80
anaconda, 269
Anaya, Ana Luisa, 462
Andrade-Lima, Dardano, 273, 349
Angola, 243–44, 252–53, 255–58, 510
anti-Vietnam war protests, 221
arctic tundra, 105, 115, 117, 120, 178, 478. *See also* Alaskan trek
Argentina, 105, 240, 261, 276–77, 385
army ants, 304
Arrhenius, Susanne, 13, 366, 394, 428
Arroyo, Mary, 324, 328
aspen forests, 128, 164
Association for Tropical Biology, 11, 335
president, 409–12, 414–18, 420–21
Association for Tropical BiologyATB, 11, 17, 335, 409–12, 414–16, 418, 420, 455–56, 458
Atolla, Jorgé, 347–48
Auntie (car), 102–3, 107, 110, 113, 121
Australia, 374–75, 377–79, 381–87, 389–91

B

Bailey, I. W., 171, 177
Bailkey, Nels, 34–35
Baker, Herbert, 256, 313
Balik, Michael, 455–56
banana slug, 288–89
Banks, Harlan, 45, 195
Barclay, Harriet, 31, 36, 39–40, 53, 91–92
Barghoorn, Elso, 160, 170, 172, 176, 184–85, 299
Barrosa, Graziella, 209
Bates, H., 274, 351, 514, 516
Bazzaz, Fakhri, 399, 421

Get Published, Inc!
Thorofare, NJ 08086
26 February, 2010
BA2010057